CLAR

CLARENDON LAW SERIES

An Introduction to Roman Law
By BARRY NICHOLAS

Natural Law and Natural Rights
By JOHN G. FINNIS

Public Law and Democracy
By P. P. CRAIG

Precedent in English Law (4th edition)
By SIR RUPERT CROSS AND J. W. HARRIS

Playing by the Rules
By FREDERICK SCHAUER

Legal Reasoning and Legal Theory
By NEIL MACCORMICK

An Introduction to the Law of Contract (5th edition)
By P. S. ATIYAH

The Concept of Law (2nd edition)
By H. L. HART

Policies and Perceptions of Insurance
By MALCOLM CLARKE

An Introduction to Constitutional Law
By ERIC BARENDT

An Introduction to Family Law (2nd edition)
By GILLIAN DOUGLAS

Discrimination Law
By SANDRA FREDMAN

The Conflict of Laws
By ADRIAN BRIGGS

The Law of Property (3rd edition)
By F. H. LAWSON AND BERNARD RUDDEN

Introduction to Company Law
By PAUL L. DAVIES

Tort Law
By TONY WEIR

Personal Property Law (3rd edition)
By MICHAEL BRIDGE

An Introduction to the Law of Trusts
By SIMON GARDNER

Equity
By SARAH WORTHINGTON

Employment Law
By HUGH COLLINS

Public Law
By ADAM TOMKINS

Contract Theory
By STEPHEN A. SMITH

Administrative Law (4th edition)
By PETER CANE

Criminal Justice
By LUCIA ZEDNER

UNJUST ENRICHMENT

SECOND EDITION

PETER BIRKS

UNIVERSITY PRESS

OXFORD
UNIVERSITY PRESS

Great Clarendon Street, Oxford OX2 6DP

Oxford University Press is a department of the University of Oxford.
It furthers the University's objective of excellence in research, scholarship,
and education by publishing worldwide in

Oxford New York

Auckland Cape Town Dar es Salaam Hong Kong Karachi
Kuala Lumpur Madrid Melbourne Mexico City Nairobi
New Delhi Shanghai Taipei Toronto

With offices in

Argentina Austria Brazil Chile Czech Republic France Greece
Guatemala Hungary Italy Japan South Korea Poland Portugal
Singapore Switzerland Thailand Turkey Ukraine Vietnam

Oxford is a registered trade mark of Oxford University Press
in the UK and in certain other countries

Published in the United States
by Oxford University Press Inc., New York

First edition 2003
Second edition 2005

British Library Cataloguing in Publication Data

Data available

Library of Congress Cataloging in Publication Data

Data available

ISBN 0–19–927698–6

3 5 7 9 10 8 6 4

Typeset in Ehrhardt
by RefineCatch Limited, Bungay, Suffolk
Printed in Great Britain by
Biddles Ltd., King's Lynn, Norfolk

For Gareth and Vivienne Jones

Foreword

On 6 July 2004, Peter Birks died of cancer at the age of 62. This new edition was important to him and, with characteristic commitment, he was still working on it, despite ever-failing health, until a few days before he died. By then, he had successfully completed it subject to the tidying up of a few sentences in the text and the checking of some of the footnotes (for which I would like to acknowledge the assistance of Dr Arianna Pretto).

Peter inspired generations of students and colleagues with his passionate enthusiasm for, and dedication to, the study of law in the universities. The power of his mind, the brilliance of his writings and teaching, and his generosity in helping others with their work and ideas, made him one of the most influential academic lawyers of our time. Words cannot express the enormity of the personal debt I owe to him, as a teacher and subsequently as a colleague and friend.

In reading this book, admiration vies with sadness. One longs for Peter still to be here to defend and develop his views and to illuminate us still further. Yet it seems only appropriate that in the pages of this book, and shining through the unique style of prose, we see right to the end the originality of his ideas, the depth of his learning, the rigour of his reasoning, and the clarity of his vision. It is the fitting final testament of a truly great scholar.

Andrew Burrows
26 November 2004

Preface to the Second Edition

The first edition of this book sought to prove to common lawyers that unjust enrichment was an indispensable category of private law, a proposition which civilians do not contest. During the 20th century common lawyers on both sides of the Atlantic were made familiar with the law of restitution and fell into the habit of regarding restitution as doing the work of the civilian's unjust or unjustified enrichment. However, the book argued that it was an error to regard unjust enrichment as coterminous with restitution. It was no more than a part of the law of restitution when that area of law was divided according to the different events from which restitutionary rights arose.

The book then sought to explain how to understand and operate the law of unjust enrichment by asking what was involved in asserting that one person had been enriched at the expense of another and in what circumstances such an enrichment might be regarded as relevantly unjust so as to give the claimant a right to restitution. The core of that work was done by the proposition that in England the judges had already begun to move towards a species of the civilian inquiry whether the enrichment had or had not occurred in circumstances which in the eye of the law sufficiently explained its acquisition. Was it explicable as having a good legal basis or was it legally inexplicable? If inexplicable, it must be given up.

Since the first edition a number of new cases have arisen on points central to its argument, and some new academic work has been published which has to be taken into account. In the latter category, although at the time of writing still on their way to publication, are the papers given and discussed at a symposium convened by Professor Andrew Burrows on 13 January 2004 at St Hugh's College, Oxford, at which two short papers were read on each of the book's five principal parts.

That symposium turned out to be a memorable occasion, showing the university at its very best. Strongly differing views joined battle in the attempt to get to the bottom of the matter in hand, but there was no hint of animosity between the protagonists.[1] Quite to the contrary, there was a

[1] Kit Barker, Andrew Burrows, Tom Krebs, Gerard McMeel, Charles Mitchell, Robert Stevens, William Swadling, Andrew Tettenborn, Graham Virgo, Sarah Worthington. Illness prevented the presence of Francis Rose, editor of the Restitution Law Review, in which the proceedings of the symposium will appear.

strong sense that the different views all shared the common purpose of understanding something which was difficult in itself and had been made more difficult by its thorny history.

At the end of that day, my sense of the debate was that the case for the conceptual independence and necessity of the law of unjust enrichment was accepted. But that consensus did not extend to unanimity on the question whether as a matter of practical wisdom one should insist on physically separating its treatment from the rest of the law of restitution. That is a relatively minor point of difference. I adhere to the view that unjust enrichment needs at least some books in which it is treated in isolation, as in this one. Part I, which is the proof of its independence, accordingly remains virtually unchanged in this new edition, which is, however, more careful to underline the fact that there is of course nothing wrong with books on the law of restitution as a whole, so long as they are internally compartmentalized to distinguish between different causative events giving rise to restitutionary rights.

In relation to the crucial Parts II and III (enrichment at the claimant's expense and unjust) it was clear that most participants found my account in important respects unconvincing. In this new edition, Part II now bears the marks of a near knock-out blow landed in defence of the view that the gain-based recovery of a claimant in unjust enrichment must be capped by the amount of his own loss. As for Part III, where blows were most expected, I had certainly failed to convince most of my colleagues that the English approach through 'unjust factors' would have to be given up in favour of an English version of the civilian '*sine causa*' approach. But there I did not feel that I had taken any knock-out punches. So far as it is new, Part III seeks to strengthen the argument, not to retreat from the position taken. It also takes into account some important new case law.

Part IV, the principal concern of which is the proprietary response to unjust enrichment, remains very little changed. Part V is about defences, the most important of which is change of position, which in this edition is once again divided between disenrichment and other changes of position. Recent attempts by the Court of Appeal to reshape the defence seem to be aimed at softening its edges, a development which is not easy to welcome and which Part V resists. Part VI is essentially historical. It reviews the figures which used to do the work of unjust enrichment. It remains almost completely as it was in the first edition.

Peter Birks
All Souls College, Oxford
15 March 2004

Preface to the First Edition

The law of restitution has crept into the consciousness of common lawyers as an indispensable addition to the traditional law school syllabus. However, energetic as it has been in recent decades, it is constantly troubled by intimations of not yet having become quite what its makers intended. A butterfly is what all along a caterpillar is destined to be. We cannot know, our early teachers used to say, what foreknowledge of its metamorphosis the caterpillar may entertain. The butterfly in this case is and will be unjust enrichment.

Every year, in each new course on restitution, we waste an unconscionable time wondering whether unjust enrichment exists and, if it does, what form it might take, and what its relationship might be to restitution. Worse still, having achieved anything but perfect unanimity, we boldly move on to waste more time endeavouring to answer questions which are literally unanswerable so long as these foundations are insecure. How, for instance, can it be decided whether property rights can be generated by unjust enrichment if unjust enrichment itself remains a camel to some, a weasel to others, and a whale to all the rest?

The one thing that really matters about this book is the goal of saving all that wasted time. Unjust enrichment does exist. It is knowable by reason, and not by faith alone. It does not change its shape from day to day, and can therefore be recognized by any eye. It is the indispensable core subject that restitution has been trying to become. Whether the book will achieve that goal is another question. If it does not, another will. The scrap of truth which it seeks to prove is not new. It is acknowledged by every civilian jurisdiction. It was all but accepted by the common law in the eighteenth century, which then contrived to obscure it so completely as to make its rediscovery seem more startling than it is. The proof does not depend on comparative law but it is confirmed by comparative law.

When I first became a Fellow of Brasenose College Oxford in 1971, the vacancy I filled was made by Barry Nicholas's elevation to the Chair of Comparative Law. He did not have to move away. For that Chair is attached to Brasenose. Later he became Principal. The advice he gave me when I started now seems to come from a world which is no more: 'Teach, do not worry about writing, nobody wants to hear from you till later.' I had no notion of defying him. Nearly fifteen years passed before I became one of those who produced a book on the law of restitution. All of us owed the same debt. In the slipstream of Robert Goff and Gareth Jones we had a relatively easy journey. All the same Barry Nicholas's advice now comes constantly back, for I see now that I wrote before I had fully understood. Almost everything of mine now needs calling back for burning.

St Paul was relatively lucky. In one flash of blinding light he knew that he must change sides. In the university the awful sense of having been wrong comes on more slowly and with it the still more awful realization that one must befriend those whom one has persecuted and persecute those who are one's friends. But universities are for getting to the bottom of things, come what may. Public apostasies may ruin a reputation and thus cost a merit point or two, but that cannot be helped. I dare not say that I am finally error-free, but in my view, for whatever it may still be worth, this butterfly, although it could certainly have been better depicted by another hand, is very beautiful and its emergence from the chrysalis of restitution is something to celebrate.

It may help the reader to know from the outset what propositions formerly defended are now renounced. There are three principal recantations. First, it was an error to think that unjust enrichment could safely be left within the law of restitution and, more particularly, it was incorrect to suggest that, within that response-based category, whatever was not 'autonomous' unjust enrichment was always restitution for wrongs. Secondly, by assuming without proving, and in fact almost certainly incorrectly, that the claimant in unjust enrichment must have suffered a loss corresponding to the defendant's gain, I adopted a much too narrow view of the extent to which cases of restitution for wrongs are susceptible of alternative analysis in unjust enrichment. Thirdly, and perhaps most importantly, the onward march of case law and academic analysis, especially comparative analysis, has both compelled and convinced me that it was a misjudgement to insist that the common law, late coming, had by good luck hit upon a better way of answering the question whether an enrichment was unjust than, with their much longer experience, the civilian jurisdictions had achieved.

My view on this issue was that to answer the question whether an enrichment is unjust English law had very usefully and clearly chosen to look for specific 'unjust factors' of a kind intelligible on the Clapham omnibus and that that was to be preferred to the more abstract civilian inquiry whether the defendant's enrichment rested on some recognized explanatory basis. In the great series of cases on void interest swaps, which are discussed in Chapter 5, the approach through unjust factors suffered a decisive defeat, partly, as I now think, because my own renewed defence of it was not done well enough. It half-persuaded one Lord Justice. My immediate reaction was to return to its defence, but the comparative literature, Dr Sonja Meier's work in particular, convinced me that that cause was hopeless. The swaps cases did not know that they were making a momentous choice, but they were, and in fact they chose the better method.

I also acknowledge a considerable debt to the work of Professor Dan Friedmann and of Sir Jack Beatson, the latter now a High Court judge. Although I did not see it at the time, they have often been one jump ahead of me.

I also gratefully acknowledge that the work on this book, especially in its comparative aspects, has been assisted through funds made available by the European Commission. Under the Commission's programme for Improving Human Potential, Oxford is one member of a network which is studying legal terminology (contract No HPRN-CT-2002-00229 'Uniform Terminology for European Private Law'). The network is coordinated by Università degli Studi di Torino (Italy). Its other members are: Universitat de Barcelona (Spain), Université Jean Moulin Lyon 3 (France), Westfaelische Wilhelms-Universitaet, Muenster (Germany), University of Nijmegen (The Netherlands), Universitat Warsawskiego (Poland).

Peter Birks
All Souls College, Oxford
1st September 2003

Contents

Expanded Contents

Part III. Unjust

Part VI. Competing Terminology

Table of Cases

Table of Statutes and Foreign Legislation

Part I

Introduction

1

A Core Case

Of the subjects which form the indispensable foundation of private law, unjust enrichment is the only one to have evaded the great rationalization achieved since the middle of the 19th century in both England and America by the writers of textbooks. Its fragments, obscurely named, were instead tucked under the edges of contract and trusts.[1] The consequence is that even at the beginning of the 21st century unjust enrichment is still unfamiliar to most common lawyers. It will have played no independent part in their intellectual formation. Its modern name, adapted from civilian equivalents, is slightly disconcerting. Suspicion of the unfamiliar is therefore compounded by instinctive aversion to the hint of revolutionary doctrine. In fact it has no tendencies of that kind. Neglect has certainly left it difficult and untidy, but the example of the civilian jurisdictions shows that it is not by nature disruptive.[2] In this chapter it is introduced through one core case. The law of unjust enrichment is the law of all events materially identical to the mistaken payment of a non-existent debt.

Such a payment gives rise to a right to restitution. The law of restitution is the law of gain-based recovery, just as the law of compensation is the law of loss-based recovery. Thus a right to restitution is a right to a gain received by the defendant, while a right to compensation is a right that the defendant make good a loss suffered by the claimant. The word 'restitution' is not entirely happy in this partnership with 'compensation'. It has had to be manoeuvred into that role. 'Disgorgement', which has no

[1] The old language of imaginary contracts and trusts is as much as possible avoided in this book. It is examined in the last two chapters.

[2] Since 'civilian' recurs it may be helpful to recall at the outset that it identifies the Roman-based systems of, and exported from, continental Europe. The Latin for 'citizen' is '*civis*'. The Romans called their law the *ius civile*, which means 'the law (*ius*) pertaining to a citizen'. As they dispensed with 'Roman', so 'common law' makes no mention of England. Anglo-American law is the common law only because in post-Conquest England the royal judges insisted that the King's law was the law common to the whole realm. Some systems are 'mixed'. Scots law, for instance, has borrowed from both the civil and the common law.

legal pedigree, might be said to fit the job more easily and more exactly. This awkwardness is encountered again later in this chapter, and it and related terminological problems are more fully discussed in Part VI.[3] At the end of this chapter we will return to the difficult question whether the right which arises from an unjust enrichment not only is, but can only be, a right to restitution. In English law it always is.

The law of restitution is better known than the law of unjust enrichment because it was under that name, starting in America in the 1930s, that the first serious attempts were made to overcome the problems of misdescription and misclassification which deprived unjust enrichment of its own place on the map of the law. The outcome was the American Law Institute's *Restatement of the Law of Restitution*.[4]

In England the law of restitution has attracted an enormous amount of attention since 1966. That year saw the publication of the first edition of the path-breaking textbook by Goff and Jones.[5] As one edition has succeeded another, that great book has grown bigger. For the practitioner it is the standard work of reference. Meanwhile, the subject has been made more accessible by a number of shorter works, of which the most widely used is the brilliant and lucid account by Professor Andrew Burrows.[6]

However, the very success of the law of restitution is now itself impeding the recognition of the law of unjust enrichment. The reason is simply stated. The law of gain-based recovery is larger than the law of unjust enrichment. Every unjust enrichment gives rise to a right to restitution and therefore belongs in the law of restitution. But that proposition cannot be turned around, because, quite often, a right to gain-based recovery is the law's response to some other causative event.

It is a grave but all too tempting error to suppose that every instance of gain-based recovery is also an instance of unjust enrichment. Restitution is not mono-causal. This chapter's final task will be to underline its multi-causality. Unjust enrichment is a distinct causative event, while restitution is a multi-causal response. To be properly understood unjust

[3] Below, 281–3.

[4] A Scott and W Seavey (reporters), *Restatement of the Law of Restitution* [:] *Quasi Contracts and Constructive Trusts* (American Law Institute St Paul 1937).

[5] R Goff and G Jones, *The Law of Restitution* (Sweet & Maxwell London 1966), now G Jones (ed), Lord Goff of Chieveley and G Jones, *The Law of Restitution* (6th edn Sweet & Maxwell London 2002).

[6] A Burrows, *The Law of Restitution* (Butterworths London 1993), now (2nd edn Butterworths London 2002); see also A Burrows and E McKendrick, *Cases and Materials on the Law of Restitution* (OUP Oxford 1997).

enrichment needs books to itself. That is not to deny that it will always occupy a large part of any book on the law of restitution, but only to assert that its distinct nature as an independent causative event cannot be securely made apparent unless and until it is also treated in isolation from other instances of gain-based recovery.

A. *TERTIUM QUID*

The classical English illustration of mistaken payment of a non-existent debt is the 19th-century case of *Kelly v Solari*.[7] Mr Solari died. He had insured his life. His widow, as his executrix, claimed under the policy and was paid. The insurers later discovered they had not been liable to pay. The policy had lapsed before Mr Solari's death. He had omitted to pay a premium. The policy had indeed been marked 'lapsed', but when the claim was made the office never checked. The Court of Exchequer held that, unless at a retrial the jury were to find that the insurers had not after all been mistaken or, even if they had been mistaken, had been indifferent to the seemingly crucial fact, the widow was bound to repay.

It was not relevant that she had not been at fault at all, nor that they had been careless. On the latter point Parke B observed:

> [If the money] is paid under the impression of the truth of a fact which is untrue, it may, generally speaking, be recovered back, however careless the party paying may have been, in omitting to use due diligence to inquire into the fact. In such a case the receiver was not entitled to it, nor intended to have it.[8]

Mrs Solari's counsel had also pressed her innocence. The widow's conscience was clean. As to this Rolfe B said:

> With respect to the argument, that money cannot be recovered back except where it is unconscientious to retain it, it seems to me, that wherever it is paid under a mistake of fact, and the party would not have paid it if the fact had been known to him it cannot be otherwise than unconscientious to retain it.[9]

This shows the danger of using the word 'unconscientious' in this context. It and other adjectives in the same family easily suggest bad behaviour at the time of the receipt. That is misleading, for there is nothing resembling a requirement of fault on the part of the defendant. Mrs Solari was indeed a totally honest and innocent claimant, but it made no difference.

[7] (1841) 9 M & W 54, 152 ER 24.

[8] Ibid 59, 27.

[9] Ibid. The language reflects that of Lord Mansfield in *Moses v Macferlan* (1760) 2 Burr 1005, 1012, 97 ER 676, 681.

The only unconscientiousness in play is unconscientiousness *ex post*, which is no more than a reflection of the prior determination that other facts require restitution to be made. It is the obligation to make restitution which renders retention unconscientious. The reason for that obligation cannot be found in any meaning of 'unconscientious'. The reason, in Parke B's words, is that 'the receiver was not entitled to it, nor intended to have it'. It is unconscientious to retain what you ought to repay. Unconscientiousness *ex post* clearly has no explanatory weight.[10]

The notion of a careless insurance company recovering from a totally innocent widow is initially shocking. But the shock induces reflection, and reflection reveals that this is indeed the essential nature of liability in unjust enrichment. Any other regime would be intolerable. This is perhaps the most important proposition in this book. If it were false, unjust enrichment would lose its claim to independence. Having been laboriously extracted from contract and trusts, the law of unjust enrichment could then be emptied into the law of wrongs. But it is not false, and unjust enrichment cannot be decanted into the law of wrongs or into any other more familiar category. A simple example will show that *Kelly v Solari* is right, although its correctness must in the end also be qualified in one important respect.

Suppose a situation in which change is overpaid. You go shopping with a friend. As you are leaving a department store an assistant comes running up to tell you that he has accidentally given you change for £50 when you had in fact paid with a £20 note. He gave you £30 more than he owed. You may be tempted to insist that you were entirely innocent. It is no doubt true that you were chatting to your friend and did not even notice how much change you were being given. But you will immediately see that a retort of that kind will not strengthen your case to keep the £30. Your innocence is irrelevant. Nor would it do you any good to make a show of anger at the shop assistant's want of care. He himself will admit to having been careless. The fact remains that, so long as you still have the mistaken money, there is no answer to the shop's demand to have it back.

It is important to notice that this does not depend entirely on your having those three £10 notes in your purse. The same conclusion can follow even if you no longer have the actual money received. Suppose that you went to the shop to buy five items and that the transaction involving

[10] To the contrary B Kremer, 'Restitution and Unconscientiousness: Another View' (2003) 119 LQR 188 commenting on *Roxborough v Rothmans of Pall Mall Australia Ltd* [2001] HCA 68, (2002) 76 ALJR 203. Compare *National Australia Bank v Garcia* (1998) 155 ALR 614, 624.

the overpayment was your first purchase. By the time you were stopped you had bought the other things. Your purse is now empty. You no longer have the money which you received. But your wealth, abstractly regarded as a single fund, is still swollen by £30. You paid cash from your purse for things you were going to buy anyhow. You would otherwise have gone to the cash machine or paid by credit card.

It is evident that in these situations the strict liability from which we recoil is actually the only acceptable regime. The reason is that the shop assistant's demand does not aim to make you bear a loss or to inflict a deterrent punishment on you. Strong facts are needed to justify unpleasant outcomes of that kind which will leave you worse off. The shop assistant is not trying to make you worse off. He seeks only that you should give up the gain obtained at the shop's expense. He asks that you return to the position you would all along have been in had you not received from the shop money to which you were not entitled. The strict liability reflects this difference between a defendant who is being asked to bear a loss and a defendant who is only being required to surrender a gain. It takes very slight facts to justify the relocation of an extant gain, and fault on the part of the recipient is not one of them. The liability is both strict and not affected by the carelessness of the claimant.

It is an important feature of the example just given that you spent the money on things that you were going to buy anyway. The outcome would be different nowadays if, still honestly believing that you had somehow underestimated your short-term liquidity, you were led into inviting your friend to lunch. Let it be that you would have spent £5 on a snack. The overpayment leads you into buying lunch for two, with a glass of wine each. The bill is £30. Having used up most of the money in an expenditure which you would not otherwise have incurred, you can now reasonably say that the shop is attempting to shift its whole loss to you. Your assets are no longer swollen beyond the £5 difference between what you would have spent and what you did spend. Repaying the mistaken £30 in full will take your wealth below the level at which it would have been had you not received the overpayment.

The strict liability becomes repugnant when the recipient's assets are no longer swollen. Nowadays this is prevented by the defence of change of position, which is discussed in Part V.[11] It takes very slight facts to generate a strict right to restitution of an extant gain at another's expense, but the fierce strict liability has to be fragile. The emphasis is on the word

[11] Below, 208–19.

'extant'. Once the enrichment has disappeared the question is transformed. The new question is about allocating a loss. One or other party must now bear the loss. The law's answer, where the defence is available, is that the loss lies with the claimant.

We do not know whether or not Mrs Solari had honestly changed her position. In those days it would have been irrelevant. A mistaken payment was treated like a loan. A borrower has to repay the sum borrowed whatever happens to the money. Suppose him mugged five minutes after receiving the borrowed money. He never gets to use any of the money, but he still has to repay the lender.

The harshness of carrying that approach over to mistaken payments was partly concealed by the fact that the incidence of restitutionary claims for mistake was heavily reduced by restrictions put on the cause of action itself. The mistake would not count unless it gave the impression of liability. Even then the maxim '*ignorantia iuris neminem excusat*' was applied, so that, if you thought that you were liable to make the payment because you had made a mistake of law, you would not be able to recover. These restrictions meant that when it came to the point there were relatively few restitution-yielding mistakes, and the analogy with loan unobtrusively prevailed. In the search for a just solution, the law thus chose a horribly blunt hammer. It now uses the sharper instrument of a sensitive defence. It is easier now to make out the cause of action, but the strict restitutionary right is fragile. It expires with the enrichment.

The previous paragraphs have shown that a striking feature of the liability to make restitution of mistaken payments is that the liability is strict, at least so long as the defendant's assets, taken as whole, remain swollen. This strictness stands out all the more sharply when juxtaposed with the irrelevance of negligence on the part of the claimant. However, the really remarkable aspect is that the 'very slight facts' which suffice to provoke the liability reveal no trace of either of the two causative events which usually explain why defendants have to pay up. In short, there is no contract and there is no wrong. This is crucial to the independence of the law of unjust enrichment. Where there is an unjust enrichment, the reason why restitution is obligatory is never a contract and never a wrong. The absence of both is evident in *Kelly v Solari*.

First, the case shows that the right to restitution of a mistaken payment is not referable to any manifestation of consent on the part of the recipient. It does not depend on the recipient's promising or in any sense agreeing to give up the enrichment. The law, endorsed as it would seem to be by the moral judgment of most of its subjects, imposes the obligation to give it up. Far from agreeing, the recipient often resists. It makes no difference. The mistaken payer's restitutionary right is not founded on contract. Mrs Solari did not promise to repay. We might say that a decent person would immediately agree to pay, but that adds nothing. A decent person would always agree to honour all obligations, but not all obligations arise from contract.

Secondly, there is no wrong. Rights do often arise independently of consent, but then they mostly arise from wrongs. Mrs Solari was not a wrongdoer. If we were to say that she committed a wrong in retaining the money which she ought to have given back, we would lock ourselves in to the same circle as those who wish to ascribe her liability to bad conscience. That is to say, we would evade the question why, without wrong or contract, she was in the first place under a duty to repay. In receiving a mistaken payment the recipient need have committed no breach of duty at all—no tort, no equitable wrong, no breach of contract.

It is therefore apparent that the remarkable strict liability illustrated in *Kelly v Solari* arises from slight facts which amount to neither contract nor wrong. If there were a contract or a wrong, the case would excite no special interest. Contracts and wrongs are familiar causative events. But this strict liability arises in the absence of these familiar events. It arises, if we confine ourselves to our core case, simply from the receipt of a mistaken payment. Beyond contracts and wrongs, there is clearly *tertium quid*, something of a third kind. The causative event of the third kind is unjust enrichment.

B. AS LABRADOR TO DOG

Although a cyclist compelled to dismount might refer to it as a canine, emphasizing with or without the addition of a coarse epithet the animal's evolutionary proximity to the wolf and dingo, in common parlance the neighbour's labrador is a dog. It is a dog, canine, mammal, and animal. As surely as a neighbour with a labrador is a neighbour with a dog, a list of causative events which includes receipt of a mistaken payment includes unjust enrichment at the expense of another. At approximately the level of generality at which a labrador is an animal, the receipt of a mistaken payment is a causative event, as is a contract of sale or the tort of defamation. These are all events which are 'causative' in the sense that they cause to come into existence rights which can be realized in court. At a slightly lower level of generality, much as a labrador is a dog, receipt of such a payment is an unjust enrichment at the expense of another. Unjust enrichment at the expense of another—unjust enrichment for short—is no more than a generic name for the receipt of a mistaken payment.

The elements of the generalization are as follows. Receipt of a payment supposes a receipt of money, and receipt of money generalizes to enrichment. 'Enrichment', like 'payment', is a verbal noun. Most such nouns hover between process and outcome. It is important to emphasize the element of process, because, no less than payment, enrichment is an event. It is something which happens in the world. Payment also supposes that the enrichment happens by transfer from another. Enrichment by transfer from another generalizes to enrichment at the expense of another. The mistake is or reflects the existence of the reason, not being a contract or a wrong, why the payment has to be given up. The generic reason why an enrichment at the expense of another has to be given up is that it is unjust.

The utility of this generic restatement is that it enables us to look for and to recognize other examples which are materially identical to the core case, if any there be. In the same way 'dog' gathers to the labrador all the rotweilers, alsatians, spaniels, pointers, terriers, dalmatians, and so on. At a certain point we inevitably approach a boundary. Boundaries are nearly always troublesome. Near the boundary of 'dog' correct usage requires to be debated, and people begin to disagree. Except in the special usage denoting the male, 'dog' is not used of foxes. It is not used of wolves. Dingos raise difficulties, for they are regularly referred to as wild dogs, whence wildness cannot be the key.

When we look for other examples of unjust enrichment the purpose is to find all the events, in whatever language they have historically been discussed, which generate a right to restitution by the same logic as explains the right to restitution in the core case. The boundary cannot but be troublesome. The noise on the boundary will immediately be taken by some people as indicating that the exercise is doomed from the outset. That is not right. Categories do not become incoherent or otherwise unsound merely because argument breaks out on their edges. Few would otherwise survive.

By generalizing from money received to enrichment we can ask whether that logic can extend to other benefits received, and, if yes, under what conditions other benefits will be treated in the same way as money. Again, by generalizing from transfer by the claimant to at the expense of the claimant, we can ask what other connections might suffice, beyond simple transfer, sufficiently to connect a would-be claimant to the enrichment which he wants the defendant to give up. Finally, by generalizing from mistake to unjust we can ask whether there are any other reasons of the same non-contract, non-wrong kind which have the effect of requiring the enrichee to give up an enrichment at the claimant's expense.

If we were to take the generalization of mistake to unjust as inviting us to search for any and every reason why an enrichment should be given up, we would gather in cases of contracts to give up gains and wrongs for which gain-based recovery is available. The most important feature of mistaken payments is the absence of contract and wrong. That shows that there really is something of a third kind, a distinct cause of action requiring explanation and exposition. Contracts and wrongs are well-trodden territory. Within the common law, the territory of mistaken payment and its congeners has never been mapped.

In recent years good maps of the response-based category of restitution have been made. But, precisely because restitution is a response, and multi-causal, those maps fall short of isolating unjust enrichment. They have gathered together each and every reason why a gain should be given up, but they have not drawn a careful line around the sub-set of those reasons which are not contracts and not wrongs or, slightly more accurately, which are not manifestations of consent and are not wrongs.

C. RESTITUTION OUTSIDE UNJUST ENRICHMENT

'Restitution' and 'compensation' are partners. Compensation is loss-based recovery. Restitution is gain-based recovery. 'Restitution' is by nature more comfortable with a slightly narrower brief but it has been compelled to become a synonym for 'disgorgement'. It will be helpful at this point to give one or two examples of restitution in which the causative event is not an unjust enrichment.

One obvious case is contractual restitution. We are clearly not in our third area when the reason why a gain must be given up is that parties have validly agreed that in given events it must be. This happens in all sorts of contexts. If I lose my wallet and ask you to lend me £30 to tide me over the weekend, my obligation is to make restitution. There is a contract for restitution. In other words a simple loan, what Roman law called '*mutuum*', generates a restitutionary debt. Again, one party sometimes pays another's demand in exchange for the other's promise to repay if it should turn out that the money was not due. Again the source of the obligation to make restitution is contract.

Less obviously distinct are cases of gain-based recovery for wrongs. In *Boardman v Phipps*,[12] for example, a solicitor who acted for a trust which held a minority shareholding became aware that the company was seriously under-performing. Using the information which he had gathered as solicitor to the trustees, he pulled off a brilliant coup. With his own money he bought out the majority holding. This yielded not only a better long-term prospect for the company but an immediate profit for all shareholders. The trust and its minority shareholding, and hence the beneficiaries of the trust too, did very well indeed. However, despite his honesty and his success, it remained true that the solicitor had acted in breach of the fiduciary duty to avoid conflicts of interest, and he had not obtained the fully informed consent of the trustees to that breach.

This breach of equitable duty put the solicitor under a restitutionary liability—a liability to give up to the trustees on behalf of the beneficiaries the gain which he had made, subject to an allowance for the work and skill he had put in. This case shows that gain-based recovery is one response to the wrong which consists in breach of fiduciary duty. The facts can easily be dressed up in the language of unjust enrichment. Boardman can be said to have been unjustly enriched at the expense of the trustees. But that language turns out on closer analysis not to be talking about a cause of action distinct from the wrong.

The proof is that it is impossible to dispense with the wrong and come up with a different not-wrong explanation of his duty to give up his profit. The words 'unjust enrichment at the expense of the claimant' succeed in concealing this. The language applies easily enough but it does not identify a cause of action materially identical to mistaken payment of a non-existent debt. In what sense was the gain obtained at the trustees' expense? It was obtained by committing a breach of fiduciary duty. In short, it was obtained by a wrong. There was no connection between claimant and enrichment other than the wrong. The facts are thus beyond the range of the logic which explains the recovery of a mistaken payment where there is a reason for restitution notwithstanding the absence of contract and wrong. An unjust enrichment is something different. It is never a wrong. In whatever language is used, the fact remains that the liability in *Boardman v Phipps* arose from a wrong.

Attorney-General v Blake[13] concerned the autobiography of a traitor. Blake had been a secret agent whose treachery cost the lives of many of

[12] [1967] 2 AC 46 (HL). [13] [2001] 1 AC 268 (HL).

his colleagues. Imprisoned in England, he had escaped to the safety of Moscow. The memoirs from which he hoped to become rich were written in breach of contract. Like all agents he had promised the Crown that he would never write an unauthorized book. The Attorney-General successfully obtained an injunction preventing the payment to him of royalties. The premiss of the injunction was that, if he were actually to receive the money, he would immediately be liable to give it up to the Crown. The House of Lords, breaking new ground, held that this was a rare case in which gain-based recovery was available for the wrong of breach of contract.

This too is restitution for a wrong. It belongs to the law of breach of contract. It has nothing at all to do with unjust enrichment. All lawyers know that dual analysis is sometimes possible. You can sometimes find two causative events in one story. A payment obtained by fraud can be presented either as the tort of deceit or, dispensing with the allegation of fraud, as a simple payment by mistake. But no such alternative analysis is possible in the *Blake* case. Just as in *Boardman v Phipps*, the Crown, without relying on the facts in their character as a wrong of breach of contract, could not have created any connection at all between it and the gain in question. Clearly, therefore, the only question at issue was whether this breach of contract gave rise to a right to restitution in place of the normal right to compensation.

The mono-causal notion of restitution easily reaches cases of this kind and, erroneously, dresses them up in the language of unjust enrichment. It infers from the defendant's liability to give up a gain that he was unjustly enriched at the claimant's expense. But that wide usage conceals the lines between different causative events. Unjust enrichment, within the logic underlying mistaken payments, requires a connection between claimant and enrichment which is independent of wrongdoing and a reason for restitution which is likewise not a wrong. These conditions cannot be satisfied in the *Blake* or *Boardman* facts. The liability there flows unequivocally from the wrong. These cases involve gain-based recovery but have nothing to do with the *tertium quid* that is unjust enrichment. In unjust enrichment 'unjust' always denotes a reason for restitution which is not a manifestation of consent and not a wrong.

Moses v Macferlan[14] is a more subtle example of the same kind. It seems at first sight to be susceptible to the alternative analysis which was manifestly impossible in the *Blake* case, but it is not. Macferlan promised

[14] (1760) 2 Burr 1005, 97 ER 676.

Moses that if Moses endorsed certain promissory notes over to him he would never seek to enforce Moses' liability on the endorsements. Moses did endorse the notes. In breach of his promise, Macferlan sued him. The first court thought it could not take notice of the contract not to sue. Having paid up, Moses began a new action in the King's Bench. This was not an appeal of any kind but simply a new action claiming, as we would now say, restitution of the sum he had had to pay. He was successful.

Macferlan was enriched by transfer from Moses. The transfer clearly suffices in itself to establish a sufficient connection between claimant and enrichment without relying on wrongdoing. There also seems at first sight to be an available unjust factor analogous to mistake, in that the money was obtained through pressure. But there is a fatal snag. The only pressure was due process of law. Macferlan had sued for this money and had obtained a judgment. Lord Mansfield's conclusion in favour of Moses has been strongly condemned for its failure to accept that due process of law cannot be a restitution-yielding pressure.[15] Another way of coming to the same conclusion is to say that the judgment provides a thoroughly sound explanation of the enrichment. It cannot be seen as an enrichment lacking any legal basis. Where a judgment has been given there can be no right to restitution unless the judgment is set aside. Capitulation after an action has begun is likewise brought within the doctrine of *res judicata*.[16] Therefore, the unjust enrichment analysis of *Moses v Macferlan* just will not work.

However, as an instance of restitution for a wrong the case appears in a different light. The difference between unjust enrichment and restitution for wrongs was not articulated in the 18th century, but Lord Mansfield's decision can be defended in retrospect on the ground that it was only the analysis in unjust enrichment, not the action for breach of contract, which encountered objections. Lord Mansfield's premiss was that Moses was indubitably entitled to an action for breach of contract.[17] Such an action was perfectly compatible with respect for the other court's judgment, which, valid as it was, had indeed been obtained in breach of

[15] *Phillips v Hunter* (1795) 2 H Bl 402, 414–16, 126 ER 618, 624–6; *Marriot v Hampton*, (1797) 7 TR 269, 101 ER 969. Cf Goff and Jones 6th edn (n 5 above) [44-001].

[16] *Res judicata* means 'a matter adjudicated' or, slightly expanded, 'a matter on which judgment has already been given': the family of 'finality' defences is considered below, 232–40.

[17] JH Baker, 'The History of Quasi-Contract in English Law' in WR Cornish and others (eds), *Restitution Past, Present, and Future* (Hart Oxford 1998) 37, 55.

contract. If the action for breach of contract remained intact, it remained intact without regard to the measure of recovery which was sought.

By 1760 it was not uncommon for claimants to seek restitution of the proceeds of wrongs under the cover of the phrase 'waiver of tort'.[18] The interpretation in the previous paragraph understands *Moses v Macferlan* as having allowed the same kind of claim for breach of contract. The history of waiver of tort was ultimately examined by the House of Lords in *United Australia Ltd v Barclays Bank Ltd.*[19] Their Lordships there exposed 'waiver' as a fiction. They had before them the case of conversion of a cheque. The defendant bank argued that it could not be sued for converting the claimant's cheque because, earlier in the same story, the claimant had once and for all waived the tort by bringing against another party an action, almost immediately discontinued, for restitution. The fallacy in that argument was that the 'waiver' on which the restitutionary action had been based was a fiction. It had been introduced to ensure that there was no question of coming back with a second claim for compensation and as a sop to the contractual form of the action in which the restitutionary claim originally had to be made.

Their Lordships held that the true reason why it was possible to seek restitution of money received by conversion was not that the tort could be genuinely waived but, much more simply, because conversion was a tort which generated two remedial rights. Without switching to another cause of action, the claimant could elect to realize either the right to compensation or the right to restitution.

The *United Australia* case shows that a claimant can have restitution for the tort of conversion. As envisaged by the House of Lords, that is restitution for the wrong as such and has nothing whatever to do with unjust enrichment. However, differently from the three preceding examples, here it seems likely that dual analysis is possible. That is to say, it may be that the victim of the tort of conversion can reach the proceeds either on the basis that the tort itself generates a restitutionary right or, in the alternative, in unjust enrichment properly so-called, not waiving the wrong but simply dispensing with that characterization of the facts. The House of Lords did not address that possibility, although it would no less effectively have answered the argument based on waiver. If you sell my car for £5,000, the question whether I can reach

[18] This practice was reluctantly approved in *Lamine v Dorrell* (1701) 2 Ld Raym 1216, 92 ER 303.

[19] [1941] AC 1 (HL).

that £5,000 without relying on the wrong of conversion or any other wrong turns out to be as important as it is difficult. It deeply affects the range of the law of unjust enrichment. It is further discussed in Chapter 2.[20]

D. CONCLUSION

Analysis of the receipt of a mistaken payment of a non-existent debt reveals a causative event of a third kind. It is not a manifestation of consent such as a contract, and it is not a wrong. The consequent liability, surprisingly at first, is strict, albeit subject to defences. The generic conception of that causative event is unjust enrichment at the expense of another. That generalization enables us to look for other examples materially identical to the core case. It does not tell us how many, if any, are to be found. Those other cases may differ as to the form in which the enrichment is received. It may not be money. They may also differ as to the nature of the connection between the enrichment and the claimant. It may not have been transferred by him. Above all, it may be unjust for a different reason. The task of the word 'unjust', which seems at first sight to be so ominously unstable, is to understand the reasons, however few or many they may be, which are neither contracts nor wrongs but are nevertheless sufficient in law to generate a right to restitution of an enrichment obtained at the claimant's expense.

The study of the core case not only does not tell us whether the *tertium quid* is large or small; it also gives no indication whether, if it be not an isolated case, the category which forms around it will be a loose confederacy, like the law of tort, or a closely knit family, like the law of contract. The law of tort, in the common law, is of the former kind, a long list of particular wrongs which are difficult to integrate one with another. In the law of contract, by contrast, the particular contracts acknowledge their subjection to the general principles of a single law of contract. To such an extent is this true that books and courses on contract for the most part treat the particular contracts, such as sale, partnership and agency, as detail to be left to specialist books which are written with a smaller compass but on a larger scale. Until a decade ago, one could predict that in the common law the mature law of unjust enrichment would look more like the law of tort—a list of unjust enrichments. Massive litigation concerning value passing under void contracts has meanwhile forced a change in

[20] Below, 78–86.

direction. Unjust enrichment now begins to look more like the law of contract in that it has acquired a tighter unity.

A second theme of this introductory chapter has been the strong differentiation of unjust enrichment from restitution. Restitution, like compensation, is a category of response, not a category of causative event. The causative event is not always unjust enrichment. It follows that the law of unjust enrichment is a sub-set of the law of restitution, when rights to restitution are divided according to their causative events. The absolute truth of that proposition supposes, as was indeed accepted above, that unjust enrichment properly so-called always gives rise to a restitutionary right and never to any other.

That proposition is sound in English law, but it is not an invariable and necessary truth. That is, in England unjust enrichment does, as it happens, give rise only to restitutionary rights, but in our core case it would be possible to understand the mistaken payer's right as compensatory, in that it makes good the loss caused to him by the gain to the other. Some systems do take that compensatory view, adding immediately that the loss which is recoverable is capped by the gain to the other. For example, the new Dutch Civil Code says the enrichee must 'make reparation for the damage suffered by [the claimant] . . . up to the amount of his enrichment'.[21] This means that the claimant recovers his loss up to the maximum of the other's enrichment, which in turn is but one way of saying that he recovers the other's gain so far as it constitutes a loss to himself. There are two crucial comments which require to be made on this approach.

The first comment is that the premiss of this capped-compensation analysis is one which in German law is robustly rejected. It assumes that there is a good cause of action only where and to the extent that the claimant in unjust enrichment has suffered a loss. Once a given jurisdiction has decided that the claimant in unjust enrichment is definitively and exclusively a person who has suffered a loss corresponding to the enrichment of the defendant, then, and only then, can it choose to describe his right as a right to have that loss made good. This is a very difficult and sensitive issue. We will see that such evidence as there is indicates that English law shares with German law the view that the claimant need not be identified as a person who has suffered a loss.

[21] Book 6 article 212.1: 'is verplicht . . . diens schade te vergoeden tot het bedrag van zijn verrijking'. The translation is taken from PPC Haanappel and E Mackaay, *New Netherlands Civil Code, Patrimonial Law* (Kluwer Deventer 1990) 324.

This will be discussed in Chapter 4, because it goes to the meaning of the phrase 'at the expense of' or, more accurately since that phrase takes its meaning from its function, to the nature of the required connection between the claimant and the enrichment which he wishes to recover.[22] To adopt the capped-compensation approach simply because it happens to fit the core case would illegitimately close down the discussion of that issue and create insuperable difficulties for the cases which indicate, albeit intuitively rather than after full and open argument, that the English choice has already fallen in line with that of the German law.

The second comment is no less important. If claims in unjust enrichment are regarded as recovering loss—compensation—it has to be loss capped by the defendant's gain. Even the systems which do use the capped-compensation approach insist on the cap. That tautology has to be emphasized, because the very words 'loss' and 'compensation' are inimical to the *raison d'être* of the law of unjust enrichment, and at their mention the cap is therefore instantly indispensable. This third kind of causative event has to be recognized as distinct from others precisely because very slight facts raise a strict liability to surrender an extant enrichment. Their very slightness means that they cannot support any claim that the enrichee should answer for consequential loss suffered by the claimant. It may well be that, because I paid you £50,000 which I thought I owed and did not, I could not save my business from receivership, or could not feed my cattle, or could not take shares in what turned out to be an immensely successful goldmine. Such losses are totally beyond the range of the slight facts which will entitle me to recover the £50,000. The strict liability in unjust enrichment is tied, as we have seen, to extant enrichment. The very slight facts not amounting to wrongs or contracts go no further than to require the relocation of extant gains.

If Dr Kremer is a reliable witness, not only Gummow J but the whole High Court of Australia is embarking on an experiment in which there will be no law of unjust enrichment.[23] If so, of all jurisdictions Australia will pay the highest price for the common law's predilection for hiding its law of unjust enrichment in unsuitable places. This time the intention seems to be to bury it on the edge of the law of civil wrongs. There it will accede to the law of equitable compensation for unconscionable conduct.

[22] Below, 77–83.

[23] Kremer (n 10 above) 188. At 189 a residual role is envisaged for it 'at a visceral level'. Such language is inappropriate, indeed inapplicable to this causative event.

But unjust enrichment does not require unconscionable conduct, except, meaninglessly, *ex post*.[24] And the slight facts which create rights to restitution of unjust enrichment make no case at all for compensation of loss save so far as the loss is capped by gain. Hence any system which attempts to do without a law of unjust enrichment is bound sooner or later to have to reverse out of the cul-de-sac in which it has placed itself.

The third kind of causative event beyond contract and wrongs, exemplified in the mistaken payment of a non-existent debt, really is both foundational and distinct. It cannot be done without. And its strict restitutionary liability is unequivocally tied to the relocation of gains. It would be a painful and expensive irony if, just as English law is finally managing to retrieve the disruptive error of hiding unjust enrichment in contract and trusts, another great common law jurisdiction were deliberately to conceal it in the law of civil wrongs.

[24] Above, 5–6.

2

Three Maps

The mapping metaphor was used by Blackstone. In 1756, in his inaugural lecture, he said that the duty of the 'academical expounder of the laws' was to make clear how the various parts of the law fitted together:

> He should consider his course as a general map of the law, marking out the shape of the country, its connexions and boundaries, its greater divisions and principal cities: it is not his business to describe minutely the subordinate limits, or to fix the longitude and latitude of every inconsiderable hamlet.[1]

This chapter is concerned with three maps which together show where unjust enrichment belongs and how it is itself divided. Unjust enrichment is a causative event. That is, it is an event from which rights arise. The first of the three maps fixes its relation to other categories of the same kind. The second relates those event-based categories, and unjust enrichment in particular, to the law of obligations and the law of property. These are not categories of causative event but of responses to events. The third map raises the level of magnification so as to expose the layout of unjust enrichment itself.

To require a good map of the law is by metaphor to insist on sound classification. Classifications answer questions. Where do animals live? Some are aquatic, some terrestrial, some amphibious, others (like tapeworms) live in other habitats. What do animals eat? Some are omnivorous, some carnivorous, some herbivorous, and others eat other things. When different classifications are combined, a complex hierarchy results, each level dividing according to its own criterion. The hierarchical combination can be undone. That is to say, one can revert to a series of single-question classifications.

Flawed classification is a source and symptom of intellectual disorder, and there are common flaws of many different kinds. Most obviously, a classification is flawed if any term at any one level is part of an answer to

[1] Sir William Blackstone, *Commentaries on the Laws of England* vol 1 (1765) 35 [facsimile of the first edition (University of Chicago Press Chicago and London 1979)].

an alien question, as where 'herbivorous' appears in the division by habitat. Equally bad is the flaw which occurs when, even though all the terms answer the same question, one of them is or may be a sub-set of another, as where 'arboreal' is included in the classification by habitat without any limit being imposed on 'terrestrial'.

A. THE FIRST MAP: EVENT-BASED CLASSIFICATION

From what events do rights arise? All rights which can be realized in court arise from some event which happens in the world. In the previous chapter we identified unjust enrichment as the generic conception of one causative event from which restitutionary rights arise. We bumped from time to time into other causative events such as contracts and wrongs, which form the two best known categories. This section briefly gives a more complete picture of the classification of rights by reference to their causative event.

1. FOUR COLUMNS

Rights always arise either from manifestations of consent or from events which operate independently of consent. Manifestations of consent include, above all, contracts, declarations of trust, conveyances, and wills. Events which operate independently of consent are wrongs, unjust enrichments, and miscellaneous others. Every wrong is a breach of duty, but in our legal system the event-based category of wrongs has rarely been visible in its entirety because it has traditionally been broken up into sub-sets according to a different criterion, namely the source of law which recognized the duty broken by the wrongdoer.

Instead of one category of civil wrongs we have therefore had four, and those four have not lived in close proximity to each other. The four are torts, equitable wrongs, breaches of statutory duty not amounting to a tort, and breaches of contract. Torts are breaches of duties directly imposed by the common law. In the other cases the primary duty is imposed by equity (meaning by the law descended from the Court of Chancery), by statute, or by the parties' own contract. The primary rights and duties arising from contract are not to be confused with the secondary rights and duties arising from the wrong of breach of contract.

After manifestations of consent and wrongs come unjust enrichments. These have already been introduced as including all events materially identical to the receipt of a mistaken payment of a non-existent debt.

The defendant is enriched at the expense of the claimant and there is in addition a reason, not being a manifestation of consent or a wrong, why that enrichment should be given up to the claimant. There are acquisitive wrongs and hence there are cases of wrongful enrichment, but an unjust enrichment is never a wrong. If the claimant relies on the facts in their character as a wrong, his cause of action arises in the law of wrongs.

Finally, there is a residual miscellany of events which fall outside the previous three categories. When a ship is holed and in danger, the obligation to pay a salvor a reward for saving it or its cargo arises from successful rescue. *Negotiorum gestio* (uninvited intervention in the affairs of another) also belongs in the residual miscellany. It has a paragraph to itself below. Liability to pay tax arises from a range of taxable events. The list of miscellaneous events beyond the three nominate heads need not be further investigated here. This is just as well since to enumerate all its members requires encyclopaedic erudition. Awareness of the existence of the residual miscellany is nonetheless important, to keep at bay a troublesome and incorrect supposition that every causative event must fit into one or other of the three nominate categories.

That error can do a number of different kinds of damage. The worst is its tendency to undermine attempts to describe the law of unjust enrichment. Gummow J, for instance, has attacked those who think it worthwhile to work in the field of restitution of unjust enrichment. He says that they encourage a futile search for a single explanation of 'all obligations which are neither contractual nor tortious in nature'.[2]

Here he hits out at an imaginary enemy. The law of restitution was indeed slow to recognize its multi-causality, but even the books on restitution did not claim to have hit upon a single explanation of every liability beyond contract and tort. That is all the more evident in the case of the law of unjust enrichment, which deals with only one of the generic events which gives rise to restitution. It claims only to reduce the size of the residual miscellany beyond contract and tort by taking out of it one more nominate event-based category. The remaining miscellany is miscellaneous. Gummow J is obviously right to insist that no single generic description can capture all the causative events within it.

Of the borderline cases which in the end need to be confined to the miscellany, one important example is *negotiorum gestio* which, translated

[2] The Hon Justice WMC Gummow AC, foreword to ID Jackman, *The Varieties of Restitution* (Federation Press Sydney 1998) iv.

literally, means management (*gestio*) of the affairs (*negotiorum*) of another (understood). It is convenient to use a looser translation and to speak of uninvited intervention in another's affairs. In the parable of the Good Samaritan, the Samaritan was prompted to intervene simply from his sense of neighbourly duty to the unconscious victim of the robbers.[3] Roman law, followed in this by its modern civilian successors, took the view that there should be a legal regime for such interventions, in part in order to avoid discouraging the giving of useful help to people not in a position to help themselves: 'because nobody would look after their affairs if there were no action to recoup his expenses.'[4]

Negotiorum gestio is not properly regarded as a species of unjust enrichment. There is no doubt that the intervener's right to reimbursement turns on the utility of the intervention, not on its success. There is no inquiry at all into the enrichment of the beneficiary and hence no tie between enrichment of the beneficiary and the amount he must pay. The measure of recovery is not gain-based. Moreover, the event has wider consequences. It binds the intervener to execute his intervention with due care and skill and to surrender anything he obtains in the course of his intervention.

For more than a hundred years the orthodox doctrine has been that English law does not recognize these liabilities other than in a few exceptional situations. That view always rested on an unsound foundation.[5] It has also been eroded by the multiplication of exceptions. It may be that the exceptions have now overwhelmed the supposed rule.

The interesting condition of the modern law cannot be explored here because it does not belong within unjust enrichment. Even in relation to the intervener's right to reimbursement, *negotiorum gestio* belongs in the fourth column of causative events, miscellaneous other events, not in the third, unjust enrichment. Moreover, in the grid which is discussed immediately below, the intervener's right is not even a right to restitution. It should appear in the compensation stripe, not in the restitution stripe. That being so, *negotiorum gestio* belongs neither in the law of unjust enrichment (an event-based category) nor in the law of restitution (a response-based category).

It is nonetheless true that, if English law really had no *negotiorum gestio*, some particular instances of uninvited intervention would be found

[3] Luke 25–37.

[4] Justinian, *Institutes* 3.27.1.

[5] The classic statement is to be found in the judgment of Bowen LJ in *Falcke v Scottish Imperial Insurance Co* (1886) 34 Ch D 234, 248, but the facts of the case were not appropriate to test the wide negative which he declared.

to conform to analysis as unjust enrichments, and those few cases would then form the kernel of a much narrower doctrine of necessitous intervention within the law of unjust enrichment. That is another story. It cannot be pursued here. It may never be pursued, because, as has been said, the old proposition denying the intervener any general right to reimbursement has probably been swallowed up by its numerous so-called exceptions.

Negotiorum gestio makes a brief appearance at this point only to illustrate the need to keep the fourth column of the grid in mind and to avoid overloading the third event-based column (unjust enrichment) under the illusion that non-contractual, non-tortious causative events can find no other home. Uninvited intervention is not a contract, a wrong, or an unjust enrichment. It belongs in the miscellaneous fourth column. In addition, the intervener's right is not a right to restitution.

2. THE GRID: STRIPES ACROSS THE COLUMNS

	Manifestations of Consent	Wrongs	Unjust Enrichments	Other Causative Events
Restitution	1	5	9	13
Compensation	2	6	10	14
Punishment	3	7	11	15
Other Goals	4	8	12	16

(a) Four Stripes

The short version of the classification of rights by causative events is that every right which courts will realize arises from consent, from a wrong, from an unjust enrichment, or from some other event. These four categories include no mention of restitution. The reason is obvious. They are categories which only appear when the question is, From what events do rights arise? Restitution and compensation, by contrast, are categories which appear when a different question about rights is asked, What goal are rights intended to achieve when, with or without litigation, they are realized? Compensation is loss-based recovery: a right to compensation is a right to have a loss made good. Restitution is gain-based recovery: a right to restitution is a right to obtain a gain made by the defendant.

Different questions provoke different classifications, which cut across each other. If we represent the four categories of causative event as four vertical columns, the goal-based categories—let us settle for restitution, compensation, punishment, and other goals—must appear as horizontal stripes. The boxes formed as the stripes cut across the columns do not necessarily have any content. Sometimes they definitely have none. The box at the intersection of punishment and unjust enrichment has no content. The boxes should be regarded as asking questions. This box asks whether the event unjust enrichment ever generates a right to punitive awards. The answer is an emphatic 'no'.

(b) The Restitution Stripe: Multi-Causality

The grid depicts the multi-causality of restitution or, more accurately, its potential multi-causality. As the restitution stripe cuts across the four event-based columns it makes four boxes, each of which asks whether restitutionary rights are ever generated by that particular causative event. In the consent box the answer is yes. If, having lost my purse, I ask you to lend me £50, the loan gives you a restitutionary right which is by origin contractual. The contract of loan obliges me to give up value received. Again, if in response to my demands you hand over money which I promise to pay back if it should turn out that you were not bound to pay, you have, arising from contract, a conditional entitlement to restitution.[6] Again a publisher generally promises an author a percentage of the profits from the book, thus incurring a gain-based liability from contract. Where contractual rights to restitution exactly mirror the operation of the law of unjust enrichment, there can be no recourse to the law of unjust enrichment.[7]

As we saw in the last chapter when examples were given of rights to restitution arising other than from unjust enrichment, the box formed by the intersection of wrongs and restitution also has content. Instances were given of restitution for breach of fiduciary duty, for breach of contract, and for the tort of conversion.[8] The next box, at the intersection of restitution and unjust enrichment, needs no discussion here. It is the business of the rest of the book. It contains the receipt of the mistaken

[6] *Sebel Products Ltd v Commissioners of Customs & Excise* [1949] Ch 409.

[7] *Pan Ocean Shipping Ltd v Creditcorp Ltd (The Trident Beauty)* [1994] 1 WLR 161 (HL) where the point is made more difficult by the use of 'restitution' to identify the cause of action in unjust enrichment.

[8] Above, 12–16.

payment of a non-existent debt and, with that core case, every event materially identical to that central figure.

The fourth box, made by the intersection of the restitution stripe and the miscellaneous column, also has content. In *negotiorum gestio* we saw a fourth column event outside the restitution stripe. But there are also instances of a right to recover a gain—hence within the restitution stripe—where the relevant event is not a contract, wrong, or unjust enrichment. This is quite difficult and must take more than a line or two. The fact that this box has content means that, even after having eliminated all cases of contractual restitution or restitution for wrongs as such, you cannot jump from gain-based recovery to the conclusion that you are looking at a case of unjust enrichment.

One who earns £1,000 usually owes the Inland Revenue a percentage of that gain, say £400. The Inland Revenue has a gain-based right—a restitutionary right according to the stretched meaning which that word is made to bear in its role as a respectable synonym for disgorgement.[9] This is restitution, but it is not restitution triggered by unjust enrichment. The taxable event, income received, is not an enrichment of the taxpayer at the expense of the Inland Revenue. Since the taxpayer makes no promise to pay and commits no wrong in earning income, the causative event belongs in none of the first three columns.

Another restitution-yielding event which belongs in the fourth column is the judgment of a court. All the four boxes made by the restitution stripe as it crosses the event-based columns are boxes of rights which, until they are realized, remain birds in the bush. If it comes to litigation, the judgment will generally order the defendant to comply with the right which the claimant has asked to be realized. Thus, where a claimant establishes a right to restitution arising from a wrong or from an unjust enrichment at his expense, the court will generally order the defendant to give up the money value of that gain.

If the defendant remains recalcitrant, the process of execution of judgment will finally turn the bird in the bush into a bird in the hand. The right exists before the judgment which replicates it, but technically the judgment novates the original right. That is to say, it extinguishes the right brought into court and replaces it with another born of the judgment itself. Although its content may be identical to that of the right brought into court, the right which goes to execution is the right created by the order of the court.

[9] Below, 281–3.

A more difficult example which also belongs in the fourth column is the receipt of a thing owned by another. Suppose that your car is stolen and comes into my possession. Your interest in the car may have arisen from consent, or from a wrong, or from an unjust enrichment, or from some other event. Whatever its origin, your property interest in the car gives you a right to possession, and my coming into possession puts me under an obligation to surrender possession to you. This is true even if I have committed no wrong. Hence, my coming into possession is not a second column event, for it may not initially be a wrong, although it will rapidly become one if I fail to comply with my obligation to surrender possession.

An honest finder commits no wrong while intending to honour his obligation to surrender possession to the owner.[10] It is not a third column event either. That is, it is not an unjust enrichment. When you assert your title you are asserting that the car is not my asset but yours or, in other words, that it is part of your wealth, not mine. To base your claim on unjust enrichment, which you can do, you have to renounce your title. You have an election. You can either insist on your title and thus deny my enrichment or forego your title and treat me as unjustly enriched at your expense.[11]

This relatively straightforward picture of a column four event within the restitution stripe is complicated by the fact that, if and when it comes to litigation, a claimant rarely stands directly on his proprietary interest. The common law knows no claim of that kind in relation to chattels. In the case of the car, therefore, it is probable that you will sue me for the wrong of conversion, in the second column. Conversion, as we have seen, is a wrong which entitles you to either compensation or restitution. Alternatively, you may sue me in unjust enrichment for the value added to my wealth. If you do that, you will be renouncing your title, for you cannot say that I am enriched while at the same time insisting that the car forms no part of my wealth. In effect you are driven into the law of obligations in order obliquely to protect your proprietary interest. You have to appeal either to an obligation arising from a wrong or to an obligation arising from unjust enrichment.[12]

On the chancery side matters proceed differently. There the claimant can directly assert his entitlement under a trust and, so long as he is entitled to the entire beneficial interest, he can demand that the defendant

[10] Compare *Costello v Chief Constable of Derbyshire* [2001] EWCA Civ 381, [2001] 1 WLR 1437 (police lawfully in possession for forensic purposes).

[11] Below, 64–8.

[12] Below, 66–8.

be ordered to transfer the legal title. The column in which his claim arises depends on the event which created the trust which he alleges. Most trusts arise from declarations of trust accepted by the trustee. The assertion of an interest under a trust created in that way will clearly belong in the first column, which contains all rights arising from manifestations of consent. The different modes, direct and indirect, of protecting property in litigation will be discussed in more detail later in this book.[13] The matter has crept in here only because we have been discussing the different causative events from which rights arise and one such event on which we paused was the defendant's coming into possession of something belonging to the claimant.

B. THE SECOND MAP: PROPERTY AND OBLIGATIONS

Rights realizable in court are responses to events. We have seen how they can be divided according to their different causative events. They can be divided by many other criteria. If a question is asked as to their goals, the answer is that they aim at restitution, compensation, punishment and other goals. If a question is asked about the source of law responsible for their recognition, the answer is that some were recognized by the courts of common law, some in the chancery, some in admiralty, some by Parliament, and others by other sources. However, their causative events aside, the most important division arises from the question about their exigibility. Exigibility is demandability. Against whom can rights be demanded?

1. RIGHTS *IN PERSONAM* (OBLIGATIONS) AND RIGHTS *IN REM* (PROPERTY)

The answer is that some are rights *in personam* and some are rights *in rem*. Rights *in personam* are in principle demandable only from the person against whom they originally arose or someone representing that person, while rights *in rem* are in principle demandable wherever the *res* (the thing) is found and hence against anyone who has it or is interfering with it. The phrase 'in principle' leaves room for contrived departures from these starting points. Thus a right *in rem* can be cut off in the interests of the security of transactions in some or all cases of bona fide purchase. And under particular conditions a right *in personam* can be made to

[13] Below, 54–8, Chapter 8.

simulate the behaviour of a right *in rem* so as to be demandable against a third party.

Rights *in personam* are rights that a person make some performance, exigible against that person. A right that a person should do something is, when looked at from the other end, an obligation incumbent on that person to do it. That perspective has always dominated our choice of vocabulary. Hence the law of rights *in personam* is better known as the law of obligations. Obligations are not events. They are responses to events. All rights which can be realized in court are responses to events. What holds for the set, holds for the sub-set of rights *in personam*, rights exigible against the person under the correlative obligation.

The law of obligations coordinates with the law of property. Obligations and property are the two pillars of private law. Just as the law of obligations is the law of rights *in personam*, the law of property is the law of rights *in rem*. Ownership of a thing, for example, follows the thing owned. My wedding ring when stolen remains mine even when, later, you buy it from a shop. A lease of land is likewise a property right. The land does not move, but whoever comes to the land must recognize the interest of the lessee. A charge by way of legal mortgage behaves in the same way. A right of way created as an easement likewise binds all those who subsequently come to the servient land. There is a finite number of rights which can take effect *in rem*. Synonymously, there is a *numerus clausus* of property rights.

We use 'property' in more than one sense. It frequently operates as a synonym for wealth. In that usage property includes obligations. A right *in personam* to be paid £1,000 is an asset. It is property when property is wealth. In the stricter sense in which there is always a tacit contrast between property and obligations the law of property is the law of rights *in rem*. In this book references to property rights or proprietary rights and every use of the language of property should be understood in that narrower sense. The same assumption underlies every law school syllabus which offers a course in property and separate courses in the event-based sub-sets of the law of obligations. Thus, if there is a course in contract and a course in property, 'property' is being used in the narrower sense, as the law of rights *in rem* as opposed to the law of rights *in personam*.[14]

[14] The tendency to blur this distinction and the danger of doing so form the theme of A Pretto, *The Boundaries of Personal Property: Shares and Sub-Shares* (Oxford D Phil Thesis 2002). Dr Pretto was my supervisee. The supervisor, as often happens, learned much more than he taught.

Property and obligations are thus sub-sets of rights realizable in court which emerge in answer to the question against whom rights are demandable. Prudence might suggest the need for a residual third category, but the words 'realizable in court' probably render that unnecessary. There are indeed other rights good against everyone, such as the right to reputation or to bodily integrity, which are neither *in rem* nor *in personam*, but they are never directly realized in court. They form the superstructure above wrongs, and it is the wrong consisting in their infringement which immediately generates rights which are realizable in court. I have a primary right to bodily integrity, which you infringe when you hit me or carelessly drive over my foot. It is the secondary right arising from the wrong that is brought into court. So, when you have run over my foot, I assert my right *in personam* that you pay me compensation for the infringement of my primary and solely superstructural right to bodily integrity.

2. UNJUST ENRICHMENT AND THE LAW OF OBLIGATIONS

When we combine classification of rights by exigibility (rights *in rem* and rights *in personam*) and classification of rights by causative event (consent, wrongs, unjust enrichments, other events) we have to create a hierarchy. The question is which to start with. Should the first level divide by events or by exigibility? There is no logically correct answer. It is merely a matter of convenience. Throughout the European tradition, the practice is to make exigibility dominant. So, at the first and highest level the *summa divisio* is between property and obligations.

(a) The second level: obligations and their causative events

One level down, within obligations, we turn to the division by causative events. As a matter of history it proved relatively easy to see that every obligation arose from a manifestation of consent, from a wrong, or from one of a jumble of other events.[15] Unjust enrichment ultimately emerged much later in the long struggle to reduce the residual jumble.[16] In the common law it is only emerging now. Its identification adds one more

[15] Already clear in Gaius in the second century AD: Digest 44.7.1 pr (Gaius, *Res Cottidianae*) amplifying Gaius, *Institutes* 3.88–91. For further discussion see below, 268–70.

[16] On the role of Grotius (1583–1645) in this: R Feenstra, 'Grotius' Doctrine of Unjust Enrichment as a Source of Obligation: Its Origin and Its Influence in Roman-Dutch Law' in E Schrage (ed), *Unjust Enrichment: The Comparative Legal History of the Law of Restitution* (Duncker and Humblot Berlin 1995) 197. For the earlier period J Hallebeek in the same volume 59–121.

nominate generic category of causative event and reduces the size of the residual fourth category. Every obligation arises from consent, from a wrong, from an unjust enrichment, or from some other event. A person who receives a mistaken payment of a non-existent debt is unjustly enriched, and from that unjust enrichment he comes under an obligation to make restitution.

This is as yet lopsided. We have made no second level statement for property rights. That is matter for the next sub-section. Otherwise there is no mystery here. It is only necessary not to be distracted by the switch between obligations and rights *in personam*. We have taken precautions against confusion. The law of obligations is synonymous with the law of rights *in personam*. A right *in personam* held by one person correlates with an obligation in another. Although the category is predominantly named from the latter perspective, it remains a sub-set of rights. What is true of the set is true of the sub-set. We have already established that all rights realizable in court can be classified by these causative events. The same is true of rights *in personam* or, synonymously, obligations.

(b) The English Curriculum in the 21st Century

Our hierarchical map looks like this: rights realizable in court are either personal, forming the subject-matter of the law of obligations, or proprietary, forming the subject-matter of the law of property; personal rights arise from consent or independently of consent, and, when independently of consent, from wrongs, from unjust enrichment, or from miscellaneous other events. To what extent is this reflected in the law school curriculum? There are courses on property, in practice often confined to one *res*, namely land. There are also always courses on two of the sub-sets of obligations, namely contract and tort, those being slightly restricted versions of consent and wrongs. There are as yet no courses at all on unjust enrichment.

Unjust enrichment has to be found, if at all, in the books and courses on restitution. Unjust enrichment is one of the events which triggers rights to restitution. Although restitution has for some years been required by the professions as part of a qualifying law degree, it makes no more than an interstitial appearance in most undergraduate curricula. There are a few full courses on that response-based subject, but they are mostly found only at the postgraduate level. Within them, some do and some do not distinguish clearly between unjust enrichment and other events giving rise to restitutionary rights.

The gap in the curriculum is reflected in the law library. The first paragraph of this book remarked that unjust enrichment, however necessary, was an unfamiliar category of the law. Its work has been done after a fashion, but incoherently under obscure names and illegitimately borrowed explanations. At this end of the law of obligations, the process of rationalization has fallen a century behind schedule.

This end of the law of obligations includes the residual fourth category of causative events. They do not lend themselves to either books or courses. Judgments are discussed in works on civil procedure and on *res judicata*, also to a certain extent under the slippery title of 'remedies'. Tax lawyers deal with one substantial sub-set, namely all those obligations arising from taxable events. The miscellany could indeed be substantially narrowed if we used a five-term classification: consent, wrongs, unjust enrichment, taxable events, and miscellaneous others. A book on uninvited intervention in the affairs of another, covering both *negotiorum gestio* and salvage, would create a sixth head. It is in the nature of a residual miscellany to yield up ever smaller nominate categories. Tidying up the non-contractual, non-tortious end of the law of obligations means being aware of the residual miscellany; it cannot mean looking for some unifying theory. The miscellany is miscellaneous.

3. UNJUST ENRICHMENT AND THE LAW OF PROPERTY

It is possible to confine the operation of unjust enrichment to the law of obligations. Civilian systems make that choice. They say it generates only rights *in personam*. One effect is that claimants in unjust enrichment, having only personal claims, all become unsecured creditors. As against an insolvent enrichee, they have to join the miserable crowd waiting to share *pro rata* the scraps left over after the secured creditors have been satisfied. One scholar has argued that English law ought to make the same choice and move as quickly as possible to the position in which unjust enrichment generates only personal claims.[17] The form of the argument shows that that is not the present law. In English law unjust enrichments do currently also give rise to property rights in some, but not all, cases.

(a) The Shape of a Categorical Error

A system which confines unjust enrichment to the law of obligations, allowing it to trigger only rights *in personam*, creates a monopoly of

[17] WJ Swadling, 'Property and Unjust Enrichment' in JW Harris (ed), *Property Problems from Genes to Pension Funds* (Kluwer London 1997) 130.

choice, not a monopoly determined by logic. Unfortunately, in recent years just as the need for a rational law of unjust enrichment has begun to assert itself, a contrary view has begun to take root. In some quarters property and unjust enrichment have been presented as categories which are mutually exclusive as a matter of logic. That is an error, which confounds the true relationship between unjust enrichment and property. A little time must be taken to weed the error out.

Once one combines different classifications in a hierarchy, one must not forget that each level divides according to its own criterion. This means that it is almost invariably unsafe to suppose an exclusive logical opposition between categories at different levels. Nobody would dream of saying of a given case that it belonged to the law of obligations and therefore not in the law of unjust enrichment. That would contradict the empirical facts. It would also be logical nonsense. One could not say of a given animal that it was terrestrial and therefore not carnivorous.

Categorical errors of that kind are in fact never seen in relation to unjust enrichment and obligations. But it is exactly this kind of error which has for the moment taken a firm but flawed grip on orthodox doctrine as to the relationship between unjust enrichment and property. Very distinguished lawyers have begun to allow themselves to assert that a given case or question belongs in the law of property as opposed to the law of unjust enrichment. Yet property and obligations are coordinate categories: rights divided by exigibility. What is obvious about the relationship between unjust enrichment and obligations (rights *in personam*) should be equally obvious of unjust enrichment and property (rights *in rem*). Unjust enrichment is the generic description of an event from which rights arise. Commonly those rights are *in personam* and hence obligations. Sometimes, however, the rights generated by unjust enrichment are *in rem*, property rights.

The relationship between unjust enrichment and the law of property is formally the same as the relationship between unjust enrichment and the law of obligations. Property rights, like obligations, are a sub-set of rights realizable in court. What holds for the set holds for the sub-set. As every right, so every property right must arise from consent, from a wrong, from an unjust enrichment, or from some other event. Although every property right must arise from one of these events, it does not follow that every one of these events must generate one or more property rights. We have just accepted that some systems choose not to allow unjust enrichment to generate any property rights and that one scholar thinks that English law should follow suit.

(b) Non-Consensual Property Rights

Non-consensual property rights arise from wrongs, unjust enrichment and other events. If I paint my car with your paint, the paint accedes to the car and becomes mine. Similarly, if I make wine from your grapes, the wine is mine. These are fourth category events. They belong in the residual miscellany. We know from *Attorney-General of Hong Kong v Reid*, if we did not know it before, that there is at least one acquisitive wrong, namely breach of fiduciary duty, which generates a proprietary right.[18] There the Hong Kong government acquired an equitable beneficial interest in bribes taken by a corrupt prosecutor in breach of his fiduciary duty. Having a property interest in the bribes, it was then able to claim such an interest in their traceable product, the farms in New Zealand in which the bribes had been invested.

The proprietary response to wrongs is rare. An opponent might condemn it on all sorts of grounds but not on the ground that it was a logical impossibility. In *Chase Manhattan Bank NA Ltd v Israel–British Bank (London) Ltd*[19] Goulding J held that a mistaken payment, the central example of an unjust enrichment, generated both personal rights and equitable proprietary rights. Again, all sorts of criticisms might legitimately be made of that decision, except that it was *a priori* impossible for a mistaken payment to cause the second of these different responses. As with wrongs, whether an unjust enrichment generates proprietary rights is a matter of choice, not logic. A system may or may not reverse unjust enrichment by means of allowing the event to generate a proprietary right.

(c) *Foskett v McKeown*

The House of Lords appears nonetheless to have endorsed just such a logical exclusivity between property and unjust enrichment. In *Foskett v McKeown*[20] the question was whether beneficiaries of a trust could claim a proprietary interest in assets obtained with money stolen from the trust. To simplify the complexities of the case itself, suppose a trustee steals £100,000 from the trust, puts it into his bank account at a time when the

[18] [1994] 1 AC 324 (PC NZ). The question whether this case, departing from *Lister & Co v Stubbs* (1890) 45 Ch D 1 (CA), represented English law applicable at the level of the High Court was answered in the affirmative by Lawrence Collins J in *Daraydan Holdings Ltd v Solland International Ltd* [2004] EWHC 622 (Ch) [78]–[87].

[19] [1981] Ch 105 (Ch). The outcome is reinterpreted in *Westdeutsche Landesbank Girozentrale v Islington LBC* [1996] AC 669 (HL) 714 (Lord Browne-Wilkinson). Forthright extra-judicial criticism by Lord Millett: The Rt Hon Sir Peter Millett 'Restitution and Constructive Trust' (1998) 114 LQR 399, 412–13.

[20] [2001] 1 AC 102 (HL).

account stands £50,000 in credit, then empties the account and uses the £150,000 to buy himself a Rolls Royce. Can the beneficiaries take a proprietary interest in the Rolls Royce? The House of Lords held that they can but insisted that that answer belonged to the law of property, not the law of unjust enrichment. With the support of Lord Browne-Wilkinson and Lord Hoffmann, Lord Millett said, 'The transmission of a claimant's property rights from one asset to its traceable proceeds is part of our law of property, not of the law of unjust enrichment.'[21]

One reason for this unfortunate opposition was reliance on what can conveniently be called the fiction of persistence. Their Lordships thought that it was correct to say that the claimants' original right in the original asset simply persisted in, or was transmitted to, the substitute. The same idea lurks in the civilian phrase 'real subrogation', which means 'thing substitution'. Real subrogation rests on an image in which a property right resembles a single fishing line which can hook one fish after another. The Rolls Royce which replaces the trust money is then just the pike which is hooked after the perch. The right, which is the fishing line, remains the same throughout.

The effect of the fiction of persistence is to assert that the right in the substitute, the Rolls Royce, is the very same right as the right in the pilfered money. Hence the event from which the right in the Rolls Royce arose was the original declaration of the express trust from which the money was stolen. The fiction conceals the need to find and reflect upon any other causative event and, in particular, upon the event which consists in the non-consensual substitution.

In contrasting the categories of property—a category of response—and unjust enrichment—a category of causative event—their Lordships, in the grip of the fiction, must really have intended to contrast causative events. They must have intended to say that the property right in the substitute arose from the original declaration of trust, not from any other event and in particular not from unjust enrichment.

The element of fiction is evident. It is odd to say that a right in a car about which at the time nobody knew anything arose from a declaration of trust of money. It is even more odd when the right itself mutates. The claimant has a choice in relation to the substitute whether to take a beneficial interest proportionate to his involuntary contribution or a security interest for the amount of that contribution.

[21] [2001] 1 AC 102, 127, 132. Lord Browne-Wilkinson and Lord Hoffmann used similar language: 108–9, 132.

Fictions express faith in the existence of a true but presently elusive explanation. The elusive explanation has to be found.[22] For the moment, however, all that matters is the proposition, seemingly denied by their Lordships, that the law of property is a category of response of the same nature as, and coordinate with, the law of obligations. There can be no logical opposition between such categories and their causative events. A right *in rem* can arise from unjust enrichment, just as can a right *in personam*. When it does, it belongs equally to the law of property and to the law of unjust enrichment, no less than a right *in personam* to recover a mistaken payment belongs equally in both the law of obligations and the law of unjust enrichment, and a lion is both terrestrial and carnivorous.

(d) Academic Support: the Virgo Position

There is no doubt that their Lordships were deeply influenced by the work of Mr Virgo of Cambridge University. His important book does indeed contend that property rights can never arise from unjust enrichment. It is definitionally impossible for them to do so. For him, therefore, it makes perfect sense to talk of 'property, therefore not unjust enrichment'.[23] Mr Virgo's position reflects complex and not fully resolved problems in this area, but in the extreme form in which he presents the proposition it must certainly be incorrect.

If my wedding ring is stolen and passes to you in circumstances in which title remains in me, it is indeed impossible to say that my title arises from your unjust enrichment. It arose before you came into the story. The ring became mine when my wife gave it to me. The consensual causative event which explains why my ring is mine remains unchanged even though the ring is now in your hands. The passive survival of my title prevents your enrichment. There is no new right, no active response to unjust enrichment. Suppose, however, that the circumstances are such that title passes. I make a gift to you of an antique silver spoon. Let it be that there was a mistake induced by an innocent misrepresentation on your part, with the consequence that property passed at law while the

[22] A Burrows, 'Proprietary Restitution: Unmasking Unjust Enrichment' (2001) 117 LQR 412. The article (i) rejects the fiction and (ii) insists, rightly in the present author's view, that the truth is that the relevant event is unjust enrichment. Not everyone who accepts (i) also accepts (ii). Mr Swadling would place non-consensual substitution in the fourth category which is 'miscellaneous other events': W Swadling in P Birks (ed), *English Private Law* (OUP Oxford 2000 with annual supplements) [4.439]–[4.481].

[23] G Virgo, *The Principles of the Law of Restitution* (OUP Oxford 1999) 15–17, 592–601.

mistake nonetheless rendered the gift invalid and left you unjustly enriched at my expense.

Nothing prevents a system which chooses to do it from reversing this enrichment by means of a proprietary right. If it purported to confer on me exactly the same kind of right as I had before, it would be merely contradicting the proposition that property had passed. That is the case of the ring, and to that extent Mr Virgo is right: it is impossible to respond to an unjust enrichment by re-creating the same proprietary right as was previously held by the claimant. But if the law confers a new and different proprietary right, as by giving me a new equitable interest which I never had before or by conferring on me a power *in rem* to vest the ring in me, that new right *in rem* indisputably arises from your unjust enrichment and in order to reverse it. We will see in Part IV that English law does respond to unjust enrichment in this manner. If it is true that a tide is running against that kind of proprietary response, it is a tide of policy, not logic, and so far it is a tide of policy which is insufficiently informed.

(e) Preventing and Reversing Unjust Enrichment

It is tempting to say that the law of property prevents unjust enrichment and the law of unjust enrichment reverses it. That attractively elegant proposition is seriously inaccurate. It falls back into the error of seeing the categories of property and unjust enrichment as being mutually exclusive. All property rights belong in the law of property. They are what the law of property is about. A property right brought into existence by an unjust enrichment, to reverse that unjust enrichment, belongs both to the law of property and to the law of unjust enrichment. The relevant contrast is not between the law of property and the law of unjust enrichment but between the survival of old proprietary rights and the creation of new rights, whether *in rem* or *in personam*, for the purpose of reversing an enrichment. The passive survival of old rights *in rem* is preventative. The active creation of new rights to undo enrichment is the business of the law of unjust enrichment. It is business done through both the law of property and the law of obligations.

Professor Stoljar saw the law of unjust enrichment, which he preferred to call the law of quasi-contract,[24] as an extension of the law of property. There are a number of ways in which that proposition can be defended.

[24] SJ Stoljar, *The Law of Quasi-Contract* (2nd edn Law Book Company Sydney 1989) 18, 250.

The strict liability in unjust enrichment does find its parallel in the irrelevance of fault in the assertion of proprietary rights against defendants in possession. But he went further. He constantly described quasi-contractual claims as having a proprietary flavour or a proprietary explanation. That language plays with fire. The relationship between property and unjust enrichment is complex and has been made more tense by persistent error. But the discussion in the preceding pages shows that it can be pinned down in terms of causative events and responses to those events. To speak of the law of unjust enrichment as 'proprietary' in any looser sense can only blur the picture. Unjust enrichment is an independent causative event which straddles the analytical distinction between property and obligations. Some rights arising from that causative event belong to the law of property and some to the law of obligations.

This section has said, in the teeth of high authority, that unjust enrichment is an event which can and does generate proprietary rights—rights *in rem* as opposed to rights *in personam*. Structurally the relationship between property and unjust enrichment is the same as that between obligations and enrichment. The really difficult question is when. That question belongs to Chapter 8. Unsurprisingly, given the confusions introduced here, that Chapter will reveal some very unsettled case law.

C. THE THIRD MAP: INSIDE UNJUST ENRICHMENT

We have been relating unjust enrichment to other better-known categories. At this point we pass inside it. We are now concerned with the layout of the law of unjust enrichment itself. Every case of unjust enrichment is materially identical to mistaken payment of a non-existent debt. The word 'materially' carries a heavy burden. On the surface all the other examples look different. The principal differences relate to the nature of the enrichment, the nature of the claimant's relationship to that enrichment, or the nature of the reason why the enrichment is unjust.

A category which is formed around a core case will inevitably have untidy boundaries. It is necessary to keep in mind the fact that the unity and necessity of the law of unjust enrichment was long denied and is only now being recognized. Even now it is still often more difficult than one would expect to identify a member of the family, disguised as it is likely to be in the deceptive language of the past. Individual figures have grown up in isolation, as for instance money had and received, subrogation, and rescission. It will be some time before there is agreement among lawyers as to all the borderline cases.

The view taken here is that the terrain is not best mapped by trying to achieve an overview of every known liability which, in whatever language it was developed, might now be said to arise from unjust enrichment. On the contrary, the better course is to emancipate the law from the welter of earlier language and to insist that unjust enrichment be more abstractly mapped in terms of the analysis to which every figure which really is materially identical to mistaken payment of a non-existent debt will in fact conform.

Every liability in unjust enrichment answers to a five-question analysis derived, with two necessary additions, from the full name of the event, unjust enrichment at the expense of another. The map of the modern law of unjust enrichment will be directly determined by that analysis. The old names of the individual figures will be transcended and replaced by this analysis. They do not make the map. They obscure it.[25]

I. THE FIVE-QUESTION ANALYSIS

Every problem in unjust enrichment can be unlocked by asking these five questions: (i) Was the defendant enriched? (ii) Was it at the expense of this claimant? (iii) Was it unjust? (iv) What kind of right did the claimant acquire? (v) Does the defendant have a defence? These questions provide the structure of the law of unjust enrichment and of the rest of this book.

The first three questions show that an unjust enrichment has happened and they thus establish a *prima facie* cause of action. The fourth (rights) principally seeks to determine whether the claimant's restitutionary right is *in personam* or *in rem* and, if the latter, whether it is immediately vested or merely a power to vest and whether, when vested, it is a beneficial interest or a security interest. The answers to that question have been rendered less than coherent by the long difficulty of seeing the subject as a whole. In the days before they began to be pulled together by the language of unjust enrichment, each centrifugal fragment became a

[25] The two chapters of Part VI, below, review the old, pre-unjust enrichment world. They seek to explain a dozen or so difficult words and phrases which have hitherto both done the work and impeded it. In the judgments that vocabulary still competes with the language of unjust enrichment. But much of it is now little understood. Money had and received, for instance, is commonly invoked, as a formula with a function but no meaning. The five-question inquiry will displace most of the old vocabulary. Some is still needed but has to be more precisely understood. Part VI discusses the old terminology. Some readers may prefer to read that discussion first. It doubles as a species of historical introduction to the modern law.

law unto itself. The aim, in relation to the fourth question, must now be to come as near to a single regime as genuine differences between groups of cases will allow. There is a long way to go.

It has become apparent in recent years that the fine tuning of the law of unjust enrichment will fall increasingly to the fifth question (defences). Restrictive interpretations of the cause of action have been relaxed as the defences have begun to take the strain. Provided the trade-off between liberal grounds for restitution and vigorous defences is kept in mind, the new strategy will do more sensitive justice. Here as elsewhere the *sine qua non* of rational development is the capacity to grasp the unity of unjust enrichment. Unless and until a contrary case is made the same defences must apply to every variety of the event and to every kind of right arising from the event.

The first three questions disentangle the three principal elements of the causative event. Question one (enrichment) and question two (at the expense of the claimant) are dealt with in Part II. In the great majority of cases neither is problematic, although when problems do arise they are rather difficult, largely because they have not often been directly confronted in the cases. Their importance could not be recognized other than intuitively so long as unjust enrichment was not acknowledged to exist as an independent causative event.

Part III is the heart of the law of unjust enrichment. It deals with the third question (unjust). Its business is to explore the reasons why an enrichment at the expense of the claimant has to be given up despite the absence of any wrong or manifestation of consent to that effect. Again the reader may prefer to take things out of order. Part III is accessible even if Part II is postponed. Whether read in or out of order, it is not easy going. The reason is that the last decade has twisted the kaleidoscope. The pattern is not as it was ten years ago. The process of understanding what has happened is only just beginning. It is exciting, but difficult. The final function of this introduction is to give a preliminary account of the way in which the picture has changed.

2. UNJUST FACTORS AND ENRICHMENT WITH NO BASIS

Nearly two hundred and fifty years ago, in *Moses v Macferlan*,[26] Lord Mansfield turned to Roman law to sort out one large sector at the non-contractual end of the English law of debt. Debt is a category of response, not a category of event. It is the sub-set of the law of obligations in which

[26] (1760) 2 Burr 1005, 97 ER 676.

the obligation is to pay a fixed sum of money or a fixed quantity of fungible goods. There are contractual debts and non-contractual debts. The spectrum of debt-creating events stretches from, at the contractual end, deeds, loans, sales, and leases to, at the non-contractual end, mistaken payments, judgments, and taxable events.

In Lord Mansfield's time it was common ground, built into the English forms of action, that one person became indebted to another when he received money for the benefit of that other. Some answer needed to be given to the question under what circumstances the law would regard a receipt as having been of that kind, 'to the use of the plaintiff'—as the old law expressed it. The answer which Lord Mansfield borrowed was immediately copied by Blackstone in his *Commentaries*, albeit embedded in a matrix of implied contract with an enthusiasm absent from the original. This is the part which Blackstone took from Lord Mansfield's judgment:[27]

> This is a very extensive and beneficial remedy, applicable to almost every case where the defendant has received money which *ex aequo et bono* he ought to refund. It lies for money paid by mistake, or on a consideration which happens to fail, or through imposition, extortion, or oppression, or where undue advantage is taken of the plaintiff's situation.

A generation later Sir William Evans identified the Roman and more recent civilian sources behind this clarification.[28] On that civilian foundation and hedged in by the form of action which Moses had used, the common law appeared to have constructed a building of its own, which was to be its law of unjust enrichment. The receipt of 'money which *ex aequo et bono* he ought to refund' needs minimal adjustment to become 'unjust enrichment'. Sadly, by the beginning of the 20th century this promising building had been completely overgrown by the ivy of implied contract. But it was not beyond reconstruction.

(a) Groups of Unjust Factors

The key to the English approach appeared to be the identification of specific non-contract, non-wrong reasons for restitution. Thus the Mansfield/Blackstone presentation already enumerated mistake, failure

[27] Blackstone (n 1 above) 3 *Commentaries* 162.

[28] Sir William Evans (tr), *Pothier's Law of Obligations* (Joseph Butterworth London 1806) vol 2, 378–81, cf his *Essays On the Action for Money Had and Received, on the Law of Insurances, and on the Law of Bills of Exchange and Promissory Notes* (Liverpool 1802) 48–9, repr [1998] Restitution L Rev 1, 7–8, 25.

of consideration, shades of fraud and pressure, and taking advantage of vulnerable people. Developed over the years, this list of 'unjust factors' could be seen to fall into groups.

(i) Intent-Based Unjust Factors

Most were variations on the nursery theme 'I didn't mean him to have it!' The full range divided in two, between imperfect intent and qualified intent. Imperfect intent in turn broke down between no intent at all and impaired intent. An intent to transfer might be relevantly impaired by mistake, by illegitimate pressure or by reduced autonomy caused by a relationship or by some personal disadvantage or from some other cause. Qualified intent covered all those situations in which the claimant did intend to make the transfer but only on a specified basis. If that underlying conditionality was not purged, the claimant could say, as in the cases of impaired intent, that, in the events which had happened, he never meant the defendant to be enriched.

(ii) Defendant-Sided Unjust Factors

At one time it seemed that it was essential to make room, alongside the intent-based unjust factors, for a fault-based and defendant-sided category called something like 'unconscientious receipt' or simply 'free acceptance'. That proved to be the result of muddled thinking. Professor Burrows was chiefly responsible for eliminating the defendant-sided category.[29]

Every supposed case turned out to be one in which, a *prima facie* unjust enrichment having already been established on other grounds, an element of culpable knowledge was additionally required on the particular facts and for a particular reason. It might be, for instance, that on some facts the defendant could not be said to have been enriched unless he knew that he was receiving a benefit offered in the expectation of payment. Or, again, it might be that an element of culpable knowledge was invoked to restrict restitution in a particular area to protect a countervailing interest, as for instance the need not to infantilize the aged. All elderly people would find it difficult to deal with their property if it were easy to obtain restitution for dementia.[30] There is no doubt that Professor Burrows was right to eliminate this defendant-sided category.

[29] A Burrows, 'Free Acceptance and the Law of Restitution' (1988) 104 LQR 576. See now A Burrows, *The Law of Restitution* (2nd edn Butterworths London 2002) 402–7.

[30] More detail in P Birks, 'The Role of Fault in the Law of Unjust Enrichment' in W Swadling and G Jones, *In Search of Principle: Essays in Honour of Lord Goff of Chieveley* (OUP Oxford 1999) 235.

One regrettable consequence of the error of creating this false category was the belief that an unconscientious receipt could operate as an indication of both enrichment and unjust. That is no longer accepted in the academic literature, but it has not yet been altogether cut out of the cases.[31]

(iii) Policy-Based Unjust Factors

The fault-based unjust factors being redundant, there remained cases inexplicable in terms of defective or qualified intent. It seemed possible to attribute all of them to the operation of specific policies which required enrichments to be given up without regard to the quality of the claimant's decision to make the payment or confer the benefit in question. Thus the reason why an enrichment had to be given up might be the need to reinforce governmental respect for the rule of law or the desirability of incentives encouraging withdrawal from illegal contracts.

Although somewhat untidy, the two lists of intent-based and policy-based unjust factors seemed to work, and they had the merit of keeping more or less in step with the way lay people thought.

(b) *Sine causa*, No Explanatory Basis

Despite its 18th-century foundation in Lord Mansfield's learning in Roman law, the down-to-earth, pragmatic and in some respects backward English law thus emerged from the heresy of implied contract in the second half of the 20th century looking very different from its civilian equivalent. Although civilian jurisdictions differ as between themselves in many ways, they all use the same basic approach to the question which asks when an enrichment must be given up even in the absence of contract or wrong. They divide enrichments between the explicable and the inexplicable. An enrichment which has no explanation must be given up. There is a limited range of recognized explanations. If the putative explanation is invalid or if there never was even a putative explanation, the enrichment is *sine causa*, it lacks the required explanatory basis and must be given up.

The last decade has seen the most important series of unjust enrichment cases ever to run through the English courts. They concerned the consequences of void contracts and, in particular, of void interest swaps.

[31] It recurs in *Rowe v Vale of White Horse DC* [2003] EWHC 388, [2003] 1 Lloyd's Rep 418. However the error did no harm, because in that case the Council seeking restitution had knowingly accepted the risk that the recipients of their services would not agree to pay. No system would have allowed recovery, so that it was not necessary to ascribe the conclusion against liability to the absence of any free acceptance.

They are explained and considered in Part III.[32] There is no escape from the conclusion that they adopted the 'no basis' approach. They do not fit in the list of unjust factors. This cannot be shuffled off or absorbed as though insignificant. It compels a radical re-orientation.

(c) Incompatible Bedfellows

Disorder in the law of torts is largely due to mixing incompatible approaches. We have torts which are degrees of fault, like negligence and deceit, and we have torts which are infringements of protected interests, like defamation, nuisance, interference with contractual relations, and interference with goods. These cannot but cut across each other. History brought us to that confusion. Nobody could voluntarily have chosen it. The law of unjust enrichment is young enough to haul itself out of a similar mess. The list of unjust factors and the inquiry into the existence of an explanatory basis are two entirely different methods of determining that an enrichment at the expense of another must be given up. Although in the vast majority of cases they reach the same destination, the two methods cannot be mixed or merged. Lord Hope of Craighead has already encouraged an assimilation.[33] But assimilation cannot mean anything like the blind co-existence of fault-based and interest-based torts, and it cannot happen without marginally changed outcomes.

Comparatists have seen this crisis coming. Dr Meier has repeatedly made a powerful case for the necessity of an English reorientation towards the *sine causa* approach.[34] Dr Krebs's timely comparative study placed English law 'at the crossroads' but came narrowly down in favour of persisting with the intent-based and policy-based unjust factors.[35] Canada, under French influence, has already become the first common law country to embrace the civilian terminology but appears to be in danger of falling incoherently between two stools, since it uses the language of absence of cause without regard to the technicalities of its operation.[36] The comparative dimension now exercises a potent and

[32] Below, 108–13.

[33] *Kleinwort Benson v Lincoln CC* [1999] 2 AC 349 (HL) 408–9.

[34] This was the theme of her book: S Meier, *Irrtum und Zweckverfehlung* (Moher Siebeck Tübingen 1999) which was the subject of a review article by T Krebs, 'A German Contribution to English Enrichment Law' [1999] Restitution L Rev 270. For her more recent contributions, below, 113 nn 20–1.

[35] Krebs, *Restitution at the Crossroads* (Cavendish Press London 2000). This book is really about unjust enrichment, not restitution.

[36] Shortcomings and uncertainties: LD Smith, 'The Mystery of Juristic Reason' (2000) 12 Supreme Court L Rev 211.

practical influence on the interpretation of the swaps cases, which were not themselves overtly aware that they were walking a watershed.

One might muster the courage to say that they were incorrectly decided, or at best incorrectly reasoned, and that the judges should have made more effort to understand the approach to which English law appeared to be committed. That is a cul-de-sac, and a dangerous one. It leads over a cliff. Anyone bold enough to go down it will find himself dashed to pieces on the sharp rocks of Dr Meier's arguments. Over many years her case has been that the lists of unjust factors must in the end collapse into the 'no basis' approach. Between the lines of Dr Krebs's defence of unjust factors it is evident that he was constantly on the verge of capitulation.

Partly therefore by the force of precedent and partly because of the power of the Meier comparative analysis, Part III now accepts that in the recent cases English law paused at the crossroads and took a new direction. There can be no half measures. This is not the kind of issue which is susceptible of fudge or deliberate compromise. After the swaps cases English law now has to work through absence of basis across the board. It is a question of method, not substance, but methods have their own message. On the margin different methods produce different outcomes. The best prescription in the short term will be to use both approaches, in full awareness that they cannot be mixed.

D. CONCLUSION

One great advantage of pulling the law of unjust enrichment out of categories to which it does not belong, and even out of restitution to which it does belong but in which it has tended to lose its identity, is that it allows us to get a better picture of the classification of private law as a whole.

The first two sections of this chapter located our *tertium quid* in what turns out to be a fourfold series of causative events and then related that series to the different division between property and obligations. These are coordinate categories of response to the series of causative events. When rights are classified the first level is usually occupied by the division between *in rem* (property) and *in personam* (obligations). The division according to causative events is placed on the second level. All the rights which we seek to realize in court arise from are either *in rem* or *in personam*, and, one step down, all arise from distinct causative events—consent, wrongs, unjust enrichment, and others. Like the events in the other three, unjust enrichment is a causative event capable of generating both rights *in personam*, in the law of obligations, and rights *in rem*, in the law of property.

The third section then took us inside the law of unjust enrichment itself. As it happens we have opened that door at a time when the common law is rejoining the tradition from which it borrowed heavily in the 18th century. Having recovered from an age wasted in the wilderness of implied contract, it had been evolving an approach of its own to 'unjust', but a series of important cases has moved it back into the mainstream. Like all the civilian systems, it will now ask whether the enrichment does or does not rest on a recognized explanatory basis. Wealth is transferred with a purpose in mind. Generally, though not invariably, the purpose is the basis. An unjust enrichment at the expense of another is an enrichment which, in those terms, is inexplicable. It fulfils no purpose and has no other basis.

Part II

Enrichment at the Expense of the Claimant

3

Enrichment

Enrichment at the expense of another is neutral in itself. A present of £1,000 given by proud parents on graduation day enriches the new graduate at their expense, but not unjustly. The two chapters of this part are therefore preparatory. They lead up to the crucial question whether the defendant's enrichment at the claimant's expense was unjust. This chapter asks only whether the defendant was enriched. The next asks whether that enrichment was at the expense of the claimant.

A conclusion that the recipient was not enriched puts an end to the inquiry. The defendant may still be liable, but not in unjust enrichment. He may be liable in one of the other three columns of the grid introduced in the previous chapter. For example, a person who has received a service but cannot be said to have been enriched may yet be liable to reimburse an uninvited intervener in his affairs. We placed uninvited intervention (*negotiorum gestio*) in the residual miscellany of causative events which forms the last of the four columns. Moreover, the intervener's claim is not gain-based. So far as concerns the stripes which run across the columns of the grid, it belongs in the compensation stripe, not in restitution.[1]

In the great majority of unjust enrichment cases the enrichment in question is passed over unnoticed. This is not because it does not require an answer but because the defendant has usually received money. Since money is the measure of wealth, there is very rarely any contest on the enrichment issue where money has been received. In our core case a mistaken payee receives money. The generalization enlarges the receipt of money to enrichment, precisely with a view to finding out whether the logic which explains restitution of a mistaken payment still works in cases in which what is received is not money. The answer may seem obvious, and in a sense it is. What works for money must work for value received in other forms. There are, however, a number of complications. Most of the problems relating to enrichment fall under one or other of two heads.

[1] Above, 22–4.

The first is the subjectivity of the value of non-money benefits. We all have our own priorities. Money is both the measure of value and the medium of freedom. We have to be allowed to put our own value on everything that money can buy. The market value says nothing of the value to you or me. The courts have no choice but to deal in market value, but there has to be some reconciliation between that practical necessity and freedom of choice. In this respect it is one thing when you pay me money by mistake, but quite another when you mistakenly paint my house.[2]

The second problem picks up the discussion of the relationship of unjust enrichment and property in the last chapter. Can a recipient be said to be enriched by some asset in his possession which still belongs to the claimant? Here 'asset' includes cash. Am I enriched when my wallet contains a £10 note which still belongs to you?

These two problems have sections to themselves below. Both prove rather difficult, partly because the case law is still thin. The need to take enrichment seriously does not assert itself so long as the law of unjust enrichment is hidden behind imaginary contracts and pretended trusts. Wherever the enrichment question does occupy attention, there is a danger of overlooking its neutrality. It does not determine liability. The enrichment question is only the first step in the five-question inquiry. Not every enrichment has to be given up, not even when it seems to attract description as a windfall.[3]

A. WEALTH AND NOT-WEALTH

There is a preliminary problem about the level of the generalization. Enrichment received is the generalization of money received. Pitching the generalization at that level has to be justified. Why not say 'thing' or 'anything'? This question also arises in relation to the law of restitution. 'Restitution' has come to denote gain-based recovery, but the word is not naturally confined within the sphere of wealth.

Even if we lay aside restitution of a person or thing to a previous condition and speak only of restitution of something to someone, there is

[2] The single market value of stocks and shares tends to mislead. Market value generally means the court's estimate of the fair value between these parties dealing with each other willingly or, where the supplier has a published tariff, the price there specified.

[3] E McKendrick, 'Incontrovertible Benefit—Postscript' [1989] LMCLQ 401–3 commenting on *Procter & Gamble Phillipine Manufacturing Corporation v Peter Cremer GmbH (The Manila)* (No. 2) [1988] 3 All ER 843.

no natural reason why the something should be wealth. There is a live question whether a court might order the giving up of body parts retained by a hospital for research without consent.[4] Again, parents turn to courts to recover abducted children. These 'things' are not wealth. Although contrary practices obtain in a particularly unpleasant sector of the underworld, there is no situation whatever in which the law allows an individual or a court to turn them into money. Textbooks on restitution do not discuss these not-wealth restitutions. The omission appears to rest on the artificial sense of 'restitution'. It is deemed to mean gain-based recovery, and 'gain' is assumed to mean material gain. Those who withhold brains and children have not gained.

Here in the law of unjust enrichment, by contrast, the restriction to enrichment is not imposed or artificial. The law of all events materially identical to the receipt of a mistaken payment is confined to enrichment because the logic of that liability extends no further. If it were objected that the word 'enrichment' could have been pitched at a still higher level of generality, say at 'things received', the first part of the answer would be that totally different considerations enter in when there is no question of making a substitutionary award in money. The logic of the strict liability to give up a mistaken payment does not stretch beyond acquisitions measurable in money. We have already seen that the character of unjust enrichment as a distinct cause of action is explained by the uncomplicated proposition that only weak facts are needed to require the surrender of a misplaced gain. Where the gain is still extant in the sense that, whether or not he still has the very thing received, the defendant's wealth remains swollen, the liability is in principle strict. The reasons why I might be able to recover £100 or the value of a gold bar or the value of a day's work are totally different from the reasons why I might recover an abducted child. While the word 'restitution' might be applied to the restoration of a child to its mother, the very notion of an extant gain is inapplicable to such a case.

Unfortunately the first part of the explanation does not go far enough. Abandoning 'thing' the hostile critic might object that the generalization should be pitched at 'wealth' or 'assets'. But this would also create a

[4] *Dobson v North Tyneside Health Authority* [1997] 1 WLR 596 (CA); *R v Kelly* [1998] 3 All ER 741 (CA); *AB and Others v London Teaching Hospital NHS Trust* [2004] EWHC 644 (QB) [136]–[161]; R Magnusson, 'Proprietary Rights in Human Tissue' in N Palmer and E McKendrick (eds), *Interests in Goods* (2nd edn Lloyds of London Press London 1998) 25–63; S Munzer, 'Human Dignity and Property Rights in Human Body Parts' in JW Harris (ed), *Property Problems: from Genes to Pension Funds* (Kluwer London–Hague–Boston 1997) 25–38.

category wider than that which centres on mistaken payment. This exposes the problems which arise from the relationship between the law of property and the law of unjust enrichment. The short answer is that 'wealth received' embraces both enrichments to be reversed and enrichments prevented. The subject which centres on the receipt of mistaken payments is confined to the former. There must be an enrichment to be reversed. When a mistaken payment is received, a new right arises to undo an enrichment. The law of unjust enrichment is the law of events which create new rights to reverse what would otherwise be an unjust enrichment. There is noise on many boundaries, not least on this one. We return to it below in section C.

In summary, the reason why the generalization of money stops at enrichment is that if it went higher, to 'thing', it would reach the receipt of non-wealth, where adjustment in money is unthinkable. And, if it went slightly less high, to 'wealth', it would cross the line between the subject represented by the core case, which is the creation of new rights to reverse enrichments, and the assertion of pre-existing property rights, the survival of which prevents the recipient's enrichment. It is extremely dangerous to say that a difficult problem is unimportant, but this may be such a case. It is certainly very difficult but it does not cause problems in the day to day work of the law of unjust enrichment.

That the positions taken here may not be perfectly right might be inferred from the choices made by the BGB, the German civil code. Having made a commitment in the title to enrichment,[5] it immediately switches in the first of the paragraphs which follow to the receipt of 'something': 'If through the performance of another or in some other way at his expense a someone receives something without legal ground, he is bound to make restitution to that other.'[6]

B. ENRICHMENT AS VALUE MEASURED BY MONEY

When the first of the five questions is put, it should be answered by looking narrowly at that which was received. Was it an enriching receipt? Surrounding facts should be ignored, even if they ultimately cancel out the conclusion that the recipient was or remained enriched. In Part V we

[5] *Titel* 26 BGB is '*Ungerechtfertigte Bereicherung* (Unjustified Enrichment)'.

[6] § 812(1) BGB: '. . . *etwas erlangt* [receives something] . . .'. Here the English 'to make restitution' represents '*zur Herausgabe*'. In the German there is no hint that givings up which are not givings back might be excluded.

will encounter enrichment-related defences. A resolution not to syphon that matter into answers to the first question makes for clarity of thought.

1. MONEY RECEIVED

It is barely necessary to say anything about money received. There is no room for argument as to the value of money. There is a question, however, as to the way in which the value of money over time should be handled. When you borrow money you have to pay for its use over time. You have to pay interest. The House of Lords has held, against the dissent of Lord Goff and Lord Woolf, that only simple interest is normally payable when judgment is given in unjust enrichment. Compound interest is reserved for the case in which the money received was trust money belonging in equity to the claimant.[7]

Outside that case it therefore appears that the defendant has to give up less than the full value of the benefit received. Money is not available in the market place on simple interest terms. However, this issue will have to be handled very carefully when next it is revisited, for the availability of money to use is not unequivocally enriching in the same degree as the receipt of money. The use of money is in itself a non-money benefit and, whether the issue is enrichment or disenrichment, it has to pass the tests applied to other non-money benefits. In the *Westdeutsche* case the local authorities were saved from borrowing on the market, so that the use of the bank's money was an incontrovertible benefit.

2. ENRICHMENTS IN KIND

Money has value and is the measure of value. Things and services have a market value measured in money. It is possible to find out how much, within a certain range, such and such a thing or service costs. However, no single one of us is bound to subscribe to the demand that creates the market value. We all have our likes and dislikes, and we match our available resources to our own sense of priorities. The market price is thus often very different from the price at which you or I would buy. There are many marketable things that we would not buy at all, not at any price. There are canine beauty parlours at which the price of a dog's haircut can run to more than £100. There is a market for that service. Some people hate the very idea. They prefer their poodles shaggy. Asked to pay for an unrequested perm, they would counterclaim for damage.

[7] *Westdeutsche Landesbank Girozentrale v Islington LBC* [1996] AC 669 (HL).

English law accepts the subjectivity of value. It accepts that recourse to the market value would violate freedom of choice. At the same time it does not pretend to attempt the impossible task of finding out at what price the particular recipient of an unrequested benefit would have bought it. The old pleadings which made claims in respect of non-money benefits invariably recited that the thing or service in question had been conferred at the defendant's special instance and request.[8] Those words, together with the absence of any other form of claim, represented on their face an extreme commitment to the proposition that an unrequested benefit must be taken to have no value at all to the recipient.

Starting from that extreme position the law began to explore its limits. There were situations in which it was unreasonable or impossible to insist on the subjectivity of value, where insistence on one's right to make one's own choice would be no more than a prevarication to defeat an unwelcome claim. In such cases the market value could safely be imposed or, where the range of market prices was broad, a market price reasonable in all the circumstances of the parties.[9] This process began within the special instance and request counts. The courts cautiously allowed other facts to substantiate the allegation of request. Where that was done, the request became a fiction.

For example, in *Exall v Partridge*[10] the owner of a carriage took it for repair, but the landlord of the repairers, as he was entitled to do, seized it as security for the payment of the repairers' rent. To release his carriage the owner paid the rent. The repairers thus received a benefit, not immediately in money, but in the discharge of a debt. The owner's claim for reimbursement was made in the standard form of action alleging that he had spent money on behalf of the repairers at their special instance and request. There had been no request at all. But the law by this time took the view that these facts were as effective to create a liability as if a request had been made.

Counsel in that case argued that the request should be implied if the defendant had been unequivocally benefited. The court disagreed. In modern terms, it was asserting that within the law of unjust enrichment the enrichment of the defendant is essential but not sufficient. The case in which the allegation of request could not be traversed and thus became a fiction was that in which there was in addition a

[8] Below, 287–8. [9] Explained in n 2 above.
[10] (1799) 8 TR 308, 101 ER 1405.

reason, not being a contract or a tort, why that enrichment should be surrendered.

In *Exall v Partridge* itself that additional requirement was satisfied by the fact that, the enrichment of the defendants being no more than the by-product of a payment made by the claimant under legal compulsion, there was absolutely no reason as between the claimant and the defendants why the latter should be enriched at the former's expense. As between these parties, it was a by-product with no substantive explanation.[11] The law no longer consists in a list of standard forms of action. The modern law therefore does not need to advance by fictionalized allegations—allegations which must be made but need not be proved. It is free to explore the natural limits of the subjectivity of value without having to play that kind of game.

3. FIVE EXCEPTIONAL SITUATIONS

The fundamental principle is that, outside contract, non-money benefits cannot be valued unless, exceptionally, the imposition of a money value will not, in the judgment of a reasonable person, do violence to the law's respect for the individual's right to choose freely how to employ available resources. It is probably impossible to make an exhaustive list of the exceptional situations, but there are five which between them cover most of the ground.

These five belong in two groups according as they turn on one of two larger conclusions, either that, contrary to first impressions, the defendant did have a sufficient opportunity for choice or that the benefit in kind was incontrovertibly enriching just as the receipt of money is incontrovertibly enriching. The third of these five, numbered (a) (iii) below, is different from the others in that it points to valuation by reference to a defunct contract between the parties, not the market. In all five cases the crucial intermediate proposition which they support is that it is not in the circumstances reasonable for the defendant to insist on his freedom to choose how to spend his money.

(a) Where the Defendant had a Sufficient Choice

In this first group the reason why a defendant who is made to pay cannot be heard to complain of interference with his freedom of choice is that he did choose.

[11] To put this in context see below, 158–60.

(i) Where he could make Specific Restitution of the Very Thing Received

If he received a free-standing asset such as a picture and all other conditions for a claim in unjust enrichment are in place, he cannot resist an action for the value on the ground that he had no opportunity to choose, because he has a continuing opportunity to give the picture up. The more worthless it seems to him, the easier to surrender it.[12] Such a case recently reached the Court of Appeal.

In *McDonald v Coys of Kensington*[13] a car had been expressly sold without its 'cherished' number plate, TAC 1. An administrative error in the operation of the statutory registration scheme resulted in the number nevertheless passing with the car, and the buyer sought to hang on to his good luck by saying, inter alia, that he had no intention of realizing its commercial value. Registration in that number was worth some £15,000 extra. But the error could easily be put right. Nothing obstructed his giving back the unintended benefit in kind. Holding that the buyer had indeed been enriched, Mance LJ, with whom Thorpe LJ and Wilson J agreed, said that in the contest over the issue of enrichment too little weight had been given to the fact that this was a benefit which was 'readily returnable'.[14]

(ii) Free Acceptance

Free acceptance, at its weakest, is foregoing an opportunity to reject the benefit. Requests and demands are *a fortiori*. The objection to market value being the law's commitment to the individual's freedom of choice, a recipient who accepted the benefit in question when he might have rejected it is in no position to resist, unless that choice was made on the assumption that it was offered gratis or at a price lower than the market price.

There are some cases which are unequivocal. In *Pavey & Matthews v Paul*[15] Mrs Paul had requested building work and had received all the work for which she had asked. For want of writing the builders had no action in contract. The High Court of Australia allowed them to recover the reasonable value of their work. In such a case the enrichment question poses no problems. There is no violation of the defendant's freedom of choice. In an earlier building case, *William Lacey (Hounslow) Ltd v Davis*,[16] the claimant builders were successful bidders for a development contract. Before any contract was signed the developer then had them do a good

[12] P Birks, *An Introduction to the Law of Restitution* (rev edn OUP Oxford 1989) 130–1.

[13] [2004] EWCA Civ 47.

[14] Ibid [27], [31], [37].

[15] (1987) 162 CLR 221 (HCA).

[16] [1957] 1 WLR 932.

deal of preparatory work. The amount went far beyond what builders often risk in the attempt to catch a contract. When the developer suddenly changed his mind and decided to sell rather than develop, the builders recovered the value of that work.

Passive acquiescence suffices. Suppose that you know that work is being done for you and you have no reason to believe that it is a gift or a simple speculation in the manner of a busker who takes his chance whether those who listen will pay. In ordinary circumstances you ought to speak out. If you could intervene without trouble to yourself, and you pass up the opportunity of finding out what is going on and putting a stop to it or making clear that you will not pay, you can hardly turn round and say that your right to choose your own priorities requires the law to abstain from putting a money value on the benefit.

In *Leigh v Dickeson*,[17] in which one owner in common failed to recover from the other a contribution to the cost of improvements to a house, Brett MR put it this way:

> Sometimes money has been expended for the benefit of another person under such circumstances that an option is allowed to him to adopt or decline the benefit: in this case, if he exercises his option to adopt the benefit, he will be liable to repay the money expended; but if he declines the benefit, he will not be liable. But sometimes money is expended for the benefit of another person under such circumstances, that he cannot help accepting the benefit, in fact he is bound to accept it: in this case he has no opportunity of exercising any option, and he will come under no liability.[18]

The negative proposition with which this passage ends had earlier been put very neatly by Pollock CB:[19]

> Suppose that I clean your property without your knowledge, have I then a claim on you for payment? How can you help it? One cleans another's shoes; what can the other do but put them on? Is that evidence of a contract to pay for the cleaning? The benefit of the service could not be rejected without refusing the property itself.

In the days when unjust enrichment was buried in contract and could not be seen as a distinct causative event, free acceptance was forced to operate through contract. These passages could not but envisage the freely accepting recipient of the benefit as impliedly contracting to pay. The artificialities which that entailed are no longer necessary. Nowadays the

[17] (1884) 15 QBD 60 (CA). [18] Ibid 64.

[19] *Taylor v Laird* (1856) 25 LJ Ex 329, 332.

passages should be understood as a guide to answering the underlying question, which is whether by passing up an opportunity to reject the recipient has shut himself out from the argument based on respect for freedom of choice.

(iii) Incomplete Contractual Performances

Very difficult questions arise where the benefit in question is part-performance of a contract which has been terminated, as for instance three-quarters of a house. They are not solved by squeezing such cases under free acceptance. Such claims may fall at the third question (unjust). However, for the moment we are concerned only with the question of enrichment. In *Sumpter v Hedges*[20] builders who ran out of money and failed to finish the houses they were putting up recovered a reasonable market price for the loose materials which the defendant had used but nothing for the incomplete houses themselves. The materials could have been rejected and were freely accepted. As for the incomplete houses they fell within the last sentence of Brett MR's analysis which is quoted immediately above: 'But sometimes money is expended for the benefit of another person under such circumstances, that he cannot help accepting the benefit, in fact he is bound to accept it: in this case he has no opportunity of exercising any option, and he will come under no liability.'

A recent analysis, hostile to such claims, looks to the third question in the five-question analysis (unjust) to explain the result in *Sumpter v Hedges*.[21] That is, the authors do not seek to say that an incomplete house is not an enrichment. They seek a more absolute negative. At this point we are only concerned with the issue of enrichment and can agree that this is not a situation of no enrichment.

It may sometimes be that the incomplete performance has been or is destined to be realized in money, as where land with incomplete building work is sold on to a new developer or waiting to be sold or it may be for some other reason as incontrovertibly valuable as a payment of money. In the absence of facts of that kind, free acceptance cannot be relied on unless the performance is genuinely divisible into accepted units.[22] An order for a whole house cannot be understood as a request for or

[20] [1898] 1 QB 673 (CA). Cf *Bolton v Mahadeva* [1972] 1 WLR 1009 (CA).

[21] B McFarlane and R Stevens, 'In Defence of *Sumpter v Hedges*' (2002) 118 LQR 569, 574. A Burrows, *The Law of Restitution* (2nd edn Butterworths London 2002) 354–6 argues that the part-performer should recover and has no difficulty in seeing the recipient of part as enriched.

[22] But most periodical payments in the nature of income accrue from day to day under the Apportionment Act 1870 s 2.

free acceptance of part of a house. Nevertheless, independently of free acceptance in the full sense this is a situation in which the recipient cannot reasonably resist valuation in money.

The valuation must not be by the market. It must be made in the light of the contract price, even though the contract is defunct. The contract supplies the evidence of the value which the parties themselves put upon the performance. Even then, the calculation is unlikely to be *pro rata*. That is to say, three-quarters of a performance will probably not merit three-quarters of the contract price. The underlying proposition is that no money valuation will be made where the defendant is in a position reasonably to insist that such a valuation would deny him his freedom to set his own priorities.

There are two reasons why it would be unreasonable to resist a contract-based valuation here. First, the order for the whole does imply a degree of acceptance of the parts and, secondly, the valuation ceiling set by the defunct contract minimizes the degree to which the defendant's own options will be overridden. By contrast market valuation of a part performance can produce bizarre results.[23]

(b) Incontrovertible Enrichment

Money is incontrovertibly enriching. It is the measure of enrichment. Even with benefits in kind, some are objectively enriching (where 'objectively' means independently of any choice made by their recipient). There seem to be two cases, the saving of inevitable expense and the realization in money of the benefit's otherwise doubtful value.

(i) Inevitable Expenditure Saved

It sometimes happens that the recipient of an unrequested benefit in kind is thereby saved outlay that he would have made anyway. In *Exall v Partridge*[24] the owner of a carriage took it for repair. The landlord of the repairers seized it as security for the payment of the repairers' rent. To release his carriage the owner paid the rent. The repairers thus received a benefit, not immediately in money, but in the discharge of a debt. The

[23] *Boomer v Muir* 24 P 2d 570 (1933) shows that an open market valuation can yield more for a part performance than would have been earned on completion. The March 2003 draft of the new Restatement proposes to subject the award (which it treats as 'damages' thus indicating that the cause of action is breach of contract not unjust enrichment) to a valuation cap based on the contract price: American Law Institute, *Restatement of the Law of Restitution and Unjust Enrichment, Tentative Draft No 3* (March 2004, for discussion in May 2004) para 38 and accompanying text.

[24] (1799) 8 TR 308, 101 ER 1405.

repairers were enriched. Their rent would have had to be paid anyhow. In *Craven-Ellis v Canons Ltd*[25] a managing director acted as such in the mistaken belief that he had a contract with the company. Unknown to him he had dealt with people not qualified to bind the company. He recovered the market value of his work. The company could not reasonably say that it would not have employed a managing director. As a matter of commercial reality a company has to have someone to manage its affairs.

In *Rowe v Vale of White Horse DC*[26] the local authority had provided sewerage services to council houses which it had sold to private buyers. For thirteen years it made no demand for payment. It seems that at first the authority, by an administrative oversight, continued to service the properties as though nothing had changed. In the years within the limitation period it had recovered from that error but abstained from issuing invoices because of a suspicion that the provision of sewerage services might be ultra vires. When that doubt was resolved in its favour, it demanded six years' payments. Lightman J accepted that Mr Rowe had been enriched at the Council's expense. The extraordinary history of this particular case made it reasonable for Mr Rowe to believe, and he did believe, that the Council did not intend to charge. He had not freely accepted. But such services were necessary and it was common knowledge that they normally had to be paid for. They constituted an incontrovertible enrichment. He had been saved an inevitable expenditure.

It is clear that the breadth of this exception depends on the interpretation of 'inevitable'. If it were taken as requiring absolute inevitability, hardly any examples would be found. Even *Craven-Ellis v Canons Ltd* might be squeezed out. However, the basic principle is founded on reasonableness. An exaggerated degree of inevitability is not looked for. In a commercial context it suffices that the expenditure was necessary as a matter of commercial reality.[27] In other contexts some guidance can be derived from the interpretation of necessaries in relation to minors' contracts. The supply of a necessary anticipates an expenditure which the minor would have needed to make. This was not confined to things

[25] [1936] 2 KB 403 (CA) 412.

[26] [2003] 1 Lloyd's Rep 418. For the reason why the Council lost, see above, 43 n 31.

[27] *Monks v Poynice Pty Ltd* (1987) 11 ACLR 637, 640. Compare *Greenwood v Bennett* [1973] QB 195 (CA) where the owner of a Jaguar car which had been repaired and improved by another without his knowledge was himself a dealer whose business entailed making cars presentable for sale.

necessary to keep body and soul together. It was always construed broadly to include all those things needed to maintain a person in the condition in life in which he found himself.[28]

The discharge of a debt is a clear case of necessary expenditure saved, because the law would have compelled payment. However, when one person pays another's debt other than under compulsion, in general the debt is not discharged without the consent of the debtor. It would be a fair inference that if the discharge failed the debtor could not be said to be enriched. That is not correct. An imperfect discharge can be an enrichment. A special technique has to be used to overcome the problem posed by the imperfection.

If the facts are otherwise suitable for a claim, the law will allow the claimant who has imperfectly discharged the debt to compel the creditor to permit him to realize the undischarged right, suing in the creditor's name. This is subrogation properly so-called. Using the name of the victim an indemnity insurer who has paid a loss can sue the undischarged tortfeasor who caused it. The tortfeasor is imperfectly discharged and hence imperfectly enriched, but it would be unreasonable to leave it at that, since it is highly unlikely that the victim, having been paid off, will ever sue him, especially since the proceeds would anyhow go to the insurer.[29]

(ii) Market Value Realized

It sometimes happens that a benefit in kind has been turned into money. If, acting under a mistake, *C*, a builder, improves *D*'s cottage, as for instance by adding to it a conservatory, and then *D* sells the cottage, it will be relatively easy to ascertain by how much money the price has been enhanced and, within that sum, the market value of *C's* input. Here *D* cannot reasonably argue that the benefit which he has received at *C*'s expense must not be measured in money terms.[30]

The picture looks quite different before sale. The market may say that *D*'s cottage is now worth £20,000 more, and that £15,000 of that can be said to have come from the builder, but *D* is fond of the cottage and has no intention of realizing that added value. *D* has not turned the conservatory into money; nor can it be said that *D* has been saved inevitable expenditure. The unchosen extension is thus not a benefit expressible in money. *D* is not enriched.

[28] *Bryant v Richardson* (1866) 14 LT 24, 26.

[29] *Lord Napier and Ettrick v Hunter* [1993] AC 713 (HL).

[30] In *Greenwood v Bennett* [1973] QB 195 (CA) the improved car had indeed been sold before action.

Goff & Jones would distinguish between a unique asset, such as a cottage, and a chattel such as a car, one car being much the same as another. In the case of the car, they take a more robust attitude. The law should not scruple to order or assume a sale.[31] Professor Burrows is of the same view, but with the further proviso that it must appear to be reasonably certain that the added value will be realized by the defendant.[32] It now seems likely that, with or without that additional qualification, this less tender approach will prevail, although it takes a considerable step back from the law's traditional sensitivity to the subjectivity of value and its respect for freedom of choice.

We have seen that in *McDonald v Coys of Kensington*,[33] where a car had been expressly sold without its 'cherished' number plate, TAC 1, but, owing to an error, in fact passed to the buyer with that valuable registration still intact, the Court of Appeal decided the enrichment issue on the basis of the easy returnability of the unintended benefit. However, the Court also considered the matter from the standpoint of incontrovertible benefit and was clearly inclined to favour the robust approach of *Goff & Jones*.[34]

4. EXTANT ENRICHMENT AND INSTANT DISENRICHMENT

It has been a question whether a pure service, meaning either one which leaves no end-product or is for the moment contemplated as distinct from an end-product which it does leave, can ever qualify as an enrichment.[35] In *BP Exploration Co (Libya) Ltd v Hunt (No 2)* a joint venture between the parties to find oil in the Libyan desert was first hugely successful and then frustrated by Libyan expropriation. Robert Goff J, applying the Law Reform (Frustrated Contracts) Act 1943 section 1(3), concluded that, in the assessment of the valuable non-money benefit conferred on the defendant by the claimant, the statute required him to look only at the end-product of the claimant's work for the defendant. By finding oil, BP had enormously enhanced the value of the concession over the empty

[31] G Jones (ed), *The Law of Restitution* (6th edn Sweet & Maxwell London 2002) [1–024], accepted as 'common ground' by Hirst J in *Procter & Gamble Phillipine Manufacturing Corporation v Peter Cremer GmbH (The Manila)* (No. 2) [1988] 3 All ER 843, 855, and preferred *obiter* by Judge Bowsher QC in *Marston Construction Co Ltd v Kigass Ltd* (1989) 46 Build LR 109.

[32] A Burrows, *The Law of Restitution* (2nd edn Butterworths London 2002) 19.

[33] [2004] EWCA Civ 47; cf text to n 13 above.

[34] Ibid [35], [36], [40]. These paragraphs are also disinclined to accept the intermediate position of Professor Burrows. Cf text to n 32 above.

[35] J Beatson, *Use and Abuse of Unjust Enrichment* (OUP Oxford 1991) 31–44.

desert which the Libyan government had granted Hunt. That was the end product. Yet at the same time he indicated that, but for the wording of the statute, he would himself have regarded exploration services as capable in themselves of counting as an enrichment, quite independently of their end-product.[36]

The terms of the debate have changed since the defence of change of position was secured. Unless the enrichee is disqualified from that defence, his liability now extends only so far as he is still abstractly enriched. Singers and violinists command handsome fees, but the song and the sonata leave behind no material end-product. Even if the circumstances would otherwise permit a claim in unjust enrichment, it could not lie here unless the defendant were disqualified from pleading the instant disenrichment.

Bad faith disqualifies.[37] Free acceptance will often but not always involve shabby, even dishonest, conduct, for the circumstances in which a recipient passes up an opportunity to reject a benefit are likely to be such that, in the words of Griffith ACJ, a man is bound by the rules of honesty not to be quiescent.[38] Freely accepting defendants of that kind will therefore be disqualified. The effect of the defence across the board is to drive the analysis away from the work itself and to the end-product, the house or the book, as opposed to the labour of building or writing. Where a pure service is such as to save an inevitable expenditure, the inevitable expenditure saved will be the relevant end-product.

C. WHERE PROPERTY DOES NOT PASS

A difficult enrichment question arises from the relationship between unjust enrichment and property, which was discussed in the previous chapter. We have to distinguish between two situations. In one, *C*'s asset falls into *D*'s hands in circumstances in which no property in that asset passes. *C* retains his pre-existing title. This may happen because the asset reaches *D* absolutely without *C*'s knowledge or, although with his knowledge, in circumstances in which his apparent consent is nullified by an extreme species of mistake or duress. In the other, property passes to *D* but in circumstances in which he is unjustly enriched and in which the law reverses that unjust enrichment by raising a new property right in *C*,

[36] [1979] 1 WLR 783, 801–2.

[37] Details in Chapter 9 below, 214–8.

[38] *City Bank of Sydney v McLoughlin* (1909) 9 CLR 615 (HCA) 625 (Griffith ACJ).

as for instance by turning *D* into a trustee and thus giving *C* an equitable beneficial interest: *C* begins as owner at law but ends as owner in equity. The difference is between surviving property rights which passively prevent enrichment and new ones which actively reverse enrichment.

1. PRE-EXISTING TITLE SURVIVES

Can it be said that *D* is enriched by *C*'s £50 note in his wallet or *C*'s car in his garage? To the layman *D*'s position is ambiguous. On the one hand he can see that there is a sense in which *D* is not enriched, because nothing has been added to his wealth, and on the other there is a robust sense in which he is enriched, since the fact is that he is in control of the asset. English law agrees with the layman that both analyses make sense. It allows *C* to choose between them. In fact, if we keep an eye on the probable availability of an action in tort, three kinds of claim can be made by *C* in this situation.

(a) The *vindicatio*

C can say 'That car is mine!' or 'That £50 note is mine!' Throughout this book that direct assertion of ownership, and nothing else, is referred to in Latin as a *vindicatio*. The Latin term is used in order to distinguish the technical term from the loose usage into which English lawyers sometimes fall in which 'vindicating property' can refer to any kind of claim which has the object of protecting or realizing proprietary rights.

Although direct assertions of property rights are common enough out of court, if it comes to litigation *C* will find that the common law does not entertain any *vindicatio* of moveables. It only protects ownership obliquely. It is different in equity, where a claimant can ask for a declaration that the defendant holds the asset in question on trust for him. If it comes to litigation, that is as near to a *vindicatio* as English law gets. In or out of court the *vindicatio* is incompatible with the proposition that *D* is enriched. The foundation of the demand is precisely that the asset forms no part of *D*'s estate.

Macmillan Inc v Bishopsgate Investment Trust plc (No 3),[39] which arose from the collapse of the Maxwell empire, provides a model of an equitable *vindicatio*. The claimant company, Macmillan, sought to vindicate Berlitz shares which Maxwell had caused it to transfer and which he had used as security for last minute loans. Legal title had passed to the

[39] [1996] 1 WLR 387 (Ch).

Maxwell company, Bishopsgate, but not equitable title. Macmillan wanted the court to declare that all the banks which held the shares as security for their loans actually held on trust. 'Declare that the banks are trustees for us' is synonymous with 'We own these shares in equity.' Hence the bold assertion that this is no less than a *vindicatio* in the technical sense.

This claim fell at the hurdle of bona fide purchase of the legal estate without notice. But what Macmillan wanted can be expressed in two simple sentences. It wanted the court to declare that the shares belonged to it in equity, or, synonymously, that the banks held as trustees for it. And it wanted the court to order the banks to transfer the legal title to them. The second sentence is a demand for restitution, but not on the basis of unjust enrichment.[40] No claim in unjust enrichment was attempted. The first of the two sentences shows that Macmillan denied that the defendants were enriched.

We have seen that debt is multi-causal. 'You owe me £100!' might be substantiated by contract or in the absence of contract. At the non-contractual end of the spectrum, it might be substantiated by unjust enrichment, as where I earlier paid you that sum by mistake. In this respect the vindication 'That's mine!' behaves in the same way. The proprietary right asserted must have arisen from a causative event, and it may have arisen in any one of the four categories. Thus, where a pre-existing property right survives a change of possession, it may have arisen from consent, from a wrong, from unjust enrichment, or from some other event. For instance, a jeweller who makes a ring from your gold acquires the ring by *specificatio*, the creation of a new thing. *Specificatio* belongs in the fourth category. It is not a manifestation of consent, not a wrong and not an unjust enrichment.

Mistaken payment is the paradigmatic unjust enrichment. Suppose that it still remains true that a mistaken payment turns the payee into a trustee.[41] If the payee uses the mistaken money to buy a picture and then gives the picture to his friend, the payer can vindicate the picture from the friend. His proprietary right will have arisen from unjust enrichment. The *vindicatio*—the assertion 'That's my picture!'—is incompatible with an allegation of present enrichment but it is not incompatible with prior acquisition from unjust enrichment. The right vindicated, which

[40] Above, 27–8.

[41] *Chase Manhattan Bank NA Ltd v Israel-British Bank Ltd* [1981] Ch 105, now under some pressure.

now denies the enrichment of this donee, arose to reverse the unjust enrichment. There is no contradiction.

(b) Wrongful Interference

The oblique protection of property rights comes in two kinds. One is an action for a wrong. The claimant then complains of a wrongful interference with his asset. At law the wrong will usually be conversion, more rarely trespass. The claim in respect of the wrong can have a variety of outcomes the most common of which is a money judgment, either compensatory or, under *United Australia Ltd v Barclays Bank Ltd*,[42] restitutionary. Payment of damages then extinguishes the claimant's title to that interest.[43]

Such a claim, no less than the direct *vindicatio*, also supposes that the asset did not become part of *D*'s estate. It is no less incompatible with an allegation of enrichment than is the *vindicatio*. *C*'s case is precisely that *D* tortiously interfered with an asset which did not belong to him. Where *C* complains of a wrong but claims gain-based damages, he is claiming that *D* was enriched by his wrong, as by receiving the price of the asset, not that the asset itself was an enrichment to him. *C*'s claim to gain-based recovery for the wrong is again absolutely incompatible with an allegation that *D* was unjustly enriched at his expense. Unjust enrichment is never a wrong, and the premiss of this particular wrong is that *D* had no right to the thing.

(c) Unjust Enrichment

The other oblique protection is an action in unjust enrichment. There is no parallel provision for extinguishing the title of the claimant. Nor should there be. The reason is that *C*'s election to assert that *D* has been unjustly enriched at his expense supposes a renunciation of his title. Asserting his title or complaining of a wrongful interference he denies the enrichment but in claiming the value of the asset as an enrichment of the defendant at his expense he is renouncing his title. That is the choice which the claimant has in this kind of situation. He can insist on his title, in which case he will either bring a *vindicatio* or complain of wrongful interference, or he can renounce his title and claim the value of the asset as an unjust enrichment. The unjust enrichment option is commonly

[42] [1941] AC 1 (HL).
[43] Torts (Interference with Goods) Act 1977 s 5.

used in respect of *C*'s money in *D*'s hands,[44] but there is no reason why it should be confined to money cases, the relevant axiom being that the law of unjust enrichment applies symmetrically to all enrichments.

Mr Virgo says that claims of this kind where no title has passed to the defendant are not properly described as actions in unjust enrichment. They belong in the law of property and have the function of 'vindicating' the claimant's property right.[45] This entails using the language of vindication in a very loose sense, to include any claim which has the function of defending or protecting a proprietary right, even obliquely. This extended notion of vindication is part of his view, encountered in the last chapter, that property and unjust enrichment are categories in exclusive opposition to each other. We have already rejected that view as akin to an assertion that no animal can be both aquatic and a mammal.

At this point it is only necessary to say that Mr Virgo's extended notion of vindication can only be supported by an analysis which very strongly favours substance over form. That is to say, analysts of his complexion must assert that the proposition which underlies the claim in unjust enrichment is a kind of fiction, which conceals what is in truth a *vindicatio*. Similarly, where the claimant sues for conversion, claiming loss-based or gain-based damages,[46] the same analysts will have to say that what is formally an action for a tort is in substance a vindication of the proprietary right.

The competing analysis will seem preferable to many jurists. The actions in unjust enrichment and conversion are not fictions. They are what they appear to be, genuine recourses to the law of obligations. They are certainly not vindications in the true sense. They realize proprietary rights obliquely, by the assertion of rights *in personam* arising from unjust enrichment or from tort. For Mr Virgo even *Lipkin Gorman v Karpnale Ltd*,[47] in which the House of Lords recognized for the first time that English law has a law of restitution of unjust enrichment, was not a case of unjust enrichment. It was a vindication of a property right.[48]

It will be recalled that the claimant firm successfully recovered a sum of money from the defendant casino. A partner in the firm had raided its client account to feed his gambling habit. The firm recovered

[44] *FC Jones & Sons v Jones* [1997] Ch 159 (CA); cf *Holiday v Sigil* (1826) 2 C & P 176, 172 ER 81; *Moffatt v Kazana* [1969] 2 QB 152.

[45] G Virgo, *Principles of the Law of Restitution* (OUP Oxford 1999) 11–17.

[46] A choice warranted by *United Australia Ltd v Barclays Bank Ltd* [1941] AC 1 (HL).

[47] [1991] 2 AC 548 (HL).

[48] Virgo (n 45 above) 591–4.

from the casino the amount of his stakes, less his occasional winnings. This was not a *vindicatio*. The firm never made any attempt to point to money in the possession of the defendant in order to say of it 'That money is ours!' Besides, by the time the case reached the House of Lords, it had by agreement been confined to the parties' common law rights, and the common law has no *vindicatio* of moveables. The firm's claim was made in the law of obligations. It was not a claim in tort. Lord Goff went out of his way to say that the casino could not be said to have committed any tort, having lawfully received money which at the moment of receipt belonged to the gambler.[49] The claim was simply that the defendant owed them the sum in question. It was a debt born of unjust enrichment. There is no element of fiction. The claim in unjust enrichment cannot be represented as a *vindicatio* in disguise. When no property has passed to a recipient in possession, the claimant has different options. One of them is to renounce his title and make his claim in unjust enichment.

2. NEW PROPRIETARY RIGHTS

The tripartite realization regime introduced above as available when an asset passes into a new possessor's hands is also encountered immediately upon some unjust enrichments. Recourse to the law of unjust enrichment can be recourse to the law of property because sometimes the unjust enrichment itself generates both personal rights and property rights. Thus, immediately on your receiving a mistaken payment from me and even if the property passes to you at law, I have both a personal claim and proprietary claim, both arising from unjust enrichment.

Everything said above applies. My *vindicatio*, if I choose that route, will say that you are not enriched, meaning no longer enriched: the new equitable interest, arising immediately from the unjust enrichment, has already carried the wealth back to my estate. My personal claim in unjust enrichment will say that you are enriched and must repay. In the latter case the animal will sometimes seem to eat its own tail. But that turns out on reflection not to be a cause for anxiety.

The only reason for separating the case of the new proprietary right from the passively surviving proprietary right is that the case of the new right demonstrates very vividly that the law has no aversion whatever to concurrency between proprietary and personal claims and in particular

[49] [1991] 2 AC 548 (HL) 573 (Lord Goff, describing the structure of rights contingent on tracing as requiring something analogous to ratification).

no hostility to an option between a personal claim in unjust enrichment and a proprietary claim. If this were otherwise, in *Chase Manhattan Bank NA Ltd v Israel-British Bank Ltd*,[50] the claimant, which had paid £2m and then, mistakenly, paid it again, could not possibly have had both kinds of claim at once.

This then reflects back on the cases in which the proprietary right is not new, as for instance *Holiday v Sigil*,[51] where the claimant simply lost his £500 note and the defendant found it. It was the claimant's note all along and, at the same time, the finder incurred a debt born of unjust enrichment. Such a claimant does indeed have two inconsistent rights, but the common law allows a choice to be made between them.

D. TWO CONCEPTIONS OF WEALTH

There are two ways of contemplating a person's wealth. Each has to be kept in mind since the law uses both, often without expressly noticing the passage from one to the other. The first sees the person's wealth as a list of particular assets, some corporeal, some incorporeal. This can be called the discrete conception of wealth, wealth as an inventory of distinct items such as a house, car, jewels, money, bank accounts, bonds, shares, and so on. The other conception envisages an individual's wealth as a single fund with a money value. When a celebrity is said to be worth millions, the speaker is thinking in terms of an abstract fund. This can be called the abstract conception of wealth.[52]

An enrichment, or gain, is an addition to wealth. The words can be used in that sense whichever conception of wealth is in play. Gain is marginally the more neutral of the two. Enrichment inclines slightly towards the abstract conception. Some people may deny that nuance and affirm that the two words are perfectly synonymous. There is not much in it. It may not be possible for any law of unjust enrichment to function entirely satisfactorily with only one of these conceptions of wealth. In the end, however, absurdities result if the abstract conception is not made dominant.

At common law money unjustly received and other benefits unjustly received through the claimant's laying out money to third parties have always created money debts. That is, they always ask for the surrender of an abstract slice of the defendant's wealth, not a discrete item. The

[50] [1981] Ch 105 (Ch).

[51] (1826) 2 C & P 176, 172 ER 81.

[52] BA Rudden, 'Things as Things and Things as Wealth' (1994) OJLS 81–97.

relevant claim for goods received was that the recipient should pay *tantum quantum valebant* (so much as they were worth) and for services received *tantum quantum meruit* (so much as he deserved).[53] These are by no means the only techniques known to English law as a whole for undoing unjust enrichment, but they have been central. Quite differently from German law, there is no suggestion that the obligation to pay the money value was to be regarded as a substitute for an obligation to surrender the very asset received. It is a legitimate inference that from the outset the law has been intuitively committed to the abstract conception of enrichment.

There are, however, particular areas in which there is a contrary commitment. The early law of rescission can be represented as a law of unjust enrichment tied to specific things transferred and consequently to all-or-nothing solutions depending on the possibility of exact reversal of the transaction. The law relating to traceable substitutes of assets received also supposes that enrichment survives, not in the level of the abstract fund, but in particular assets in which the value of the original is re-invested.

In both those areas the law is currently struggling, at the level of defences, to ensure that the discrete conception of wealth is always ultimately trumped by the abstract conception. A mistaken payment invested in a painting will, by the one conception, survive in that substitute, even although according to the other the enrichment may have been eliminated from the fund by a banquet thrown to celebrate the purchase. If the abstract conception, represented by the defence of disenrichment, did not trump the discrete conception, represented by the rights in the traced substitute, a single event would concurrently produce inexplicably diverse responses.

A mistaken payer would then have an indefensible incentive to pursue those which happened to suit him best, as where the innocent payee has, in the abstract perspective, totally disenriched himself by making a wild investment in reliance on his enrichment but still happens to hold the discrete sum actually received or its traceable substitute.[54] It is a matter of pure chance whether the relevant disenrichment uses up the very money received or other funds. That is why the defence of change of position, which deals solely in the abstract conception of wealth, has to apply to every species of claim which arises from the generic event which we identify as an unjust enrichment.

[53] Below, 286–8. [54] Below, 209–10.

E. CONCLUSION

The first of the five questions usually slips past unnoticed, because money received unequivocally swells the abstract fund which is the sum of the recipient's wealth. Non-money benefits are more problematic. They will be given a reasonable market value where that can be done compatibly with respect for the subjectivity of value. In the most recent case of *McDonald v Coys of Kensington* the Court of Appeal, taking the same line as *Goff and Jones*, has indicated, *obiter*, a willingness to incline to a less tender attitude to the subjectivity of value. Within strict limits, that will be beneficial. For instance, it will strengthen the view that part performance under a defunct contract will be valued subject to a ceiling set by the contract—a valuation ceiling—which a too fastidious respect for subjectivity cannot fully explain.

Where money or some other asset passes to a recipient who acquires no title to it, the claimant who still has title has a choice whether he will assert his title and thus deny the recipient's enrichment or assert the recipient's enrichment and thus forego his title. There is no other satisfactory explanation of the English cases.

The law of unjust enrichment operates for the most part on an abstract conception of enrichment. That is to say, it views the enrichee's wealth as a single fund measured in money. The enrichee remains enriched so long as that abstract fund is swollen. Sometimes, however, the law falls back to the discrete conception of wealth which sees wealth as locked in particular assets which are rolled over from time to time, thus in effect reinvesting those particular units of value. This is most evident in relation to traceable substitutes. In the past that part of the law of unjust enrichment which is represented by the law of rescission has also operated on the premisses of the discrete conception of wealth. To avoid the absurdities which could arise if claimants were able to exploit the different implications of the two conceptions of wealth, the abstract conception has to be made dominant.

The vital instrument which guarantees that dominance is the defence of change of position. The defence ensures that all claims arising from unjust enrichment are in principle capped by the amount of abstractly surviving enrichment. We will see in Chapter 9 that the defence of change of position has to be cut in half, between the defence of disenrichment and other, non-disenriching changes of position. The treatment of enrichment and the treatment of disenrichment must increasingly be seen as two parts of the same discussion.

In the phased inquiry which unlocks all problems in unjust enrichment, enrichment is question 1, while disenrichment belongs to question 5. However, since extant enrichment—that is, abstractly extant enrichment—is the key to the peculiar normativity of unjust enrichment, this relation between the two must always be kept in mind. When it is overlooked the development of the defence of change of position threatens to come off the rails.

4

At the Expense of the Claimant

Categories which are conceptually certain are rare. The blood relatives of *X* are those who share a common ancestor with *X*. The class is conceptually certain because that test will determine whether any person is or is not a member and has no competitors. It leaves only evidential difficulties outstanding. Unjust enrichment is a category of the much more common kind, with a core where all agree and a periphery where reasonable people begin to differ. At a certain point all agree once more that an outer limit has been overstepped. If a tidier boundary is to be defined, it has to be artificial. The law is used to that. It makes choices all the time to iron out uncertainties which would otherwise leave the law unstable. Such peripheral doubts beset the limits of 'at the expense of the claimant'. The choices which every system therefore has to make turn out to have a profound effect on the range of its law of unjust enrichment.

This book began in the core of the core with the case of the receipt of a mistaken payment of a non-existent debt. In that example the connection between the claimant and the enrichment in the hands of the enrichee is a transfer knowingly, albeit mistakenly, made by himself. In the great majority of cases that is all there is to it. However, the generic description of the event contemplates the money as having been received 'at the claimant's expense'. This phrase of imprecise meaning is used to identify the full range of proper claimants.[1] It asks what variations upon knowing transfer are possible without losing touch with the logic which explains the right to restitution of a mistaken payment. When I drop my wallet and you pick it up, there is a transfer but one which happens without my knowledge or active participation. That suffices.[2] What other departures from the core case are possible?

This inquiry turns inevitably into a discussion of the meaning of 'at the expense of', but the real question is not what those words mean but what

[1] *Re Byfield* [1982] 1 All ER 249, 256.

[2] *Holiday v Sigil* (1826) 2 C & P 176, 172 ER 81; *Neate v Harding* (1851) 6 Ex 349, 155 ER 577; *Moffatt v Kazana* [1969] 2 QB 152.

constitutes a sufficient connection between the would-be claimant and the enrichment he wants to claim. The words are there to label the right answer to that question.

A. THE 'WRONG' SENSE

There are usages of 'at the expense of' which have to be ruled out. A joke might be said to have been made at my expense, meaning that it was calculated to diminish or embarrass me. Closely related is the 'wrong' sense. *C* is beaten up by *D*. *D* was paid £5,000 by *X*. Here *D* is enriched at *C*'s expense in the sense that he has obtained money by doing a wrong to *C*. We encountered this sense in Chapter 1 when we introduced the notion of restitution for wrongs as something different from restitution for unjust enrichment. Had the spy Blake been paid his royalties he would have been enriched at the Crown's expense in that he would have committed a profitable breach of his contract not to write without clearance.[3]

This is the 'wrong' sense of 'at the expense of': *C* relies on a wrong to connect himself to *D*'s enrichment. It is also the wrong sense in that it cannot be admitted to the law of unjust enrichment. A wolf in sheep's clothing is not a sheep. Where a claimant identifies himself as the victim of a wrong he is relying on the wrong and, albeit in the language of unjust enrichment, asking the court whether that wrong is one which yields a right to a gain-based award. The law of unjust enrichment cannot answer that question. It belongs to the law of wrongs. Failing any general answer, the question whether defamation, conversion, breach of fiduciary duty, and so on, yield rights to gain-based awards is a matter for the law of each particular wrong.[4]

B. THE 'FROM' SENSE

That leaves only the subtractive sense according to which an enrichment at the expense of another is one which is drawn from that other. The subtractive sense is the 'from' sense. 'From' is not straightforward. It is at this point that choices need to be made. There are questions which different legal systems answer differently. In the core case there is a simple transfer from claimant to defendant, and the transfer entails a plus

[3] *A-G v Blake* [2001] 1 AC 268 (HL), introduced above, 12–3.

[4] A large step towards sound general answers has now been taken by J Edelman, *Gain-Based Damages* [:] *Contract, Tort, Equity and Intellectual Property* (Hart Oxford 2002).

to the defendant corresponding to a loss to the claimant. Both limbs require examination. The subtraction can take the form of an interception. And it is a difficult and doubtful question whether the claimant must have suffered a loss.

1. INTERCEPTIVE SUBTRACTIONS

In the standard case the asset moves from the claimant's possession to that of the defendant. Is it sufficient that it was on its way from a third party to the claimant when the defendant intercepted it? Where there is an interceptive subtraction the enriching assets are never reduced to the ownership or possession of the claimant. They will have been on their way, in fact or law, to the claimant when the defendant intercepted them. The choice has gone in favour of accepting the sufficiency of interceptive subtractions, albeit without much analysis and hence with many untidy loose ends.

(a) Illustrations

One early example was where *D* usurped an office of profit which ought to have been occupied by *C*. *D* thus received fees which ought to have been paid to *C*. *C* could claim those profits intercepted by *D*.[5] In 1998 in *Montana v Crow Tribe of Indians* the Supreme Court of the United States upheld the principle, although on the facts the majority found that it did not apply, that where authority *D* has wrongfully levied a tax payable to authority *C*, *C* can recover from *D*.[6] Similarly, a self-appointed executor or administrator who receives what was due to the estate is liable to make restitution to the incoming rightful personal representative.[7] Again, if *D* receives rent from *X* which was due to *C*, he will have to account to *C*.[8] Of the same kind but rather more difficult are the cases, which are discussed by Professor Chambers, of land intended to be conveyed by *X* to *C* being mistakenly conveyed to *D*. In such a case *C* has sometimes been allowed to claim against *D*.[9]

[5] *Arris v Stukely* (1677) 2 Mod 260, 86 ER 1060; *Howard v Wood* (1679) 2 Lev 245, 83 ER 530. Although these provide a root for waiver of tort, they do not need to be analysed as instances of wrongful enrichment.

[6] 523 US 696 (1998) 715–16 (Souter and O'Connor JJ dissenting, 722–3). Both majority and minority approved *Valley County v Thomas* 109 Mont 345, 97 P 2d 345 (1939) where one county recovered vehicle tax levied by another.

[7] *Jacob v Allen* (1703) 1 Salk 27, 91 ER 26; *Yardley v Arnold* (1842) C & M 434, 174 ER 577.

[8] *Official Custodian for Charities v Mackey (No 2)* [1985] 1 WLR 1308, where Nourse J acknowledged the principle but found it not to apply on the particular facts.

[9] *Leuty v Hillas* (1858) 2 De G & J 110; *Craddock Brothers v Hunt* [1923] 2 Ch 136 (CA). R Chambers, *Resulting Trusts* (OUP Oxford 1997) 127.

However, the claimant has a heavy onus when his case rests on a factual rather than a legal inevitability the enrichment was en route to him. In *Hill v van Erp*[10] a solicitor's negligence caused a will to be invalid. The solicitor was liable in tort, but it was said that the intended beneficiaries could not sue the next of kin to whom the estate had gone. They could not say that those who benefited under the intestacy had intercepted assets which were on their way to those who, but for its invalidity, were entitled under the will.

If the boot had been on the other foot and the money been paid out under the invalid will, the mispaid beneficiaries would have been held to have intercepted money destined to those who were indisputably entitled as a matter of law, as in *Ministry of Health v Simpson*.[11] There, failing to notice the nullity of the bequest, the executors of Caleb Diplock had paid to charities sums which ought as a matter of law to have gone to the next of kin. The next of kin recovered directly from the charities. The money which the charities received was, as a matter of law, destined to go to them.

Professor Lionel Smith has exposed difficulties in all these cases, arguing that, where the defendant has received from a third party money which the claimant says should have come through to him, the claimant should never be allowed to recover if his rights against the third party are still intact.[12] He points out that if executors pay the wrong people they remain liable to pay the true beneficiary. Hence those who ought to have been paid cannot be said to have suffered an interceptive subtraction, because they are no less entitled to be paid by the executors after the misdirection than they were before. *Ministry of Health v Simpson* can only be explained, in his view, by understanding the Court to have complied with the requirement that the next of kin's continuing claim against the executors be discharged by insisting on prior exhaustion of all possible remedies against them.

[10] (1997) 188 CLR 159 (HCA). In *Lac Minerals Ltd v International Corona Resources Ltd* [1989] 2 SCR 574, 61 DLR (4th) 14 the Supreme Court of Canada found that the defendants had intercepted a goldfield which as a matter of fact would otherwise have been acquired by the claimants, but the case was decided in favour of the claimants as the victims of the wrong of either abuse of confidential information or breach of fiduciary duty. Once the case was presented as restitution for a wrong, the finding of factual interception ceased to be relevant.

[11] [1951] AC 251 (HL).

[12] LD Smith, 'Three-Party Restitution: A Critique of Birks's Theory of Interceptive Subtraction' (1991) 11 OJLS 481.

That requirement has few defenders.[13] It is incompatible with the principle *cuius commodum eius periculum* (the one who takes the advantage also bears the risk).[14] The money which the executors had paid to the charities, viewed as a mistaken payment, was at the time irrecoverable by the executors themselves, since in those days a payer had to bear the risk of a mistake of law. But the executors' liability to the next of kin should have been regarded as secondary to that of the charities, who enjoyed all the associated benefits, with the consequence that, in respect of such sums as they repaid the next of kin, the executors should have been entitled to reimbursement from the charities, just as a surety is entitled to reimbursement from a principal debtor. That in turn makes nonsense of the requirement that the next of kin recover from the charities only those sums irrecoverable from the executors.

The only general answer to Professor Smith's keen analysis is that the law sometimes prefers the reality to the technicality. In *Agip (Africa) Ltd v Jackson*,[15] for instance, the claimant company's account with a bank in Tunisia was debited with large sums on the basis of forged payment warrants. Technically their claim against the bank remained intact. They had not authorized the debiting of their account. Strictly, the bank should have been the claimant, but factually the Agip account had been debited. Agip had not been able to induce the Bank of Tunis to re-credit the account. They were allowed to sue the defendant accountants who had acted for the fraudsters and had received the money into their account. The reality was that the recipients had intercepted money due to Agip. On some facts of this pattern a solution can be found by subrogating the claimant to the third party's right against the defendant.

(b) False Interceptions

Sometimes what looks at first sight to be a clear case of interceptive subtraction turns out on closer inspection not to be. Suppose that, intending a gift to you standing below, I throw down a bundle of notes from an upper window, expecting you to catch them. *D* jumps up to intercept them. At law the notes are mine, since you have not obtained the

[13] G Jones (ed), *Goff and Jones on Restitution* (6th edn Sweet & Maxwell London 2002) [30–002].

[14] Digest 50.17.148 (Paul), more congruent to which is *Eaves v Hickson* (1861) Beav 136, 54 ER 840.

[15] [1990] Ch 265, aff'd [1991] Ch 547 (CA). On this aspect see E McKendrick, 'Tracing Misdirected Funds' (1991) LMCLQ 378.

possession which is essential to the perfection of the gift by delivery. But equity raises a beneficial interest in you as soon as I have done all that lies in me to do in order to transfer the legal title.[16] The physical interception comes a second or two later, when you already have a proprietary interest in the notes. The subtraction is not interceptive. The money is yours and is taken from you.

Again, suppose that I give *X* £50 to give to you. We might say that that money is now on its way to you. However, if *X* absconds with it, the question whether he is enriched at my expense or, interceptively, from you admits of no natural answer. The law therefore adopts an inevitably artificial criterion. The claim stays with me until *X* has attorned to you, which means until *X* has informed you that he is holding for you. But the attornment passes the property at law with the result that when *X* pockets the money the subtraction is no longer interceptive. He has taken the money from you.

Such an interception is not always short-circuited in this way. In *Shamia v Joory*[17] there was no identified fund, so that no property could pass. The defendant, who owed a sum of money to a third party, was told by that creditor to pay the claimant. The defendant attorned to the claimant. The claimant, though not owner, was able to obtain restitution. It is sometimes said that the case was wrongly decided for the very reason that no property could pass. But it is defensible as an instance of interceptive subtraction. The attornment, though it could not pass the property in any specific thing, nevertheless served as an indication that the sum in question was finally en route to the claimant. Accordingly, in withholding it the defendant had enriched himself by interceptive subtraction from the claimant.

2. CORRESPONDING LOSS?

The narrowest understanding of a sufficient connection between claimant and enrichment requires an arithmetic subtraction, a plus to the defendant and a corresponding minus to the claimant. In all the interceptive examples which have just been reviewed, the claimant does suffer a loss in that he fails to receive that which he was about to receive. Our two big questions—interception and corresponding loss—are separate questions, although they do overlap on some facts.

[16] *Re Rose* [1952] Ch 499 (CA).

[17] [1958] 1 QB 448.

(a) An Argument Finely Balanced

Under French influence transmitted through Quebec the law of Canada now uses words which appear to insist that the claimant must always have suffered such a corresponding loss.[18] However, 'from' does not necessarily imply loss, and English law appears not to insist that the claimant must have suffered one.

Suppose that when I am taking my summer holidays you use my bicycle for a month without my permission, then put it back in perfect condition; or that you stow away on my ship intending to take a free ride across the Atlantic. In these cases you have gained a valuable benefit but I have suffered no loss. I am no worse off. As long ago as 1776 in *Hambly v Trott* Lord Mansfield indicated that a claim for the value of these benefits would lie.[19] Such a claim might be explained as restitution for a wrong, but it is not obvious that it should be and it is very unlikely that Lord Mansfield was thinking on those lines.

There is other evidence that a claimant in unjust enrichment need not have suffered a loss. Attempts have been made to forge a defence out of facts which show that, if the claimant suffered a loss initially, he has since eliminated it. These arguments have been thrown out in Australia[20] and England.[21] One reason has been that loss is beside the point, an action in unjust enrichment being concerned with gains not losses. This is also what the German jurists say.[22]

[18] *Pettkus v Becker* [1980] 2 SCR 217, 227–8; M McInnes, 'The Measure of Restitution' (2002) 52 U Toronto LJ 163; M McInnes, 'At the Plaintiff's Expense: Quantifying Restitutionary Relief' [1998] CLJ 472. This Canadian position is vigorously supported by RB Grantham and CEF Rickett, 'Disgorgement for Unjust Enrichment' [2003] CLJ 159.

[19] (1776) 1 Cowp 371, 375, 98 ER 1136, 1138. The later refusal in *Phillips v Homfray* (1883) 24 Ch D 439 (CA) to treat use, and hence saving of expense, as an enrichment is roundly repudiated by Goff and Jones (n 13 above) [36–003]. Compare the case of the stowaway on the plane to New York BGH NJW 609 (7.1.1971) translated by G Dannemann in B Markesinis, W Lorenz, and G Dannemann, *German Law of Obligations Vol 1 The Law of Contracts and Restitution: A Comparative Introduction* (OUP Oxford 1997) 771.

[20] *Roxborough v Rothmans of Pall Mall Australia Ltd* (2002) 76 ALJR 203 (HCA), Kirby J dissenting; *Commissioner of State Revenue v Royal Insurance Australia Ltd* (1994) 182 CLR 51 (HCA), where Mason ACJ adopted the view of Windeyer J in *Mason v NSW* (1959) 102 CLR 108, 146.

[21] *Kleinwort Benson v Birmingham City Council* [1996] 4 All ER 733 (CA).

[22] 'In this area of law only the enrichment of the person liable is relevant. Whether the enrichment-creditor has been impoverished is of no significance. . . . It would therefore be a serious mistake to withhold a claim founded on unjust enrichment on the ground that the enrichment-creditor had suffered no detriment' HJ Wieling, *Bereicherungsrecht* (Springer Berlin 1993) 1–2 (my translation).

There is a counter-argument to be found in *BP Exploration Co (Libya) Ltd v Hunt (No2)*.[23] It carries great weight, because the judge was Robert Goff J, co-author of the leading textbook. He had to consider the question of enrichment in the context of the Law Reform (Frustrated Contracts) Act 1943 section 1(3). Before oil was discovered in the Libyan desert BP and Hunt entered into a joint venture to exploit a concession obtained from the Libyan government by Hunt. BP took a half share in the concession and then, under the terms of the joint venture, began prospecting. Success vastly enhanced the value of the concession, but the joint venture was later frustrated by expropriation. Where one party has conferred a valuable non-money benefit on the other the Act gives the court a discretion to make an award of a just sum, within a limit set by the value of that benefit. Robert Goff J assessed the enhancement of Hunt's half-share of the concession at some $85m but ordered him to pay, by way of just sum, less than one-quarter of that valuable benefit.

While the discretionary nature of the jurisdiction conferred by the Act, which was emphasized when the case went on appeal, may to some extent distort the picture, Robert Goff J clearly thought of it as a statutory application of the law of unjust enrichment. Against that background it is certainly possible to understand his premiss as having been that a claimant in unjust enrichment must have suffered loss. Otherwise it is not obvious why, having already made an allowance in the valuation of the benefit for that element which was not due to the efforts of BP, he nevertheless allowed them to recover only a much lower amount, seemingly the amount that it cost them to confer that benefit. The same premiss appears to be assumed in the treatment of 'at the expense of' by *Goff and Jones*, which, however, does not directly confront the issue.[24]

The requirement that the claimant must have suffered a corresponding loss is a choice which some systems make, thereby giving themselves a

[23] [1979] 1 WLR 783, aff'd [1981] 1 WLR 232 (CA), [1983] 2 AC 352 (HL).

[24] *Goff & Jones* (n 13 above) [1–045]–[1–046]. Very recently *Re BHT (UK) Ltd* [2004] EWHC 201 (12 February 2004) decided that a liquidator could not recover on behalf of the insolvent company an overpayment made to a secured creditor, one ground being that the company had suffered no loss: even if it recovered it would not be able to keep the money but would have to pay the sum over to preferential creditors [24]–[27]. This is certainly incorrect. It suffices here to say that, in the same paragraphs, the deputy judge showed that he contemplated the law of unjust enrichment as part of the law of wrongs and the law of wrongs as requiring a loss: especially [26]. This case is not even properly one in which the claimant suffered no loss, merely one in which it was likely that if it recovered it would be swiftly disenriched.

narrow law of unjust enichment. English law appears not to have made that choice. Germany certainly has not. Arguing for the narrow view, Grantham and Rickett have recently maintained that a system which abandons the requirement of corresponding loss cannot have an independent law of unjust enrichment. The choice of the broader view is, in their view, a choice in favour of merging the law of unjust enrichment and the law of restitution for wrongs.[25]

That is incorrect. As will become apparent in the next sub-section, the effect of the broader view is to enlarge the incidence of alternative analysis. That means that there will be more cases in which a claimant will have two distinct restitution-yielding causes of action, one in unjust enrichment and one in civil wrongs. The two different events remain analytically distinct. It is not even true that every example of restitution for wrongs will be susceptible of alternative analysis. There will be facts on which the law of civil wrongs will give the claimant a right to the defendant's gain (restitution for the wrong) but the law of unjust enrichment will be excluded for want of any not-wrong connection between claimant and enrichment. *A-G v Blake* is one such case.

Nevertheless, a very powerful new article in the Cambridge Law Journal by the Canadian Professor Mitchell McInnes will persuade many people that the law of unjust enrichment must restrict itself to those cases in which the claimant has suffered a loss corresponding to the defendant's gain.[26] In that article he quite rightly decouples the issue of interception and the issue of corresponding loss.[27] He is also right in insisting that the rationale for restitution is at its strongest when the defendant is occupying an extant gain *and* the claimant has suffered a corresponding loss.[28] It does not follow, however, that this or indeed any subject must be confined to the case in which it is most strongly underpinned. We might also concede, more generally, that there is nothing particularly desirable about the broad version of the law of unjust enrichment which emerges when the requirement of corresponding loss is abandoned, especially in a system which, unlike German law, does not shrink from gain-based recovery for wrongs.

There is nonetheless one serious weakness in this excellent study, namely that it has nowhere to put the cases which chiefly compel the adoption of the proposition that English law does not insist on loss to

[25] Grantham and Rickett (n 18 above) 174–5.

[26] M McInnes, 'Interceptive Subtraction, Unjust Enrichment and Wrongs—A Reply to Professor Birks' [2003] CLJ 697.

[27] Ibid 705.

[28] Ibid 706.

the claimant. Those cases, starting with *Hambly v Trott* itself, appear to be satisfied with a proposition the short version of which would be 'from my property, therefore sufficiently from me'. One cannot create and adopt an elegant view of the law of unjust enrichment by sweeping awkward bits of it into no-man's land.

(b) From My Property

It is clear that if I invest your money and double it, you are entitled to the doubled proceeds. That is the law. This is what happened in *FC Jones (Trustee in Bankruptcy) v Jones*.[29] There Mr Jones had transferred money from the firm's bank account to Mrs Jones. As the law then stood, in the firm's insolvency the account then vested retrospectively in the trustee in bankruptcy. She multiplied the money she had received fivefold by speculation in potato futures. The trustee in bankruptcy recovered all that she had made. There is no hint that the outcome turned on wrongdoing. The only satisfactory explanation is that she was unjustly enriched at his expense to the extent of the whole sum.

More recently, as we have already seen, the House of Lords has held, in *Foskett v McKeown*,[30] that, where a trustee misappropriates trust property, the beneficiaries under a trust are entitled to choose between a security interest and a beneficial interest in the traceable proceeds. In the case itself they thus obtained many times what they had lost. This outcome is fully compatible with, if not dictated by, the law relating to resulting trusts based on contributions to the purchase price of a house or other asset.[31]

The taxonomy of these cases is disputed.[32] They fit the unjust enrichment analysis if we say that the earning opportunities inherent in an asset are attributed to its owner. Anyone who takes those opportunities intercepts what is already attributed in law to that owner. In speculating with the firm's money Mrs Jones intercepted the firm's earning opportunities. The actual loss to the firm and its trustee was one fifth of that which they recovered from her. The fivefold increase was from the firm's property and therefore from it.

[29] [1997] Ch 159 (CA). The analysis of this case in Grantham and Rickett (n 18 above) 170–5 is vitiated by their view that it is 'property, not unjust enrichment', as to which see 32–8 above.

[30] [2000] AC 51 (HL) discussed above, 34–6.

[31] Compare below, 304–7.

[32] Above, 32–8.

(c) The Future

There is a great deal at stake. The taxonomic disputes surrounding such cases as *Jones* and *Foskett* will determine the scope of the English law of unjust enrichment. Are these cases in which the defendant was enriched 'at the expense of the claimant' within the way that the law understands the 'from' sense of that phrase? Or, bearing in mind that we are not construing a statutory phrase, are they cases in which the connection between the claimant and the enrichment is sufficient to keep them within the logic which drives the recovery of the mistaken payment of a non-existent debt? If they are, the reach of the law of unjust enrichment is much longer than we thought.

Chapter 1 observed that in *United Australia Ltd v Barclays Bank* the House of Lords held that conversion was a tort which generated both compensatory and restitutionary rights.[33] The House did not say whether a claimant could also reach the proceeds of a conversion through an alternative analysis in unjust enrichment. If the previous paragraphs are correct, the answer is yes. If I sell your bicycle for £200, I usurp the earning opportunities inherent in your ownership of the bicycle and intercept £200 which the law attributes to you. On these facts there are therefore two paths to restitution, either by standing on the tort but asking for restitution rather than the more usual compensation or by ignoring the tort and treating the facts as an enrichment at your expense and absolutely without your consent.

A claimant who takes the second route is not waiving the tort, merely ignoring it. Since the *United Australia* case there has been no such thing as 'waiver of tort' except in the rare case of one who, without authority, holds himself out as an agent for a principal. There, by ratification, the principal does extinguish any tort the originally unauthorized agent committed. That genuine case apart, the *United Australia* view was that 'waiver of tort' was nothing but a fiction disguising the first of the two routes to restitution, where the cause of action remains the tort itself but the claimant seeks, and the law allows, gain-based recovery. *United Australia* said nothing about the other route to restitution, where there is a sufficient connection between the claimant and the enrichment even if the character of the facts as a wrong is entirely ignored. If you by fraud induce me to believe that I owe you money, and I then pay, I may choose to ignore the fraud and treat the facts only as revealing a mistaken payment of a non-existent debt. Our question is whether the same is true

[33] [1941] AC 1 (HL) on which see above, 15–6.

of these cases where there is no correspondence between the gain obtained from the claimant's property and the loss suffered by the claimant?

If future cases confirm that the implication of *Jones* and *Foskett* is that the choice has gone in favour of treating the victim of these interceptive subtractions as a proper claimant in unjust enrichment, we will have intuitively chosen a broad law of unjust enrichment on the German lines, rather than the narrower version of the jurisdictions which follow France. One consequence will be a much greater overlap with restitution for wrongs. The *Jones* case, where nothing was said of any wrong, leads directly to the proposition that the House of Lords in *United Australia Ltd v Barclays Bank Ltd* should have recognized the two different routes to restitution after the tort of conversion, neither of them requiring a genuine waiver of tort. Moreover, no line can be drawn between, on the one hand, sale and exchange of another's asset and, on the other, hiring it out. If I hire out your car the rental which I receive is an interceptive subtraction from you, of the same kind as in the case of a sale, and much more obviously may exceed the loss to you.

Edwards v Lee's Administrator,[34] the case of the Great Onyx Cave in Kentucky, was an example of a profitable trespass. Edwards found on his land the entrance to a wonderful scenic cave. He started up a thriving tourist business. Unfortunately one third of the cave extended into Lee's neighbouring land. Far below the surface the trespassing tourists caused no loss, but profits were being made from the use of his land. Edwards had to pay Lee's estate one-third of his profits.

The result is easily explained as restitution for the trespass itself. In that light it is an instance of gain-based recovery for a wrong. Can it be understood, by alternative analysis, as restitution of unjust enrichment at Lee's expense? The language used by the court is equivocal, not to say muddled, but once we break away from the requirement of corresponding loss the answer must be that it can. *Jones* and *Foskett* tell us that we have, unequivocally, made that break.

In order to understand the likely future reach of our law of unjust enrichment we need to distinguish between the use of the land and the profits of that use. These are two steps on one path. The use of the land was taken directly from Lee. Despite Lee's having suffered no loss, he would clearly have had a claim in unjust enrichment for the reasonable

[34] 96 SW 2d 1028 (Kentucky CA 1936).

rental, being the value of what Edwards had taken.[35] But he wanted and got a share of the profits. The money came from the tourists, and its receipt by Edwards even more obviously caused Lee no corresponding loss. Nevertheless, the case is materially indistinguishable from the *Jones* case discussed above. Edwards earned that money from Lee's property and hence by interceptive subtraction from Lee. It follows that Lee's estate did not have to rely on the trespass to connect himself to Edwards' profits. Ignoring the wrong, he could say that it was money obtained, interceptively, from him: from his property and therefore from him.

The discussion of this case is then a model for many. For example, gain-based recovery in respect of infringements of intellectual property is amenable to the same dual analysis. Indeed early relief by way of account of profits in equity may in retrospect be more easily understood as based on interceptive unjust enrichment rather than as applying the analogy with tort which nowadays seems elementary.[36]

It is tempting to push these cases where there is no corresponding loss back into restitution for wrongs. There are insuperable obstacles. One is illustrated by *Jones*.[37] The wife in that case received the trustee's money by two cheques. To explain the outcome in the law of wrongs, one must, as the court did not, tie it to conversion of the cheques. But that would mean that, if the transfer had been paperless, the result would have been completely different. That is probably acceptable to nobody. The other obstacle concerns traced substitutes in general. Again, tracing depends on substitutions, not on wrongful substitutions. *Foskett*[38] shows that, if it is not explained by unjust enrichment, the right in the substitute has to be explained by a fiction of persistence.[39] It is very doubtful whether the law could now withdraw from the broad version of unjust enrichment, to which it has committed by not requiring corresponding loss, without retreating into that fiction. We are in the business of escaping fictions. We

[35] In *Olwell v Nye & Nissen Co* 26 Wash 2d 282, 173 P 2d 652 (SC Washington 1946) this difference between use and profits was centrally in issue. The defendant was liable for the profits of wrongfully using the claimant's egg-washing machine. *Beck v Northern Natural Gas Company* 170 F 3d 1018 (10th Cir 1999) confines the recovery of profits to cynical deliberate wrongdoing. On this see J Edelman, *Gain-Based Damages* (Hart Oxford 2002) 138–9. The law of wrongs takes that stance, but the analysis in the text above, showing that an action lies in unjust enrichment, cannot.

[36] *Watson v McLean* (1858) EB & E 75, 120 ER 435; *Edelsten v Edelsten* (1863) 1 De GJ & S 185, 46 ER 72; *Neilson v Betts* (1871) LR 5 HL 1.

[37] [1997] Ch 159 (CA).

[38] [2001] AC 102 (HL).

[39] Above, 35–6 and below, 198.

have to find out why, by way of holding operation, the fiction seemed acceptable. The only answer is unjust enrichment.

C. THE IMMEDIATE ENRICHEE

It is usually perfectly obvious who is enriched at whose expense. The reason is that in most cases there are only two parties in view. Even when there are more than two players it is often obvious who is whose immediate enrichee. I pay you money by mistake; you make a present of it to *X*. We can arrange these three parties in a straight line. You are my immediate enrichee, and *X* is your immediate enrichee. So far as *X* can be said to be enriched at my expense, he is a secondary or remote enrichee. Immediacy matters. I can only sue a remote enrichee if the rules of leapfrogging do not forbid it. 'At the expense of the claimant' means, in the first instance, 'immediately at the expense of the claimant'. Thereafter the problems of leapfrogging set in. It is essential to be able to recognize the immediate enrichee. One cannot otherwise tell whether the claimant faces leapfrogging problems.

1. THE PROPRIETARY CONNECTION

There is one recurrent three-party situation in which the intervention of a third hand makes no difference at all. If the defendant has received the claimant's property, it does not matter how many intermediate hands it has passed through. There is an illusion of leapfrogging, but in reality there is none. In *Lipkin Gorman v Karpnale Ltd*[40] a partner in a firm of solicitors who was addicted to gambling fed his addiction from the firm's client account. He gambled the money away at the defendant's casino. There was no point in suing the gambler. He was penniless and in prison. The firm succeeded in recovering from the casino, seemingly leapfrogging the addicted gambler. Although the facts were actually more complex, the model from which the House of Lords worked was this. If *X* takes *C*'s money without *C*'s consent and gives it to *D*, then, subject to possible defences, *D* becomes indebted to *C* in the sum received.

A number of cases show that the model holds good where the claimant's interest in the thing is a power to avoid a voidable title. In *Banque Belge pour l'Étranger v Hambrouck*[41] the bank had paid out money

[40] [1991] 2 AC 548 (HL).

[41] [1921] 1 KB 321 (CA). Cf undue influence: *Bainbrigge v Browne* (1881) 18 Ch D 188, 196–7; *Midland Bank v Perry* [1988] 1 FLR 161, 167.

to a fraudster who had forged cheques. On the strength of its power to avoid his title, it was able to go against his mistress, to whom he had given some of the money. On a larger scale *El Ajou v Dollar Land Holdings Plc*[42] is structurally similar. The claimant was the victim of a huge share-selling fraud. He was able to reach across a world-wide money laundering operation to the defendant company in cooperation with which the rogues had invested in the development of New Covent Garden.

It is necessary to bear in mind the operation of the defence of bona fide purchase. Where bona fide purchase destroys prior property rights, there will be no proprietary connection between the claimant and the bona fide purchaser, and in the case of money bona fide purchase always does clear off earlier interests.[43] In *El Ajou v Dollar Land Holdings Plc* the defendant developers were found to have known of the provenance of the funds in question. They were not bona fide purchasers. Subject to that caveat, where there is a sufficient proprietary connection there are no remote recipients. If I find your wallet it makes no difference whether I am the first recipient or the second or the twenty-second. Suppose a pickpocket took it and, in alarm, threw it down, and then I found it. My position would be exactly the same as if your wallet had fallen from your pocket into the road in front of me without your noticing its loss. A receipt of your money is always a receipt directly from you.

2. ENRICHMENTS CONFERRED BY ONE BUT PROCURED BY ANOTHER

Appearances can deceive. It is quite often true that a defendant is not the immediate enrichee of the person who actually conferred the enrichment. This happens where that person, in conferring the enrichment, acts at the behest of and on the credit of another. If I want to pay off a debt to you or build you a garage, I will almost certainly do it through another person. To pay my debt to you, I will draw a cheque in your favour which my bank will honour. To build the garage, I will employ a builder to do the work. The builder works under a contract with me and on my credit. Likewise my bank in making the payment to you. In such cases you appear at first sight to be immediately enriched by the builder and the bank, but the builder and bank act for me and look to me to pay them. You are my immediate enrichee.

[42] [1993] 3 All ER 717 (Millett J) rev'd on one point as to attribution of knowledge [1994] 2 All ER 685 (CA). In the CA the defendants were no longer seen as bona fide purchasers.

[43] Below, 240–5.

Although they conferred the enrichment and although it is true that you are enriched at their expense, you are as regards them a remote or secondary enrichee. You are my immediate enrichee, and you are their remote enrichee. If I fail to pay the builder or the bank, they may want to go against you. Because there is no direct enricher-enrichee relationship between them and you, they have to satisfy the rules which control leapfrogging. We will come back in the next section to cases of this kind, where the defendant is a remote enrichee. The liability of a remote enrichee depends on the rules of leapfrogging.

In *Khan v Permayer*[44] the claimant restaurateur and his partner, in financial trouble, wanted to sell the restaurant and the sub-lease of its premises to *X*, who was willing for them to continue to run it as his employees. The landlord, Permayer, made it a condition of the assignment of the lease that a debt owed to him be paid. It was agreed that *X* would pay it and the partners would repay him. *X* then by deed assumed responsibility to Permayer and paid off the debt, and the restaurateurs repaid *X* from their salaries. Much later it emerged that the supposed debt had not existed. In earlier insolvency proceedings which played no part in this story, it had been extinguished. That was before *X* ever came into the picture. Nobody argued that the debt survived even as a natural obligation, like a debt barred by limitation.

The Court of Appeal allowed the restaurateur to recover directly from Permayer, the supposed creditor. However, the Court made the problem more difficult than it was. Despite holding that there was no separate and distinct deal between *X* and the defendant but only a mechanism for the discharge of the restaurateur's debt, the Court treated the restaurateur as though it were leapfrogging *X* to attack a remote enrichee. In fact the defendant was the immediate enrichee of the restaurateur, since *X* had paid on the partners' credit, just as a bank pays on the credit of its customer. If *X* himself had not been repaid and had then attempted to recover the money from the defendant, he would have had to sue the defendant as a remote enrichee and would almost certainly not have been allowed to leapfrog the restaurateur. He would have been a person who conferred an enrichment on another on behalf of and on the credit of a third party. The next section deals with actions brought by persons in that position.

[44] [2001] Bankruptcy and Personal Insolvency Rep 95 (CA).

D. LEAPFROGGING

There is no absolute bar against leapfrogging. This section asks when, if ever, the claimant in unjust enrichment is confined to his action against the immediate enrichee. If I mistakenly pay *X* £1,000 and *X* is thereby enabled to give to you £500, it is not nonsense to say that you have been enriched at my expense. However, you are manifestly not my immediate enrichee. Can I leapfrog *X* and recover from you? It is important that you are a donee. Many remote recipients will be bona fide purchasers from the immediate enrichee and will therefore have a defence. We are only concerned here with those who do not have that protection. A remote enrichee, properly so-called, is one who would not have been enriched but for the enrichment of the immediate enrichee. The connection is causal. We have already seen that if there is a proprietary connection the requirement of immediacy is satisfied all down the line.

It is not easy to state the law for merely causal connections, for two reasons. First, the question whether the remote enrichee can be liable has never been directly addressed in the English cases. Secondly, the incidence of the proprietary connection is unclear because of the confused state of cases on the proprietary consequences of unjust enrichment.[45] If, for example, it is true that a mistaken payment turns the recipient into a trustee, the payee's donee is not a remote enrichee of the payer, because there is a proprietary connection between them. The donee receives that which in equity belongs to the claimant. We can hardly do more than nibble at the problem here.

The picture seems to be that there is one common case in which leapfrogging is ruled out. For the rest the policy of the law is not hostile to leapfrogging. It leaves remote recipients to the protection of normal defences.

1. INITIALLY VALID CONTRACTS

At this point we return to those cases in which one party confers an enrichment which is procured by another. Where a defendant receives a benefit from or because of the performance of a contract between two others and the party making the performance and thus conferring the benefit had a valid contractual right to be paid for that performance by the other party to the contract, the recipient of the enrichment is the

[45] On which see Chapter 8, below, esp 203–4.

immediate enrichee of the latter party, the party bound to pay, and the remote enrichee of the former, the party conferring the enrichment. In such a case the former, who procured the performance, may never be leapfrogged by the latter, who conferred it. Leapfrogging out of an initially valid contract is not allowed. One may never attack one's contractual counter-party's immediate enrichee.

A simple model is an unsecured loan. If a bank extends overdraft facilities to a customer, and the customer thus has funds enough to give £1,000 to his son, the bank will have no recourse against the son. If the father becomes insolvent, the bank will have to line up with the other unsecured creditors. One reason for not allowing the bank to sue the son is precisely that the bank must not wriggle round the risk of insolvency inherent in its contract with the father. Contracts entail the risk of insolvency.

The cases often do not declare on their face that they are of this kind. In *Lloyds Bank Plc v Independent Insurance Co Ltd*[46] the bank paid its customer's creditor a large sum with its customer's authority but by reason of a grave mistake as to the funds available to the customer. It thought a very large cheque in favour of the customer had been cleared, but it had not. The customer became insolvent. The bank tried and failed to recover from the creditor-payee. The reason given was that the bank got what it paid for. It obtained the discharge of the debt. That cannot be quite sufficient. It is inconceivable that the result would have been any different if the payee had been a donee receiving a birthday present by the wish of the customer.

The stronger reason is that, even though the bank made the payment directly to the customer's creditor, the bank's immediate enrichee was the customer against whom it had a valid contractual claim for repayment. The bank lent the customer more money which, at the request of the customer, it paid directly to the creditor. The creditor was indeed enriched at the expense of the bank, but only through the customer. It was the bank's remote enrichee. The enrichment which the bank wanted to get back from the remote enrichee was initially the subject of a valid contract between the bank and its customer under which the bank had a right to be repaid by the customer.[47] No leapfrogging is allowed in that situation. Any other rule would subvert the insolvency regime. This case

[46] [1999] 2 WLR 986 (CA).

[47] This explanation also applies to the leading case of *Aiken v Short* (1856) 1 H & N 210, 156 ER 1180, the facts of which were materially identical.

is the opposite of *Khan v Permayer*, discussed immediately above. There the claimant was the party who paid for the performance which enriched the defendant, not the party with a contractual right to be paid for it. The defendant was the claimant's immediate enrichee.

Brown and Davis v Galbraith illustrates the same rule in a different context.[48] A garage does work on a car which has been damaged in a crash. The car's owner is the ultimate beneficiary of the work. In almost all cases the garage works under a contract with an insurance company. If after the work is done and the customer has taken the car back into his possession, the insurance company becomes insolvent, the unpaid garage has no claim against the owner. The enrichment of the owner of the car was initially the subject of a contract between the garage and the insurance company. The latter is thus the garage's immediate enrichee. The customer is its remote enrichee. The garage has to take the risk of the insolvency of the insurance company with which it validly contracted. If the contract is terminated and a claim is made in unjust enrichment, it too must be made against the insurance company. There can be no leapfrogging out of a disappointing contract.

Pan Ocean Shipping Co Ltd v Creditcorp Ltd (The Trident Beauty)[49] is more difficult. It has excited controversy.[50] But it ultimately reduces to a similar analysis. The facts are best taken in two stages. Pan Ocean were the charterers of the Trident Beauty. Her owners were in financial trouble. They were bound to pay the hire in advance, which they did. It turned out that they had paid for some periods when no freight had been carried. Had there been no complications, that money would have been recoverable as having been paid on a basis which failed.

There were, however, two complications. One was that the contract contained a term covering the return of hire paid in advance which was not earned. Lord Goff appears to say that such a term, creating a contractual debt, displaces the law of unjust enrichment altogether.[51] The

[48] [1972] 1 WLR 997 (CA); *Gray's Truck Centre Ltd v Olaf L Johnson Ltd* (CA 25 January 1990).

[49] [1994] 1 WLR 161 (HL).

[50] A Burrows, *The Law of Restitution* (2nd edn Butterworths London 2002) 348–50 favours Lord Goff's second reason [1994] 1 WLR 161, 166, which was that Creditcorp were in a position analogous to a bona fide purchaser in that they had given value for the assignment and should not have their bargain undermined. Cf A Burrows 'Restitution from Assignees' [1994] Restitution L Rev 52. Rather different: D Visser in D Johnston and R Zimmerman, *Unjustified Enrichment in Comparative Perspective* (CUP Cambridge 2002) 526, 548–50.

[51] [1994] 1 WLR 161 (HL) 164, made more difficult by the fact that he calls unjust enrichment 'the law of restitution'.

other and greater complication was that they had not in fact paid the owners at all, but rather the owners' assignee. The owners had borrowed heavily from Creditcorp and the security which they gave included the assignment to Creditcorp of their right to receive the hire from the charterers. Pan Ocean had therefore paid Creditcorp. They argued that this was nonetheless a payment made upon a basis which had failed. They were denied recovery and thus remitted to their claim against the insolvent owners.

If Pan Ocean had merely been requested to pay Creditcorp by the owners, this case would have been indistinguishable from the others. There was a valid contract between Pan Ocean and the owners which obliged Pan Ocean to take the risk of the creditworthiness of the owners. Pan Ocean would have conferred the enrichment on Creditcorp but it would have been the owners' payment, made through Pan Ocean. Creditcorp would have been the remote enrichee of Pan Ocean, barred by the rule that there can be no leapfrogging out of a valid contract. The direct enricher-enrichee relationship would have been between the owners and Creditcorp.

It is at first sight strange to say that it makes no difference that Pan Ocean were liable to pay, by virtue of the assignment. Can it be that a payer liable to the payee was not in an immediate enricher–enrichee relationship with the payee? The answer is yes, because recourse to the machinery of assignment does not alter the facts that the payment to Creditcorp was procured by the owners on the faith of their either earning it or repaying it, and that to allow the restitutionary claim against Creditcorp would be to allow Pan Ocean to wriggle out of the risk of insolvency which their contract with the owners entailed. The fact that their contract contained a term for repayment may make this extra-clear. But the result would have been the same without it. What we know from this case, although we could have worked it out without its help, is that the veto on leapfrogging out of an initially valid contract is very strong, strong enough to protect even an assignee.

At first sight the numerous *O'Brien* cases[52] seem to defy this rule. The *O'Brien* doctrine stands guard at the gate where business, red in tooth and claw, comes knocking at the door of the cosier world of family and friends. Two parties, usually but not necessarily man and wife, agree that one of them, usually the wife, will mortgage or join in the mortgage of the

[52] *Barclays Bank plc v O'Brien* [1994] 1 AC 180; *CIBC Mortgages plc v Pitt* [1994] 1 AC 200, reviewed in *Royal Bank of Scotland v Etridge (No 2)* UKHL 44, [2001] 3 WLR 1021.

family home and stand surety for the other's business borrowing. The security once given, the lender, usually a bank, makes the advance. Later, when the pound of flesh is called for, the security-giver wants the mortgage and the guarantee set aside, maintaining their invalidity on the ground of misrepresentation or undue influence. This bid for restitution sometimes can succeed. It is not an attempt to leapfrog out of a valid contract between the security-giver and the business borrower. It belongs in the next sub-section.

2. NO INITIAL CONTRACT

In the *O'Brien* configuration there is no valid contract between security-giver and the business borrower. Even if the deal between them survives the presumption in family matters against intent to create legal relations, it will be invalid from the outset for misrepresentation or because of the impaired autonomy of the security-giver. Although it appears to be a three-party situation, with one party seeking to leap out of a bad contract which has benefited a third party, the now defendant, in fact the threesome resolves itself into a simple two-party transfer between the security giver and the lender.

This resembles the case in which a bank mistakenly pays its customer's creditor believing it has its customer's authority but in fact having none. There the bank can recover directly from the creditor. For the enrichment of the creditor is not the subject of a valid contract between bank and customer, merely a mistaken payment by the bank to the creditor-payee, who is the immediate and only enrichee.[53] None of these apparently three-party situations are attempts to leapfrog. It will be recalled that we said the same of *Khan v Permayer*.[54] In that case there was an arrangement whereby the outgoing sub-tenants' supposed debt would be paid off by the new sub-tenant, who was to be, and was, repaid by the supposed debtors. We said that there was a direct enricher–enrichee relationship between the supposed debtors and the supposed creditor.

Leapfrogging supposes a claimant who could, however unsatisfactorily, sue an immediate enrichee but who wants to sue a remote enrichee instead,

[53] *Barclays Bank Ltd v WJ Simms & Son Ltd* [1980] QB 677. Compare *Customs and Excise Comrs v National Westminster Bank Plc* [2002] EWHC 2204 (Ch), [2003] 1 All ER (Comm) 327 where the claimant Commissioners owed money to a taxpayer creditor but recovered their payment to the defendant Bank. They had thought that they had their creditor's agreement and authority to pay the Bank, which was indeed his bank, but they had overlooked instructions forbidding payment via the Bank and requiring payment via named solicitors.

[54] Above, 88.

on the ground that, but for the unjust enrichment of the first recipient, the remote recipient would not have been enriched. In the previous subsection we saw that there is no hope of leapfrogging out of an initially valid contract with the immediate enrichee. But in the absence of any such contract, it seems that such leapfrogging is permitted. This is controversial. Professor Burrows assumes a general principle against actions against anyone but the immediate enrichee, but recognizes a series of exceptions.[55] Professor Tettenborn takes a strongly negative stance. He puts this case:

> C inadvertently overpays his creditor A by £1000; A, pleasantly surprised on reading his next bank statement but entirely unsuspicious . . ., proceeds to give £1000 from his other account to his son B. . . . A can almost certainly plead change of position as a defence. Hence the potential significance of a direct claim by C against B; can C say (in effect): 'I have paid money by mistake; but for this B would not have been enriched; therefore B has been unjustifiably enriched at my expense and ought to refund'?[56]

His answer is no. In German law it is certainly yes, for this very case is provided for in the BGB.[57] The answer must also be yes in English law. The paragraphs which follow show that our law is not absolutely averse to leapfrogging claims.

Professor Tettenborn's example is one in which the claimant's rights against the first recipient, the immediate enrichee, are extinguished as a matter of law by the defence of change of position. The same is true of the case in the BGB. It is impossible at the moment to say whether that or some other restrictive requirement must be satisfied in addition to the requirement of 'but for' causation. A slightly milder restriction would be that remedies against the first recipient must have been exhausted. A more severe precondition would be traceability: the remote recipient would then have to be shown (i) to have received because the first recipient received and (ii) to have received the very assets which the first recipient received or their traceable substitutes. The severest restriction of all would be to insist, in addition to 'but for' causation, on both extinc-

[55] Burrows (n 50 above) 31–41. His basic rule is not specific to leapfrogging. It is much wider: 'the claimant is not entitled to the restitution of benefits conferred by a third party rather than himself' 32.

[56] A Tettenborn, 'Lawful Receipt—A Justifying Factor' [1997] RLR 1, 1. Cf Burrows (n 50 above) 41.

[57] 822 BGB: If the recipient disposes of the thing received to a third party gratuitously, then, so far as the first recipient's restitutionary obligation is thereby barred, the third party incurs a restitutionary obligation just as though the disposition had been made to him by the creditor without legal ground (my translation).

tion or exhaustion and traceability. The only purpose of such restrictions would be to reduce the incidence of leapfrogging claims. If there is no well-founded objection to leapfrogging, other than to leapfrogging out of a valid contract, there is no real justification for additional restrictions. The remote recipient will anyhow have the protection of defences.

It will be noticed that Professor Tettenborn's example is carefully constructed to exclude traceability. The father's gift to his son came from a separate account, but the gift was nonetheless caused by the arrival of the unjust enrichment. Traceability figures in this discussion merely as a restriction, not as a preliminary to the assertion of a proprietary right, but by eliminating it from the example Professor Tettenborn also sidesteps the possibility of there being a sufficient proprietary connection between the bank and the son, which would render the inquiry into the causal connection superfluous.

The validity of the proposition that a remote recipient can be reached on the basis of the causal argument rests partly on the real state of things in *Lipkin Gorman v Karpnale Ltd*, which differed markedly from the model on which their Lordships relied. If its peculiarities cannot be fitted to that model, the outcome may have to be explained on the basis that it is possible to reach a secondary recipient on a purely causal basis.[58] One nagging worry, if that revision were otherwise acceptable, is that there was a contractual relationship between the partners. If the property connection breaks down, other explanations would very likely be caught by the bar against leapfrogging in that context.

The difficulty with the *Lipkin Gorman* case is that the money in the gambler's hands, though taken from the firm's account, belonged to the gambler. He was an authorized signatory on the account, although his gambling was of course not an authorized purpose. It was expressly held that the property passed to him.[59] The money was traceably money from the account. But tracing does not in itself confer proprietary rights. Tracing identifies substitutes. The proprietary right in the substitute depends on there being a proprietary right in the first asset received. The *Lipkin Gorman* judgments do not say that the gambler's title to the money first received was voidable, so as to give the firm at least a power *in rem* in it.

If I give you £100 for your birthday and then trace the £100 to a watercolour on your wall, I will not give myself any right in the watercolour. Nor will I obtain any such right by pointing to the fact that, a moment before I

[58] Above, text to n 40. [59] [1991] 2 AC 548 (HL), 578 (Lord Goff).

handed it over, the money was mine. There is a certain danger that, in starting the tracing chain from the bank account, which certainly belonged to the firm even if the money withdrawn did not, the case may have fallen into the error of finding the proprietary base too early in the story. If that is what happened, the outcome needs a new explanation.

A reinterpretation of one major case would not suffice if the causal argument were not rooted in other decisions. There is a group of cases, lucidly explained by Mitchell,[60] in which mistaken payments have been recovered from remote recipients on proof that the enrichment did come through to them. In *Bannatyne v D&C MacIver* the London agents of the defendant firm borrowed money for them without authority. The claimant lenders mistakenly believed that they did have authority. The Court of Appeal upheld the claim against the firm to the extent that the money had been turned to their advantage. Romer LJ said:

> Where money is borrowed on behalf of a principal by an agent, the lender believing that the agent has authority, though it turns out that his act has not been authorised, or ratified, or adopted by the principal, then, although the principal, cannot be sued at law, yet in equity, to the extent to which the money borrowed has in fact been applied in paying legal debts and obligations of the principal, the lender is entitled to stand in the same position as if the money had originally been borrowed by the principal.[61]

This is the same doctrine as underlies *B Liggett (Liverpool) Ltd v Barclays Bank Ltd*,[62] a decision of Wright J which was reinterpreted by the Court of Appeal in *Re Cleadon Trust Ltd*.[63] In the *Liggett* case a bank had paid out money believing that it had the authority of a company which was its customer, when in fact it had only the insufficient authority of one director of the company. It was allowed to debit the company's account.

The explanation of the *Liggett* case which was advanced by the majority of the Court of Appeal in *Re Cleadon Trust Ltd* was that the money must be regarded as a mistaken payment to that one director but that the company nevertheless had to make restitution because he had discharged the company's debts. In short it was enriched and it would not have been enriched but for his enrichment. He had no authority to borrow, but he

[60] C Mitchell, *The Law of Subrogation* (OUP Oxford 1994) chapter 9, especially 124–9, 133–5.

[61] [1906] 1 KB 103 (CA) 109. In *Reid v Rigby & Co* [1894] 2 QB 40 recovery was allowed at law, the facts being materially identical.

[62] [1928] 1 KB 48.

[63] [1939] Ch 286 (CA), discussed by Mitchell (n 60 above) 127–8, 162–5.

did have authority to discharge debts.[64] The emphasis on discharge may be misplaced. Imperfect discharge should not have been fatal, since the bank could still have been subrogated to the creditors' imperfectly extinguished rights against the company. That is what subrogation proper is for.[65]

Butler v Rice,[66] though in some respects confusing, is factually more straightforward. Butler, who had been misled by Mr Rice, mistakenly thought that Mr Rice owned a house subject to a charge. He made a payment to him thinking he was lending to discharge that particular charge. Mr Rice had no such interest and in fact used the money to discharge a mortgage on property belonging to his wife. Mrs Rice, who had not known of her husband's doings, regarded herself as entitled to a windfall, leaving Butler to his remedy against her husband. But Warrington J held that Butler was entitled to be subrogated to the claim and security which had been paid off. In other words Mrs Rice, as second recipient, had to surrender the enrichment which she would not have received but for the unjust enrichment of the first recipient. Butler was not leapfrogging out of a valid contract.

Mr Rice had misrepresented the facts. The contract with him was therefore voidable. The voidability not only shows that there was no leapfrogging out of a valid contract but also allows the case to be explained on the basis of a proprietary connection between claimant and defendant. However, before adopting that explanation it is necessary to ask whether there is any reason at all why the causal connection should not suffice. When one bargains one does not take the risk of mistakes induced by misrepresentation. It seems to follow that one does not take the risk of the insolvency of the misrepresentor. One cannot leapfrog out of a valid contract because one has taken the risk of one's counter-party's insolvency. Where the law relieves you of that risk, there is no convincing objection to leapfrogging.

Although the principle of these cases is found chiefly in relation of mistakes in the context of agency, it is both attractive and deeply rooted in the western legal tradition.[67] It cannot reasonably be confined to one particular context. It would not be rational to admire the clarity and good sense of Romer LJ's statement of principle while at the same time adhering

[64] [1939] Ch 286 (CA) 318 (Scott LJ), 326 (Clauson LJ).

[65] Below, 296–9.

[66] [1910] 2 Ch 277.

[67] It comes from the *actio de in rem verso* (the action for things applied to the defendant's use): R Zimmermann, *The Law of Obligations Roman Foundations of the Civilian Tradition* (OUP Oxford 1996) 878–87.

to the stern opinion that a donee should be immune from suit even though he would have received no gift but for the unjust enrichment of his donor at the mistaken claimant's expense.

E. CONCLUSION

This chapter has considered questions of great importance to the scope of the English law of unjust enrichment. When offered choices the cases have inclined to the broader options. They do not seem to insist that the claimants must have suffered loss. They do not exclude claimants who found their claim on interception. In consequence they enlarge the number of situations in which a claimant seeking restitution can claim in the alternative, in the law of wrongs and in the law of unjust enrichment. Since there is no question of cumulating both claims, there is no obviously pressing reason for imposing restrictive requirements. A pressure may, however, build up in relation to the defence of change of position. There is such a thing as an innocent wrong. Defendants in conversion are often innocent wrongdoers. The defence of change of position does not apply to wrongs. It may be difficult to hold that line, but it will also be difficult to know how to cross it.[68]

When it comes to suing remote enrichees, the choice again goes in favour of allowing such claims, so long as the claimant is not trying to escape the insolvency of a contractual counter-party. To allow leapfrogging out of an initially valid contract would make a mockery of the insolvency regime.

A considerable degree of uncertainty persists. For one thing the questions have so far been answered without being explicitly asked. For another, until there is a secure and stable answer to the fourth of the five questions, which determines the incidence of the proprietary response to unjust enrichment, we will not be able to see clearly when causation-based leapfrogging is rendered superfluous by a sufficient proprietary connection between the claimant and the enrichment. In the meantime, it is best to assume that such leapfrogging is permissible. Remote recipients, like other defendants, are nowadays sufficiently protected, where they need to be, by vigorous defences.

[68] Below, 213.

Part III

Unjust

5

Changing Direction

Part I introduced a core case. If you receive a mistaken payment of a non-existent debt you are unjustly enriched at the expense of the payer. In Part II, Chapter 3 addressed the first of the five questions, Was the defendant enriched? It explored the proposition that what is true of money received must be true of all enrichments received. That truth is narrowed in application but not contradicted by the need to reconcile the measurement of the enrichment in money with the law's respect for the subjectivity of value. Chapter 4 then turned to the second question, Was the enrichment at the expense of the claimant? It had to examine the necessary connection between a would-be claimant and the enrichment which he wants to claim. The enrichment must have been obtained at his expense in the sense of having come from him, but it is a sophisticated 'from', not a simple one. There need be no corresponding loss, and interception suffices. Immediate enrichees have to be distinguished from remote enrichees. Against a remote enrichee the claimant encounters obstacles. In some situations he is not permitted to leapfrog the immediate enrichee.

The first two questions of the five-question analysis having been discussed, the business of the two chapters of Part III is to address the third, Is the enrichment at the expense of the claimant unjust? The answer must not wander from the logic of the core case, the most important feature of which is the negative proposition that the liability does not arise from contract or wrong. The positive is more elusive. There are competing ways of stating the reason why payment by mistake of a non-existent debt gives the payer a right to restitution. A stream of litigation about the consequences of void contracts has, to borrow Dr Krebs's image, brought English law to a crossroads.[1] Compelled to rethink, it has chosen a new direction. This chapter gives an account of this change of

[1] T Krebs, *Restitution at the Crossroads: A Comparative Study* (Cavendish London 2001) in which Krebs presents the choice which, on reflection, the swaps cases have already made.

approach to 'unjust', of its vocabulary, and of its principal implications. The next chapter examines its operation.

A. TWO METHODS

It will be recalled that in *Kelly v Solari* an insurer paid a death benefit having forgotten that the policy had lapsed. Parke B observed:

> [If the money] is paid under the impression of the truth of a fact which is untrue, it may, generally speaking, be recovered back, however careless the party paying may have been, in omitting to use due diligence to inquire into the fact. In such a case the receiver was not entitled to it, nor intended to have it.[2]

The last sentence conveys Parke B's understanding of the reason why the enrichment is unjust: 'In such a case the receiver was not entitled to it, nor intended to have it'. The ambiguity slips by almost unnoticed. Does the claimant recover because he did not intend to enrich the recipient or because on the true facts the recipient was not entitled to the enrichment? One easily assumes that these are two sides of one penny, but in the marginal case it matters where the emphasis is put. The common law has, until recently, looked chiefly for incomplete intent. Civilian systems emphasize disentitlement.

1. THE CIVILIAN APPROACH: NO EXPLANATORY BASIS

It is not right to think of civilian jurisdictions as homogeneous. They share their root in the Roman law library, but national codifications broke up the unity of the *ius commune*. Even in the field of unjust enrichment there are marked differences, especially between the German model and the earlier French model. It is no less an error to think of any one civilian system as having reduced its law of unjust enrichment to orderly stasis. Their books are still replete with argument and debate. It is nevertheless true that all civilian jurisdictions share a particular angle of approach to 'unjust' which is ultimately derived from the Roman action of debt.

They begin from the proposition that every enrichment at another's expense either has an explanation known to the law or has not. Enrichments are received with the purpose of discharging an obligation or, if without obligation, to achieve some other objective as for instance the making of a gift, the satisfaction of a condition, or the coming into being of a new contract. These outcomes succeeding, the enrichment is

[2] (1841) 9 M & W 54, 59, 152 ER 24, 27.

sufficiently explained. An enrichment which turns out to have no such explanation is inexplicable and cannot be retained. The recipient is not entitled to it. The shorthand for this, in Latin, is '*sine causa*'. The inexplicable enrichment lacks a *causa*. In English that reduces to 'no basis'. Enrichment *sine causa* is enrichment with no explanatory basis. The English rendering has a subsection to itself below.

(a) 'No Basis' in *Kelly v Solari*

English law had settled to understanding *Kelly v Solari* as turning on impaired intent. The insurer made the decision to pay on incorrect data. The mistake caused the payment. A decision impaired by a mistake which causes a payment gives rise to a right to restitution.[3] Subject to a complication which will be addressed immediately below, the civilian approach, by contrast, sees *Kelly v Solari* as a case in which the putative explanation of Mrs Solari's enrichment was that it was received in discharge of an obligation arising from a contract of insurance. The truth was that there was no such obligation. The putative basis therefore failed, and there was no other. The money was received *sine causa*. She was not entitled to it. This inquiry makes nothing of the mistake as impairing the intent to pay. The absence of basis is established by applying the law to the true facts. The basis was a debt to be discharged and there was no debt.

There was a complication. It is easy to overlook the fact that the actual judgment in *Kelly v Solari* was for a new trial. Against the balance of probabilities the widow might yet have proved facts upon which a jury should find for her. It might have been that the insurer was never mistaken or, though mistaken, was actually indifferent to the truth or falsity of what seemed to be the crucial belief. It is after all not unknown for insurance companies to make payments ex gratia, whether from compassion or from anxiety not to be depicted in conflict with widows.

We have been assuming that the basis of the payment must unequivocally have been discharge of the insurance obligation. But for the civilian observer the new trial would serve the purpose of checking whether it might after all have been gift. On the hypotheses to be tested at the new trial the insurer either positively intended a gift or was indifferent whether the outcome was gift or discharge. In such a situation one who is not mistaken at all knows that he is not liable to pay. He intends a gift.

[3] *Barclays Bank Ltd v WJ Simms & Son Ltd* [1980] QB 677, where the judgment of Robert Goff J reviews all the mistake cases to produce this basic ground-rule.

One who could not care whether he is mistaken or not also, but less graciously, intends a gift. In the end, therefore, the causative mistake is not irrelevant. It negatives gift.

(b) Submerged Relevance of Intent

Although in general pushed out of sight, in the civilian *sine causa* inquiry the claimant's intent is nevertheless not irrelevant. If the claimant had no intent at all to make the transfer, as where the defendant was a pick-pocket, there could generally be no basis for the defendant's enrichment. If he did consciously make the transfer, he will have intended some particular basis for it. The crucial question is whether that intended basis held good. On the *Kelly v Solari* facts it was necessary to find out whether the insurer intended discharge or gift. If it was discharge, the basis failed. The policy had lapsed for non-payment of the premium. There was no obligation to be discharged. Again, in some cases, although not in this one, the very reason why the intended basis fails will be that the intent to make the transfer was defective or otherwise incomplete.

Viewed in this way, 'no basis' is a method of finding out whether the claimant intended the enrichment by treating every transfer which is consciously made as made with qualified intent, conditional on the achievement of one of the explanatory outcomes. If I intend to pay a debt to you, and there is no debt, the condition for my intending you to have the money fails. On the true facts, I did not mean you to have the money. This ultimate dependence on qualified or, synonymously, conditional intent is generally submerged. So, in *Kelly v Solari*, the right to restitution follows from there being no obligation to discharge and no gift, no other possible basis being in sight. It is not necessary to make the connection with qualified intent and in practice the fact that it can be made remains a silent truth.

(c) Two Elementary Propositions

The previous paragraph partly explains why the civilian approach, so different on its surface, nearly always comes to the same conclusions as the common law reaches through its list of unjust factors. It is a different method of showing that the claimant did not intend the defendant to be enriched at his expense. The English unjust factors for the most part address intent directly. This identity of goal in turn invites two elementary and related propositions which have to be defied by anyone minded to deny the change of course which the English law of unjust enrichment has made in the last ten years.

One is that 'no basis' cannot be simply absorbed into the English approach through intent-based unjust factors. An alternative method of reaching a conclusion is an alternative method. The other is that an alternative method is not an alternative cause of action. The fact that the two methods can be applied to one set of facts, as for instance to the facts of *Kelly v Solari*, cannot mean that these are facts in which, as sometimes happens, there are two alternative causes of action. The same pudding is cooked in some houses on gas, in others by electricity.

2. THE COMMON LAW APPROACH: UNJUST FACTORS

Before its position was properly tested in the recent litigation on void contracts, it was possible to say with tolerable confidence that the common law had come down overtly on the side of 'was not intended to have it'. As we noticed immediately above, it viewed mistake as in itself a sufficient reason for restitution, and it saw the mistake as having that effect because it impaired the decision to make the transfer. Over time the notion of a sufficiently impairing mistake was enlarged. Restrictive requirements which were satisfied in *Kelly v Solari* were relaxed. It ceased to be necessary to show that the mistake gave the payer the impression of being bound to pay and that the mistake was as to fact, not law.

The upshot was that in order to operate as an unjust factor the mistake had to be as to the present or past, not the future, must have caused the enrichment, and must not be such that restitution would disturb risks distributed by a bargain. In the modern English view the facts which Mrs Solari was to be allowed to test at a new trial would have shown that there was no impairment of the insurer's decision to pay. On the one hypothesis there was no mistake at all, and on the other there was a mistake but it had not caused the payment.

(a) Two Groups of Unjust Factors

This understanding of the nature and role of mistake made it possible to compile a list of other factors which could be seen to operate in a similar way. A reasonably coherent law of unjust enrichment thus began to appear under the proposition that, in the absence of contract or wrong, an enrichment at the claimant's expense was unjust when the claimant had not intended the recipient to have it. It might be that he had given no consent at all, as where his pocket had been picked, or that his consent had been impaired, or that his consent had been qualified and the qualification had not been purged.

Amongst the impairments there were, alongside mistake, illegitimate pressure, undue influence, personal handicaps such as minority, dementia, and illiteracy; also transactional inequality, where the nature of the transaction in itself cripples autonomy. Examples of unpurged qualified intent are pre-payment for a counter-performance which fails to materialize and an uncle's gift to his niece for her forthcoming marriage, the marriage then being called off.

Since the cases showed that these three categories of incomplete intent—no intent at all, impaired intent, and qualified intent—did not cover every case in which in the absence of contract or wrong a claimant could recover an enrichment received at his expense, it proved necessary to admit a secondary or supplementary proposition to the effect that a claimant might also recover by showing that, whether the enrichment had been perfectly intended or not, there was a specific reason why the enrichment should be given up, as for instance to reinforce governmental respect for the rule of law or to encourage withdrawal from illegal transactions. Critics pounced on this supplementation as destroying the unity of the category.[4] There is no doubt that it weakened it.

Taken together, these two groups of unjust factors meant that in broad terms an unjust enrichment at the expense of the claimant was one to which the claimant had not fully consented or one in respect of which some policy militated in favour of restitution. Under the first limb the list of unjust factors had to identify all the situations in which the claimant's intent was sufficiently defective or qualified, while under the second it had to enumerate all the policies regarded as demanding restitution.[5]

(b) Development over a Quarter of a Century

In 1978, 12 years after the publication of the first edition of *Goff and Jones*, Lord Diplock said:

> My Lords, there is no general doctrine of unjust enrichment recognised in English law. What it does is to provide specific remedies in particular cases of what might be classified as unjust enrichment in a legal system that is based on the civil law.[6]

[4] I Jackman, *The Varieties of Restitution* (Federation Press Sydney 1998), in which the first chapter sets out the theme already captured in the title. For him the multi-causality of restitution penetrated even the category of unjust enrichment.

[5] Above, 41–3.

[6] *Orakpo v Manson Investments Ltd* [1978] AC 95 (HL) 104.

The second sentence of this difficult dictum should be understood as observing that the work of the law of unjust enrichment was still being done under a variety of different heads, which were not co-ordinated under that or any other common name. Lacking such a bond, the fragments did not admit to shared principles and tended to go each its own way.

Slightly more than a decade later the House of Lords unanimously affirmed that English law did recognize a law of restitution of unjust enrichment.[7] The wandering sheep thus became a single flock. However, while the dominant name remained that of the response-based category of restitution, they still found themselves mixed with disruptive goats. Despite that, they began to behave better.

The first sentence of Lord Diplock's dictum—'My Lords, there is no general doctrine of unjust enrichment recognised in English law'—can be understood as condemning the law of unjust enrichment to the condition of the law of tort. There the generic description of the causative event, tort or, slightly larger, civil wrongs, brings together particular figures such as defamation, negligence, nuisance, conversion, abuse of confidence, breach of fiduciary duty, and so on. But the outcome is still no more than a list of particular wrongs which history has thrown up and which obstinately resist stronger unification.

In the same way, so long as the list of unjust factors persisted, the law of unjust enrichment seemed destined to be no more than a collection of particular unjust enrichments. Beyond the three categories of non-voluntary transfer—no intent, impaired intent, and qualified intent—the list degenerated into miscellaneous other reasons for restitution not amounting to a wrong or contract. The single term 'policy-motivations' did no more than confess the miscellany. It left an unbridged gap between 'miscellaneous other reasons' and non-voluntary transfer.

Although the example is not edifying, the law of tort proves that a legal category can subsist in that condition. Had unjust enrichment clung to its list of unjust factors, it would have been an untidy heap, like tort, but its one compensating merit would have been that, in any one case, it was accessible to ordinary intelligence. The layman who wants restitution says 'It was a mistake', 'I was forced to hand it over', 'I was under his thumb', 'It was for a purpose which never came off', and so on. In 1990

[7] *Lipkin Gorman v Karpnale Ltd* [1991] 2 AC 548 (HL) 558 (Lord Bridge), 559 (Lord Templeman), 568 (Lord Ackner), 578 (Lord Goff). Lord Griffiths concurred with the Lord Templeman and Lord Goff; endorsed in *Banque Financière de la Cité v Parc (Battersea) Ltd* [1999] 1 AC 221 (HL).

the common law still spoke much the same language as the Clapham omnibus.

The past tenses accept that there has been a change of course. Heavyweight cases have adopted the 'no basis' approach. That approach achieves the tighter unification which Lord Diplock said we did not have. The 'general doctrine' is that enrichment at another's expense has to be given up if it lacks an explanatory basis. And, as we have seen, that approach works on a single if often unacknowledged foundation, namely that in the events which have happened the claimant did not intend the recipient to be enriched.

That makes the law of unjust enrichment look less like the law of tort and more like the law of contract. The law of contract is a much tighter unity than the law of civil wrongs. The particular contracts, such as sale, partnership, agency, and carriage of goods, are not islands in a non-contractual sea but distinct features in one contractual landscape.

This metamorphosis has been brought about in the wake of a cataclysm unleashed in 1992. *Hazell v Hammersmith & Fulham BC*[8] was nothing less. The decision of the House of Lords in that case let it be known that billions of pounds had changed hands under void contracts. It did not say what consequences followed. The resolution of that question fell to the wave of swaps cases which followed. These are the subject of the next section.

B. THE SWAPS CASES

> The cases where contracts are void, but not attended with any circumstances which are illegal or immoral, are involved in some confusion, and will hardly admit of any settled principle being confidently ascribed to them in respect to the obligation of returning money actually paid.[9]

At the very beginning of the 19th century when Sir William Evans wrote these words, his chief anxiety was to resist the notion that the nullity of a completely executed void contract might automatically require mutual restitution. The civilian approach leads to that conclusion, save so far as it can be cut off under the fifth question, which asks after defences. In the pages which followed Evans sought to prevent English law from going

[8] [1992] 2 AC 1 (HL).

[9] Sir William Evans, *Essays on the Action for Money Had and Received, on the Law of Insurances, and on the Law of Bills of Exchange and Promissory Notes* (Liverpool 1802) 48–9, repr [1998] Restitution L Rev 1, 15. I have cut out a comma after 'principle'.

down that path. That which he resisted has now come to pass, and in the most unequivocal manner.

1. SWAPS AND VOID SWAPS

In an interest swap, one party promises to pay the other a fixed rate of interest on a notional sum for a fixed period, say 5 per cent on £5 million for five years with quarterly settlement dates, and, on otherwise identical terms, the counter-party promises to pay a floating rate determined by a formula. If interest rates fall the floating payer will pay less and will thus win; vice versa if they rise. There is a vast market in swaps worldwide.

Up and down the United Kingdom hundreds of local authorities were players on that field. Their counter-parties were usually banks. Huge sums of money were involved. Many swaps were of the 'deeply discounted' kind, under which the bank paid a large sum of cash up front, in anticipation of its later obligations under the swap contract. At a time when their taxing powers were being capped, it was attractive to the authorities to be able to improve their liquidity by such devices. Present liquidity was bought at the risk of running up big bills for a later generation of local voters. In the public sphere swaps were not without a political dimension.

In *Hazell v Hammersmith & Fulham BC*[10] the axe fell. The House of Lords decided that contracts for interest swaps made by local authorities were not within the authorities' money management powers and were consequently void. The revelation of nullity brought swaps which were still in progress to an immediate halt. Performance ceased at once. Others had already been fully performed, the parties had played out the game and had received exactly what they thought they had contracted for.

2. CLOSED SWAPS AND INTERRUPTED SWAPS

A series of test cases was brought to the courts to determine the consequences. The contracts all conformed to the same basic pattern, but different parties found themselves in slightly different situations. One case could not decide all. The most important of these shades of difference was that between the closed swaps and the interrupted swaps. It seemed possible that the closed swaps could be left quietly in their graves. That hope was dashed. Without exception, *Hazell v Hammersmith & Fulham BC* was held to require mutual restitution, with the effect that the

[10] *Hazell* (n 8 above).

winner, the party who had received the greater sum, has had to repay the winning difference.

(a) One Ground for All

In the first major decision, Hobhouse J had before him two cases. One was an interrupted swap, *Westdeutsche Landesbank Girozentrale v Islington LBC*, and one was a closed swap, *Kleinwort Benson Ltd v Sandwell BC*.[11] He took the view that there was no relevant difference between the two. The ground for restitution was the nullity of the contract under which the payments had been made, which he called 'absence of consideration'. He expressly said that it was not possible to hold, in relation to the interrupted swap, that the ground was failure of consideration (in the sense of failure of contractual reciprocation).[12]

There was no appeal in *Kleinwort Benson Ltd v Sandwell BC*, Hobhouse J's closed swap, but later when another closed swap finally reached the Court of Appeal his decision was affirmed. In *Guinness Mahon & Co Ltd v Kensington & Chelsea Royal London BC*[13] it was decided that the invalidity of the contracts was in itself decisive. From their nullity it followed that the basis of the payments failed *ab initio*. That absence of basis entitled the loser to recover the difference, notwithstanding full performance by both sides.

The invalidity of the contracts gave rise to what is variously described in the judgments as 'absence of consideration' or 'failure of consideration'. In accordance with the resolution, explained more fully later in this chapter, once and for all to renounce the ambiguities of 'consideration', that has to be rendered as 'absence of basis' or 'failure of basis'. The important point lies below the terminology. The appearance of the word 'consideration' in the name of the reason for restitution had nothing to do with performance or non-performance of the contract. In a closed swap both parties had by definition fully performed. 'Absence of consideration' was an immediate inference from the invalidity of the contract under which the parties supposed themselves to be operating. Restitution in these cases followed directly from the invalidity of the supposed basis of the payments.

[11] Both reported together [1994] 4 All ER 890.

[12] The principal meanings of 'failure of consideration' are considered later in this chapter, 117–19.

[13] [1999] QB 215 (CA). This was in effect the long-delayed appeal from Hobhouse J's decision in the *Sandwell* case (n 11 above).

(b) A Second Ground in Interrupted Swaps

Interrupted swaps and the closed swaps differ in that, despite the opinion of Hobhouse J, the former seem to admit of a different explanation of the ground for restitution, possibly alternative, possibly exclusive. As Sir William Evans himself had observed, in void contracts incompletely performed the right to restitution could be understood to arise, not from the initial nullity, but from the subsequent failure of contractual reciprocation.[14] In *Westdeutsche Landesbank Girozentrale v Islington BC*, which was an interrupted swap, this different analysis, denied by Hobhouse J at first instance, was accepted by the Court of Appeal.[15] It was accepted as an alternative. No doubt was thrown on the applicability to interrupted swaps of Hobhouse J's other ground, namely absence of consideration deriving immediately from the invalidity of the contract.

In the House of Lords there were dicta which, on their face, prefer the explanation in terms of failure of contractual reciprocation.[16] Moreover, the preference appears to be for an exclusive rather than an alternative application of that ground. This, being inapplicable to closed swaps in which by definition there can have been no failure of performance, raised questions whether automatic restitution would indeed be required other than in interrupted swaps. It will be recalled that there had been no appeal on Hobhouse J's closed swap. As we have seen, however, that doubt was later blown away.

Even when these *Westdeutsche* dicta in the House of Lords were uttered, they were fragile, for two reasons. One was the inveterate ambiguity of 'failure of consideration', to which we will return. The other was that by the time that *Westdeutsche* reached the House of Lords the nature of the reason for restitution was, as was then thought, no longer an issue in that case itself. The appeal was limited to the rate of interest which was payable. As we shall see in Chapter 7, the assumption that that restriction made it unnecessary to examine and identify the reason for restitution was in fact a serious error.

[14] Evans (n 9 above) 54–5 (Restitution L Rev reprint 16).

[15] [1994] 4 All ER 890, 924 (Hobhouse J), 960–1 (Dillon LJ, with whom Kennedy LJ agreed).

[16] Especially Lord Goff [1996] AC 669 (HL) 683. Compare E McKendrick, 'The Reason for Restitution' in P Birks and F Rose (eds), *Lessons of the Swaps Litigation* (LLP Mansfield London 2000) 84, 108.

(c) A Third Ground

Later, in *Kleinwort Benson Ltd v Lincoln CC*,[17] the only closed swap to reach the House of Lords, their Lordships decided that the automatic restitution which was the invariable outcome of the swap cases could also be attributed to mistake of law. That was important to parties whose swaps were long dead, since it had the effect of stopping the limitation clock until the mistake was discovered through the judgment in *Hazell v Hammersmith & Fulham BC*.[18] Here there is no doubt that their Lordships were thinking of an alternative ground. They had no intention of saying that the explanation must be mistake of law rather than absence of consideration.

Whatever additional strains it would have placed on their Lordships' already overstretched notion of mistake, to have said that the explanation must be mistake of law would have vindicated the common law's list of unjust factors. It would have eliminated the incompatible competitor 'absence of basis'. The case cannot be understood to have done that. It merely said, mixing two incompatible methods, that the outcome could be understood as turning on mistake.

3. NO GOING BACK

Once *Kleinwort Benson Ltd v Lincoln CC* had upheld the dual analysis for closed swaps, it followed that perhaps all three analyses were possible in the interrupted swaps, absence of basis, failure of contractual reciprocation, and mistake. With hindsight, these multiple analyses can be seen to be unsound. From the premiss that animals can be hairy, carnivorous, and black, one cannot infer that in a census of the local canine population the labrador next door should count as three. The next section seeks to prove the categorical incompatibility between absence of basis and the list of unjust factors.

The *Lincoln* case was the last chance for the common law's list of unjust factors. It perfectly exemplifies the dilemma of those whose initial instinct, even after the swaps litigation, was to continue to defend that approach. It showed, at the very least, that the House of Lords thought that the outcome of every swaps case could be fitted into the list under mistake. Hence it was possible to argue that their Lordships should have insisted on sticking with the English approach.

[17] [1999] 2 AC 349 (HL), applied in *Nurdin & Peacock plc v DB Ramsden & Co Ltd* [1999] 1 WLR 1249 (Ch D).

[18] [1992] 2 AC 1 (HL). The limitation point is further discussed in below, 239–40.

But comparatists instantly pointed out that any such insistence would make the outcomes of the swaps cases turn on the uncertain metaphysics of mistake. In the light of the acceptance of 'absence of basis' in the swaps cases themselves, any such exercise would be senseless because the latter approach yielded a clean and indisputable answer as plain as *Kelly v Solari* itself:[19] the swaps money had been paid to discharge a contractual obligation and that obligation did not exist.[20]

There is no answer to that. To force the swaps cases back into the list of unjust factors requires their acceptance of the 'no basis' approach to be rejected and replaced with other grounds from the list of unjust factors. But those other grounds would have to be constantly massaged to ensure that they dictated an answer as stable as is reached by the shorter 'no basis' route.[21] It would also have to be done against the authority of Professor Sir Guenter Treitel, who endorses the use of that shorter route.[22] For him it is a starting point, meaning that any overkill can still be prevented in other ways. As we shall see in Chapter 10, the vigour of modern defences to actions in unjust enrichment ensures that that is correct. It would therefore be perverse to insist on going back to the list of unjust factors. And it is not possible to mix the two methods. The next section underlines the fact that that is not an option.

C. NO POSSIBILITY OF INTEGRATION

The swaps cases show that the invalidity of a contract is in itself the reason why there has to be restitution of enrichments transferred under it. The invalidity means that those enrichments have no explanatory basis. They are transferred *sine causa*. After the swaps cases English law is bound to use this civilian method of answering the third question. In a system which was getting used to consent-based and policy-based unjust

[19] For 'no basis' as applied to that case, see below, 114, 132.

[20] S Meier and R Zimmermann, 'Judicial Development of the Law, *Error Iuris* and the Law of Unjustified Enrichment' (1999) 115 LQR 556, esp 560–5.

[21] This is the core of Dr Meier's criticism of unjust factors, that they constantly impose a superfluous task, evading restitution where *sine causa* would not permit it and ensuring restitution where it would. We have in effect been covertly resting 'unjust' directly on the absence of legal ground: Meier, 'Restitution after Executed Void Contracts' in Birks and Rose (eds) (n 16 above) 168 esp 206–13; cf Meier, 'Unjust Factors and Legal Grounds' in D Johnston and R Zimmermann (eds), *Unjustified Enrichment: Key Issues in Comparative Perspective* (CUP Cambridge 2002) 37, 67–75.

[22] Sir Guenter Treitel, *The Law of Contract* (11th edn Sweet & Maxwell London 2003) 1058–60.

factors it has been tempting to absorb this conclusion by adding absence of basis to the list. That cannot be done.

1. ABSENCE OF BASIS IS NOT ANOTHER UNJUST FACTOR

The list of unjust factors was already miscellaneous. In principle it could admit another reason for restitution, just as tort can admit new wrongs. But absence of basis is not a deficiency of consent; nor is it a policy dictating that the enrichment should be reversed; it is also not a reason for restitution independent of the other members of the list. This means that it cannot join either of the two groups of unjust factors, and it cannot make a third group of its own. One could not smuggle 'vertebrates' into a list of mammals. In the same way absence of basis cuts across the list of unjust factors.

The first group comprises all the intent-based unjust factors. Absence of basis cannot go in that group. We have already seen that the mistake in *Kelly v Solari* can be used as an impairment of intent or as the reflection of a non-existent basis for the enrichment. It would be absurd to suggest, as would be suggested by including absence of basis in the list of unjust factors, that by demonstrating two approaches applicable to that case that we have revealed the presence of two different causes of action. Then, when we look down the list of the unjust factors in this group, one after another they all invalidate the contract or gift which would otherwise provide the explanatory basis of the recipient's enrichment—no consent, spontaneous mistake, mistake induced by misrepresentation, pressure, undue influence, and so on. These cannot stand beside absence of basis, only under it.[23]

The other group of unjust factors comprises policies which call for restitution. Policies behind invalidity can fit in the list of reasons why an enrichment should be given up. The effect of treating the policy behind the invalidity as the reason for restitution is to select certain invalidities as meriting that response and thus to prevent all invalidities from automatically presenting themselves in that character. Invalidity is then not a reason for restitution unless the policy behind it is one which is reinforced by and not undermined by restitution. There are hints in *Guinness Mahon v Kensington & Chelsea Royal London BC* that the courts could have made restitution under void interest swaps turn on such a

[23] '[I]t is remarkable that these unjust factors do nothing else than mirror the reasons why the contract is invalid': S Meier in P Birks and F Rose (eds), *Lessons of the Swaps Litigation* (LLP Mansfield London 2000) 168, 211.

policy. They could have said that it was essential in the longer-term interests of the community to compel respect for the limits put upon the authorities' powers by ordering restitution of money obtained beyond those powers: public authorities had to learn that they must not play ducks and drakes with the limits on their powers.[24]

However, that is not how the case was decided. Except perhaps in the judgment of Waller LJ, the outcome is squarely rested on the invalidity of the swaps contract and the attendant absence of basis for the payments made under it. Absence of basis tells us that invalidity is a reason for restitution in itself. In that state of affairs the group of policy-motivated unjust factors becomes redundant. Invalidity in itself destroys the basis of the enrichment. It is obvious therefore that absence of basis cannot be integrated into this group.

If absence of basis cannot be assigned to either of the two groups of unjust factors, the list could only admit it as constituting a third group of its own. That possibility is shut out by the fact that it is also not independent of the two groups but, on the contrary, is instantiated in every member of the intent-based group, and it overwhelms and enlarges the policy-based group. In the end, therefore, there is no question of integrating absence of basis anywhere in the list of unjust factors. Its recognition and application in the swaps cases is a rejection of the approach through unjust factors. They are incompatibly alternative methods of deciding which enrichments are unjust.

Absence of basis is now the only unjust factor in English law. This makes for lawyer's law. No passenger on the Clapham omnibus ever demanded restitution for want of legally sufficient basis. But the change of course is not a disaster. Nor is it to be regarded as dictated only by the doctrine of precedent. The civilian method at which our courts have arrived, although it too leaves room for many arguments in difficult cases, is efficient, tried, and tested. We borrowed some of it in the 18th century, only to be diverted into the heresy of implied contract.

Emerging from that nonsense, we attempted a more homely development of what we then borrowed. It served us well enough but occasionally led us into severe difficulties, even into downright error. The dangers which Evans foresaw in the civilian method will one way or another be overcome under the fifth question. Defences are infinitely more vigorous than they were even 20 years ago. The best course will be to welcome the change. Surgeons now operate on babies *en ventre*. In effect the law of

[24] *Guinness* (n 13 above) 229 (Morritt LJ), 232–3 (Waller LJ).

unjust enrichment has been repaired even before finally escaping from the law of restitution.

2. THE PYRAMID: A LIMITED RECONCILIATION

The previous pages show that a limited reconciliation between the two approaches lies in making the intent-based unjust factors subservient to absence of basis, which itself then becomes an intermediate generalization between the unjust factors and unjust. A pyramid can be constructed in which, at the base, the particular unjust factors such as mistake, pressure, and undue influence become reasons why, higher up, there is no basis for the defendant's acquisition, which is then the master reason why, higher up still, the enrichment is unjust and must be surrendered. There is no room at the base of this pyramid for policies dictating restitution. The logic of the pyramid is that a policy which does not invalidate the basis of an enrichment has no relevance at all, and a policy which does destroy that basis is irrelevant, since the invalidity is sufficient in itself, without regard to the reason for it. Hence 'policies dictating restitution' becomes 'any other reason for invalidity', where 'other' means 'other than non-voluntariness'.

The base of the pyramid thus consists of all the categories of deficient intent (no intent, impaired intent, and qualified intent) together with all other causes of invalidity. All these work through 'absence of basis'. A single proposition covers every case: an enrichment at the expense of another is unjust when it is received without explanatory basis. Subject to some very rare exceptions,[25] it will be true of every case in which an enrichment is received without any explanatory basis that its claimant will not have intended it to accrue to the defendant, for in every case it will either have accrued absolutely without his consent or, if with his consent, on a particular basis which has failed.[26]

Policies underlying invalidities will in future have their say in relation to the fifth question. Selectivity under the third question, based on policies which favour restitution, will be replaced by selectivity under the fifth question, based on policies which would be damaged by the automatic restitution now in principle available in all cases of invalidity. For example, an adult who made a bad bargain with a minor should have no hope of recovering his money, because, if for no other reason, it would make nonsense of the minor's protection if the protective invalidity of the contract were turned against him. That now has to be expressed under

[25] Below, 158–60. [26] Above, 104.

the fifth question. In Chapter 10 we will see that a claim in unjust enrichment always encounters a defence if the effect of upholding it would be to stultify a considered position taken by the law. It is there that, when necessary, the *prima facie* automatic consequences of absence of basis will have to be restrained.

D. FOUNDATIONS OF ABSENCE OF BASIS

From this point on, this chapter has to do three things which together lay an essential foundation for the next one. It has to stabilize the language of absence of basis and, in particular, the relation between 'basis' and 'consideration'. It must then kill stone dead the ambiguities of 'total failure of consideration'. Finally, it must relate 'invalidity' and 'failure of basis'. The second and third of these two tasks grow out of the first, to which we now turn.

1. THE LANGUAGE OF ABSENCE OF BASIS

The English word 'consideration' is woven into the history of this subject and must be eliminated from it. Blameless in itself, it now plays havoc with our attempts to think clearly. It has to be replaced in this context by 'basis'. 'Absence of basis' appears in the cases as 'absence of consideration' and as 'failure of consideration', while 'failure of consideration' has also been appropriated to claims arising from failure of contractual reciprocation. The ambiguities have produced something close to intellectual breakdown. Again and again we slip from one meaning to another without noticing. Precautions have to be taken. It is impossible to exaggerate the potential for chaos of these ambiguities.

(a) Meanings of 'Consideration'

When a person considers something, he reflects upon it, he takes it into consideration. The noun 'consideration' denotes the process of reflection, as where we say that an appeal is currently under consideration. It can also denote a matter considered in coming to a decision, as where we say that there were two considerations which weighed with the court in allowing the appeal. In this sense a consideration is a reason, ground or basis for doing something. It serves and has long served as the English translation for the no less slippery Latin '*causa*'. In the 18th century Lord Mansfield used it for that purpose.[27]

[27] Evans (n 9 above) 8, 25 (Restitution L Rev repr 4, 9), cf below, 289–90.

(i) *Specialization as* quid pro quo

In the formation of contract it is elementary that a promise, if it is to be binding, must be supported by consideration. Deep down that means that it must be made for a legally sufficient reason, but ever since the early 19th century the law has taken the view that there is only one legally sufficient reason, namely some reciprocation from the promisee demanded as the price of the promise, some *quid pro quo*.

The law of contract has almost forgotten that a consideration is a reason. It has so specialized the meaning of the word that in or near that context it now denotes nothing but the reciprocation which is the price of the promise. This specialization has seeped into the lay world so that even there 'consideration' can mean *quid pro quo*. 'May I ask you a favour?' might meet the ungracious reply, 'What's the consideration?'

(ii) Reason, Ground, or Basis

There is no doubt whatever that, when that part of the law which is now becoming the law of unjust enrichment first began to use 'consideration', it did so in the sense of reason, ground or basis, not in the specialized sense of contractual reciprocation. In *Moses v Macferlan* when Lord Mansfield spoke of money received upon a consideration which happens to fail,[28] he was borrowing the Roman *condictio causa data causa non secuta* (debt for things given for a reason, that reason not following).[29] He was not speaking narrowly of failure of contractual reciprocation. There has been a constant danger that this broader sense would succumb to the specialized contractual meaning. Beneath the surface the proximity of the specialized meaning has exercised an inhibiting influence. At first instance in the *Westdeutsche* case the danger broke the surface. There Hobhouse J said: 'The phrase "failure of consideration" is one which in its terminology presupposes that there has been at some stage a valid contract which has been partially performed by one party.'[30]

It is important to notice that this quotation entails not one but two constrictions of the broad meaning of consideration as reason, ground or basis. The lesser of these two restrictions was almost certainly already present in the Roman category which Lord Mansfield was following, which appears to have concerned only subsequent failures of the reason

[28] (1760) 2 Burr 1005, 1012, 97 ER 676, 679.

[29] Sir William Evans, *Pothier on Obligations* vol 2 (Joseph Butterworth London 1806) 380; also his 'Essay on the Action for Money Had and Received' (1802 reprinted in [1998] Restitution L Rev 1) 25–34 (repr 9–11).

[30] *Westdeutsche Landesbank Girozentrale v Islington London BC* [1994] 4 All ER 890, 923.

for the payment which had been made. But Hobhouse J cuts much deeper. He excludes all subsequent failures which are not failures of reciprocation under an initially valid contract. The Court of Appeal thought that he had cut too hard. It was not true that the cause of action traditionally called 'failure of consideration' lay only for failure of contractual reciprocation under an initially valid contract. It could certainly reach the case of failure of reciprocation under a supposed contract which was in fact no contract at all.[31] As we shall see, it can reach cases in which there is no trace of non-reciprocation.

(b) Clearer Vocabulary

To prevent the persistence of confusion it is necessary to steer altogether clear of the word 'consideration'. This has its own risks, which are however minimized when the strategy is implemented with rigour. The first rule has to be that where failure of consideration in the cases signifies the claimant's failure to receive an expected *quid pro quo*, this must be spelled out as 'failure of reciprocation'. That formulation allows the expected reciprocation to be contractual or non-contractual.

The second rule must be that where, as in the swaps saga, the cases speak of absence, failure, or non-existence of consideration as the invalidity of the legal reason, ground or basis of the enrichment, we must stick to failure or absence of basis (choosing 'basis' as preferable to 'ground' and 'reason'). Absence of basis and failure of basis are synonyms. And both differ from failure of contractual reciprocation. Only stylistic reasons determine the choice. 'Failure' tends to be favoured when the absence of basis supervenes after the receipt.

In almost all cases, failure of contractual reciprocation is not in itself a failure of basis but precipitates that failure. If I pay you £10,000 in advance for the building of a garage, and you abscond, the failure of contractual reciprocation, namely the building of the garage, precipitates the failure of the contract, which itself was the basis of my payment. That is a case of subsequent failure of basis which might equally be called supervening absence of basis.

2. TOTAL FAILURE AND PARTIAL FAILURE

The commitment to vocabulary which distinguishes between the different applications of the word 'consideration', and the resolution to abjure the use of 'consideration' itself, makes it possible to deal immediately with

[31] Ibid 959–60 (Dillon LJ, with whom Kennedy LJ agreed).

two important propositions which, in the unregenerate language of consideration, appear to be flatly contradictory. The first is that English law no longer insists on total failure of consideration. The second is that there is no such thing as partial failure of consideration. When we renounce the use of 'consideration', the two propositions sit quite happily together. The first then says that, when an enrichment has no basis, the fact that the claimant has received some *quid pro quo* by way of reciprocation is no longer fatal to his claim to restitution. The second asserts that a claimant seeking to establish that an enrichment has no basis must establish a total failure of its basis. There is no such thing as a partial failure of basis.

(a) No Requirement of Total Failure of Reciprocation

In the *Fibrosa* case[32] a Polish company had paid in advance for textile machinery which it never got because the contract was frustrated by the Nazi invasion of Poland and the outbreak of the Second World War. The House of Lords decided that the company's remnant in London was entitled to restitution. One reason why the Law Reform (Frustrated Contracts) Act 1943 was nonetheless necessary was the assumption in *Fibrosa* that, even where a contract was brought to an end, a party would not be able to obtain restitution if he had received in exchange anything which could not be returned in kind exactly as it had been received. In the old ambiguous language this was expressed as a requirement that there must have been a total failure of consideration, meaning total failure of reciprocal *quid pro quo*.

Leaving on one side the habitual bias towards restrictive interpretation in the period before liability in unjust enrichment was rendered more fragile by the defence of change of position, the absoluteness of this bar chiefly appears to have been due to an extreme reluctance to value part-performances so as to allow counter-restitution in money by way of a substitute for the return of the very asset received.

For frustrated contracts the 1943 Act overrode that reluctance. Without the aid of further legislation, the common law has achieved the same development where the contract is not terminated for frustration but has become terminable for repudiatory breach. That is to say, it is no longer fatal for the claimant to have received some part of the contractual

[32] *Fibrosa Spolka Akcyjna v Fairbairn Lawson Combe Barbour* [1943] AC 32 (HL). On the need to reassess this great case in the light of the proposition that a failure of contractual reciprocation is not in itself a failure of basis, below, 140–2.

reciprocation so long as counter-restitution can be allowed for in money.[33] All the swaps cases, where there was never more than the illusion of a contract, show that the same applies in the case of non-contractual reciprocation.

In Australia, *Dillon v Baltic Shipping, 'The Mikhail Lermontov'*[34] appears at first sight to deny this. Owing to bad seamanship the Mikhail Lermontov sank in mid-cruise. At first instance the claimant passenger was allowed to recover her whole fare, the judge taking the view that the termination of the contract had nullified the benefit received in the days before the disaster. The High Court of Australia, however, insisted that she could not be said to have suffered a total failure of reciprocation. She had enjoyed one pleasant week. This now looks very old-fashioned, but only because it is easy to overlook one crucial fact. She had already received a pro rata refund. She wanted a full refund. It was only for that reason that she had to show that she had received nothing.

There are many cases in which the claimant in unjust enrichment has himself received some exchange benefit. They all now answer to a single principle, which is that he may not have restitution unless he makes counter-restitution. The discussion of that principle will be taken up again in the discussion of defences under the head of 'counter-restitution impossible'.[35] There is no requirement of total failure of consideration in the sense of total failure of the defendant's reciprocation.

(b) Total Failure of Basis

The basis of an enrichment either fails or it does not. There is no such thing as a partial failure of basis. This proposition can be examined in the light of the many cases in which the putative basis of the enrichment is a contract or, more precisely, the discharge of a contractual obligation. In the swaps cases, for instance, the parties thought, when they made their payments, that they were discharging contractual obligations.

(i) Obligation Non-Existent Despite Valid Contract

An insurance company which pays up believing the insured event has happened, when it has not happened, has a right to restitution.[36] An employer bound to pay an employee according to some formula can

[33] *D O Ferguson & Associates v Sohl* (1992) 62 Building LR 95 (CA); *Goss v Chilcott* [1996] AC 788 (PC).

[34] (1993) 176 CLR 344 (HCA).

[35] Revisited below, 225–9.

[36] *Norwich Union Fire Insurance Ltd v William Price Ltd* [1934] AC 455 (PC).

likewise recover the excess if he applies the formula incorrectly.[37] These are cases in which the mistake is as to the application of the contract to the facts. On the true facts there is a good contract but there is no contractual obligation to make the payment. There is then a total failure of the basis of the payment—the supposed but non-existent debt—even though the contract remains in being.

(ii) Obligation Valid Unless Contract Eliminated

The value of a performance which is required by a contract cannot be recovered unless the contract itself is eliminated. In *Bell v Lever Brothers*[38] Lever paid golden handshakes to executives at the time of a take-over. Later, after the takeover had been completed, Lever found out that the executives could all along have been dismissed out of hand for misconduct. Lever would never have paid handsomely for something which could have been had for nothing. But the causative mistake was not enough. Its claim for restitution was rejected. The contract and contractual obligation being valid, this was not a case in which the executives' enrichment had no basis.

(iii) Valid Contract Performed but One Obligation Unlawful

A claimant sometimes wants to say that some part of what he paid should never have been charged. In *Green v Portsmouth Stadium*[39] a bookie had long been made to pay more than the statutory maximum for entry to the defendant's racecourse. He failed to recover the difference. In *Orphanos v Queen Mary College*[40] a student's contract had incorrectly applied the much higher overseas tariff. He should have been charged home fees. He also failed to recover the difference. These cases seem to say that the validity of the contract is conclusive.

However, others have gone the other way. They appear to put the orthodox doctrine under pressure. In *Queen of the River Steamship Co v Conservators of the River Thames*[41] the claimant company was charged mooring fees higher than the statutory tariff and recovered the excess. In *Solle v Butcher*[42] the claimant tenant had been paying the agreed rent which was higher than the statutory regulated rent. At first instance he was allowed to recover the difference, but the lease was left standing. The

[37] *Larner v London CC* [1949] 2 KB 683; *Avon CC v Howlett* [1983] 1 WLR 605 (CA). *National Mutual Life Association v Walsh* [1987] 8 NSWLR 585, so far as it appears to deny this, is inconsistent with *Norwich Union Fire Insurance v William Price* (previous note). It was incorrectly decided.

[38] [1932] AC 161 (HL).

[39] [1953] 2 QB 190 (CA).

[40] [1985] AC 761 (HL).

[41] (1899) 15 TLR 474.

[42] [1950] 1 KB 671 (CA).

Court of Appeal, by treating the entire lease as voidable, brought the case within the orthodox doctrine and by imposing terms ensured that both sides gave up what they had obtained under the voidable contract. Now *Great Peace Shipping Ltd v Tsavliris Salvage (International) Ltd*[43] holds that that course was not open to the Court of Appeal but does not say that the decision at first instance was incorrect. In Australia, *David Securities Pty Ltd v Commonwealth Bank*[44] resembled *Solle v Butcher* at first instance. A foreign currency loan obliged the borrower to bear, inter alia, the burden of withholding tax, in contravention of the relevant Act. The High Court of Australia allowed the claimant borrower to recover the money paid under that head as paid by mistake of law. The outcome was, as in *Solle v Butcher* at first instance, that the contract stood, but on terms less favourable to the other party than would ever have been agreed.

More recently, against a determined dissent by Kirby J on the very ground that the law does not allow awards of restitution within a valid contract, the High Court of Australia has again come firmly down on the side of the apparently unorthodox cases. In *Roxborough v Rothmans of Pall Mall Australia Ltd*[45] the appellant retailers bought a month's supply of cigarettes from the respondent wholesalers for a price which included, separately quantified, a tax disguised as a recurrent licence fee. Both parties understood that the wholesalers would pass that sum over to the New South Wales government, while the retailers for their part would pass the tax on to the smoking public. Then, before the wholesalers paid over but after the retailers had sold the cigarettes, it was established that the tax was void.[46] The majority of the High Court held that the retailers could recover the tax element of the price because the basis upon which it was paid had failed.

Cases of this complexion seem to say that even within a perfectly valid contract there can be a partial failure of basis. That cannot be. What they stand for is that in a rare case there can be a failure of a particular obligation within a valid contract. There is a total failure of basis. When the obligation goes, the basis of the enrichment which it purported to explain fails totally.

Professor Beatson, as he then was, argued that the real question was whether restitution would upset the contractual distribution of risks.

[43] [2002] EWCA Civ 1407, [2002] 3 WLR 1617.

[44] (1992) 175 CLR 353 (HCA).

[45] [2001] HCA 68, (2002) 76 ALJR 203.

[46] *Ha v New South Wales* (1999) 187 CLR 465 (HCA).

Exceptionally, he said, it is right to treat in isolation an invalid element within a contract which was non-negotiable, as to which the parties therefore took no risks.[47] That seems right but it needs some reinforcement to show why it does not derogate from the necessity of total failure of basis. If an item is genuinely non-negotiable, the payment of any excess is as much a payment of a non-existent debt as when the contract itself is misapplied so as to cause an overpayment. Provided the excess is cleanly identifiable and independent of the other obligations in the contract, the basis for that payment totally fails, because the money is paid to discharge an obligation and the obligation does not exist.

Many cases will need to be reconsidered. Beatson himself has said that his approach could not reach *Roxborough v Rothmans of Pall Mall Australia Ltd*.[48] He says the facts were not sufficiently unusual to warrant the invocation of his exception, but others may think it a clear case. There never was an obligation to pay the non-negotiable but void tax. Had the nullity of the tax come to light before payment the parties would simply have struck out that part of the contract. Once it appears that a particular obligation within a contract was invalid so that its performance was totally without legal basis, it may be that the claimant must in addition show either that, as in *Roxborough*, it is clear that the parties would have struck it out without further adjustment or that the disciplinary policy of the law is such as to justify imposing on the defendant a contract to which he would never have agreed, which might account for *David Securities* but doubtfully for *Solle v Butcher*.

(iv) Valid Contracts Still to be Completed

There is one other troubling group of cases. In them the contract between the parties remains valid and undischarged. One party has failed to complete his performance to the point at which he would qualify to be paid, as where logs to be cut in 25 cm lengths have so far been cut only in 50 cm lengths or where limited industrial action results in one aspect of contractual work being left undone. There are occasional hints that the incomplete performer might be able to obtain restitution for the work

[47] J Beatson, 'The Temptation of Elegance: Concurrence of Restitutionary and Contractual Claims' in W Swadling and G Jones (eds), *The Search for Principle: Essays in Honour of Lord Goff of Chieveley* (OUP Oxford 1999) 143, 151–3. Compare J Beatson, 'Restitution and Contract: Non-Cumul?' (2000) 1 Theoretical Inquiries into Law 83, 88.

[48] J Beatson and G Virgo, 'Contract, Unjust Enrichment and Unconscionability' (2002) 118 LQR 352, 356.

which he has actually done.[49] But no claim in unjust enrichment is possible if and so long as the contract remains in being. The work has been incompletely done in discharge of a contractual obligation and that obligation which is its basis still stands. So far as the hints of a right to recover can be defended at all they must refer to the possibility of finding a new contract alongside the incompletely performed contract.[50] It is quite different once the contract has been terminated.

3. DEGREES OF INVALIDITY

The previous subsection affirms that there is no such thing as a partial failure of the basis of an enrichment. There are, however, degrees of invalidity. The basis of a transfer must fail totally, but different degrees of invalidity count as failure and at least one degree of invalidity does not. In the swaps cases the contracts were absolutely void. In the *Fibrosa* case the initial validity of the agreement to sell did not impede the Poles' claim for restitution of their pre-payment.[51] The contract had been subsequently terminated by frustration. The supervening automatic termination, although it did not operate retrospectively, meant that there was no valid basis for the payment. The Law Reform (Frustrated Contracts) Act 1943 is a statutory liberalization of the common law founded on the same principle.[52]

Subsequent termination is already one degree different from absolute nullity. In the post-swaps world we cannot say that the failure of contractual reciprocation was itself the relevant failure of basis. The Polish payment was made under a valid contract and therefore had a good basis until the termination. It must therefore be that the termination of the contract was a sufficient invalidation. It sufficed to show that the basis of the payment, the contract, had failed.

A third degree of invalidity is found where a contract is terminable for breach. While frustration terminates automatically, a repudiatory breach renders the contract terminable by the other side. There is no termination until the other side exercises its power to terminate. For the same

[49] *Miles v Wakefield DC* [1987] AC 539 (HL) 553 (Lord Brightman), 561 (Lord Templeman), criticized by B McFarlane and R Stevens, 'In Defence of *Sumpter v Hedges*' (2002) 118 LQR 569, 590–592. Contrast SA Smith, 'Concurrent Liability in Contract and Unjust Enrichment' (1999) 115 LQR 245.

[50] *Steele v Tardiani* (1946) 72 CLR 386 (HCA).

[51] *Fibrosa Spolka Akcyjna v Fairbairn Lawson Combe Barbour* [1943] AC 32 (HL).

[52] *BP Exploration (Libya) Ltd v Hunt* [1979] 1 WLR 783 (Robert Goff J). On appeal the House of Lords emphasized that the discretion conferred by the Act was not fettered by this interpretation: [1983] AC 352 (HL).

reason as was given in relation to frustration, failure of contractual reciprocation through breach is not in itself the failure of basis. The failure of reciprocation is only the event which invalidates the basis of the claimant's performance, namely the contractual obligation. The terminability of the contract is nonetheless sufficient.

Similarly, where a contract is voidable *ab initio*, as for instance for misrepresentation, pressure, or undue influence, it is the voidability of the contract which shows that the basis of the enrichment has failed. The power to terminate in the one case and the power to rescind and revest in the other arise from the unjust enrichment precipitated by the invalidity. They are the means of reversing that enrichment. If you obtain my car by misrepresentation, the contract between us is immediately invalid. Because your receipt of the car lacks a valid basis, I am entitled to restitution.

Nullity (voidness) and automatic termination are not the only degrees of invalidity which amount to 'failure of basis' or 'absence' of basis. If we were to say that terminability and voidability were insufficient in themselves and that the absence of valid basis only began from the termination or the rescission, we would not be able to explain the origin of the powers to terminate or to avoid, which are not granted by contract and cannot be said to arise from their own effects. These powers arise from the enrichment rendered unjust by the invalidity of the contract under which it was transferred.

To this it is only necessary to add in the case of terminability and voidability that both these phenomena look only one way. Thus, in the case of repudiatory breach, it is only from the victim's point of view that the contract is terminable. Similarly in the case of, for example, misrepresentation, it is only for the representee that the contract is voidable. The consequence is that if the party in breach or the representor were to have recourse to the law of unjust enrichment as claimant, he would fail. From their standpoint the enrichment cannot be unjust until the other has brought the contract to an end. Nullity and automatic termination, by contrast, work both ways. Both parties can allege a failure of basis. Terminability or voidability work only one way. At the first stage only one party can allege a failure of basis.

Subject to that caveat, nullity, termination, terminability, and voidability all suffice to show that an enrichment has no valid basis. Mere unenforceability does not. The word 'unenforceable' is by convention reserved for a good contract on which no action can be brought. Thus, if a contract is rendered unenforceable in the absence of a memorandum in writing, it must in addition be voidable or terminable on some other ground before value transferred under it can be regarded as having no basis and hence as an unjust enrichment.[53] Thus in *Pavey & Matthews Pty Ltd v Paul*,[54] where the High Court of Australia allowed a builder to recover the value of work completed under such a contract, the refusal of Mrs Paul to pay was a repudiatory breach which rendered the contract terminable. The unenforceability of the contract was not itself a sufficient invalidity. It was because of the breach of that good but unenforceable contract that the basis of her enrichment failed.

E. CONCLUSION

In the swaps cases English law changed direction. This took some time to sink in. The first instinct was to integrate absence of basis in the list of unjust factors. That turns out to be absolutely impossible. There is now no turning back.

The 'no basis' method of establishing that an enrichment is unjust creates a serious dilemma for the exposition of the answer to the third question in the five-question analysis. One horn is near-impossibility, the other jejune abstraction. If the unjust enrichment is the enrichment with no valid explanatory basis, should the expositor set out all the conditions under which obligations are invalid and all the circumstances in which purposes other than discharge fail to be validly achieved? That verges on the impossible. The jejune alternative is to begin the account at invalidity and abstain altogether from explaining the causes of invalidity. That has the unfortunate consequence that it leaves the law of unjust enrichment abstract and further out of touch with the Clapham omnibus.

It may be that the abstract option is inevitable. A full-scale textbook will have to decide. A short book has no choice. It has to take the abstract line. However, the great merit of the common law being its dependence on cases, the abstraction can never be absolute. The next chapter introduces the operation of the 'no basis' approach. The account which it offers comes with a warning that it makes no pretence of explaining all the causes of invalidity. Its brevity also means that it cannot investigate all the controversies on the outer edges of the 'no basis' approach.

[53] *Thomas v Brown* [1876] 1 QBD 714.

[54] (1987) 162 CLR 221 (HCA). The contract was unenforceable under the Builders Licensing Act 1971 s 45 (NSW).

One point important to emphasize is the Englishness of what follows. Nationalism is always out of place in legal thought and argument. When it does push in, it always strikes a note which is either absurd or repulsive or both. The assertion of Englishness is not an outburst of chauvinism. It is merely a warning that, although the no basis approach is very civilian and although there is now guidance to be obtained from civilian jurisdictions, what has happened is not a passive reception of German or French law to fill a vacuum.

Lord Mansfield did indeed do some deliberate borrowing of that kind from the *ius commune*. By contrast, the modern English judges have simply been drawn to an approach to 'unjust' which, with hindsight, is both incompatible with the list of unjust factors with which they were previously managing and reflects the method which, in different sub-forms, is already familiar in civilian jurisdictions. This time there is no evidence in the cases of deliberate borrowing.

Just as there are differences between civilian interpretations, so in matters of detail the English application of no basis will be different again. It has to be founded on the interpretation of the same corpus of cases as until recently seemed to warrant the use of the approach through a list of unjust factors. If that case law had been firmly settled, there would have been no room for the change of direction. There was room, and a new direction has now been chosen. Since 1760 the direction which now seems attractive has all along been one of the possible futures, but now the fit with the recent past will have to be re-worked.

6

Absence of Basis

The two chapters of this part are concerned with the meaning of 'unjust'. The previous chapter discussed the transition from lists of unjust factors to absence of basis and from the language of 'consideration' to the language of 'basis', that being preferred to 'reason' or 'ground'. This chapter turns to the operation of what in England has to be regarded as a new approach. In most situations the 'no basis' test works with a surgical simplicity which the lists of unjust factors could not emulate.

Every enrichment comes about either with or without the participation of the claimant. Non-participatory transfers are those over which the claimant has no control, as where a pickpocket takes money from his pocket. Such an enrichment at the claimant's expense almost invariably has no explanatory basis.

Participatory enrichments are perceived as either obligatory or voluntary. If the purpose is discharge of an obligation and there is indeed a valid obligation which is discharged, the enrichment has an explanatory basis and cannot be unjust. If there turns out to be no valid obligation discharged, the enrichment is inexplicable. It has no explanatory basis. Voluntary enrichments are those which are transferred without obligation but in order to achieve some outcome. If that purpose is achieved, the basis has not failed. If it is not achieved, the enrichment has no explanatory basis.

The previous paragraph can be restated in the form of three questions which will resolve nearly all cases. (1) Was the enrichment perceived to be obligatory? If it was, its basis will have failed if there was in fact no obligation. (2) If it was not obligatory but voluntary, what end was it intended to achieve or depend upon and, in particular, was it intended to bring about or depend upon a contract, trust, gift or other outcome? If that outcome did not come about, the basis of the enrichment will have failed. (3) If the enrichment was acquired without the participation of the claimant or his agents, was there any legal authority for its acquisition by the defendant? The premiss of the third question is that in general enrichments of that kind necessarily have no basis.

In relation to both 1) and 2) it is tempting to enter an immediate caveat, namely that the claimant must not have knowingly taken the risk that the desired outcome would not be achieved. But that caveat is actually supererogatory, for one who takes such a risk desires one outcome but intends two. A busker desires to be paid for his music but intends a gift to those who choose not to pay. It follows without more that, in relation to the latter, there is no failure of basis.

A. OBLIGATORY ENRICHMENTS

The vast majority of cases fall under this head. The enrichment is transferred in discharge of an obligation owed to the recipient. It turns out that there was no obligation. The money was not due. The absence or invalidity of the obligation means that from the outset the basis of the enrichment failed. It can happen that the basis is good at the moment of receipt but fails afterwards, as where a contract under which a payment is made subsequently becomes terminable or void.[1] It is convenient to separate initial and subsequent failure.

The right to recover something which turns out not to have been due goes all the way back to the first life of Roman law, where the claim was referred to as the '*condictio indebiti*'. Since the Latin term crops up recurrently, it is as well to know from the outset what it signifies and why. The *condictio* was the Roman action of debt. '*Condicere*' meant 'to give notice'. The action took its name from the fact that the claimant originally had to make a solemn declaration giving notice to the defendant to take a judge in a month's time.

The legal category of debt is always multi-causal. That is, a debt arises from different events, sometimes from contract, sometimes from other events. The word '*indebitum*', which becomes '*indebiti*' in the genitive just as 'John' becomes 'John's', names one of the causative events in the non-contractual sector of the spectrum.'*Indebitum*' is 'something not owed'. Thus the *condictio indebiti* is the action of debt 'in respect of a non-debt' or 'in respect of something not due'.

The English word 'indebted' has no negative connotation and therefore means more or less the opposite. 'Indebtedness' is the condition of owing, whereas an '*indebitum*' is something not owed. Historically omnipresent

[1] Subsequent nullity is rare, but see *Goss v Chilcott* [1996] AC 788 (PC): subsequent alteration of a deed by the obligee renders the deed void under the rule in *Pigot's case* (1614) 11 Co Rep 26b, 77 ER 1177.

in this context in England was the action which, from its principal words, was called '*indebitatus assumpsit* (having become indebted he promised)'. It is not unlikely that squeamishness about juxtaposing '*indebitum*' and '*indebitatus*' was at least part of the reason why English law did not make a more thoroughgoing reception of the Roman categories at and after the time when Lord Mansfield borrowed from the civilian learning on the *condictio* to explain the scope of the sub-species of *indebitatus assumpsit* called the action for money had and received. These mysteries are revisited later.[2]

It was said only a few years ago, and by no less an authority than Lord Goff, that English law knew nothing of the *condictio indebiti*.[3] At the time of that dictum the unjust factors still held sway. It can no longer be true, for the *condictio indebiti* embraces every claim in which the supposed basis of the enrichment was the discharge of an obligation and there was in fact no obligation to discharge. All the swaps cases were of that kind.

1. INITIAL FAILURE OF BASIS

An enrichment received as due when it was not due cannot be retained unless the payer knew it was not due or willingly took the risk that it might not be. The old list of intent-based unjust factors is often completely irrelevant. They need only be invoked, indeed can only be invoked, where one of them is the very reason why the supposed obligation is invalid. In the background qualified intent is, however, omnipresent, but only in the way described in the previous chapter, namely that one who pays on a particular basis only intends the recipient to be enriched if that basis holds good.[4]

The discussion which follows deals first with cases in which the supposed obligation is invalid for a reason other than deficient intent on the part of the claimant. It then comes back to cases where deficiency of intent is the reason for the invalidity.

(a) Invalidity Independent of Intent

We have already seen that the swaps cases all involved payments which were thought to be due but were not. The supposed obligation was a contractual obligation which was void because the contract was of a kind which fell outside the powers of local authorities. The cause of the

[2] Below, 285–90.

[3] *Woolwich Equitable BS v IRC* [1993] 1 AC 70 (HL) 172. Compare Lightman J in *Rowe v Vale of White Horse DC* [2003] 1 Lloyd's Rep 418, 422.

[4] Above, 104.

invalidity was incapacity. Mistake and other impairments of intent were irrelevant, save in relation to the subsidiary question whether the claimant had willingly taken the risk that there might be no valid contract. Similarly, in an illegal contract, as for instance to sell osprey eggs, to evade exchange control regulations, or to defraud an insurance company, the reason that there is no obligation is the illegality itself. If value passes, it passes without any basis. The cause of action in unjust enrichment is in principle made out, although it may be defeated under the fifth question in the five-point analysis which asks whether the enrichee has any defence.

This book began with the example in which a shop gives you change for a £50 note when you paid with a £20 note. Chatting to your friend, you did not notice that you received £30 too much. The shop-assistant intended to discharge an obligation. Every time a customer tenders more than the price, there is a genuinely implied contract that the shop will return the excess. This is a good example of a restitutionary obligation arising from contract. The shop intended to discharge that contractual obligation. The failure of the putative basis of your receipt of the £30 excess depends solely on finding facts which are unrelated to the shop's intent, namely that you paid with a £20 note and received change for a £50 note. As to the excess, there was no basis for it, for the shop was under no obligation to pay that sum. Theoretically you might show that the basis was not discharge but gift, because the shop knew or knowingly took the risk that it did not owe, but there would have to be some very peculiar additional facts if you were to run that argument.

In *Kelly v Solari*[5] the insurer's supposed obligation could be negatived simply by showing that the policy had lapsed, but there the court did think that Mrs Solari was entitled to put to a jury the question whether the intended basis might not have been gift rather than discharge. If the intended basis of the payment was discharge, the fact that the policy had lapsed was in itself sufficient to entitle it to restitution. In *Craven-Ellis v Canons Ltd*[6] a company's managing director had, unknown to him, worked under a contract which was void because it had been made by persons not qualified to be directors. His work was done under the impression of an obligation. There was no obligation. The absence of basis turns on the disqualification of the directors. The mistake of the claimant has nothing to do with it. Its only role is to indicate that he did not know that there was no obligation and did not take the risk that there

[5] (1841) 9 M & W 54, 59, 152 ER 24, 27. [6] [1936] 2 KB 403 (CA).

might not be. In construing the basis of an enrichment, one can never take one's eyes off that secondary possibility, however remote.

With hindsight it is now possible to see that before the change brought about by the advent of 'absence of basis' in the swaps cases, the common law often wasted energy in a superfluous struggle to identify an unjust factor which would demonstrate that the claimant's consent to the enrichment was deficient. Duress, which is illegitimate pressure, is one such impairment. The Australian case of *Mason v New South Wales*[7] has become a leading illustration of restitution for illegitimate pressure, but if the facts recurred now it is unlikely that duress would even be mentioned.

Duties levied by New South Wales on the border with Victoria had been held unconstitutional. This was the successful attempt to recover what had been paid. The High Court of Australia was able to find that the intent to pay had been systematically impaired by duress. It was not a case in which the officials had confined themselves to threatening legal proceedings, which is never illegitimate to do. The void statute under which they had been operating purported to entitle them to impound the lorries of those who did not pay. In perfect good faith but without lawful authority, they had backed their demands with duress of goods. The right result was reached, but, in the light of the swaps cases, the diversion through duress was completely unnecessary. The money was paid to discharge an obligation, and there was no obligation. The enrichment of the government of New South Wales had no basis. There were no facts to suggest that the basis might have been a generous or grudging gift.

In England, in *Woolwich Equitable Building Society v IRC*,[8] a similar scenario was played out on facts which did not admit of reliance on duress or any other impairment of intent, so that the outcome had to be made to turn on an unjust factor from the other family, namely 'policy motivations'.

Regulations had been enacted to deal with tax payable by building societies. The Woolwich all along maintained that the regulations were ultra vires. It evidently judged that public conflict between a financial institution and the revenue would be more seemly after payment. It therefore paid up some £57m and then successfully challenged the validity of the regulations in the courts. The Inland Revenue returned the £57m but took the view that the payment was made ex gratia and that its grace did not extend to interest. In a second action the Woolwich successfully established that, on the contrary, it had been entitled to repayment as of right. It was therefore able to recover another £7m in interest.

[7] (1959) 102 CLR 108 (HCA).
[8] [1993] 1 AC 70 (HL).

It proved an uphill struggle to show that the Inland Revenue had been under an obligation to return the money. One reason was that the Woolwich had not made any mistake of fact and, unlike the claimant in *Mason v New South Wales*,[9] had not been subjected to any illegitimate pressure outside the ordinary working of the due process of law. Even if the mistake of law bar to restitution had not still been in place, it could not be said that the Woolwich had made any mistake. Its position had been from start to finish that the regulations were void. In the end the constitutionally important victory was won in the supplementary group of unjust factors, in which the reason for restitution was always a policy dictating restitution. So here the unjust factor was that it was essential that the servants of the state stay within their powers and, within that, especially important that the principle of no taxation without Parliament be upheld.

There is no denying the significance of the *Woolwich* case. However, if it had been decided after the impact of the swaps litigation had been fully appreciated, neither the diversion through principles of public law nor the difficulties subsequently experienced in defining the precise limits of the principle which was applied[10] would have been necessary. The Woolwich had paid to discharge a debt. There were no facts to suggest that it intended a gift or had knowingly taken a risk that the money was not due. All the evidence was that it had constantly contended that it was not liable to pay. And the courts upheld that view. After the swaps cases we can see that there was all along nothing special about this case. It was simply a payment made to discharge a non-existent debt. It is not possible to decide the swaps cases on the ground of 'absence of basis' and at the same time to decline the short cut to the *Woolwich* conclusion. Dr Meier justly shows that here our unjust factors have tied us in knots. She points out that Lord Goff himself came very close to admitting that none was needed.[11]

[9] Note 7 above.

[10] In *Waikato Regional Airport v A-G of New Zealand* [2003] UKPC 50 [80] the Privy Council, applying *Woolwich*, found it necessary to hold that ultra vires charges for the New Zealand biosecurity system were not a tax nor a charge for a service. Drawing that kind of distinction is exacerbated by the fact that non-tax cases such as *South of Scotland Electricity Board v British Oxygen Company* [1959] 1 WLR 589 (HL) played a part in the *Woolwich* argument, even though an overcharge for electricity is certainly not a tax or levy.

[11] S Meier, 'Unjust Factors and Legal Grounds' in D Johnston and R Zimmermann (eds), *Unjustified Enrichment: Key Issues in Comparative Perspective* (CUP Cambridge 2002) 37, 61–5 emphasizing [1993] AC 70 (HL) 173 (Lord Goff).

At the time when these cases were decided the rule was, and had been for some 200 years, that there could be no restitution for mistake of law. Under the regime of the unjust factors that meant simply that mistake of law was not an unjust factor. It is important to notice that, so long as the rule was maintained, it hid the attractions of the 'no basis' approach. If, for instance, the claimants in *Mason v New South Wales* had tried to run a 'no basis' argument, they could have showed that there was no obligation to discharge, but they could not have shown that they did not know that there was none. So long as they were deemed to know the law, they could not show that they did not know that the Act imposing the duties was unconstitutional. The artificial inference would have been drawn that the intended basis of their payments had been gift and had not failed.

This problem has been swept away. When in *Kleinwort Benson Ltd v Lincoln CC*[12] the House of Lords persuaded itself that, by way of an analysis alternative to 'no basis', the swaps cases could be regarded as turning on mistake, it also decided that mistakes of law should be treated in the same way as mistakes of fact. Outside the criminal law there is no more deeming that everyone knows the law. Mistake of law thus becomes one way—and the *Woolwich* facts show that it is only one way—of excluding the unlikely suggestion that what appears to be a payment to discharge an obligation was in reality intended, grudgingly or not, to be a gift.

(b) Invalidity Dependent on Deficient Intent

In the cases above the invalidity of the supposed obligation had nothing to do with mistake or pressure or any other impairment of intent. Sometimes, however, as the pyramid graphically represents, such a deficiency of intent is the very reason why the obligation is invalid.

Although many protections have been introduced in recent times, especially for consumers, in general bargaining is still a dangerous business. When you make a contract you hope to do well, but you take the risk of disappointment. However, even before the spate of consumer protection, the playing-field was not without rules. There were, and are, risks which as a matter of law nobody takes. If the obligation arises from a contract obtained by misrepresentation,[13] or illegitimate pressure,[14] or

[12] [1999] 2 AC 349 (HL), applied in *Nurdin & Peacock plc v DB Ramsden & Co Ltd* [1999] 1 All ER 941.

[13] *Redgrave v Hurd* (1880) 20 Ch D 1 (CA).

[14] *Barton v Armstrong* [1976] AC 104 (PC); *Universe Tankships v ITWF, The Universe Sentinel* [1983] AC 366 (HL); *B& S Contracts and Design Ltd v Victor Green Publications Ltd* [1984] ICR 419.

undue influence,[15] it will be voidable, and the value which passes will be recoverable. More rarely, a contract will be voidable because one party's autonomy was reduced by some severe personal handicap, such as education and up-bringing inadequate to cope with transaction,[16] post-divorce stress,[17] or an immigrant's inability to understand the language or culture.[18] Sometimes the transaction is itself disabling. When business borrowing seeks financial support from the domestic sphere, as where a home is mortgaged by one spouse to support the other's commercial activity, the contract is often set aside on the ground of undue influence,[19] but the invalidity could equally well, or better, be explained on the ground of transactional inequality. That phrase indicates that the nature of the transaction is in itself calculated to disable an adult's standard capacity for self-management.[20]

These special cases apart, either the contract places the risk of a given disappointment on your counter-party, or it must be borne by you. If the watercolour which you bought for £100,000 turns out after all not to be by Turner, the seller will be liable to pay you damages if you managed to get a term to that effect included in the contract. If not, you have to live with the disappointment of having paid ten times too much. In general there is no hope in a bargaining situation of appealing to the law of unjust enrichment. It is no use your saying that you want your money back because you would never have bought the picture but for your mistaken belief. The law of unjust enrichment has nothing to say, and never has, except in the vanishingly few cases in which a foundational mistake renders the contract void. Mutual restitution will then return the parties to square one.

Bell v Lever Brothers Ltd[21] illustrates how rarely a disappointing contract will be invalidated by spontaneous, as opposed to induced, mistake. Lever Brothers sought restitution of golden handshakes which they had paid to get rid of two executives at the time of a takeover. It emerged later that the executives could have been peremptorily sacked for misconduct.

[15] *O'Sullivan v Management Agency and Music Ltd* [1985] QB 428 (CA); *Goldsworthy v Brickell* [1987] 1 Ch 378.

[16] *Fry v Lane* (1889) 40 Ch D 312.

[17] *Creswell v Potter* [1978] 1 WLR 255.

[18] *Commercial Bank of Australia v Amadio* (1983) 151 CLR 447 (HCA).

[19] *Barclays Bank plc v O'Brien* [1994] 1 AC 180 (HL); *CIBC Mortgages plc v Pitt* [1994] 1 AC 200 (HL); *Credit Lyonnais v Burch* [1997] 1 All ER 144 (CA); *Royal Bank of Scotland v Etridge (No 2)* [2001] UKHL 44, [2001] 3 WLR 1021.

[20] The same principle applied to marriage broking: *Hermann v Charlesworth* [1905] 2 KB 123 (CA).

[21] [1932] AC 161 (HL).

Lever would never have paid if it had known. But the causative mistake was not enough. The company's claim for restitution was rejected. Lever's mistake had not invalidated the contract, with the consequence that the obligation under which it paid had been valid.

On these facts there was no foundational mistake. Whatever words are used to capture the nature of such a mistake, they must be construed against that background. The mistaken belief must go to the foundation of the contract in the sense that its truth was the necessary basis of all the obligations which the parties undertook. It must be a mistake which manifestly lay outside all the risks taken by the parties. If parties are buying and selling a horse which, unknown to them, has just been struck dead, the falsification of their belief that it was alive renders the contract void. That the horse was alive was an assumption outside the risks of the bargain. But in the context of the take-over in *Bell v Lever Brothers Ltd* the parties could perfectly intelligibly bargain for the executives' quiet and immediate departure whether or not there might be a ground for dismissing them. When the dust settled after the takeover Lever Brothers had the leisure to ascertain the true facts. It was then, so to say, that they discovered that they had bought a watercolour by Turner that was not one. They had paid to discharge a valid contractual obligation. There was no question of restitution. The basis of the defendants' enrichment had not failed.

This fierce outcome has recently been underlined. An attempt was made to soften it, and for half a century it was precariously maintained that there were two degrees of foundational mistake, the greater rendering the contract void at law, the lesser making it voidable in equity. That was the position taken by the Court of Appeal in *Solle v Butcher*[22] in relation to the lease of a flat made on the incorrect assumption that the parties were free to fix their own rent. In fact the pre-war rent applied, and once the lease was running no application could be made to reset it. The lease was held to be voidable in equity, and mutual restitution followed. However, the logical impossibility of there being two degrees of foundational mistake was exposed in *Great Peace Shipping Ltd v Tsavliris Salvage (International) Ltd, The Great Peace*.[23]

There the Great Peace was chartered for a minimum of five days on the assumption that it was near enough to effect an immediate rescue from a tanker in danger of sinking. In fact it was a full day away, and another ship met up with the stricken vessel within hours. The five-days' hire still had

[22] [1950] 1 KB 671 (CA).

[23] [2002] EWCA Civ 1407, [2003] QB 679.

to be paid. First Toulson J and then the Court of Appeal exposed the fallacy of *Solle v Butcher*: either the mistake was foundational and outside all the risks of the contract, or it was not. The common law had occupied all the available ground.

In *Bell v Lever Brothers* and *Solle v Butcher* the injustice of the enrichment depended on establishing the invalidity of a contractual obligation. In the one, the basis never failed; in the other it was said, but incorrectly, that it had. *Deutsche Morgan Grenfell Group plc v IRC*[24] will also have to be condemned. Although it came after the swaps cases, it followed the old method of looking for unjust factors. It came to an indefensible result.

The facts were intricate. The Income and Corporation Taxes Act 1988 section 247 provided for an exemption from payment of advance corporation tax. It worked as follows. Companies within a group could give notice of a 'group income election' which then became effective to exempt the members of the group after a lapse of three months, unless an inspector of taxes rejected it within that time. A rejection by an inspector was subject to appeal. Having the exemption, companies within the group could pay dividends without having to pay advance corporation tax. They had to pay mainstream corporation tax later. However, the Act confined such group elections to companies resident in the United Kingdom. The European Court of Justice held that that restriction was unlawful.[25] The claimants constituted one group which would have made such an election but for the supposedly valid restriction. The effect was that they had paid millions of pounds earlier than necessary. With some reluctance Park J concluded that they were entitled to restitution of the value of that money over time, measured in interest. The government later announced that further recoveries of the same kind would have to be barred by statute.

The learned judge reached his conclusion in the old way, by recourse to unjust factors. The claimants were either mistaken in law[26] or entitled to the benefit of the policy against ultra vires taxation.[27] Even following that approach and despite the totally different context, the outcome is at odds with the principle underlying *Bell v Lever Brothers*, namely that

[24] [2003] 4 All ER 645 (Ch D).

[25] *Metallgesellschaft Ltd v IRC* and *Hoechst AG v IRC* C-397/98 and C-410/98 [2001] All ER (EC) 496, [2001] Ch 620 (ECJ).

[26] *Kleinwort Benson Ltd v Lincoln CC* [1999] 2 AC 349 (HL), discussed above, 112–3.

[27] *Woolwich Equitable Building Society v Inland Revenue Commissioners* [1993] AC 70 (HL).

one cannot, even via unjust factors, have restitution of an enrichment transferred under a valid obligation. On the 'no basis' approach that merely becomes doubly clear. A payment made to discharge a valid obligation cannot be said to lack a sufficient legal basis. In *Deutsche Morgan Grenfell* the claimants succeeded even though the tax which they recovered had been due. It had been paid under a valid obligation. Every company was bound to pay advance corporation tax unless it did the things necessary to earn an exemption. The claimants had not done those things. They had abstained from doing them in the belief, later falsified, that they were not entitled to.

Since 1980 the central proposition in relation to mistake has been that restitution will follow provided that the mistake caused the enrichment. One works outwards to the qualifications and exceptions. The central test was deduced from a very large body of cases by Robert Goff J in *Barclays Bank Ltd v WJ Simms & Son Ltd*.[28] The effect of starting from that disarmingly simple proposition was to create an immediate need for the peripheral 'exceptions'. These were in reality major concessions to the 'no basis' approach. If one treats *Bell v Lever Brothers* as central 'no basis' requires no exceptions at all. In the case of the watercolour which was not by Turner you undoubtedly made a causative mistake. You would not have paid £100,000 for it if you had not thought that it was by him. But you obtain no right to restitution. Common as such a case is, it has had to be presented as an exception from the normal rule.[29] The exception had to be justified. It protected the common interest in the bargaining process. It needs no such treatment. The contract is valid. The payment was made under a good contractual obligation, to discharge that obligation. The only enrichment which has to be given up is the enrichment with no legal basis.

As we shall see immediately below, this unnecessary clash between the supposed ground-rule and an exception recurs with judgments. There can be no recovery under a mistaken judgment unless and until the judgment has been set aside. That too had to be seen as a departure from the attractively simple ground-rule promising restitution for causative mistakes. And once again the departure from the basic rule could be explained. There must be an end to litigation. There must be no untended back door through which to reopen closed disputes.

The 'no basis' approach means that these exceptions have become the rule. Payment under an obligation is irrecoverable unless the supposed

[28] [1980] QB 677. [29] [1980] QB 677, 695, Robert Goff's exception, numbered 2b.

obligation was or later became invalid. So long as a contract or judgment or other obligation remained in place and was discharged as intended the enrichment cannot be unjust.

2. SUBSEQUENT FAILURE OF BASIS

In the cases discussed so far the obligation which the claimant supposed to exist was already invalid at the time when the enrichment was received. In other cases it is valid at that time but invalidated afterwards. For example, if a payment is made under a judgment which is later quashed, it cannot be said not to have been due when the payment was made. It was undoubtedly due once the judgment had been made. Its basis was the judgment itself. Even in the pre-swaps time there could be no restitution so long as the judgment stood.[30] However, when the judgment is quashed a right to restitution arises.[31] The reason is the subsequent failure of the basis of the obligation.

Of the same kind is the common case in which a performance is made under a valid contract which is subsequently automatically terminated by frustration or becomes terminable for breach by one or other side. This kind of case now requires closer analysis. Here the swaps cases have unsettled what was once a totally reliable beacon, but, once one has reconciled onself to meddling with a scriptural text, the repair is relatively straightforward.

The modern law is largely founded on the great *Fibrosa* case.[32] It will be recalled that shortly before the outbreak of the Second World War, a Polish company ordered some textile machinery from manufacturers in England and made a part-payment in advance. With the Nazi invasion of Poland, the contract was frustrated. The Polish company had received nothing for its money. The House of Lords held that, suing through its surviving officers in London, it had a right to restitution. The consideration on which it had made its payment had failed. There is no doubt that 'failure of consideration' here meant both failure of contractual reciprocation, the supply of the machines, and failure of basis. That is to say, their Lordships took the two to be the same: the supply of the machines was the basis of the payment. This now has to be adjusted.

With hindsight from the swaps litigation, this case appears in one important respect to have taken the wrong track. The principal obstacle

[30] *Barder v Caluori* [1988] AC 20 (HL).

[31] *Commonwealth v McCormack* (1984) 155 CLR 273 (HCA); B McFarlane 'The Recovery of Money Paid under Judgments Later Reversed' [2001] Restitution L Rev 1.

[32] *Fibrosa Spolka Akcyjna v Fairbairn Lawson Combe Barbour* [1943] AC 32 (HL).

which the Polish claimants had to surmount was *Chandler v Webster*.[33] The Court of Appeal there took the law to be that, where the claimant had suffered a failure of contractual reciprocation, the fact that there had initially been sufficient consideration to bind the contract made it impossible ever after to speak of a failure of basis unless the contract were rescinded *ab initio*. *Fibrosa* did not confront that directly. It evaded it by saying that the relevant basis was not the contract but the performance of the contractual reciprocation.[34] Sensible as that seems to be, it leaves unanswered the objection that the restitutionary right would then have arisen despite the validity of the contractual obligation under which the payment was made.

We can see now that *Fibrosa* should have confronted *Chandler v Webster* head on by accepting that the contractual obligation under the sale was the only relevant basis of the Polish payment. The error in *Chandler v Webster* was the assertion that the contractual obligation could only be sufficiently invalidated if it were void or voidable *ab initio*. The House of Lords should have said that it was sufficient that the contractual obligation was prematurely terminated. This revision is inescapable after the swaps cases, on pain of our being forced to the undesirable conclusion that *Chandler v Webster* was all along right. We have to say that the failure of contractual reciprocation in circumstances of frustration brought about a failure of basis, in the form of supervening invalidity of the contract and, further, that the invalidity of the contract which was the basis of the payment was sufficient even though it was a termination and not a rescission *ab initio*.

The unjust enrichment recognized in the *Fibrosa* case was itself heavily restricted by the old view that it was confined to the case in which the claimant had received nothing at all. This was almost immediately overtaken by legislation. The Law Reform (Frustrated Contracts) Act 1943 eliminated the requirement that the claimant must have received nothing at all of the expected contractual reciprocation and made it clear that, freed from that restriction, the *Fibrosa* claim was available in the event of frustration both to the party who had paid money and the party who had conferred a valuable benefit other than money. We have seen that the restriction to total failure of reciprocation has now been abandoned across the board.[35]

Where the premature termination of the contractual obligation supervenes because of breach rather than frustration, a party in breach

[33] [1904] 1 KB 493 (CA).

[34] [1943] AC 32, esp 52 (Lord Atkin), 65 (Lord Wright).

[35] Above, 120–1.

has the same cause of action as the victim, albeit subject to liability in damages for any loss which he has caused to the other.[36] However, one important difference is that, since only the victim of the breach has the option to terminate, the party in breach cannot found on the mere terminability of the contract. From his perspective the obligation under which he paid is not terminable. For him, it is not invalidated until it is terminated.[37]

Here too, as in the case of frustration, the failure of reciprocation can no longer be regarded as the immediate ground for restitution but only the sub-reason, at the base of the pyramid, why the master unjust factor operates. If you agree to build me a garage and I pay £10,000 in advance, and you then default, your failure to build the garage invalidates the obligation under which I paid you. I have a power to terminate it and a right to recover my money. That is how the pyramid works: the failure of reciprocation invalidates the obligation and the invalidity of the obligation constitutes the absence of explanatory basis which renders the enrichment unjust. Provided the obligation is invalidated, there is no longer a requirement that I must have received nothing at all.

B. VOLUNTARY ENRICHMENTS

With the exception of those that are non-participatory, to which we will return, enrichments which are not perceived to be obligatory are made with a purpose in mind. Nearly all can be comprehended within the three heads, according as the purpose is contract, trust, or gift. These are not perfectly distinct. A trust, for example, is often the vehicle for a gift. The question is always whether the purpose for which the transfer was made was achieved. In deciding what that purpose was, great care has to be taken to see whether the claimant knowingly took the risk that his primary purpose might not be achieved, for if he did his purposes, taking those desired with those intended but not desired, will not have failed.[38] In the absence of mistake or some other impairment of intent, risk-taking is commonly negatived by revealing the purpose of the transfer and thus creating an opportunity for the other side to reject, but there is no need to communicate the purpose to a recipient to whom it is or appears to be manifest.

[36] *Dies v British and International Mining and Finance Corp* [1939] 1 KB 724; *Rover International Ltd v Cannon Film Sales Ltd* [1989] 1 WLR 912 (CA).

[37] Above, 125–6.

[38] Above, 103–4.

I. CONTRACT

'On the basis of contract' is too sweeping to be useful. Nearly every enrichment conferred on the basis of contract is made for the purpose of discharging a contractual obligation and is, as such, obligatory under the previous heading, not voluntary, under this heading. Those enrichments that fall under the present heading are made voluntarily, which means without any sense of obligation, either on the basis that a contract will come into existence or actually to make a contract.

(a) On the Basis that a Contract Will Come About

Often the basis of the enriching transfer is that a contract must later come into existence. In *Chillingworth v Esche*[39] the claimant, intending to buy property, had paid a pre-contractual deposit 'subject to contract'. When no contract eventuated, the money was held to be recoverable. The court did not use the language of failure of consideration or failure of basis, but the ground should now be so understood. The corruption of the word 'consideration' left no convenient name for the reason for restitution and forced the court to cobble together an *ad hoc* explanation. Construction of the phrase 'subject to contract' showed, at least in that context,[40] that there would be no basis for retaining the money unless a binding contract came into existence.

In *William Lacey (Hounslow) Ltd v Davis*[41] a builder was told that he had been successful in the tendering process and would be awarded the development contract. He then did a great deal of preparatory work for the developer, much more than builders customarily risk in pursuit of contracts. In the end the developer changed his mind. He decided not to do the development and sold on instead. The builder was allowed value of his work. This is not an uncommon scenario. Surprisingly, it quite often happens that even a very large project will proceed towards completion before any contract has been signed. In such cases the work is all done on the basis that a contract will come into existence.[42]

[39] [1924] 1 Ch 97.

[40] That the exercise of construction must be context-specific is shown by *Attorney-General of Hong Kong v Humphries Estate* (1987) AC 114 (PC) where value transferred at the pre-contractual phase was held to have been transferred entirely at the transferor's risk. See also *Regalian Properties plc v London Docklands Development Corporation* [1995] 1 WLR 212.

[41] [1957] 1 WLR 932; cf *Countrywide Communications Ltd v ICL Pathway Ltd* (QBD 21 October 1999, 1996 C No 2446).

[42] *Peter Lind & Co v Mersey Docks and Harbour Board* [1972] 2 Lloyd's Rep 234; *British Steel Corporation v Cleveland Bridge & Engineering Ltd* [1984] 1 All ER 504.

One eye has always to be kept on risk-taking. It is one thing to want a contract to come into existence and another to act solely on the basis that it will. Every builder and architect risks sprats to catch mackerel. It was an essential feature of *William Lacey (Hounslow) Ltd v Davis* that in the circumstances it was entirely reasonable for the builder to understand that the developer knew that the work which the builder was doing for him had gone far beyond that kind of speculation and was being done on the basis that a contract would be made later.

In *Rowe v Vale of White Horse DC*[43] the local authority had provided sewerage services to council houses which it had sold to private buyers. For 13 years it made no demand for payment. It seems that at first the authority, by an administrative oversight, continued to service the properties as though nothing had changed. In the years within the limitation period it had recovered from that error and intended to charge, but it abstained from issuing invoices because of a suspicion that the provision of sewerage services might be ultra vires. When that doubt was resolved in its favour, it demanded six years' payments. Lightman J accepted that Mr Rowe had been enriched at the Council's expense but found that, although it was common knowledge that such services had to be paid for, the extraordinary history made it reasonable for Mr Rowe to believe, and that he did believe, that the service was free. This went to unjust, not to any defence. The enrichment was not unjust.

This is best explained in terms of risk. In the special circumstances there was no shared basis between the parties. The District Council for a reason of its own had not disclosed its intention to charge. It had hoped that if it continued to provide the service the recipients would later agree to pay for it. It had taken the risk that its request for payment would be repudiated. The result would have been different if it could have shown that it could reasonably claim to believe that the householder knew all along that the services would have to be paid for.

(b) On the Basis that the Transfer Will Conclude a Contract

The transfer may itself be intended as the offer or acceptance of a contract. If you ask me to lend you £50, and I do so, my payment is made voluntarily but with the purpose of imposing a contractual obligation upon you to repay. Depending on the precise facts I may be accepting your offer or making an offer for you to accept. Similarly in unilateral

[43] [2003] 1 Lloyd's Rep 418. Earlier discussion, above 43 and 60.

contracts, a performance may be voluntarily done to accept an offer.[44] Slightly different is a payment made to satisfy a condition of entitlement, as where the payment of a premium is the condition of an insurer's liability.

In *R E Jones Ltd v Waring & Gillow Ltd*[45] both parties were deceived by a rogue called Bodenham. The claimants paid thinking that they were putting down a deposit on a number of Roma cars, and the defendants thought they were receiving payment of the rogue's debt. In *Dextra Bank & Trust Co Ltd v Bank of Jamaica*[46] the claimant thought it was lending US$3m and the defendant thought it was buying them. Again both had been comprehensively deceived by fraudsters. In the former case the House of Lords held that the claimants could recover; in the latter the Privy Council held that the Bank of Jamaica had changed its position and had a cast-iron defence[47] but, still following the pre-swaps path, it also held that the claimant bank had no cause of action. In the earlier case the House of Lords accepted that Jones had been mistaken; in the later the Privy Council found that Dextra had merely mispredicted that the Bank of Jamaica would contract with it. Its instructions were that the cheque was only to be handed over if the Bank of Jamaica agreed the strict terms of a promissory note which it had drafted. The fraudsters took care to ensure that that instruction and the promissory note were suppressed.

Whether or not there is a fine factual distinction between these two cases justifying the conclusion that in the one there was a mistake and in the other only a misprediction for which no relief could be given, both now need to be reconsidered according to the 'no basis' approach to the injustice of an enrichment. The claimants both paid on the basis of a contract to be concluded by acceptance of the payment. Deceived, they never managed to communicate that purpose to the recipients, but they could not be described as risk-takers. In each case the parties were irredeemably at cross-purposes. The claimants should have recovered, either because their intended basis was never fulfilled and they were not risk-takers or, which is not quite the same, because where parties are at cross-purposes there is no basis *ab initio* at all for the retention of benefits.[48] The latter species of failure of basis *ab initio* was famously

[44] Sir Guenter Treitel, *The Law of Contract* (11th edition Sweet & Maxwell London 2003) 37–8, 847.

[45] [1926] AC 670 (HL).

[46] [2002] 1 All ER (Comm) 193 (PC).

[47] Discussed below, 211–2, 214.

[48] *Burgess v Rawnsley* [1975] Ch 429 (CA) may have to be reconsidered. Not having been deceived, the parties could be said to be risk-takers, but it is not obvious that the cross-purposes analysis would not have produced a different result.

illustrated in *Raffles v Wichelhaus*.[49] There, however, no more was decided than that, when cotton arrived ex *Peerless* from Bombay, the buyer did not have to pay if, there being two ships of that one name sailing from Bombay and nothing to indicate which one was meant, the buyer had been thinking of the October one and the seller of the December one.

The 'no basis' approach suggests that, on one or other of these analyses, the *Dextra* case was wrongly decided so far as its claim was excluded under question three (unjust). There was no basis for the Dextra payment. In view of the Bank of Jamaica's defence, no damage was done. If the third question had been put entirely independently of the fifth question (defences), the probable error would immediately have been revealed. The factual premiss would then have been that the Bank of Jamaica's assets were still swollen by the $3m. It would have been difficult to conclude that Dextra had no cause of action.

2. TRUST

A transfer upon trust is commonly voluntary in the sense that it is not made to fulfil any obligation. It is a transfer made to bring about a trust, and that purpose can fail for many reasons.

The most common cause of failure arises from the requirement that a trust, unless charitable, must have human beneficiaries ascertainable with sufficient certainty. Thus the *Vandervell* litigation[50] arose from the mode in which millionaire Tony Vandervell arranged a benefaction to the Royal College of Surgeons. He intended to do it in a tax-efficient way by giving the College shares and then declaring a dividend on those shares. Having shed their dividend on the College, the shares were to be recovered by his family's trust company. To that end he gave the trust company an option to acquire the shares at a fixed price. He named no beneficiaries. The Inland Revenue successfully maintained that the company was intended to hold the option and afterwards the shares on trust and that the trust had failed *ab initio* for want of beneficiaries. The consequence was that the benefactor had not escaped his liability for surtax. A restitutionary resulting trust had arisen, carrying the beneficial interest back to himself. More recently, in *Air Jamaica Ltd v Charlton*[51] the ultimate trust of the airline's pension fund, intended to be triggered by the discontinuation of the fund, was found to be void for perpetuity.

[49] (1864) 2 H & C 906, 159 ER 375.

[50] *Vandervell v IRC* [1967] 2 AC 291 (HL); *Re Vandervell's Trusts (No2)* [1974] Ch 269 (CA), reversing [1973] 3 WLR 744.

[51] [1999] 1 WLR 1399 (PC).

Again, unless saving legislation intervened, a resulting trust arose for contributors.

Sometimes the trust is initially valid but later fails. Thus, in *Re Abbott Fund Trusts*[52] a fund was created to look after two disabled ladies. There was no out-and-out gift for them. Nor was their interest restricted to a life estate. The fund was to be used, as to capital and income, to look after them, but nothing at all was said as to what was to happen to any surplus after their death. When they died and it turned out that there was indeed a surplus, the trust failed and a restitutionary resulting trust carried the surplus back to the donors. The line between initial and subsequent failure is very thin. In *Re Gillingham Bus Disaster Fund*[53] money was given by subscription to the mayors of the Medway Towns, first to relieve the victims of the disaster and thereafter for other 'worthy causes'. The gift for 'worthy causes' was immediately void as being a non-charitable purpose trust, but that nullity lay dormant until it turned out that there was a surplus.

In all these cases the basis of the trustee's receipt is that he shall hold on trust, and that basis fails. It used to be confidently asserted that the settlor must be presumed to have intended the benefit to return to him in the event of failure of the express trust. The resulting trust which brought about that effect (where 'resulting' means 'jumping back', from the Latin '*resulto*') was to be regarded as a trust arising from that genuinely implied intent, assisted by an evidential presumption.

Although saved from extinction, *obiter*, by Lord Browne-Wilkinson,[54] this presumption is unreal. It is a fiction of the same order as the implied contract which was used to explain restitution of mistaken payments. As Harman J said in *Re Gillingham Bus Disaster Fund*,[55] the true fact is that the transferor never gave a thought to the possible failure of the dispositions which he intended to make. Time and again a true presumption of intent to create a trust would therefore be rebutted by evidence that there was no such intent.

[52] [1900] 2 Ch 326.

[53] [1959] Ch 62 (CA) aff'g [1958] Ch 300.

[54] *Westdeutsche Landesbank Girozentrale v Islington BC* [1996] AC 669 (HL) 689 (Lord Goff), 703, 707–8 (Lord Browne-Wilkinson), drawing support from WJ Swadling 'A New Role for Resulting Trusts' (1996) 16 Leg St 110. However, Swadling himself does not apply his intent-based interpretation to the supposed presumption generated by a trust which fails. It is only in the other case—apparent gifts, discussed immediately below—that he thinks that there is a genuine implication that the asset be held on trust.

[55] [1958] Ch 300, 310.

The unforced explanation of these restitutionary trusts arising where an express trust fails lies in unjust enrichment. Unless, against the balance of probabilities, it can be shown that the settlor intended the fund to default to the benefit of the trustee or intended to abandon it, the basis of the transfer can be seen to have failed and, to reverse the trustee's unjust enrichment, the resulting trust arises and effects restitution. There is no need for a presumption because the balance of probabilities is that the settlor did not entertain these unusual intentions. At the most the presumption eliminates an advocate's exploitation of barely existent doubts as to where the natural onus might lie. The English for what has happened is failure of consideration, but the corruption of 'consideration' has forced us to prefer 'basis'.

3. GIFT

A gift, being by definition gratuitous, always lacks consideration in the sense of *quid pro quo*, but a birthday present is not an enrichment without a basis. Gift is a recognized explanation of enrichment. It is a basis which can fail either initially or subsequently. The reason why a gift fails *ab initio* is often impairment of intent.

(a) Initial Invalidation from Impaired Intent

A valid gift requires *animus donandi*, the intention to make a gift. If the gift is invalidated for want of the necessary intent, the basis of the transfer fails. Impaired intent renders the transfer voidable.[56] A common impairment is undue influence. In the leading case of *Allcard v Skinner*[57] a young Anglican nun had given all her worldly possessions to her order under the influence of the defendant, the Mother Superior. When she later left the order, she wanted her property back. She failed because she had let too much time pass. Had she acted less dilatorily she would have been able to recover the gift, save so far as it had been spent on good works. Within the relationship with the Mother Superior her autonomy had been heavily reduced. She had not been emancipated from that influence by independent advice.

Very recently in *Hammond v Osborn*[58] a middle-aged neighbour who for years cared devotedly for an elderly retired schoolmaster in very poor health received from him some time before he died a spontaneous gift of

[56] On degrees of invalidity, above, 125–7.

[57] (1887) 36 Ch D 145 (CA).

[58] [2002] EWCA Civ 885, *The Times* 18 July 2002; compare *Pesticcio v Huet* (also known as *Niersmans v Pesticcio*) [2004] EWCA Civ 372, (2004) 154 NLJ 643.

nearly all his wealth. She had not induced it, but he had become dependent on her and lacked access to the outside world. The Court of Appeal held the gift must be returned to the estate for his next of kin. In that relationship he too had lost his autonomy. He had not been given independent advice as to the consequences of his gift for his liability to tax or for his medical needs.

In Australia, in *Louth v Diprose*,[59] a solicitor, lovesick almost to the point of mental illness, likewise gave away nearly all that he had before he recovered his autonomy. In that case the High Court rested his right to restitution on her having played upon his weakness. It happened that he could show that she had concocted stories which exaggerated her need for help. The result should have been the same without that element of exploitation. The cases on undue influence offer no warrant for that requirement. It is not clear why the case was not fought on that ground. The perception of undue influence as a fault-based wrong constantly lurks just below the surface, but it has recently been twice repudiated by the Court of Appeal, first in *Hammond v Osborn* and then, with emphasis, in *Pesticcio v Huet*.[60]

Bargains are rarely invalidated for mistake because the ground rule is that each party to a bargain bears all those risks of disappointment which the contract does not place upon the other. Gifts are not bargains, and, although gift-givers do run some risks, as for instance of ingratitude, the giving of a gift is not in anything like the same degree a risk-taking enterprise. Consequently gifts are relatively easily invalidated on the ground of causative mistake, as where the donor made a gift to her daughter forgetting that she had done it once already[61] or where a voluntary settlement was made under a misapprehension of its tax consequences.[62] It remains to explore what is meant in this context by the proposition that the gift must have caused the enrichment. If an uncle gives £1,000 each to all his nephews and nieces and then finds that one of them is gay, the fact that he is a notorious homophobe will not in itself show that he made a mistake which caused that gift. At the very least the uncle would have to

[59] (1992) 175 CLR 621 (HCA).

[60] [2004] EWCA Civ 372 [1]–[2], [20]. See also P Birks, 'Undue Influence as Wrongful Exploitation' (2003) 120 LQR 34.

[61] *Lady Hood of Avalon v Mackinnon* [1909] 1 Ch 476; cf *Ogilvie v Littleboy* (1897) 13 TLR 399, 15 TLR 294.

[62] *Re Butlin's Settlement Trusts* [1976] Ch 251; *Gibbon v Mitchell* [1990] 1 WLR 1304; cf *Barclays Bank Ltd v WJ Simms & Son Ltd* [1980] QB 677 (QBD) 697 examples (1) and (2).

show that his belief as to sexual orientation was actively in his mind when the gift was made.

(b) Subsequent Invalidation from Unpurged Qualified Intent

Gifts can also fail after the donee receives them. In *Hussey v Palmer*[63] a mother-in-law recovered money which she had given to her son-in-law to enable him to extend his house so that she could live there with her daughter and him. The house was extended and she moved in. Relations became strained. In the end she had to find accommodation elsewhere. It was money given and received on the basis of a family arrangement, that she would live out her days in the son-in-law's house. From the outset it had been qualified and not absolute.

Muschinski v Dodds[64] is similar. A woman recovered money which she had invested in a home for her and her male partner. The home was co-owned, so that her input accrued in part to him. The relationship broke down. The High Court's view of the facts was that from the beginning the gift to the co-owner had been tied to the success of the personal and business relationship between the two of them. Before he took anything out of the house he had to repay her. The earlier Irish case of *P v P*[65] is the same. Money paid in contemplation of marriage was recoverable when no marriage ensued. By statute engagement gifts between the parties to the engagement are presumed to be absolute in the absence of evidence to the contrary.[66]

(c) The Presumption Against *animus donandi* (Gift-Giving Intent)

In the examples above, where gifts have failed from the outset or subsequently, the claimant has adduced positive evidence of impairment or conditionality in order to show that the gift was or became invalid. It is not easy to see how this onus of proof on the claimant can be satisfactorily related to the second presumption of resulting trust. The first such presumption, which was said to arise when an express trust failed, is, as we have seen, a fiction designed to explain consequences now better explained by unjust enrichment, and the presumption against gift to the intended trustee runs in harness with the natural onus.

The second presumption arises where the externalities indicate a gift to the defendant. The externalities of gift are gratuitous benefit, by a

[63] [1972] 1 WLR 1286 (CA).

[64] (1985) 160 CLR 583 (HCA).

[65] [1916] 2 IR 400; cf *Re Ames' Settlement* [1946] Ch 217.

[66] A gift such as an engagement ring is now presumed to be absolute until the contrary is affirmatively proved by the claimant: Law Reform (Miscellaneous Provisions) Act 1970 s 3.

direct transfer or by the provision of the resources for the acquisition. In the case of direct gratuitous transfers of land, but not provision of resources for the purchase of land, there is a doubt whether the presumption still arises.[67] The presumption reflects a reluctance on the part of the court of Chancery to accept that outside relationships of advancement—roughly those where in earlier centuries a court would not be surprised to find gifts given—a gratuitous benefit can have been intended as a gift. The externalities of gift were thus made to generate a presumption of resulting trust. Stripped of fiction, the presumption again presumes that the apparent donor had no *animus donandi*, no intent to make a gift or, as Professor Chambers has put it, no beneficial intent.[68] As the law stands it would seem therefore that, outside the relationships of advancement, the onus should always be on the apparent donee to show that a gift was intended.

If the nun in *Allcard v Skinner* was not entitled to that shift of the normal onus of proof, it would seem that the presumption against *animus donandi* can be rebutted by proof of defective intent, the very proof of which once again destroys the gift. It would make better sense to say that the presumption presumes the absence of *animus donandi* and to treat evidence of defective intent as corroborative. Certainly the outcome under the fourth question (rights) ought to be the same in all cases whether the beneficial intent is negatived by evidence or by presumption.

The shift of onus is often overlooked, and in some cases it is renounced. In *Hodgson v Marks*, which was a case of gratuitous transfer of land, the Court of Appeal itself preferred to decide the matter on the evidence without the help of the presumption rather than resolve the doubt mentioned above.[69] A woman transferred her house to her lodger to secure him against her nephew who held him in suspicion and wanted him out. The lodger promptly sold the house with her still in it. She established a resulting trust by relying directly upon the evidence that she positively intended that, beyond the paper title, he should take no benefit. In some cases where the presumption is relied upon an actual intent of that kind can anyhow be seen. In *Tinsley v Milligan*[70] a woman contributed a share of the price to the purchase of a house by her lover, the plan between the two being to allow the contributor to appear qualified for social security housing benefit. In such a case the intention of the

[67] This arises from the Law of Property Act 1925 s 60 (3). In *Hodgson v Marks* [1971] Ch 892 (CA) the Court of Appeal found itself able to evade an opportunity to resolve it.

[68] R Chambers, *Resulting Trusts* (OUP Oxford 1997) 32–3, 38.

[69] Note 67 above.

[70] [1994] 1 AC 340 (HL).

transferor or contributor is clearly an affirmative intention that, beyond the paper title, the transferee should take no benefit from the transfer. That does amount to an intention to create a trust, although where, as in these two cases, the subject matter is land the requirement of writing in the Law of Property Act section 53(1) prevents its taking effect as an express trust.

Mr Swadling maintains that this presumption, arising from the externalities of gift, always mimics these cases. That is, the presumption presumes the trust intent apparent on these facts. He goes one step further. He says that the presumed trust is to be treated as express trust.[71] It is difficult to follow him in this view. It does admittedly have the advantage that it makes sense of the non-application of the presumption in cases of gifts made by mistake or under undue influence, for evidence of defectively intended gift is indeed incompatible with an affirmative intent to create a trust. But a presumption of intent to create a trust would be randomly rebutted depending only on whether evidence could be found to show that in truth the transferor had never given any thought to the matter.[72] The simple presumption against *animus donandi* is, by contrast, merely corroborated by such evidence.

The mess in which the law finds itself in this area arises directly from the failure to recognize the law of unjust enrichment and from the consequent necessity of explaining reactions to failure of basis by the invocation of fictitious manifestations of intent. Fictitious contracts have at length been abandoned. Fictitious declarations of trust have proved more obstinately persistent. The persistence is doubly complicated by their being divided between two types of trust, constructive trusts and resulting trusts. The last chapter of this book tries to sort out that division, not to preserve it for use but to understand it well enough to eliminate it.[73]

4. OTHER PURPOSES

We have been considering transfers the purpose of which has been contract, trust, or gift. The threefold division is useful for exposition and illustration, but the reader will certainly have realized that it has little or no technical significance, for the principle is always the same, namely that if the goal of the enrichment is not achieved the recipient must make

[71] W Swadling, 'A Hard Look at *Hodgson v Marks*' in P Birks and F Rose, *Restitution and Equity* vol 1 (Mansfield Press LLP London 2000) 75, returning to the defence of Swadling, 'A New Role for Resulting Trusts' (1996) 16 LS 110, reprinted in *Restitution and Equity* vol 1, 285.

[72] Chambers (n 68 above) 21.

[73] Below, 301–7.

restitution: the basis of the enrichment will have failed. The same is true even in the group which was dealt with first, where the enrichment was believed to be obligatory and there was no obligation to discharge. The legal insignificance of the division needs to be underlined as we come to the residual fourth category, to avert the danger of a sterile anxiety as to whether any given example really is a failure of a nominate purpose or belongs here under 'other purposes'. It is often open to argument.

In *Kerrison v Glyn, Mills, Currie & Co*[74] the appellant claimant was bound by contract to reimburse American bankers who in their turn were to cover certain liabilities of a Mexican silver mine. He deposited a sum to the respondent bank in anticipation of that liability, which in the event never materialized because the American bankers became bankrupt before laying out any money for the Mexican mine. The House of Lords held that he could recover, explaining the outcome on the ground of mistake, overlooking the fact that, even under the old regime of specific unjust factors, a mistake as to the future, a misprediction, would not have been a ground for liability.

The result could not be reached through mistake, but payment made on the basis of a liability to be met in the future is a perfectly good payment on a basis which may or may not hold good. The Roman equivalent here was not the *condictio indebiti* but the *condictio causa data causa non secuta* (debt for things given on a basis, that basis not having followed).[75] This corruption of 'consideration' again meant that English lawyers had no words to describe a payment made on the basis of, say, an obligation later to come into being. 'To discharge a future liability' is not a purpose which fits in any of the three previous categories, unless one would wish to construe it as an offer to be accepted by a promise so to apply it. One who prefers that construction will place it with 'contracts to be concluded', 1(b) above.

In *Re Cleadon Trust Ltd*,[76] a director paid off liabilities of his company without authority, merely assuming that the company would later agree to repay him. In the event it did not repay him. Without his own necessarily disqualified vote, the board was inquorate and could not pass the necessary resolution. He was understood merely to have taken the risk that it

[74] (1911) 81 LJKB 465 (HL).

[75] For Lord Mansfield's adoption of this Roman model, Sir William Evans, *Essays on the Action for Money Had and Received, on the Law of Insurances, and on the Law of Bills of Exchange and Promissory Notes* (Liverpool 1802), 25–34 (repr [1998] Restitution L Rev 1, 9–10).

[76] [1939] Ch 286 (CA).

might not reimburse him. However, there is nothing wrong with construing a payment for a voluntary reciprocation as a payment made on a basis which may or may not hold good.

A non-contractual reciprocation does not fit into any of the three previous categories. However, very fine variations of fact can affect the classification. The old case of *Holmes v Hall* illustrates.[77] Some papers of the claimant's testator were in the hands of the defendant. The claimant 'to get the writings, gave him so much money, whereupon he promised to give up the writings, but afterwards refused.'[78] Taken literally this yields the improbable interpretation that the payment was for a non-contractual reciprocation. More plausibly, it might have been a payment intended as an offer to conclude a contract, in which case it would again fall back in 1(b) above. A third possibility is that there was first a contract—money for papers—and then an obligatory payment under that contract, subsequently terminated for repudiatory breach. That case would fall under the *condictio indebiti*, the payment being originally due but the obligation being subsequently terminated.[79] In a case such as *Re Cleadon Trust Ltd* the facts which would negative risk-taking would very likely also move the construction of the story towards the second or even the third of these possibilities.

This discussion makes it necessary to emphasize once more that these categories are expository. So far as we can see from the report, in *Holmes v Hall* Holt CJ quite rightly allowed the claimant's action for money had and received without feeling the need to resolve the factual ambiguities. On each of the three possibilities, the basis of the enrichment failed.

C. NON-PARTICIPATORY ENRICHMENTS

One person can be enriched at another's expense absolutely without that other's collaboration. The clearest case is where the enrichee acts without the other's knowledge. When a pickpocket takes my wallet I am totally ignorant of the haemorrhage of my wealth. A service can also be taken secretly, as with a stowaway or free-riding freight. Ignorance, in the sense of not being aware of what is happening, is not the only case. The enrichment may accrue to the enrichee with my knowledge but in circumstances in which I am powerless to prevent it. A burglar may tie up his victims, who then see but cannot prevent the taking of their jewellery.

[77] (1704) Holt KB 36, 90 ER 917. [78] Ibid.
[79] For these kinds of invalidity, see above, 125–7.

Or it may be just a matter of distance: I am too far away to stop the enrichee breaking my car window and snatching my camera. There is a more complex sub-set of these cases of powerlessness, which we might call by-benefits (by analogy with by-products). If I irrigate my allotment, yours lower down the hill will also benefit, and if I arrange to graze my sheep on your field you will need no fertilizer. These by-benefits need to be considered separately.

1. AT LAW

In general, an absolutely involuntary enrichment will have no explanatory basis at all. There is not even any putative basis. Questions 1 (enrichment) and 2 (at the expense of the claimaint) can give rise to awkward problems, as we have seen,[80] but question 3 (unjust) is relatively straightforward. However, the curse of dualism has again created problems in that on the Chancery side there has been an inadvertent disapplication of the law of unjust enrichment, which, even though it is no more than one of the legacies of the failure to recognize the independence of the law of unjust enrichment, is proving difficult to overcome.

At law the picture is clear enough. In *Holiday v Sigil*[81] the claimant had lost a £500 note. The defendant who found it owed the claimant that sum as money had and received to his use. That is the simplest model. The leading case is now *Lipkin Gorman v Karpnale Ltd.*[82] A solicitor addicted to gambling took hundreds of thousands of pounds from his firm's client account. He gambled it away in the casino at the Playboy Club in Park Lane. The House of Lords held that the casino, which was taken to have had no reason at all to believe that it was dealing with a thief, was under an obligation arising from unjust enrichment to repay the amount received, less its own consequential payments out made on the few occasions when the gambler won. Although, as we have seen, the facts were actually more complex because of the gambler's being an authorized signatory on the client account,[83] the model from which their Lordships worked was that in which *X* steals *C*'s money and gives it to *D*.

The restitutionary liability is of exactly the same structure as that which arises from the mistaken payment of a debt not due. No fault need be shown, and no wrong proved. In the *Lipkin* case the tort of conversion was explicitly ruled out.[84] The strict liability can, however, be defeated by

[80] Above, 63–9, 86–7, 93–8.
[81] (1826) 2 C & P 176, 172 ER 81; cf *Moffatt v Kazana* [1969] 2 QB 152 (QB).
[82] (1991) 2 AC 548 (HL), followed in *Trustee of Jones v Jones* [1997] Ch 159 (CA).
[83] Above, 95–6.
[84] [1991] 2 AC 548 (HL) 574, 578 (Lord Goff).

defences. In particular, it is absolutely defeated where a recipient from a third party gives value in good faith for the money under a valid contract.[85] If the gambler had been addicted to expensive food, the restaurants which he patronized would not have been liable at all. Gambling contracts, even of licensed casinos, are void. In the *Lipkin Gorman* case, the effect was to push the casino back to the defence of change of position. It could not say that it was a bona fide purchaser for value. Its liability was instead reduced by the amounts it had been caused to pay out when, occasionally, the gambler won.

2. IN EQUITY

One consequence of the long failure to recognize the law of unjust enrichment is a misguided intuitive resistance to the strict liability, subject to defences, which it requires.[86] This error arising from unfamiliarity is the only possible explanation of the fact that, as against a recipient out of possession, those who have only equitable title behind a trust have been confined to a fault-based claim. The *Lipkin Gorman* claim has been withheld.

In *Re Montagu's Settlement Trusts*[87] trustees, in breach of trust, had released some trust assets to the tenant for life, the 10th Duke of Manchester. The Duke was thus a donee. He had not given value. The assets in question were valuable chattels, such as paintings and furniture. The trustees had a power to release them but only after taking certain steps, which they had not taken. The action was brought against the estate of the 10th Duke by his successor, the 11th Duke, who was a beneficiary under the trust. It had not been shown that the 10th Duke's estate still included any of the trust assets or their traceable proceeds, so that the only question was whether he had been under a personal obligation to repay the value he had received. Megarry V-C took the view that, even against a donee, the claimant had to establish that the old Duke had been at fault.

The required degree of fault has proved elusive. Megarry V-C thought only dishonesty would do. More recently, in *Bank of Credit and Commerce International (Overseas) Ltd v Akindele*,[88] the Court of Appeal unhelpfully confined itself to saying that the defendant must have behaved unconscionably, which covers all possibilities. Defences aside, Chief

[85] The casino's defences are discussed below, 210–12, 240–5.
[86] Above, 5–9.
[87] [1987] Ch 264.
[88] [2000] 4 All ER 221 (CA).

Akindele appears to have escaped liability for the receipt of BCCI money as a result of a factual inquiry resembling an inquiry into constructive notice: he neither knew of nor ought reasonably to have discovered the improprieties going on inside that bank.[89]

In the absence of a cogent explanation to the contrary, to insist on fault is to disapply the law of unjust enrichment in favour of the law of wrongs. The equitable wrong is 'knowing receipt'. Professor LD Smith has attempted to defend the disapplication of the law of unjust enrichment.[90] However, his arguments are chiefly historical, and history cannot justify the muddle it has made. His valiant effort is further disabled by inconsistency within the Chancery cases themselves. The *Lipkin Gorman* claim has not been disapplied where money is misdirected from the estate of a deceased person.

In *Ministry of Health v Simpson*,[91] the House of Lords confirmed that Caleb Diplock's next of kin had strict personal and proprietary claims against all the beneficaries to whom his residual estate had been misdirected, the executors having failed to spot the nullity of the bequest. On occasion, moreover, this has crept beyond the law of succession. A claim of the same strict *Lipkin Gorman* kind has been recognized as in principle available to a beneficiary against a donee from a dishonest fiduciary,[92] and to a company against persons overpaid by its liquidator.[93]

A powerful recent dictum of Lord Millett now gives notice that the anomalous disapplication of the law of unjust enrichment from misdirections under *inter vivos* trusts will be put right.[94] Lord Nicholls, writing extra-judicially,[95] has indicated that this should not be done by insisting that the wrong of 'knowing receipt' be stripped of 'knowing' and transferred to the law of unjust enrichment but rather by recognizing a liability in unjust enrichment alongside the wrong. That will be the better course.

[89] [2000] 4 All ER 221 (CA) 237–8.

[90] LD Smith, 'Unjust Enrichment, Property and the Structure of Trusts' (2000) 116 LQR 412.

[91] [1951] AC 251 (HL) upholding *Re Diplock* [1948] Ch 465 (CA).

[92] *GL Baker Ltd v Medway Building & Supplies Ltd* [1958] 2 All ER 532 (Danckwerts J), [1958] 3 All ER 540 (CA).

[93] *Butler v Broadhead* [1975] Ch 97 (Ch).

[94] *Twinsectra Ltd v Yardley* [2002] UKHL 12, [2002] 2 WLR 802 [105]. So also Birks in earlier work: P Birks, 'Misdirected Funds: Restitution from the Recipient' [1989] LMCLQ 296.

[95] Lord Nicholls of Birkenhead, 'Knowing Receipt: The Need for a New Landmark' in WR Cornish, R Nolan, J O'Sullivan, and G Virgo (eds), *Restitution, Past, Present and Future: Essays in Honour of Gareth Jones* (Hart Oxford 1998) 231.

The present muddle has been brought about by trying to make one cause of action do the work of two.

Ignorance and powerlessness do not automatically connote absence of basis. In a rare case there will be a sufficient legal explanation for the taking of the claimant's wealth. An obvious case is execution of judgment. Prerogative requisition, outside the War Damage Act 1965, probably does not entitle the Crown to take without paying.[96]

3. BY-BENEFITS

If I live in a flat, and you live above me, in winter my central heating will cut your fuel bills. Heat rises. Investment in insulation may minimize the escape of the warmth for which I am paying, but it is true in a sense that I am powerless to prevent this benefit accruing to you. You are enriched in that you are saving heating expenditure which you would inevitably incur if I turned my heating off, and the enrichment is coming from me. Similarly, if you have a flat which overlooks the Oval you will be able to watch test matches without paying.

In cases of this kind one person is enriched at another's expense and that other is powerless to prevent it. But this is not an unjust enrichment. There is no right to restitution.[97] The best explanation seems to be that the basis of the enrichment is gift. Matters must be judged at the commencement of the principal activity. If the principal activity is freely intended, in the way that I intend to heat my flat, the incidents of that activity are also intended, however little they may be wanted. A terrorist who plants a bomb in a shopping centre may not want to kill the shoppers but obliquely intends their death. In the same way I may indeed be powerless to prevent your enrichment, but I obliquely intend the inevitable by-benefit to accrue gratuitously to you, my upstairs neighbour. The rising heat is thus a gift, although possibly not warmly wished.

It is quite different when, judged at the time of the principal activity, the actor is not acting of his own free will. If, for example, two people are liable for the same debt and one is called upon to pay, the other's obligation is discharged. If, as between the party paying and himself, that other was primarily liable, as where the principal debtor paid and the party paying was his surety, he is enriched at the payer's expense as to the whole amount which he was bound to pay. If both were liable in the same degree, then he was enriched to the extent of the share that he was bound

[96] *Nissan v Attorney-General* [1968] 1 QB 286 (CA) 349–51 (Winn LJ).
[97] *Edinburgh Tramway Co v Courtenay* 1909 SC 99.

to pay. These enrichments are by-benefits arising from the payment to the creditor. In the former case the payer is entitled to reimbursement, in the latter to contribution.

In the case of the upstairs neighbour, the would-be claimant cannot show that the enrichment was unjust because in choosing to heat his own flat he intends gratuitously to heat the neighbour's flat. In the case of the discharged debt, the initial act which was the debtor's discharge of his debt was not freely chosen but obligatory. In such a case the by-benefit to the defendant, who was also liable, was indeed one which was also not intended. In the first case, the cause of enrichment is a grudging gift, in the second it has no basis at all. The discharged debtor can offer no explanation at all as to why he should retain his enrichment. It is an enrichment without any explanatory basis. This is one area in which 'no basis' does come close to lay usage, for the truth is that the reason why we think the defendant should reimburse or contribute is that there was no reason at all why he should reap the by-benefit.

It is a difficult question whether one who pays under a liability which is voluntarily incurred can make the same argument. In *Owen v Tate*[98] the claimant, by offering his own personal guarantee instead, induced a bank to release security given by his friend for the defendant's debt. The bank called on him to pay. He was denied reimbursement. Scarman LJ stated that 'if without antecedent request a person assumes an obligation . . . for the benefit of another, the law will, as a general rule, refuse him a right of indemnity.'[99] That is a tenable position, but as a matter of authority it appears to be wrong. It overlooked the Mercantile Law Amendment Act 1856, section 5, which allows all sureties to be subrogated to the creditor's claim. That Act apart, it is out of step with *Edmunds v Wallingford*,[100] where the opposite view was taken when one person's goods were lawfully taken to pay another's debts.[101]

All that has been said of discharge applies equally to imperfect discharge, as described above.[102] Thus an insurance company which pays a loss is entitled to go against the imperfectly discharged tortfeasor who caused it. But the imperfection of the discharge means that that claim must be made by subrogation to the still unextinguished right of the insured against the tortfeasor. When one of its oil tankers spilled oil on

[98] [1976] 1 QB 402 (CA).

[99] [1976] 1 QB 402 (CA) 411–12.

[100] (1885) 14 QBD 811 (CA) 816, disapproving *England v Marsden* (1866) LR 1 CP 529.

[101] Compare C Mitchell, *The Law of Contribution and Reimbursement* (OUP Oxford 2003) [6.37]–[6.40]

[102] Above, 61. Also below, 296–9.

coastal crofts, Esso paid the loss under an agreement then in force between all such companies.[103] The spillage had been caused by negligent construction of the engines of a tugboat. Esso tried to sue the negligent manufacturers and failed. Its only claim, if it had any claim at all, was to be subrogated to the unextinguished rights of the crofters. The argument from *Edmunds v Wallingford* which suggests that *Owen v Tate* was wrongly decided, applies equally to this case of imperfect discharge.

D. CONCLUSION

The previous chapter sought to show that English law has to abjure the two families of unjust factors—deficient intent and policy imperatives—and re-orient its law of unjust enrichment to 'no basis'. Accepting the risk of over-simplification, this one has outlined the way in which 'no basis' works. The question is always the same. What, if any, was the 'consideration' for the enrichment? But we could not use the corrupted word 'consideration'. Instead, preferring 'basis' from the choice between 'reason, ground, or basis', what, if any, was the basis of the enrichment? The unjust enrichment is the enrichment which has no basis.

The chapter divided enrichments between participatory and non-participatory, and, within the former, between obligatory and voluntary, and, within voluntary, between contract, trust, gift, and other bases. The division serves a useful expository purpose. It allows us to review a full range of possibilities. But it does not alter the fact that there is no more than one question. 'No basis' has a surgical simplicity. The unjust factors will seem increasingly cumbersome. They have also proved unreliable, capable of producing wrong results. A sub-theme throughout has been that the basis of an enrichment cannot be identified without an eye kept constantly on risk-taking. The busker wants to be paid but takes the risk of getting nothing. The basis of his offering is not reciprocal payment but gift.

[103] *The Esso Bernicia* [1989] AC 643 (HL).

Part IV

The Right to Restitution

7

Rights *in personam*

The fourth question asks what kind of right the claimant acquires. Above various sub-sets of each, the choice always lies between a right *in personam* (a personal right) and a right *in rem* (a property right), or both. In cases in which both kinds of right arise the claimant must elect which one he wants to realize. The election need not finally be made until judgment. That proposition is not incompatible with another, noticed above,[1] to the effect that, when title to the asset allegedly constituting the enrichment is in the claimant, the assertion of a personal claim arising from unjust enrichment entails its renunciation. The election is essentially between strategies. Until judgment one can pursue both.

Throughout this part it will be helpful to bear in mind two extreme positions, neither of which turns out to be correct in English law. One, which might be called the civilian extreme, is that the only response generated by the event called unjust enrichment is a right *in personam* entitling the claimant to restitution from the enrichee. The other is that every instance of unjust enrichment generates both a right *in personam* and a right *in rem*.

The position taken in this book is that the *in personam* response is indeed invariably available, but the *in rem* response is not. However, the *in rem* response is found as an additional response in a large and on reflection homogeneous class of case. That restitution of unjust enrichment is also effected through rights *in rem* or, synonymously, by property rights is, as we shall see, denied by some scholars and deplored by others. Denial is not an option. The least contentious example is also the most common. It is provided by all those cases in which the enrichee acquires a voidable title. There the claimant's title passes to the enrichee but, because the recipient is unjustly enriched, the claimant obtains a sub-species of right *in rem* which takes the form of a power *in rem* and enables him to rescind the transaction and revest in himself the thing which he has transferred.

[1] Above, 66–8.

The principal task of this chapter is to establish that the right *in personam* is invariably available. Restitution of unjust enrichment through rights *in rem* belongs in the next chapter. The discussion in this chapter entails a certain degree of anticipation of the business of the next, because in the past it was assumed in some situations that the standard *in personam* response was displaced by the response *in rem*. That is no longer true. The right *in personam* is always available. It is undeniable, however, that there are some patches where the generality of that assertion rests on principle which is as yet imperfectly instantiated in authority.

A. THREE SYNONYMS

It will already be apparent that there is a distracting number of different ways of saying what is said in the introductory paragraphs. The multiplication of vocabulary easily multiplies entities. First, already signalled, the Latin in 'rights *in personam*' is often anglicized to produce 'personal rights'. There is nothing worrying about that, but it requires vigilance against a misleading reorientation. 'Personal rights' suggests rights of a person, whereas a right *in personam* is a right against a person in the sense that it is a right that that person make some performance. The claimant holds the string and the other end is around the other's neck. Where a claimant has a right that the defendant pay him the value of an enrichment, the right is not called 'personal' because it belongs to a person but because it is exigible against, and only against, the person who must make the performance. The string is around that person's neck.

Secondly, instead of rights *in personam* or personal rights, we can speak of obligations. The law of rights *in personam* is usually called the law of obligations. *C*'s right against the person of *D*, that *D* make some performance, necessarily correlates with *D*'s obligation to make that performance. It follows that when we say that obligations arise from, among other events, wrongs and unjust enrichments, we can as easily say, looking from the other end, that rights *in personam* so arise, or personal rights.

Again, if we say that the English law of unjust enrichment belongs largely but not exclusively in the law of obligations, we mean exactly the same as when we say that the routine response to unjust enrichment is a right *in personam*. 'Obligation' contains within it the metaphor of being tied or bound to a performance. '*Ligare*' means 'to tie' and gives us both 'ligament' and 'liable'. In Justinian's famous definition of an obligation the metaphor within the word recurs more than once: 'An obligation is a legal bond which ties us to the necessity of making some performance in accordance with the laws of our state (*Obligatio est iuris vinculum quo necessitate adstringimur alicuius solvendae rei secundum nostrae civitatis iura*).'[2]

Just as the law of obligations is the law of rights *in personam*, so the law of property is the law of rights *in rem*. A right *in rem* is a proprietary right or simply a property right. The string in the claimant's hand is attached, at the other end, to a *res*, a thing. We will return at the beginning of the next chapter to the difference between *in personam* and *in rem* or, synonymously, between the coordinate categories of obligations and property. The law of unjust enrichment straddles the boundary between the two. Unjust enrichments give rise to both rights *in personam* (obligations) and rights *in rem* (property rights). The same, as we will see in the next section, is true of wrongs.

Thirdly, rights *in personam* and rights *in rem* can often be referred to as 'remedies'. Whether a particular right can be called a remedy depends entirely on whether its relation to its causative event triggers the metaphor of cure. If I promise to build you a house, you acquire a right *in personam* exigible against me, that I so build. That right cannot be called a remedy, because its causative event, the contract, is not a grievance or anxiety. There is therefore nothing bad to trigger the metaphor of cure. But if I commit a wrong against you, as where I defame you or injure your foot or break my contract with you, your right that I pay you damages can be called a remedy, because it serves to cure the wrong from which it arose. Unjust enrichments are never wrongs. By definition an unjust enrichment at the expense of another is an enrichment which must be given up for a reason which is not, or is not being treated as a contract or a wrong. Nevertheless, an unjust enrichment of one person is a trouble, grievance, or anxiety to another. For that reason, the metaphor of cure is not out of place and the claimant's right to restitution can be called a remedy.

It is advisable not to fall too easily into the habit of calling a right a remedy. It has the consequence, because 'remedy' is such a sloppy word, that things which need to be contrasted find themselves being yoked together. A right of whatever kind, so long as it remains unsatisfied, is a bird in the bush. In the case of this particular causative event, the bird in the hand is restitution of the enrichment to the claimant. The bird in the bush becomes a bird in the hand when the enrichee willingly complies or, if he will not, when the court makes its order and that order is executed.

[2] Justinian, *Institutes* 3.13 pr.

Even the court's order is still only a bird in the bush, although we often speak, over-optimistically, as though, when once the court has spoken, the rest will certainly follow. Many judgments remain unsatisfied.

There are thus at least two distinct steps to the final realization of rights, first the order and then the execution. Both, or both together, have a better claim to the word 'remedy' than does the right born of the event. The judge's order novates the rights which the claimant brings into court. It may also transform them. In the case of rights *in personam* arising from unjust enrichment the order of the court novates but does not transform; it only replicates the right with which the defendant would not willingly comply.[3] Nevertheless it is the replicating right born of the judge's order, and not the right which the claimant brought into court, that goes to execution. In this book we are for the most part not concerned with these later stages in the realization of rights but only with the rights which immediately arise from the causative event, and here those rights are not called remedies.

B. STRUCTURAL SYMMETRY WITH WRONGS

It will be helpful to bear in mind from the outset the parallel model of the law's response to wrongs. The structural symmetry serves as a constant reminder that there is nothing bizarre about a causative event which has one foot in the law of obligations and the other in the law of property. When a civil wrong is committed the routine response gives the victim a right *in personam* entitling him to recover money from the wrongdoer. There are sub-forms of that response. First, there is a right *in personam* to compensation. The level of compensation varies according to the base from which the loss to be compensated is measured. Secondly, some wrongs generate a right *in personam* to recover the wrongdoer's gain, a right to restitution rather than compensation. Some generate both compensatory and restitutionary rights, although the victim can never fully realize both. Thirdly, still on the obligations side, outrageous wrongs sometimes give rise to a right to recover punitive damages.

In contrast to these species of response *in personam*, the law occasionally responds to an acquisitive wrong by giving the victim a property right in the wrongdoer's ill-gotten gains. *Attorney-General of Hong Kong v Reid*

[3] The distinction between 'replicative' and 'transformative' is borrowed from Rafal Zakrzewski, whose doctoral thesis (Oxford 2003) introduced me to this illuminating terminology for the classification of remedies, where 'remedy' is the order of a court and the right arising from it. The book of this thesis is due to be published by OUP in 2005.

was such a case.[4] A corrupt prosecutor received bribes in flagrant breach of his fiduciary duty to the government of Hong Kong. It was held that each bribe received, though his at law, instantly became in equity the property of the victim of the breach. In other words, the law turned the corrupt prosecutor into a trustee of the bribes.

The regime for unjust enrichments is structurally, but not quantitatively, symmetrical with the regime for wrongs. Here, in comparison with wrongs, the *in personam* response is less various and the *in rem* response is less rare. When an unjust enrichment happens, the routine response is a right *in personam*, which is always restitutionary and never compensatory.[5] Not routinely but certainly not as rarely as with wrongs, an unjust enrichment gives rise to a right *in rem* in the enriching asset. The incidence of that proprietary response is the subject of the next chapter.

C. THE CONTENT OF THE RIGHT *IN PERSONAM*

The right *in personam* which arises from unjust enrichment is a right to restitution, a right that the enrichee give up his gain. The difficulties of the word 'restitution' are discussed in more detail in last part of this book.[6] For the moment it suffices to say that its meaning is stretched beyond ordinary usage. The functional equivalent in German law is the noun '*Herausgabe*' from the verb '*herausgeben*'.[7] These words are unequivocal in reaching all givings up, with no hint of a restriction to giving back.

A substantive point hides behind this. We saw in Chapter 4 that there is an important question whether the claimant in unjust enrichment must have suffered a loss corresponding to the defendant's enrichment.[8] By insisting, artificially but firmly, on an enlargement of the everyday sense of 'restitution' we avoid being accidentally trapped by the choice of a word into believing that the answer must be yes. If 'restitution' meant

[4] [1994] 1 AC 324 (PC). Compare *Daraydan Holdings Ltd v Solland International Holdings Ltd* [2004] EWHC 622 (Ch) where Lawrence Collins J considered the High Court free to follow *Reid* in departing from Court of Appeal authority which had stood for more than a century.

[5] For a possibly accidental statutory exception in the case of innocent misrepresentation, see 176–7 below.

[6] Below, 277–83.

[7] Para 812 BGB. BS Markesinis, W Lorenz, and G Dannemann, *The Law of Contracts and Restitution: A Comparative Introduction* (OUP Oxford 1997) 755–6.

[8] Above, 78–86.

'giving back', no other answer would be possible. The larger meaning leaves the matter open. An alternative strategy to the same effect would be to switch from 'restitution' to 'disgorgement', which has no restrictive overtone.

We concluded, not without anxiety, that the answer should be no, there is no need for corresponding loss. There is nothing to add at this point to the earlier discussion, the only point being that such crucial questions as whether the claimant must have suffered a loss corresponding to the enrichee's gain must be decided by rational argument and analysis, independently of the accidents of available vocabulary. The broader word binds no-one to the broader view. The narrower term mesmerizes. So, let it be that, subject to all the anxieties and without prejudice to them, the entitled claimant's right *in personam* is a right that the enrichee give up to him the enrichment obtained at his expense.

1. AN IMMEDIATE RIGHT TO THE VALUE OF THE ENRICHMENT RECEIVED

The enrichment is measured in the first instance at the moment of its receipt, although the operation of defences may reduce the amount for which judgment is finally given. The defence of disenrichment, in particular, has the effect of reducing liability to the amount of the enrichment still abstractly surviving at the moment at which the state of the defendant's knowledge becomes such that good faith requires him not to regard the enrichment as being at his disposition. This and other defences are discussed in Chapters 11 and 12. The word 'abstractly' has the meaning assigned to it in Chapter 3.[9]

In German law the obligation to make restitution is expressed as being in the first instance an obligation to surrender the specific asset received. The right to its value in money arises only when it becomes impossible for the claimant to have back the specific thing.[10] English law takes a markedly different line. From the outset the claimant's right *in personam* is a right that the enrichee surrender the money value of the enrichment.

This is unequivocal in the words of the old actions.[11] In the action for money had and received, the claimant declared that the defendant was indebted to him in such and such a sum, the cause of the indebtedness being the receipt of that much money for his benefit. The claim was not

[9] Above, 69–70.

[10] § 818 (II) BGB.

[11] The actual wording of the four relevant actions, somewhat abbreviated, is given in Chapter 12 below, 287.

for the coins or notes received. It was from first to last a claim to an abstract debt measured by the amount of that receipt. The same is true of the other relevant members of the *assumpsit* family. It is true, for example, of money paid to another to procure some benefit for the defendant and of *quantum meruit* for services and *quantum valebant* for goods. All these lay directly for the money value of that which the defendant received.

Just as the right is not a right to a pecuniary quantification of a prior right to have a specific thing, so also it is not a right to damages for the wrong of not giving up a specific thing. Rights born of wrongs are secondary rights, because every wrong is an infringement of an antecedent right which is itself independent of wrongdoing and as such primary.[12] The receipt of a mistaken payment is not a wrong. Nor is any other unjust enrichment. The right to restitution which is born of that event is a primary right to be paid the value of the enrichment. That right arises in most cases at the moment of the receipt.[13] In cases in which the basis fails after the receipt, the cause of action cannot be complete until then.

2. NO PERSONAL RIGHT TO BE GIVEN SPECIFIC THINGS

Subject to one exceptional case which will be considered immediately below, there is no case at all of a right *in personam* arising from unjust enrichment in which the claimant has what used to be called a *ius ad rem adquirendam*, a right to the acquisition of a specific thing.[14] Such a right supposes a specific thing in which the claimant has as yet no proprietary right, and a defendant who has come under an obligation to convey it to the claimant. A right of that kind is unequivocally personal. It is a right *in personam* to have an asset transferred. But there appears to be no example in the law of unjust enrichment.

At law such a right would not be specifically enforceable, so that it would anyhow be turned into money by the judgment. In equity, where rights are under certain conditions specifically enforceable, it seems that

[12] For further discussion P Birks (ed), *The Classification of Obligations* (OUP Oxford 1997) 1, 23–4.

[13] *Baker v Courage Co Ltd* [1910] 1 KB 56, endorsed in *Kleinwort Benson v Lincoln CC* [1999] 2 AC 349 (HL) 386, 409.

[14] Already known in England in the 17th century this is discussed by John Austin: R Campbell (ed), J Austin, *Lectures on Jurisprudence or the Philosophy of Law* (3rd edn John Murray London 1869) 386, 993: A Pretto in P Birks and A Pretto (eds), *Themes in Comparative Law in Honour of Bernard Rudden* (OUP Oxford 2002) 74. The phrase '*ad rem*' is painful Latin; it is an abbreviation of the longer form with the gerundive, as in the text above. Neither the abbreviated nor the fuller version were known in the first life of Roman law.

the maxim that equity treats that as done which ought to be done will turn the person owing such a duty into a trustee and thus raise a proprietary interest in the claimant.[15] Professor Sir Roy Goode resists that proposition. He thinks it should be possible to recognize an equitable obligation to make such a transfer, and to make it specifically enforceable, without attracting the maxim and hence without automatically turning the *ius ad rem* into a *ius in rem*.[16] In America, by denaturing the constructive trust and ignoring or disapplying the maxim, some cases do appear to have achieved a free-standing duty to transfer a thing. But those cases are muddled and suspect even in their native land. They are unlikely to prove attractive in any jurisdiction with a stronger historical sense of the nature of trusts which arise by operation of law.[17]

3. A SPECIALIZED CASE: THE RIGHT TO BE SUBROGATED TO A CLAIM

The conclusion from the previous paragraphs does not mean that specific restitution is unknown to English law, only that it is unknown through rights *in personam*. Where a right *in rem* arises, the courts will sometimes order specific restitution. There is, however, one relevant but highly specialized exception on the *in personam* side. The Chancery maxim which treats obligations to transfer things as immediately constitutive of proprietary rights bites on obligations to give, not on obligations to do or abstain from doing. Subrogation, so far as it is not merely metaphorical, rests on an obligation to abstain.

In the particular configuration of facts which we have called 'imperfect discharge',[18] the law, instead of giving the claimant a direct restitutionary right against the imperfect enrichee, puts him in charge of the realization of the right-holder's unextinguished right against that imperfectly enriched defendant. This is subrogation properly so-called, which Dr Mitchell calls 'simple subrogation' in contrast with purely metaphorical 'reviving subrogation'.[19] In subrogation proper the active

[15] In *A-G for Hong Kong v Reid*, a case of restitution for a wrong, Lord Templeman said that each bribe as it came in was immediately caught by the maxim so as to create a constructive trust, [1994] 1 AC 324 (PC) 331.

[16] RM Goode 'Property and Unjust Enrichment' in AS Burrows (ed), *Essays on the Law of Restitution* (OUP Oxford 1991) 221–3, 244, 246.

[17] Condemned by the reporter for the new Restatement: A Kull, 'Restitution in Bankruptcy: Reclamation and Constructive Trust' (1998) 72 American Bankruptcy LJ 265.

[18] Above, 61.

[19] C Mitchell, *The Law of Subrogation* (OUP Oxford 1994) 4–7; C Mitchell, *The Law of Contribution and Reimbursement* (OUP Oxford 2003) [2.33]–[2.44].

claimant is substituted for the inert right-holder as the manager of the right-holder's litigation. This substitution rests on a right *in personam* which correlates with a duty on the right-holder to remain inert and to permit something which he could otherwise prevent.

Subrogation proper mostly goes on at law. That is to say, in the days of the institutional separation of law and equity, it was the management of legal claims in courts of common law which was taken out of the hands of the right-holder and given to the substitute. The obligation of the right-holder not to interfere is nowadays taken for granted, as though the subrogation were no more than a procedural step on the way to a particular kind of restitutionary claim. However, it rests on the substitute's right against the right-holder that he not object or interfere, and it ultimately relies on equity's willingness to enjoin the right-holder not to interfere in the litigation relating to his own right.

By way of belt and braces insurers generally contract to be subrogated to such rights as diminish any loss they have to pay. One then sees the substructural right *in personam* with especial clarity in the content of the insured's promise to permit the insurer to take over those claims. However, the right to be subrogated to another's claim is not tied to contract but arises by operation of law in all cases of imperfect discharge where the claimant is neither a gift-giver nor a risk-taker. One might be brave enough to propose a theorem to this effect: wherever the claimant would have a direct restitutionary claim of his own against a defendant enriched by the perfect discharge of his debt, there, in a case of imperfect discharge, he will be entitled to be subrogated to the right-holder's unextinguished claim.

D. UNIVERSALITY

The difficult question is whether the standard personal response is universal. Is it true of every unjust enrichment that it gives rise to a right *in personam* to the surrender of the value of the enrichment received, diminished by such defences as may be available to the enrichee? There certainly used to be exceptions where the standard claim was not found, but, as the unity of the law of unjust enrichment has begun to be appreciated and common principles have asserted themselves across all instances, those exceptions have been weakened and may now have disappeared. No obvious reason suggests itself why, the accidents of history aside, some unjust enrichments should not attract the elementary restitutionary response.

We noticed earlier the difference between two concepts of wealth, abstract and discrete.[20] The abstract conception of a person's wealth as a fund measured in money is now in the ascendant. The stronger that ascendancy the more difficult it is to explain why any unjust enrichment should be immune from adjustment in money and through pecuniary obligations.

I. SURVIVING ENRICHMENT

It appears to have been assumed in the past that if a claim in unjust enrichment needed to be restricted to the amount of the enrichment still surviving in the defendant's hands the only way it could be done was to deny the availability of a personal claim and switch to a proprietary claim in respect of traceable substitutes. Thus, in *Sinclair v Brougham*[21] the Birkbeck Building Society had run an ultra vires bank and the question was whether the depositors could recover their money. The House of Lords held that they had no personal claim. The reasoning in 1914 was distorted by the prevailing implied contract heresy,[22] but it can be translated into the proposition that a personal claim would stultify the law by giving the claimants precisely that which the ultra vires doctrine, as it then stood, said they could not have.

The underlying thought seems to have been that the ultra vires doctrine nevertheless did not warrant the retention of such enrichment as survived in the Birkbeck coffers. To allow that more limited claim their Lordships felt compelled to find the depositors a proprietary right in still traceable proceeds. In other words, they switched to the discrete conception of wealth and to proprietary rights in those discrete stores of value. The conclusion that the depositors had a right to restitution of surviving enrichment could not be given effect through a personal claim. It had to be operated through rights *in rem*.

The same assumptions can be perceived, albeit less unequivocally, in the handling of attempts to obtain restitution from minors under the regime of the Infants Relief Act 1874. In *R Leslie Ltd v Sheill* the Court of Appeal said that 'restitution stopped where repayment began' and seems to have meant, not only that recovery must be limited to surviving enrichment, but also that the claim must then be a proprietary claim to traceably surviving enrichment.[23]

[20] Above, 69–70.

[21] [1914] AC 398 (HL).

[22] Below, 271–4.

[23] [1914] 3 KB 607 (CA) 618; cf *Stocks v Wilson* [1913] 2 KB 235.

The picture changed dramatically when it became clear that, in the absence of some good reason to the contrary, the defence of change of position would always restrict liability in unjust enrichment to the amount of the enrichment abstractly surviving in the fund constituted by the recipient's wealth at the moment at which good faith first required him to conserve it for the claimant. *Westdeutsche Landesbank Girozentrale v Islington LBC*[24] accordingly overruled both limbs of *Sinclair v Brougham*. In retrospect their Lordships thought that it had not been necessary to deny the personal claim in unjust enrichment because that claim did not after all stultify the doctrine of ultra vires.[25] Further, the House of Lords in 1914 not only need not have but also ought not to have discovered a proprietary claim on the facts before them.

Whatever the future of the proprietary response to unjust enrichment, the need to restrict restitution to surviving enrichment is no longer a reason for knocking out the routine personal claim. Wherever it ought to be so restricted, the defence of change of position ensures that it will be, survival being judged in all cases by the abstract, not the discrete, conception of wealth.

2. VOIDABLE TRANSFERS

In all cases of voidable transfer, the unjust enrichment is reversed by rescission and steps taken consequentially upon rescission. On closer analysis the right to rescind combines a power to untie the contract or other transaction and a power to revest the assets which passed to the transferee. Misrepresentation, pressure, undue influence, and non-disclosure are the principal factors which invalidate transactions to the extent of rendering them voidable in this way.

If the routine *in personam* response is also available in such cases, the claimant who has these powers is concurrently entitled to receive the money value of that which he transferred less the value of anything he received in exchange. The wealth of the parties, contemplated as two abstract funds measured in money, will thus be returned to square one. This is exactly what happened in the swaps cases, although there the invalidity consisted in immediate nullity, not voidability. In principle, as between the original parties themselves, there should be no difference

[24] [1996] AC 669 (HL).

[25] A shadow is thrown on this by *Goss v Chilcott* [1996] AC 788 (PC) because that later case suggested, perhaps incorrectly, that the personal claim in unjust enrichment was no more fragile than a claim in contract where from the beginning the recipient of money knew that on one ground or another it would have to be repaid, 799 (Lord Goff).

between the law's response to void exchanges and its response to voidable exchanges. If there is a principled difference it concerns only the position of bona fide third parties who subsequently acquire things transferred between the parties.

In the past the dominant conviction in relation to voidable transfers appears to have been that, if the parties were to be put back in their original position, it would have to be done exactly and *in specie* or not at all. The degree to which this conviction caused the law to depart from the standard model of the personal response to unjust enrichment differed according as the rescinding party sought to recover money or other assets and according as he claimed in equity or at law.

(a) Recovering Payments

A rescinding party who has paid money has in principle always had the normal personal claim for restitution of that sum. It has never been suggested that he has only his power to revest the money in himself if he can find it, nor is his claim barred when the money passes to a third party who honestly gives value for it and thus acquires ownership of it. His claim is not against a third party. The sum is simply owed to him by his payee. In the old language, the amount is recoverable from that payee as money had and received to his use.[26] In this respect, one who has paid money under a voidable contract which has been rescinded is in exactly the same position as one who has paid under a void contract or otherwise without explanatory basis. All the swaps cases illustrate the kind of personal claim which he has. The divergence was encountered only in relation to value which the claimant himself has received.

In the typical case in which the payer had received some non-money benefit from his payee in exchange, his claim would once have been abruptly barred if he could not make counter-restitution of the very thing received.[27] Since counter-restitution was a condition of restitution, the payer's normal personal claim thus became abnormally fragile because of the unwillingness to allow pecuniary counter-restitution by way of a substitute for counter-restitution *in specie*.

This rigidity was mitigated on the Chancery side, which was all along cautiously more flexible in allowing money to balance an imperfect

[26] *Clarke v Dickson* (1858) EB & E 148, 120 ER 463.

[27] *Hunt v Silk* (1804) 5 East 449, 104 ER 1142; *Blackburn v Smith* (1848) 2 Ex 783, 154 ER 707, relied on in *Clarke v Dickson* (previous note).

counter-restitution,[28] especially against a party guilty of fraud.[29] In recent decades that practice has been further developed and generalized.[30] Thus, where the claimant has paid money under a voidable transaction, his position has come progressively closer to what is seen in the swaps cases where the invalidity took the form of immediate nullity.

(b) Recovering Non-Money Benefits

The same squeamishness about treating wealth as an abstract fund calibrated in money meant that the party who had parted with a non-money benefit was confined to his power *in rem*. Once he had exercised that power and made the thing his again, he had all the rights which he would have had if he had not parted with it. But what he seemingly could not do was to proceed immediately to the routine personal claim in unjust enrichment, for the value of the other's enrichment. That may now have changed, as in the end it must. So long as one eye is kept on the subjectivity of value,[31] the abstract conception of wealth, which is in the ascendant, removes the objection not only to counter-restitution in money but equally to restitution in money.

In *Mahoney v Purnell*[32] a son-in-law had bought out his elderly father-in-law's shares in a hotel at a considerable undervalue. The contract was in principle voidable by the older man for undue influence, but May J found that, in view of the subsequent history of the company, it had become impossible for there to be any restitution of the shares *in specie*. He then proceeded to make a money award instead. The son-in-law had to pay the value of the shares, less what he had paid for them.

This accords with principle. It mirrors the swaps cases. While the right to rescind and revest is still available, this claim may look like the fifth wheel on a coach. It may seem to add nothing useful. However, when the right to revest has become barred by the intervention of third party rights or for some other reason it is crucial to know whether the personal claim for the value, which does not threaten third parties, does or does not lie.

[28] *Erlanger v New Sombrero Phosphate Co* (1878) 3 App Cas 1218, 1278–9 (Lord Blackburn); compare *Alati v Kruger* (1955) 94 CLR 216, 223 (Owen Dixon CJ).

[29] *Spence v Crawford* [1939] 3 All ER 271 (HL).

[30] Below, 225–9.

[31] Above, 53–62. It may yet be held that, in addition to the tests set out at 55–62, one who has, for example, gained through undue influence or misrepresentation cannot ever reasonably appeal to the subjectivity of value to defeat the other's claim to restitution.

[32] [1996] 3 All ER 61.

Mahoney v Purnell ought to open the way to full recognition of the non-money transferor's personal claim in unjust enrichment symmetrical with the claim which the payer of money undoubtedly has. It would be absurd to cause it to succumb to bars protecting interests which it does not threaten. Since, for example, the personal claim cannot threaten third parties, it would not be rational to make it vulnerable to the intervention of third-party rights in the subject matter.

If rescission has traditionally been the exercise of the twin powers to destroy the contract and to revest property transferred, the pecuniary claim in unjust enrichment can certainly be contemplated as, in the language of section 2(2) of the Misrepresentation Act 1967, 'in lieu of' the power to revest. It is not in lieu of the power to destroy the contract between the original parties, but that power is exercised merely by bringing the claim to restitution in money. The contract is undone, but third parties are not threatened. It is not clear, however, that 'in lieu of' is a helpful way of putting it. The personal claim to the unjust enrichment is better contemplated simply as distinct from the power to revest, capable of surviving supervening events which destroy the latter power. The voidability of the contract sufficiently destroys the basis of the transfer even when, as events turn out, one response, namely the power to rescind and revest, is barred.

When you obtain my car by misrepresentation, you are unjustly enriched at my expense in that, the contract being voidable from the moment it was made,[33] you have received my car with no valid explanatory basis, and that unjust enrichment gives rise to the standard obligation to pay the value of that enrichment and concurrently to the power to revest. On this view, if and when third party rights have intervened, I lose my power to revest but not my personal right to reverse the performances in money.

(c) Competition from the Law of Wrongs

It is probably too late to enlist as another example the claim provided for innocent misrepresentation by section 2(2) of the Misrepresentation Act 1967. That section gives the court a discretion to award 'damages in lieu of rescission'. Whatever awards 'damages' can embrace, the word is strongly tied to wrongs. 'Damages' are money awards for wrongs. Moreover, the words 'in lieu of rescission' have been interpreted as meaning that the discretion is only available if all the conditions for rescission are

[33] On invalidity see above, 125–7.

fulfilled and no bars have supervened.[34] The element of judicial discretion is also difficult to integrate in the general picture of unjust enrichment. The statute thus appears to give the court a contorted jurisdiction to treat an unjust enrichment as though it were a tort. If in 1967 it had been fully possible to take unjust enrichment into account, the sub-section might have been differently drafted.

There is a real danger that *Mahoney v Purnell* may itself be interpreted as turning on the commission of a wrong. Unjust enrichment is still vulnerable to the greater familiarity of neighbouring explanations. It has always been possible for a party entitled to rescission to turn instead to an action for a wrong, provided only that the facts disclose not only a factor rendering the transaction voidable but also and concurrently an actionable wrong such as the tort of deceit or, in recent times, negligence. In such a case the action for the wrong is independent of rescission for unjust enrichment. The wrong is suffered even when the contract and its consequences are left in place.[35]

Undue influence in itself is no more a wrong than is misrepresentation, which only becomes a wrong when additional facts are present, such as deceit or negligence or breach of fiduciary duty.[36] In recent years, it has nonetheless been repeatedly described as a wrong, albeit without the least attempt to justify that important reclassification.[37] An equitable wrong is a prime candidate for an award of equitable compensation: meta-damages for a meta-tort.[38] If this development continues, it will tend to conceal, but it will not negative, the availability of pecuniary restitution in cases

[34] *Government of Zanzibar v British Aerospace (Lancaster House) Ltd* [2000] 1 WLR 2333, in which HHJ Jack sitting in the High Court held, reviewing the cases and the legislative history, that, because an aeroplane in question had been sold on, the jurisdiction under s 2(2) was extinguished even against the misrepresentor.

[35] Compare *Halifax Building Society v Thomas* [1996] Ch 217 (CA).

[36] Above, 149; also P Birks, 'Undue Influence as Wrongful Exploitation' (2004) 120 LQR 34.

[37] *Barclays Bank v O'Brien* and *CIBC Mortgages v Pitt* [1994] 1 AC 200 (HL) where undue influence is repeatedly referred to as a wrong; *Attorney General v R* [2003] PC NZ 22, where only Lord Scott, dissenting, insists on the traditional understanding of undue influence as markedly reduced autonomy. Compare the parallel attempt to turn non-disclosure into a wrong capable of supporting a claim for compensatory damages: *Banque Keyser Ullmann SA v Skandia (UK) Insurance Ltd* [1990] 1 QB 665 (CA), appealed as *Banque Financière de la Cité v Westgate Insurance Co Ltd* [1991] 2 AC 249 (HL).

[38] In this vein: Lusina Ho, 'Undue Influence and Equitable Compensation' in P Birks and F Rose (eds), *Restitution and Equity* vol I (Mansfield LLP London 2000) 193. Burrows, who agrees that undue influence is not a wrong, sees the *Mahoney* award as equitable compensation for the wrong of breach of fiduciary duty: A Burrows, *The Law of Restitution* (2nd edn Butterworths London 2002) 247.

of unjust enrichment in which a right to rescind has hitherto been the standard response.

This is the tip of a much bigger and more dangerous iceberg. The great difference between an unjust enrichment and a wrong is that unjust enrichment, being by definition not a wrong and not a contract, can only explain the adjustment of extant gains. It cannot explain a liability to make good the claimant's consequential losses. Unjust enrichment is an independent subject precisely because facts which are not wrongs and cannot therefore justify compensation for loss can and do create strict liability to relocate extant gains. This is why the Australian project to empty the law of unjust enrichment into the law of equitable compensation for unconscionable conduct cannot work, or, if it is made to work, will only do so by denying good claims in unjust enrichment or allowing bad claims for compensation.[39]

E. CONCLUSION

This chapter was able to deal very shortly with the general nature of the standard response to unjust enrichment, namely a right *in personam* that the enrichee surrender the money value of the enrichment received at the claimant's expense, correlating with an obligation on the part of the enrichee to pay that value. Defences, above all disenrichment, may reduce the measure of recovery. The chapter then asked whether the standard response was universal within the law of unjust enrichment. Modern authority teeters on the brink of making it universal, even if it has not unequivocally done so already.

The personal right, universal or near universal as it is within the law of unjust enrichment, is nearly always a right to the abstract value of the enrichment. Only one highly specialized exception was found. In cases of imperfect discharge restitution is effected—or, more accurately, enabled—by putting the right-holder under an obligation to allow the person by whom he has been paid to take over the realization of his right. Subrogation properly so called, as opposed to metaphorical subrogation, rests on that obligation.[40]

Once the universality of the right *in personam* has been made secure, the one critical question in this phase of the five-question analysis will be whether the claimant has a proprietary claim in addition. That is the subject of the next chapter. It is a question which becomes of first

[39] Below, 275–7. [40] Below, 296–8.

importance when the enrichee is insolvent. The most important recent case, *Westdeutsche Landesbank Girozentrale v Islington LBC*,[41] reminds us, however, that other issues also turn on it. That was a void interest swap in which the defendant enrichee was a local authority. There was no insolvency issue. The nature of the claimant bank's right determined the choice between simple and compound interest.

[41] [1996] AC 669 (HL).

8

Rights *in rem*

Westdeutsche Landesbank Girozentrale v Islington LBC[1] decided, and all the other swaps cases accepted, that a claimant recovering enrichment transferred under a void contract had no right *in rem*. The Latin word '*res*' means 'thing', and '*rem*' is its accusative case. Rights *in personam* and rights *in rem* are differentiated according to their exigibility. Rights *in personam* can be exacted only from the person against whom they first arise, and rights *in rem* are exigible wherever the thing in question is found and hence against anyone who has it or interferes with it. The law of obligations and the law of property are the two great pillars of private law. The law of obligations is the law of rights *in personam* and the law of property is the law of rights *in rem*.

The law as to the incidence of rights *in rem* in response to unjust enrichment is in a very poor state. If one thought one could see a clear picture ten years ago, the swaps cases have shattered the illusion, so much so that the cases now seem to offer a choice between very different interpretations. They might be said to point to the extinction of the proprietary response to unjust enrichment. Mr Swadling applauds this development, on grounds of policy, not logic:

> There is no logical reason why the event of unjust enrichment should not meet the response of rights *in rem*. It is simply an observable fact that in civilian systems this never happens. . . . [I]t is highly desirable that, so far as possible, this should also be the position in English law.[2]

If that is to happen, there are nonetheless good reasons not to regard it as having happened yet. First, the degree of disruption of established principles which it requires has been underestimated, because, as so often in unjust enrichment at this stage in its development when it has barely emerged from restitution, important steps have been taken without the advantage of any overview of the subject as a whole, unmixed with

[1] [1996] AC 669 (HL).

[2] WJ Swadling, 'Property and Unjust Enrichment' in JW Harris, *Property Problems: From Genes to Pension Funds* (Kluwer The Hague 1997) 130, 130.

extraneous matter. The House of Lords overruled its own decision in *Sinclair v Brougham*[3] without any attempt at such a review.

Secondly, the assertion that it would be 'highly desirable' to eliminate the proprietary response is not self-evidently true. It would make the law simpler, but that is a blessing that often has to be foregone. The issue most prominently affected is priority in insolvency, because those with property rights take out their assets before the personal creditors, those with only rights *in personam*, get anything. It is far from obvious that assets which ought never to have been added to the insolvent's estate ought to be available to his unsecured creditors.

Thirdly, whatever the merits of the argument, the law of such a sensitive matter as insolvency, where many must necessarily suffer undeserved misfortune, should not be reviewed from case to case but left to Parliament, typically acting on the advice of a Royal Commission. Taken in combination with the fact that no insolvency issue was directly at stake, this is a strong argument for not accepting that, in addition to transforming the method of deciding whether an enrichment is unjust, the swaps cases have also overturned the rules as to the proprietary responses to unjust enrichment. It is preeminently a question of policy for reflection and legislation, not for the courts. The rationality of 'women and children first' may require re-examination, but shipwreck is not the time to attempt a re-assessment.

A. LAYING THE CARDS ON THE TABLE

This chapter first describes the different rights *in rem* which can be generated by unjust enrichment and then turns to their actual incidence. The subject is so difficult that the only safe course is to state at the beginning both the position which will be taken and the principal obstacle to it. It is possible that the courts will go another way, but if they do they must not do so piecemeal, on the facts of single cases. The law of unjust enrichment must be considered as a whole.

We noticed extreme positions—no proprietary responses, and proprietary responses in every case. The central proposition of this chapter is that neither extreme correctly states the law. Looking behind the swaps cases, the best interpretation of the English cases is that they should be divided between those in which there is no moment in which the

[3] [1914] AC 398 (HL) overruled in *Westdeutsche Landesbank Girozentrale v Islington LBC* [1996] AC 669 (HL).

enrichment is held free of any claim, and those in which for however short a time the enrichee holds the enrichment freely at his own disposition. This distinction almost exactly corresponds with the line between initial and subsequent failure of basis. In the former case, where the enrichment is never freely at the enrichee's disposition, there is always a proprietary response alongside the common or garden right *in personam*. In the latter case, where the value in question has been freely at the disposition of the defendant before the basis of the enrichment fails, there is no proprietary response.[4]

These assertions have to cope with a double obstacle. One is that pre-swaps cases themselves belong in the period in which unjust enrichment was not recognized and was made to work through imaginary contracts and trusts, sometimes even through supposed wrongs. Unsurprisingly their message is itself in many respects unclear and has to be interpreted on the precarious assumption that lawyerly intuition often reaches the correct result even when the steps to that result are less than sound.

The other obstacle is that the swaps cases themselves are cases of initial failure of basis, from which it would seem to follow that, on the picture being defended, they ought to have recognized the proprietary nature of the response. They did not. But they did start on that foot. The House of Lords then held in the *Westdeutsche* case that the claimants had no proprietary claims. But, as we shall see, when they made that decision the Law Lords clearly did not take into account the difference between initial and subsequent failure. More than that, their Lordships decided that the issue before them did not require them to analyse the nature of the ground for restitution operating on the facts before them. With hindsight we can see that that was not so. It constitutes a serious flaw. In a system committed to the doctrine of precedent, this is a combination of factors which calls for a doctrine of occasional *tabula radenda*. Litigation has a wonderful facility for producing the opportunity for a completely clean start.

B. DIFFERENT PROPRIETARY RESPONSES

Rights *in rem* come into existence as either beneficial interests or security interests. We will leave security interests until last. Both beneficial and

[4] This is the line drawn by Professor Chambers: R Chambers, *Resulting Trusts* (OUP Oxford 1997) 110, 155–70.

security rights can begin as immediately vested beneficial interests or as a power which allows the power-holder to alter the status of a thing in the enrichee's hands. This contrast is not entirely happy, for a power to give oneself an interest in a thing is itself a perfectly vested right, albeit limited by its nature as a power. Nevertheless we will continue to distinguish between powers *in rem* and immediately vested rights *in rem*.

1. IMMEDIATELY VESTED BENEFICIAL RIGHTS *IN REM*

One way of reversing an unjust enrichment is immediately to turn the enrichee into a trustee. The claimant acquires the full equitable proprietary interest. He becomes the owner in equity. As the holder of the entire beneficial interest, he can then call for the enrichee to transfer the legal interest to him. For convenience this response is consistently referred to below as the 'immediate trust'. The equitable interest is immediately vested. The legal interest in that configuration is 'voidable' in the sense that it remains in the recipient until recalled in the second stage. But here the recalling has to be done through a court, for the equitable owner has no power to give himself the legal title.

By contrast it is generally impossible to use ownership at law as a means of reversing an unjust enrichment. The reason is that if a recipient acquires possession of an asset and in the given circumstances the previous possessor is the owner, it can only mean that the property has not passed. The passive survival of the pre-existing right prevents enrichment and does not reverse it. Before this story began, the surviving right might have arisen from unjust enrichment, but it cannot have arisen from the unjust enrichment of the new possessor at the expense of the owner.

Exceptionally, in relation to an asset not previously owned by the claimant, it is possible actively to use immediately vested legal ownership as an instrument to reverse unjust enrichment. If I use your money to buy myself a picture, the law might actively undo that enrichment at your expense by making you the owner of the picture, which was never yours before. In fact, as we shall see later in the chapter, it does not quite do that. It stops short at giving you a power *in rem*, a power to make yourself the owner of the picture. You can exercise your power in relation to the traced substitute for your money and, if you do, you will make the picture yours.

2. POWERS *IN REM*

At law a right to rescind is, or, more accurately, includes a power *in rem* to alter the status of the thing transferred. The transferee gets a voidable title. By publicly manifesting his intention to excercise the power, the transferor can divest him of his acquisition and vest it in himself.[5]

According to relatively recent re-analysis, voidability in equity conforms closely to this legal model. In equity a power to alter the status of the thing transferred only allows the claimant to give himself an equitable beneficial interest, thus reducing the transferee's interest to the bare right of a trustee. The exercise of the power produces the trust. As with the immediate trust, the claimant is then in a position to call for a reconveyance of the legal estate.[6] He cannot give it to himself but he can compel it to be given by the trustee.

The American *Restatement of Restitution* assumes an older model which dispenses with the power. In that model a transfer which is voidable in equity produces an immediate trust for the transferor, who is then able on ordinary principles to recall the legal title.[7] The word 'voidable' is used but focuses on the legal title. There is an immediate trust, and the existence of the trust enables the transferor to get the court to compel the reconveyance. The analogy of the legal power *in rem* appears to have taken root. The cost is the creation of two responses where, arguably, one would have sufficed.[8] We may go back to one, if the power analysis captures more ground.

3. SECURITY INTERESTS

In practice, unless we were to count consensual interests revived by 'reviving subrogation',[9] the only security interest which ever arises directly from unjust enrichment is an equitable lien.[10] The name should not be allowed to give the impression that all that is involved is, as with common law liens, a right to retain possession by way of security. An

[5] *Car & Universal Finance Co Ltd v Caldwell* [1965] 1 QB 525 (CA).

[6] *Lonrho Plc v Fayed* [1992] 1 WLR 1, 11–12 (Millett J); *Bristol and West BS v Motthew* [1998] Ch 1, 22–3 followed in *Twinsectra Ltd v Yardley* [1999] Lloyd's Rep Banking 438, 461–2 (CA) aff'd on other grounds [2002] UKHL 12, [2002] 2 WLR 802 (HL).

[7] A Scott and W Seavey (reporters), *Restatement of the Law of Restitution Quasi Contracts and Constructive Trusts* (American Law Institute St Paul Minn 1937) ss 163, 166, with comments thereto.

[8] The old model was defended by R Chambers, *Resulting Trusts* (OUP Oxford 1997) 170–84. Compare id, 'Constructive Trusts in Canada' (part II) (2002) 16 Trust Law Intl 2, 15. That battle may now have been lost. Nevertheless, the power analysis cannot be said to be completely secure, as is shown by *Collings v Lee* [2001] 2 All ER 332 (CA) and *Halley v Law Society* [2003] EWCA 97, noted Tang Hang Yu, 'Proprietary Relief without Rescission' (2004) 63 CLJ 30.

[9] C Mitchell, *The Law of Contribution and Reimbursement* (OUP Oxford 2003) [14.13]–[14.21].

[10] Below, 261.

equitable lien is an abstract charge on assets. 'Abstract' is used here as the opposite of 'possessory'.

C. INCIDENCE

Having reviewed the different property interests which can arise, we must now ask when they do arise. The 'no basis' approach makes unjust enrichment a tighter and more coherent unity than it was. The tighter the unity the more obvious it becomes that the proper starting point is that every manifestation of unjust enrichment should elicit the same response.

There are, however, two important lines which can be drawn through the generic event. One divides cases of initial failure of basis from cases of subsequent failure. The other lies between cases in which the claimant wishes to assert a proprietary interest in the thing originally received and those in which his attention is directed to a traceable substitute for that original asset. In practice most proprietary claims are directed to substitutes. Whether a proprietary claim lies in respect of the substitute depends on whether such a claim would have been available in respect of the original immediately after its receipt. A claimant who has no proprietary base in the original can have no proprietary right in the substitute.

Those two lines are crucial. The rest of the chapter therefore considers the incidence of the proprietary response to unjust enrichment in cases of initial failure and subsequent failure on the assumption that the claimant is interested in the original asset received by the defendant. The third section then turns to traceable substitutes. The assumption in those three sections is that the interest in question is a beneficial interest, not a security interest. The final section addresses the incidence of security interests.

1. INITIAL FAILURE

Most cases fall within the *condictio indebiti*.[11] That is to say, they are cases in which the claimant has paid or performed in the belief that he was under an obligation to do so, usually a contractual obligation. The first and general requirement for a proprietary right is that the thing claimed must be identifiable. 'That's mine!' is meaningless if there is no 'that' in sight. For the moment we are assuming that the thing claimed is the thing originally transferred and that it is identifiable.

[11] Above, 130–1.

(a) Before the Swaps Cases

There used to be substantial evidence of the proprietary response in cases of initial failure and no hard opposition. We might list six items:

(i) Sinclair v Brougham[12]

The Birkbeck Building Society had been running an ultra vires bank. All the banking contracts were void. The question in the winding up was whether the depositors had any claim at all. The House of Lords held that they had no personal claim. The modern version of the reason is that, their contracts being ultra vires and void, non-contractual recovery would stultify the ultra vires doctrine. However, they were regarded as having a proprietary interest too, and their Lordships thought that there would be no stultification if they were confined to that right *in rem*. By nature it could not yield more than what the Society still held. The ultra vires doctrine did not require that the Society be allowed to hold on to ultra vires money which it still had. This case, now overruled, suffered from an ambiguity identical to that which is found in the swaps case which overruled it. It was not completely clear whether it was to be regarded as an example of initial or of subsequent failure. We will come back to that.

(ii) Chase Manhattan Bank NA Ltd v Israel–British Bank (London) Ltd[13]

The claimant bank paid the defendant bank $2m and then, by mistake, paid it again. The recipient bank became insolvent. Goulding J held that the effect of the mistaken payment was to turn the recipient into a trustee and thus give the claimant bank an equitable proprietary interest in the money paid. In the case itself the proviso was simply left hanging. Goulding J decided that Chase Manhatten had a proprietary right arising from its mistaken payment, which it could realize if they could identify the money. It is known that the bank did afterwards satisfy the liquidator that its money was traceable and, without further litigation, it got back its money before the unsecured creditors got anything.

(iii) Neste Oy v Lloyds Bank[14]

Five payments had been made in advance in respect of services to be rendered to ships arriving in port. The payments were made under a contract. They were payments in advance under that contract. The

[12] [1914] AC 398 (HL). [13] [1981] Ch 105.
[14] [1983] 2 Lloyd's Rep 658 (Bingham J).

services were not rendered. Bingham J held, in relation to the first four payments, that the failure of basis gave only personal claims. In relation to them the basis failed after the payment, when the contractual reciprocation was not forthcoming. We would now have to say that the basis of the payment, the contract, was not invalidated until that reciprocation failed. Meanwhile the money had been freely at the disposition of the recipients. The fifth payment was different. The recipient was turned into a trustee because at the time of the payment it was already certain that the service would not be forthcoming. The payee had already decided to cease trading. From the standpoint of the payer the invalidity had already supervened. The contract was already terminable. The basis had failed *ab initio*. The payer had an equitable proprietary interest in that payment.

Neste Oy and *Chase Manhattan* are indistinguishable under both approaches to unjust. The basis failed *ab initio*, in that the payer's putative contractual obligation did not exist. In the one case it had been paid off earlier in the day and in the other it had already been repudiated. In terms of unjust factors, it could be said of both that the payer's intention was impaired by a mistake, in the one case a mistaken belief that the sum had not been paid, in the other a mistaken belief that the recipients intended to make the contractual reciprocation. The Court of Appeal later sought to narrow *Neste Oy* by confining it to instances in which the recipient had acted with a high degree of improbity.[15] An attack on *Neste Oy* is an attack on *Chase Manhattan*. We will return below to the misconceived attempt to make the proprietary right depend on fault. Timing, not fault, is the key.

(iv) Failure of Trusts

The above cases have to be placed alongside two large and indisputable groups. The first includes the numerous cases in which a transfer upon trust fails. Here the basis of the transfer to the trustee is that he shall hold upon trust. If that basis fails it usually fails immediately, and the failing interest results (jumps back) to the settlor.

That immediate failure can have many causes. The simplest is the settlor's omission to nominate any beneficiaries.[16] In a recent case a pension fund had been set up in disastrous breach of the rule against perpetuities.[17] In such cases there is an immediate trust for the settlor. It is

[15] *Triffit Nurseries Ltd v Salads Etcetera Ltd* [2000] 1 All ER Comm 737 (CA).
[16] *Vandervell v IRC* [1967] 2 AC 291 (HL).
[17] *Air Jamaica Ltd v Charlton* [1999] 1 WLR 1399 (PC).

not an express or genuinely implied trust. There is no presumption of an intent to create a trust. If there were it would be constantly rebutted by evidence that the settlor never thought about consequences of failure.[18] The failure of the trust is a straightforward failure of basis. There is a remote possibility that the settlor intended an alternative basis by default, as for instance that the trustee should take beneficially or that the asset be abandoned, but, the balance of probability being the other way, it is for the one who alleges such things to prove them. The onus naturally falls in such a way as to render a presumption redundant. The trust fails. There is an immediate failure of basis. The law responds with an immediate restitutionary trust.

We tend to take this for granted as simply a well-worn truth of the law of trusts. But it is no more than equity reacting to an initial failure of basis. *Chase Manhattan* and *Neste Oy* are the same. Equity reacts to the initial failure of basis with an immediate trust which carries the enrichment back to the person at whose expense it would otherwise have been made. These are all unjust enrichment trusts. The beneficial interest jumps back. It results. It is not illuminating to call them 'resulting trusts' because the jumping back does not indicate the causative event.

In the same way the trust in *Attorney-General for Hong Kong v Reid*[19] was a wrongs trust in which the beneficial interest jumped forward, and no importance attaches either to its pro-sulting pattern or the deeming of a declaration of trust which attracts the label 'constructive trust', because, again, neither 'pro-sulting' nor 'constructive' gives the least hint as to the nature of the causative event, except, in the latter case, that that event is deemed to be but is not a declaration of trust.

The generic event in these cases where trusts fail is enrichment with no explanatory basis. The basis of the trustee's receipt was that he should hold on trust. That failing, his enrichment must be reversed.

(v) Voidability

The next group is a large one and often neglected when this matter is discussed. It comprises all those cases in which the law responds to invalidity by giving a transferor a power *in rem* to revest the thing in himself. There is apparently no immediate trust, but in a case governed by the common law the transferor can make himself owner of the thing at law and in a case governed by equity he can give himself a full equitable

[18] Thus in *Vandervell* (n 16 above) there was nothing that the settlor less wanted than the creation of a trust but still there was a trust.

[19] [1994] 1 AC 324 (PC).

interest and thus turn the other into a trustee. This happens wherever the invalidity arises from induced mistake, whether the misrepresentation is fraudulent, negligent, or totally innocent, also in cases of non-disclosure, in cases of illegitimate pressure, undue influence, and personal disadvantage. All these vitiating factors have in common that they render transfers voidable. Wherever a transfer is rendered voidable, the transferor obtains a new right *in rem*, namely a power to divest the transferee and vest the asset transferred in himself.

It should be immediately evident that it is not possible to embark on an attack against *Chase Manhattan* without taking account of voidability. On another day the second payment might have been induced by misrepresentation, fraudulent or innocent. On a third day some illegitimate pressure might have been applied. There has to be consistency across the whole law of unjust enrichment.

One inconsistency is the difference between, on the one hand, the immediate trust, found in *Chase Manhattan* and *Neste Oy* and in all the failing trust cases, and, on the other, the power *in rem* in these cases of voidability. That difference is partly but not exclusively the product of modern reinterpretation of voidability in equity.[20] In the absence of material differences between different fact situations, there should be no variations of this kind. At all events, it would be folly to attempt to sweep away *Chase Manhattan*, a case of spontaneous mistake in a non-bargaining situation, without comparing the consequences which follow from an innocently induced mistake in both bargaining and non-bargaining situations. The difference between immediate trust and power is not great enough to allow an attack on the former which ignores the latter. Any attack on voidability for induced mistake immediately becomes an attack on the settled law of misrepresentation, duress, undue influence, and so on. The whole picture has to be taken into account.

(vi) Where the Property Does Not Pass

The whole picture must include the relationship between all these cases and others where no property passes at all. Where the property does not pass, as where I lose my money, my continuing property right does not arise from the unjust enrichment of the finder or taker. Nevertheless cases of that kind lie nearby, and very nearby in the case of a mistaken transfer where the mistake may be so fundamental as to prevent the legal property passing. Again, when a claim is made to traceable substitutes the law is

[20] Above, 184.

the same for situations in which title passed voidably and those in which it did not pass at all. It is reasonable to expect a measure of consistency across that line.

(b) After the Swaps Cases

The swaps cases are on the face of things incompatible with the proposition that where the enrichment is unjust *ab initio* the law always responds with a proprietary right. In *Westdeutsche Landesbank Girozentrale v Islington LBC* the House of Lords not only held that successful claimants had no proprietary right but also overruled *Sinclair v Brougham*.[21] That knocks away one of the earlier foundations. Lord Browne-Wilkinson also distanced himself from *Chase Manhattan Bank NA Ltd v Israel-British Bank (London) Ltd* and proposed a new interpretation of it.[22] That goes far towards demolishing another of the foundations. Their Lordships appear to have moved a long way down the path to the elimination of the proprietary response to unjust enrichment.

On the other hand they made no attempt at all to integrate the other groups of cases. Failing trusts were pushed out of sight by a surprising reassertion of the presumption of intent to create a trust.[23] Voidability and the concomitant power to revest, which are probably impregnable, were simply not discussed. But they would jut uncomfortably out of a plain of personal claims. However, this hostility to the proprietary response may come to nothing. Even though it was not questioned in any subsequent swap, the *Westdeutsche* case has a fatal flaw.

At the time when the *Westdeutsche* case was decided it was not yet clear that all swaps cases turned only on initial absence of basis. Hobhouse J at first instance had insisted that they did. For him initial absence of basis was the proper explanation of restitution under both interrupted and closed swaps.[24] The Court of Appeal had upheld him, adding that in the

[21] [1914] AC 398 (HL).

[22] *Westdeutsche Landesbank Girozentrale v Islington LBC* [1996] AC 669 (HL) 714. Compare Sir Peter Millett, as he then was, writing extra-judicially: The Rt Hon Sir Peter Millett, 'Restitution and Constructive Trust' (1998) 114 LQR 399, 412–13. Compare too the parallel treatment of *Neste Oy v Lloyds Bank* [1983] 2 Lloyd's Rep 658 in *Triffit Nurseries Ltd v Salads Etcetera Ltd* [2000] 1 All ER Comm 737 (CA).

[23] Surprising, because ever since *Vandervell v IRC* (n 16 above) nobody has believed in that understanding of the failing trust resulting trust and even Mr Swadling whose views were adopted by Lord Browne-Wilkinson, supports that understanding of the presumption only in the case of apparent gifts: WJ Swadling, 'A New Role for Resulting Trusts?' (1996) 16 Legal Studies 110.

[24] *Kleinwort Benson Ltd v Sandwell BC* (decided and reported with the *Westdeutsche* case) [1994] 4 All ER 890.

interrupted swap, which alone had been appealed, the ground could equally have been subsequent failure of basis due to the interruption of the contractual reciprocation.[25]

If the money was received on trust, as Hobhouse J thought, it would attract compound interest. The House of Lords had to decide only the interest question and did not regard it as raising or requiring examination of the precise reason why the enrichment was unjust. Hence it is not knowable whether the House of Lords regarded the *Westdeutsche* case as an instance of initial or of subsequent failure. On the premiss that it was a case of subsequent failure, from want of full reciprocation, it certainly could not support a proprietary response.[26]

Given his preference for 'absence of consideration', Hobhouse J's conclusion that the claimants did acquire a proprietary right was absolutely in accord with the proposition advanced above for all cases in which the enrichment is unjust from the outset. The House of Lords reversed him, having before it no unambiguous closed swap and without disagreeing with the Court of Appeal's opinion that Hobhouse J could have decided on the case as one of subsequent failure. The later cases on closed swaps focused on other points and, although they necessarily proceeded on the basis of initial failure, they never re-opened the issue of the proprietary response.

The single source of these difficulties is the assumption in the *Westdeutsche* case that it was possible to decide for or against a proprietary response without analysing the nature and operation of the causative event. This flaw infects the overruling of *Sinclair v Brougham*[27] the facts of which present the identical ambiguity. The depositors with the ultra vires Birkbeck Bank lent their money to the Bank. The deposits were void. They were not repaid. We cannot tell whether in *Westdeutsche* the House of Lords thought the depositors were claiming because the contractual reciprocation had not been forthcoming or because their contract had been void *ab initio*. On the one view *Sinclair v Brougham* was, in their eyes, a case of subsequent failure and certainly needed to be overruled. On the other view it was a case of initial failure and could not be overruled without taking into account the other groups of cases which have just been discussed, whether of immediate trust or power to rescind and revest.

[25] [1994] 4 All ER 890, 924 (Hobhouse J), 960–1 (Dillon LJ, with whom Kennedy LJ agreed).

[26] It would then have belonged alongside *Re Goldcorp Exchange Ltd* [1995] 1 AC 74 (PC), discussed in text to n 31 below.

[27] [1914] AC 398 (HL).

(i) The Pro-Proprietary Future

The law's best hope of coherence is to accept the proposition that a proprietary interest is generated by every initial failure of basis. The swaps cases will have to be reviewed and their exclusion of any proprietary response confined to subsequent failure. They were not cases of subsequent failure. But, at the time, it was still possible to contemplate both *Wesdeutsche* and *Sinclair v Brougham* as being of that kind.

If *Chase Manhattan* is saved in that way, there will remain the tiresome problem of ironing out the difference between the immediate trust and the power *in rem* which is more widely present in the cases. However, since claimants are usually interested in the traceable proceeds of the original asset rather than the original asset itself and since the right in traceable proceeds is always a power whatever the nature of the proprietary base in the original asset, in practice this difference has much less consequence than it otherwise might.

(ii) The Anti-Proprietary Future

If *Chase Manhattan* does not survive, there are two possible scenarios, neither of which is attractive. The first is that the proprietary response will be confined to the established cases of voidability. These cannot be eradicated but will have to be pruned to reduce the visibility of their anomalous survival. The law cannot tolerate a situation in which the payment of a sum not owed has totally different consequences depending on whether the cause was a spontaneous mistake or an innocently induced mistake.

That is not to say that different mistakes do not have different consequences. They undoubtedly do. A ground-rule of bargaining is that one takes the risk of one's own mistakes, not of those induced by the counterparty's misrepresentations. But such differences are anterior to the finding that money was not due. As between one payment not due and another, no distinction can be taken so far as concerns the kind of right which then arises. One might as rationally discriminate between payments made on Mondays and payments made on Tuesdays. Development along this line, leaving voidability isolated but pruned to be less conspicuous, seems very unlikely to happen. It does not admit of much pruning.

The alternative cul-de-sac is the unprincipled compromise which would not eliminate the proprietary interest arising on initial failure of basis but would rather restrict it to cases of improbity, both initial and supervening, on the part of the recipient enrichee. In the *Westdeutsche* case Lord Browne-Wilkinson goes even further, for he seems to say that all cases of unjust enrichment can yield a proprietary response if the enrichee retains the enrichment with guilty knowledge that he ought to give it back. He would then be turned into a trustee to the extent that, when that guilty knowledge supervened, he still held identifiable proceeds of the original unjust enrichment.[28]

This is not really an unjust enrichment trust. It is a wrongs-based trust superimposed on an unjust enrichment. The wrong is knowing withholding. That would reduce but not eliminate the inconsistency on the borderline with voidability. But this new wrongs-based trust encounters a string of other objections.

First, if the law is minded to take away the proprietary priority which currently attaches to some unjust enrichments, it is hard to see how it could give it back again where it detects a wrongful withholding on the defendant's part. This sense of the irrelevance of wrongful withholding in turn arises because (a) claims arising from wrongs have never been looked on favourably in an insolvency and, which is the same point made from a different angle, instances of proprietary rights arising from wrongs are very few and far between, and (b) an insolvent's knowledge of an otherwise unprivileged debt cannot rationally affect the priority of the creditor and could not save a repayment from being a voidable preference.

Secondly, since rights arise from unjust enrichment independently of fault,[29] making the *in rem* response turn on dishonesty looks like a lop-sided outbreak of the heresy which says that there can be no unjust enrichment without fault. That heresy is a sub-form of all attempts to nudge the law of unjust enrichment into the law of wrongs. It is a manifestation of failure to recognize the very proposition to which this area of law owes its independence.

Thirdly, if it were generally true that the proprietary response turned on guilty knowledge, that doctrine would instantly eliminate the power to rescind for innocent misrepresentation and, to the extent that a high degree of fault were insisted upon, for negligent misrepresentation too. That would be to double back on the Chancery's supplementation of the common law's response to misrepresentation.

Fourthly, while it is true that rights *in personam* can sometimes be made to simulate the effects of property rights by being made enforceable

[28] *Westdeutsche Landesbank Girozentrale v Islington LBC* [1996] AC 669 (HL) 714 (Lord Browne-Wilkinson). Cf *Triffit Nurseries Ltd v Salads Etcetera Ltd* [2000] 1 All ER Comm 737 (CA).

[29] Above, 5–9.

against strangers who knowingly interfere with them, and that some property rights have historically developed from that kind of simulation,[30] the fault involved in such simulations is always that of the third party sought to be affected. Any development on those lines would suggest an inquiry into the question whether other creditors should be compelled to acknowledge the priority of a mistaken payer because they knew that the enrichee had received money not due. What is being proposed here is quite different. It is that dishonesty on the part of the enrichee himself can transform obligation into property.

The pro-proprietary future clearly offers the best hope of coherence. If there is ultimately to be an anti-proprietary future, it must come by the legislative route, after expert reflection.

2. SUBSEQUENT FAILURE

The explanatory basis of an enrichment often fails after its receipt. In such cases there is no question of a proprietary response. There is an exception which requires separate treatment. We noticed earlier that the incidence of the proprietary response does not perfectly coincide with the line between initial and subsequent failure of basis. The deviation has to be made for cases in which, despite the fact that the failure supervenes and is not initial, there is another reason why the enrichment has not been freely at the disposition of the recipient. This can be called the case of the ring-fenced fund. A proprietary response in such a case carries through the principle underlying the proprietary response to initial failure, that the proprietary interest arises where the enrichee never held the enrichment free of any claim. Correspondingly it does not arise when, for however short a time, it has been freely at his disposition.

(a) No Ring-Fenced Fund

If I pay money to you on the basis of a contract binding you to make some reciprocation, as to build me a garage, a later repudiatory breach on your part will invalidate the contract in that it will render it terminable by me. In every insolvency the unsecured creditors who have to wait for such crumbs as may fall from the secured table have all suffered such a failure of basis. They paid and did not receive, or delivered and were not paid. We know that these people have only rights *in personam*. That is what it

[30] Compare restrictive covenants from *Tulk v Moxhay* (1848) 2 Ph 774, 41 ER 1143. There is no general doctrine allowing this simulation: *Port Line Ltd v Ben Line Steamers Ltd* [1958] 2 QB 146, a classic judgment of Diplock J.

means to be an unsecured creditor. The reason that they have no proprietary claims, no rights *in rem*, is that the value passed before the basis of the recipient's enrichment failed. For a while it was not an unjust enrichment. On the contrary, it was freely at the disposition of the recipient, at least in the sense that no claim at all lay for its return.

Re Goldcorp Exchange[31] vividly illustrates the negative certainty that on these facts there is no proprietary response. Many New Zealanders had invested heavily in a scheme run by Goldcorp under which the gold which they bought from the company was supposed to become their gold but be safely kept for them and insured. No gold was ever appropriated to any contracts and no attempt was made to maintain the promised store of customer gold. Goldcorp kept some gold in hand, enough to honour the demands of those investors who from time to time requested physical delivery. By the time the company became insolvent the majority of the investors, having paid for gold and further services, had received nothing. They undoubtedly had a personal claim for the amount of their payments, but in the insolvency the crucial question was whether they had any proprietary right in the money which they had paid over. As unsecured creditors they would get nothing. They needed priority, not only over the unsecured creditors but over the Bank of New Zealand's now crystallized floating charge.

They had no proprietary right. There was no point in even beginning a tracing exercise to find out whether there were substitutes still in Goldcorp's hands because, at the moment that the basis of the payment failed, the property in the money had already passed to Goldcorp and the money had been freely at the company's disposition. An attempt to argue that Goldcorp had obtained the money by misrepresentation and therefore voidably *ab initio* never got off the ground. The New Zealand Court of Appeal's conclusion that the money had been received as ring-fenced trust money was rejected. There was nothing beyond an ordinary agreement to sell, broken by Goldcorp. It was a simple case of failure of consideration, in the old sense of failure of contractual reciprocation. The failure was subsequent to the receipt. Meantime the money had been freely at the disposition of Goldcorp.

(b) Ring-Fenced Funds

The picture changes dramatically if, for the period between receipt and failure of basis, the proper construction of the parties' intentions is that

[31] [1995] 1 AC 74 (PC).

the value was not to be at the disposition of the recipient but on the contrary was to be ring-fenced so as to be available only for a specified application. If the ring-fence is construed as a trust, the failure of the purpose certainly raises a proprietary interest in the claimant-settlor.

(i) Ring-Fencing by Trust

In *Re Abbott*[32] a fund had been subscribed to care for two disabled ladies. After they died it turned out that the fund had not been exhausted and that no provision had been made for the surplus. Similarly, in *Re Gillingham Bus Disaster Fund*[33] money was raised after sea cadets had been crushed by a bus. The terms of the appeal included provision for the event in which there was a surplus. That provision proved to be void.

These are both cases in which, in respect of the surplus, the basis of the transfer failed. The basis was that the money be held on trust, but, when the surplus emerged, there were no beneficiaries. The money was held on resulting trust for the donors. The money having been ring-fenced all along, it remained true, even if the facts were construed as subsequent failure, that the funds had never been freely at the disposition of the holders. The proprietary restitutionary right of the donors is thus perfectly consistent with the exclusion of such a right in a case of the *Goldcorp* kind.

Money is often donated or lent for a particular purpose which, as things turn out, cannot be pursued. Suppose, for example, that money is subscribed to a campaign to stop the building of a new road and then the plan to build the road is abandoned; or suppose that money is lent to pay a particular creditor but it becomes impermissible to pay him. It would be difficult to come to the conclusion that the parties did not intend the money to be ring-fenced. But there are often obstacles in the way of understanding the ring-fencing as having created a trust which subsequently failed, not least when the purpose to which the money is tied is an abstract purpose. An abstract purpose is one the execution of which will not enure to the benefit of any certain class of human beneficiaries. The campaign against the road is an abstract purpose.

A trust for an abstract purpose is void *ab initio* unless charitable. To construe a fund for preventing the building of a new road as a trust would thus be to construe it as instantly void, so that the basis would fail from the moment of the transfer, whether or not it could in fact be pursued. The courts therefore incline towards a different construction. They

[32] [1900] 2 Ch 326. [33] [1959] Ch 62 (CA).

construe the tied transfer as creating an immediate express trust for the transferor, with a concurrent grant of a power to apply the money to the purpose.[34] The failure of the purpose then terminates the power. The proprietary interest of the donor or lender does not then arise from that failure but is in place all along under the express trust. That construction leaves no work to be done by the law of unjust enrichment.

(ii) Ring-Fencing by Contract

It is not altogether clear what cases will not attract one or other of these two trust analyses. If our 'stop the road' subscription were construed simply as a transfer caught by a contract to apply the money to the purpose,[35] the failure of the purpose ought if possible to lead to the same legal outcomes as those to which the trust constructions apply. In substance it is still a case of a ring-fenced fund the purpose of which has failed. Professor Chambers's view ought to prevail, namely that the element of ring-fencing is sufficiently established if injunctions will be available to prevent the money being spent on other purposes.[36]

The failure of the purpose would then arise from a species of failure of contractual reciprocation, the holder having in the eye of the law merely promised to apply the fund to the campaign. But it would be a failure of reciprocation unlike all others, not a failure of counter-performance in exchange as typified in *Re Goldcorp* but a failure to apply the fund to its designated purpose.

A variation of the contractual construction is found in transfers to clubs and other unincorporated associations. The condition of their members taking as co-owners is construed to be their assent to the assets being caught by the multilateral contract constituted by the association's rules. Generally that contract, through which the dedication to the purpose is achieved, includes a term empowering the members to dissolve it and distribute the fund among themselves. If so, the basis of transfers to the association includes that eventuality, and the failure of the association will not amount to a failure of the basis of those transfers.[37] Otherwise the

[34] *Twinsectra Ltd v Yardley* [2002] UKHL 12, [2002] 2 AC 164 (HL), reworking *Barclays Bank Ltd v Quistclose Investments Ltd* [1970] AC 567 (HL).

[35] *Conservative and Unionist Central Office v Burrell* [1982] 1 WLR 522. In the case of a will the simple contract explanation cannot work. A condition is made to do the work: *Re Recher's Will Trusts* [1972] Ch 526.

[36] R Chambers, *Resulting Trusts* (OUP Oxford 1997) 87.

[37] *Re St Andrews Allotment Association* [1969] 1 WLR 421, *Re Bucks Constabulary Widows Fund* [1979] 1 WLR 936; cf on different grounds *Re West Sussex Constabulary Widows Benevolent Fund* [1971] 1 Ch 1.

failure of the purpose expressed in the contract will still engender a failure of the basis of a ring-fenced fund, and contributors to that fund will have not only a personal right to restitution but also a proprietary right under a resulting trust. On this view, even subsequent failure of ring-fenced funds always generates a proprietary response, whether or not the ring-fencing is done by trust.

3. TRACEABLE SUBSTITUTES

At this point we turn from the original asset received to its traceable substitute. Let it be supposed that the rules of tracing allow us to conclude that a Rolls Royce in the recipient's garage is wholly or partly the traceable product of £200,000 earlier received. If the claimant had a proprietary interest in the £200,000 when it was received, he will be able to claim a proprietary interest in the Rolls Royce. That proposition holds good both at law and in equity.[38] The right in the substitute asset may ultimately be either a beneficial interest proportionate to the contribution or a lien for the amount traceable to its acquisition. The general rule is that the claimant may choose.[39] Substitution without consent has that effect. It is an effect which the House of Lords has declined to attribute to the law of unjust enrichment, preferring a fiction to the effect that the right in the original asset persists in the substitute. That is not a sustainable position.[40]

(a) The Right in the Substitute is Always a Power

Whether a claimant's right in the asset originally received was created upon the receipt or survived from before the story began, and whether it was an immediately vested right or a power, his right in the substitute after non-consensual substitution is always a power. It is a power to vest the currently traceable substitute in himself. There may have been a long chain of substitutions.

The analysis of the right as initially a power is not uncontroversial, but it was clearly adopted in *Lipkin Gorman v Karpnale Ltd*.[41] The other view, that there is a vested interest in every link of the chain, still has support, even though it leads to grave practical difficulties.[42] In practice

[38] *FC Jones & Sons v Jones* [1997] Ch 159 (CA); *Foskett v McKeown* [2001] 1 AC 102 (HL).

[39] *Foskett* (n 38 above) 131.

[40] Above, 34–6.

[41] [1991] 2 AC 548 (HL) 573.

[42] LD Smith, *The Law of Tracing* (OUP Oxford 1997) 358–61, preferring *Cave v Cave* (1880) 15 Ch D 639, a decision of first impression of Fry J criticized in *Re Ffrench's Estate* (1887) 21 LR Ir 283 (Ir CA). This view may also have been assumed, without argument, in *Halifax Plc v Omar* [2002] EWCA Civ 121, [2002] 2 P & CR 26.

the analysis of the right in the substitute as a power goes some way towards smoothing out the picture of the proprietary response to unjust enrichment.

(b) The Rules of Tracing

The rules of tracing do not themselves confer rights. They answer the question whether one asset is wholly or partly the substitute for another. Sometimes this can be done simply by producing evidence that the value of the one was employed to obtain the other. It might be that they were exchanged, or, more likely, that the one was sold and the money thus raised was used, with or without the addition of additional funds, to buy the other. However, the proof of substitution by evidence runs quickly into obstacles.

In the example just given, if we add one more fact, namely that the price of the original asset is paid into an active bank account, we run almost immediately into an evidential impasse. There is no natural way of saying which credit is represented by which debit. That being so, there is no natural answer to the question whether the second asset was bought with the price of the first. Since the only alternative would be to allow the process of tracing to be blocked at the first evidential impasse, this kind of problem has led to the introduction of artificial rules whose purpose is to prevent the defendant from having a wholly fortuitous defence.

It is these rules which have made tracing a complex subject, but they do not completely explain why a process of identification should have needed a whole book to itself.[43] Before Professor Lionel Smith wrote his masterly study of the subject, its intricacy, or impenetrability, was due to two other complicating factors. One was the constant failure to distinguish between the process of tracing and the business of establishing a right in the identified substitute. Professor Smith conveniently calls this the difference between tracing and claiming. The other, partly textured into the confusion between tracing and claiming, was the notion that the identification rules were different at law and in equity, that equity was better at seeing through evidential impasses than the law but would only open its far-seeing eyes in special situations. Thanks to the success of Smith's work,[44] these confusions have been largely blown away. Tracing

[43] Smith, *The Law of Tracing* (see n. 42).

[44] In *Boscawen v Bajwa* [1996] 1 WLR 328 (CA), which was decided shortly before the publication of the book, the Court of Appeal accepted the main lines of Smith's analysis, so far as it had already been revealed in the periodical literature. In *Foskett v McKeown* this was further endorsed: [2001] AC 102, 131.

remains a complex process. It still needs at least a short book to itself. But it is founded on three fairly straightforward rules for breaking evidential impasses. All three belong to both common law and equity. A moment's reflection reveals that it would be absurd, and was absurd, to suppose that an evidential difficulty could be overcome on one side of the old jurisdictional division but not on the other.[45]

First, there is the default rule that a mixed fund diminishes equally for all who have innocently contributed to it: the *pari passu* rule. This was applied in the ill-fated case of *Sinclair v Brougham*.[46] The actual outcome is only intelligible against the background of a series of agreements between different classes of claimant, but the core of their Lordships' decision was that all ultra vires depositors were entitled to share *pro rata* in the fund in the liquidator's hands

Secondly, there is the principle used in banking law to determine which of several debts to a single creditor is discharged by a payment made by the debtor and hence which debit against an active bank account corresponds to which credit. The rule is 'first in, first out', always called the rule in *Clayton's Case*.[47] This rule is very fierce, in that, if the money of a number of people has been paid into an account, it can bring about a situation in which the earlier contributors bear all the loss. Consequently, where all the contributors have a common interest and common complaint, 'first in, first out' rather easily gives way to *pari passu* even where the fund was nothing other than a bank account. It is not open to the court simply to prefer *pari passu*. There has to be some reason to justify not using *Clayton's Case*.

Russell-Cooke Trust Co v Prentis was such a case.[48] A solicitor whose financial services were regulated by the Law Society offered the investing public a guaranteed yield several times greater than was otherwise available. Short term lending always commands very high interest. His scheme was to invest only in secured bridging loans. His offer attracted some £6m, but irregularities precipitated Law Society intervention. There then turned out to be a substantial and unexplained shortfall in the client account in which as yet uninvested funds were kept. The more recent contributors naturally favoured the application of *Clayton's Case*. Lindsay J justified spreading

[45] More detail in P Birks, 'The Necessity of a Unitary Law of Tracing' in R Cranston (ed), *Making Commercial Law* (OUP Oxford 1997) 239.

[46] [1914] AC 398 (HL); cf *Barlow Clowes International Ltd v Vaughan* [1992] 4 All ER 22 (CA).

[47] (1816) 1 Mer 529, 572, 35 ER 767, 781.

[48] [2002] EWHC 2227 (Ch), [2003] 2 All ER 478.

the loss *pari passu* among all contributors, on the basis that there was evidence that when the scheme was running the solicitor had not in fact been dealing with his contributors in chronological order. Later investors had sometimes been preferred to earlier ones when the size of their investment more conveniently matched the lending opportunity.[49]

Thirdly, when evidential difficulties have been created by a wrongdoer, the resulting impasse can legitimately be resolved against the interest of the wrongdoer who created it. So, where a trustee pays trust money into his own account, and then draws on the account and dissipates some of the money, the beneficiary can insist that what is left is the trust money,[50] and *vice versa* if he invests some of the money from the account and dissipates the rest, the beneficiary is no less able to insist that the trust money was the money which was taken out and invested.[51]

4. BENEFICIAL INTEREST OR SECURITY INTEREST

The previous paragraphs have assumed that, whether immediately or through the exercise of a power, the interest in question was a beneficial as opposed to a security interest. Subject to what will be said below about subrogation, the only security interest encountered as a response to unjust enrichment is an equitable lien. *Foskett v McKeown* confirms that a claimant who is in a position to assert a proprietary interest in a traceable substitute may elect to take either a beneficial interest or an equitable lien for the amount of his input.[52] Thus if it is shown that the defendant used £50,000 of the claimant's money and £100,000 of his own to buy a Rolls Royce, so that the car is as to one third the traceable substitute for the claimant's money, the choice will be between a one-third beneficial interest and an equitable lien for the amount of his input, £50,000. The choice will depend on whether a one-third undivided share in the car is now worth more or less than £50,000. Cars generally lose value quickly. Since the lien is security for £50,000, the lien will be the more attractive option if that is what has happened.

In general therefore the claimant in unjust enrichment who has a proprietary right in the asset originally received by the enrichee now has this choice between beneficial and security interest in the traceable substitute. However there appear to be some situations in which, as a matter of authority, the claimant has no more than an equitable lien. In *Foskett v McKeown* the Court of Appeal had thought that the beneficiaries

[49] Ibid [56]. [50] *Re Hallett's Estate* (1880) 13 Ch D 696 (CA).
[51] *Re Oatway* [1903] 2 Ch 356. [52] [2001] 1 AC 102 (HL) 131.

of the trust could have no more than a lien for the amount of money actually used to pay premiums due on the life policy of the dishonest trustee. It drew an analogy between paying premiums and maintaining or improving another's land.[53]

In *Lord Napier & Ettrick v Hunter*[54] the House of Lords had to answer the question whether an insurer had more than a mere personal claim in respect of money received by an insured person in diminution of a loss for which he had already been indemnified. The answer was that the insurer had a lien over the sum received, not a beneficial interest. The principle underlying these cases is difficult to articulate. It has to explain not only why a lien is an appropriate response but also why a beneficial interest is not.

There may be no principle. It is a fact, albeit not an occasion for pride, that security interests arising by operation of law, seem to rest on nothing but authority. In this the non-possessory equitable lien is no different from the possessory liens known to the common law, the incidence of which has to be learned by heart.

Where one person discharges another's debt[55] and the creditor was secured, there is an important question whether, by reviving subrogation, the intervener is entitled to take over the security. In such cases of perfect discharge where the subrogation is purely metaphorical because the creditor's rights have been extinguished, the right to the security is certainly not invariably triggered.[56]

It seems that the intervener will be allowed to 'revive the security' if he was legally liable to pay.[57] If he was not legally liable, reviving subrogation may still work for him so far as it will not put him in a better position than he would have been in if either things had worked out as he intended or, had his money had been used to buy a thing rather than to discharge a secured debt, he would have acquired a proprietary interest in the substitute asset.[58]

[53] [1998] Ch 265, 278; *Unity Joint Stock Mutual Banking Association v King* (1858) 25 Beav 72, 53 ER 563.

[54] [1993] AC 713 (HL).

[55] On the difficulty of knowing when third party payment discharges: J Beatson, *The Use and Abuse of Unjust Enrichment* (OUP Oxford 1991) 177, esp 199–205.

[56] *Re Wrexham Mold and Connah's Quay Railway* [1899] 1 Ch 440; *Burston Finance Ltd v Speirway Ltd* [1974] 1 WLR 1648 (Ch D).

[57] Sureties and co-contractors derive their rights not from these principles but from the Mercantile Law Amendment Act 1856 s 5, on which see C Mitchell, *The Law of Contribution and Reimbursement* (OUP Oxford 2003) [14.13]–[14.21].

[58] Interpreting *Banque Financière de la Cité v Parc (Battersea) Ltd* [1999] AC 221 (HL) 231–6 (Lord Hoffmann). Cf C Mitchell, *The Law of Subrogation* (OUP Oxford 1994) 27–34.

Genuine subrogation and metaphorical subrogation have in the past been insufficiently distinguished.[59] The entitlement to the securities may be more absolute in the case of the genuine subrogation, on the ground that none of the rights superfluously held by the creditor should be left in his hands.

D. CONCLUSION

The swaps cases, taken together, amounted to the most sustained judicial application of the English law of unjust enrichment that there ever has been. In relation to the method of deciding whether an enrichment is unjust they effected a radical reorientation of our law towards the approach preferred in civilian jurisdictions. In Part III we concluded that that reorientation must be accepted, even though the choice between two methods was never explicitly confronted. One powerful reason for not resisting was that the academic literature, and especially the comparative literature, makes it plain that, properly understood, the 'no basis' method, which is ultimately derived from the Roman action of debt, yields results which are more economically reasoned and more reliably consistent than the English unjust factors ever achieved.

This part has been about responses to the event. The swaps cases moved strongly and deliberately against the proprietary response to unjust enrichment. In contrast to Part III, however, this part says that here the authority of the swaps cases ought to be resisted. This conclusion is reached against the current of the comparative literature and influence, because civilian systems do not have any proprietary responses to unjust enrichment, against the apparent dictates of the doctrine of precedent, and against the trend of American case law, which in recent years has been back-pedalling from its formerly liberal recognition of such proprietary rights. It is also not to be denied that the question of the proprietary response was more directly and overtly before the judges than was the choice as to the method of handling 'unjust'. Despite all these considerations, the fact remains that the swaps cases give an unreliable lead in this matter.

It may well be that hostility to proprietary rights arising from unjust enrichment will ultimately be vindicated by the legislature, but it is impossible at the moment to accept that it represents the position of English law. Three reasons bear repetition. First, the steps which were

[59] Below, 296–9.

taken against the proprietary response were taken on too narrow a front. Nothing was done to ensure consistency across the whole range of unjust enrichments. Secondly, no strong case was made as to why the law should wish to withdraw the proprietary response where it had previously been conceded. The onus is on the side arguing for change, because there is a good *prima facie* case in favour of the earlier instinct that enrichments which were never for one minute freely at the disposition of the enrichee, and which the law therefore characterizes as unjust, should not be available to unsecured creditors. Thirdly, it has since appeared, in *Foskett v McKeown*,[60] that a disabling heresy as to the relationship between property and unjust enrichment has gained surprising ground. The heresy supposes, indefensibly, that property and unjust enrichment are systematically opposed categories. With that belief in the background it is impossible to contemplate with equanimity the proposition that in all cases of initial failure of basis, and in some others, property rights are born of unjust enrichment.

The policy underlying the hostility to proprietary responses to unjust enrichment may yet be clearly articulated and may then prevail. It is clear, however, that the ground has never been sufficiently prepared for a reliable examination of the question. Neither unjust enrichment itself nor its relation to the law of property have been clearly enough seen to allow a reliable judgment on the merits or the technicalities. If the picture presented in this chapter is destined for rejection, it will at least provide a stable platform from which to drive the law in another direction.

[60] [2001] 1 AC 102 (HL). Above, 34–7.

Part V

Defences

9

Disenrichment and Disimpoverishment

The fifth question is whether the enrichee has any defences. These have become immensely more important than they were 25 years ago. The liberalization of the grounds for restitution, which continues in the change of method determined by the swaps saga, has left them bearing a greater burden. Blunt restrictions placed on the cause of action did rough justice. That crude strategy has been given up. Instead the right to restitution is now selectively weakened. This kind of fine-tuning is chiefly the responsibility of the defences. Sir William Evans' anxieties as to the extreme consequences of recognizing rights to restitution under void contracts have to be met here, if they can be met at all.

All the defences work by trumping the injustice of the defendant's enrichment. The defendant simply adds further facts which overwhelm the claimant's *prima facie* entitlement to restitution. However, there are two which operate in this way specifically by attacking 'enrichment at the expense of the claimant'. This chapter deals only with those two. It is convenient to distinguish them from all the rest, so that the rest become unjust-related defences, while these two are enrichment-related and expense-related. The next chapter deals with unjust-related defences so defined.

The enrichment-related defence is here called disenrichment, and the expense-related defence is called disimpoverishment. Can an enriched defendant resist a claim if one way or another that enrichment has been eliminated? And does he have a defence if the claimant makes good from third parties such impoverishment as he may have suffered? Neologisms are in principle to be avoided, but 'disenrichment' and 'disimpoverishment' are vivid and save an immense number of more familiar words. There is sometimes an overlap between these two defences and one or more nominate unjust-related defences of possibly uncertain scope and rationale. The final section of the chapter briefly discusses the strategy for dealing with that kind of overlap.

A. DISENRICHMENT

The independence and necessity of the law of unjust enrichment derives from the peculiar normativity of extant gain. Chapter 1 demonstrated the truth of the proposition that very slight facts suffice to require the relocation of a misplaced gain so long as the gain is still extant. The defence of disenrichment ties the defendant's liability to the amount of his extant gain, and disqualification from the defence allows the liability to persist on the basis of the disqualifying fault. So central to the logic of unjust enrichment is this defence that it comes as a surprise to realize that it is not fully recognized in English law. It has to be extracted from the supposedly much broader defence of change of position, itself reborn only a dozen years ago.

1. DISENRICHMENT AND CHANGE OF POSITION

In *Lipkin Gorman v Karpnale Ltd* the House of Lords introduced, or revived, the defence of change of position. To the extent that restitution would no longer be equitable because of changed circumstances, the defendant must be relieved from liability.[1] This broad language, on its face, extends far beyond the single fact of disenrichment. Yet all known examples can be covered by a much narrower formulation in which the defence would be confined to disenrichment. The narrower formulation would be on the following lines. Unless the defendant is disqualified from the defence, his liability in unjust enrichment is extinguished to the extent that, by reason of an event which would not have happened but for the enrichment, his wealth is reduced.

It must be regarded as doubtful whether any non-disenriching changes of position will ever be found to give rise to a defence distinct from all the other unjust-related defences. There are two reasons. One is that it is part and parcel of the peculiar normativity of extant enrichment that it is difficult to come up with any argument for retaining a misplaced enrichment which one still has. The other is that such good arguments as can be

[1] [1991] 2 AC 548, 579–80 (HL); cf *Restatement of the Law of Restitution* (American Law Institute St Paul Minn 1937) s 142. The defence was already foreshadowed in *Moses v Macferlan*: 'This is equally beneficial to the defendant. It is the most favourable way in which he can be sued: he can be liable no further than the money he has received; and against that, may go into every equitable defence, upon the general issue; he may claim every equitable allowance; . . . in short, he may defend himself by every thing which shews that the plaintiff, ex aequo & bono, is not intitled to the whole of his demand, or to any part of it' (1760) 2 Burr 1005, 1010, 97 ER 676, 681.

found will probably turn out to be covered by a nominate unjust-related defence, as *res judicata* covers previous litigation and limitation covers delay. Nevertheless, recent dicta in the Court of Appeal in *Commerzbank AG v Gareth Price-Jones*[2] vigorously reject the suggestion that the broad defence should be cut down to disenrichment. The safe tactic is to divide the wide defence in two, between disenrichment and non-disenriching change of position. The latter, if it has any content, must clearly be an unjust-related defence. It will be revisited in the next chapter.

2. RATIONALE

The rationale of the defence of disenrichment can itself be divided into two. First, the defence draws a necessary line around the typically strict liability in unjust enrichment. That strict liability, triggered by relatively weak facts, is at first sight counter-intuitive, even repulsive. But we have seen that no other regime can be satisfactory in the business of relocating extant gains. The defence ensures that the defendant, unless disqualified, will be strictly liable only to the extent that his assets remain swollen. Only a recipient who is disqualified will remain liable despite disenrichment, but for him the liability will not be strict, since on all views disqualification supposes fault on the part of the recipient. Secondly, in the same breath the defence reconciles the interest in obtaining restitution of unjust enrichment with the competing interest in the security of receipts. There is a general interest in our being free to dispose of wealth which appears to be at our disposition. The defence avoids the need to sterilize funds against the danger of unsuspected unjust enrichment claims.

A consequential benefit, now that the defence is securely in place, is that it is not necessary to maintain the old restrictive posture in relation to the cause of action. The fragility of claims in unjust enrichment takes care of the fear of too much restitution. There is a price to pay. Deserving claimants will sometimes be defeated. The existence of the defence means that the claimants bear the ultimate risk of loss. Their plight must not narrow the interpretation of the defence. We cannot have the cake and eat it.

Every unjust enrichment has to be subject to the defence of disenrichment unless for some specific reason the defendant is deprived of its protection. This means in particular that the defence must apply not only to personal but also to proprietary claims arising from unjust enrichment. If this were not so, there would be a stampede towards

[2] [2003] EWCA Civ 1663, [65]–[66], [71]–[72] (Munby J).

proprietary claims. That must not happen. It is the event, not the kind of right born of the event, that determines the available defences. If the House of Lords were to maintain its flawed doctrine of the logical opposition between unjust enrichment and property,[3] all proprietary claims would escape the defence and the stampede would begin. Suppose that an enrichee buys gold with his enrichment and then, because he feels securely better off, disenriches himself by making a gift to charity from his current account. If the gift would not have been made but for the enrichment, the defence of disenrichment indisputably applies to the personal claim, reducing the enrichee's liability by the amount given away. If the proprietary claim to the gold were immune to the defence, the defence would be stultified and there would be a strong but irrational incentive to switch to the proprietary claim whether or not the defendant was insolvent.

The application of the defence to proprietary claims is less straightforward than to personal claims. Where the claimant has a lien, the sum secured will diminish step by step with the disenrichment. Where he has a power to vest an asset in himself, that power must be barred unless he allows for or compensates any disenrichment. The courts have from time to time acknowledged this in relation to rescission.[4] Where the claimant claims to have a full beneficial interest, the mode in which the defence should be made to apply remains to be explored. He must be put on terms, so that his payment of compensation for the defendant's disenrichment becomes a precondition of his claim. In equity, such putting on terms presents no problem.[5] At common law, except in relation to land, the court does not have to order specific delivery.[6] Any money judgment can easily allow for the defendant's disenrichment. One way or another, except against a defendant disqualified from the defence the claimant must bear the risk of loss.

3. RELEVANT DISENRICHMENTS

The fact that the defendant no longer has the money or other asset received is not conclusive of disenrichment. If I spend a mistaken £100

[3] *Foskett v McKeown* [2001] 1 AC 102 (HL).

[4] *Cheese v Thomas* [1994] 1 WLR 129, noted in M Chen-Wishart (1994) 110 LQR 173, who points out that in *Allcard v Skinner* (1887) 36 Ch D 145 (CA) it was accepted that the defendant could not have been made to restore expenditure on charitable works.

[5] Compare *Cooper v Phibbs* (1867) LR 2 HL 149; *Solle v Butcher* [1950] 1 KB 671 (CA) which even now remains the best example of a judgment on terms.

[6] Torts (Interference with Goods) Act 1977 s 5.

on the weekly trip to the supermarket and then the family eats up the food, I have nothing left of the money received or of its immediate product. So long as I would have done that shopping anyhow, my wealth, viewed abstractly as a single fund, remains swollen to the extent of £100. A recipient who is induced to pay off a mortgage or a credit card debt pays what would have to have been paid anyhow. Except to the extent that some figure can be put on the value of his educed liquidity over time, he has not been disenriched.[7]

If, by contrast, the money is lost or stolen or used up in expenditure induced by its availability, the disenrichment will be set against the enrichment, and the recipient's liability will thereby be reduced. The example which Lord Goff used in the *Lipkin Gorman* case was a donation to charity which would not have been made but for the enrichment.[8] In the case itself, the casino was *prima facie* liable to make restitution to the solicitor claimants of all the sums staked by the gambling partner. But the gambler had occasionally won. When it paid him his winnings, the casino reduced its wealth in a way in which it would not have done but for the receipt of the gambler's stakes. Its liability was therefore reduced by the amount of his winnings.

An enrichee often allows his standard of living to drift up to match his additional liquidity. In such case the courts will take a broad view and will not look with eagle eyes for proof that every item was induced by the enrichment.[9] In Australia, an enrichee who gave up salaried work in order to return to university was entitled to have taken into account the money that would have been earned but for the change induced by the enrichment.[10] Again, where a computer company's account was mistakenly credited with a sum which it believed represented long-awaited payment of a customer's debt, its having then released more goods to the non-paying customer was a relevant disenrichment.[11]

Resolving a troubling hesitation,[12] *Dextra Bank and Trust Company v Bank of Jamaica* held that there was no reason to insist that the

[7] *RBC Dominion Securities v Dawson* (1994) 111 DLR (4th) 230; *Scottish Equitable plc v Derby* [2001] 3 All ER 818 (CA).

[8] *Lipkin Gorman* (n 1 above) 579.

[9] *Phillip Collins Ltd v Davis* [2000] 3 All ER 808, 829–30; *Scottish Equitable plc v Derby* [2001] 3 All ER 818 (CA) 827–8.

[10] *Gertsch v Atsas* [1999] NSWSC 898 (Foster A-J).

[11] *National Westminster Bank v Somer* [2002] 1 All ER 198 (CA).

[12] *South Tyneside Metropolitan BC v Svenska International plc* [1995] 1 All ER 545, where, however, there was arguably no reliance specifically on the relevant enrichment, which was the rolling difference between the payments made by each party.

disenrichment must come after the enrichment.[13] There the disenrichment was anticipatory. Dextra Bank sent the Bank of Jamaica a cheque for US $3m. Both banks were the victims of an elaborate fraud. The Bank of Jamaica thought that it was buying foreign currency. Dextra Bank believed that it was concluding a foreign currency loan. The Bank of Jamaica was so comprehensively deceived that, even before it actually received the cheque, it reimbursed those who had supposedly paid the price of the US dollars. Effect can precede cause when the medium is reliance. The causal connection between the money received and the payment out was absolutely clear. It gave the Bank of Jamaica a complete defence.[14]

The Court of Appeal has since followed the Privy Council in this. In *Commerzbank AG v Gareth Price-Jones*[15] the defendant banker contested the notification of his guaranteed bonus of £250,000. The bank, meaning to add £15,000, sent a second notification saying that it would pay £265,000. Later it paid both the £250,000 and the £265,000. The banker maintained that he had understood the second notification as raising his entitlement to £515,000 and that, in the months after notification but before payment, he had therefore abstained from seeking higher remuneration with another merchant bank. His employer unsurprisingly took the view that he was bound to repay £250,000 and in due course deducted that sum from money otherwise owed to him.

The Court of Appeal did not question Mr Price-Jones's honesty. He was not disqualified from the defence. And the Court accepted that a relevant change of position in anticipation of an enrichment was to be treated in the same way as one which came afterwards. Hence it was no objection that it was before he received the money that he had, as he maintained, foregone better prospects elsewhere. He could not, however, show any definite, quantifiable disenrichment. We will return to this case in the context of non-disenriching changes of position, although in fact the claimant also failed under that limb of the defence. His employer had rightly insisted that he was under an obligation to repay in full the unintended £250,000.

[13] [2002] 1 All ER Comm 193 (PC) [35]–[39].

[14] This may now explain a minor mystery in *Lipkin Gorman* (n 1 above) in that the casino was allowed credit for all the winnings. On a strict view the firm would have recovered all the losing stakes in full while the casino would have been allowed to keep the few winning stakes. However, the winnings can perhaps be contemplated as having been paid in response to the winning stakes and in anticipation of his continuing to indulge his addiction.

[15] [2003] EWCA Civ 1663.

4. DISQUALIFICATION

Once you know of your disentitlement you cannot expect to escape liability by hurriedly disenriching yourself. The enrichee in *McDonald v Coys of Kensington*[16] appears to have snatched at that vain hope by making a gift of the enrichment to his partner. A few lines sufficed to dismiss his defence.[17] But the disqualification must be narrow. The question is how exactly it should be expressed.

In the *Lipkin Gorman* case Lord Goff said that the defence was only open to those who acted in good faith. Those in bad faith were disqualified, as also wrongdoers.[18] Wrongdoers will usually be disqualified on the ground of bad faith, but the existence of torts of strict liability, conversion for instance, means that an innocent recipient can be disqualified as a wrongdoer. However, Lord Goff was speaking of claims for restitution, not of claims in unjust enrichment. The same is true of the *Restatement*.[19] The disqualification of innocent wrongdoers is probably confined to wrongdoers sued as such or, in other words, to restitution for wrongs as opposed to restitution for unjust enrichment. A wrongdoer sued as such has no defence of change of position, but a wrongdoer sued in unjust enrichment will have the defence, unless disqualified by bad faith.

The logic which requires disenrichment to be a defence to claims in unjust enrichment, namely that only extant enrichment supports strict liability, does not apply to gain-based recovery in respect of wrongs. In relation to any wrong for which the choice goes in favour of gain-based recovery a second choice has to be made as to the measure of the recoverable gain. The measure is again a matter of choice, not logic. If the choice then went in favour of abstractly surviving gain, disenrichment would appear to be a defence, but it will always be true that the defence has no necessary application to wrongs. So far there appears to be no example in which the choice has gone in favour of giving the acquisitive wrongdoer credit for all disenrichments, although *Boardman v Phipps*[20] comes close to being one. For the moment therefore it remains true that, even when the claim is to restitution, not compensation, wrongdoers sued as such are not entitled to the defence or any simulation of it.

16 [2004] EWCA Civ 47.

17 Ibid [41]. Primarily relevant to the issue of enrichment, this case is discussed above, 56.

18 *Lipkin Gorman* (n 1 above) 579–80.

19 *Restatement* (n 1 above) s 143(2).

20 [1967] 2 AC 46 (HL), discussed above, 12.

(a) Disqualification on the Ground of Bad Faith

In the *Dextra Bank* case Lord Goff and Lord Bingham emphasized that only bad faith would disqualify. To disqualify recipients on the ground of negligence would draw the courts into the guessing game of apportioning blame between incommensurable acts of negligence—of the claimant in parting with the money and of the defendant in allowing himself to believe that he was entitled to it.[21] The reason is that it would appear intolerable to any defendant disqualified for negligence that the claimant's claim should continue to be unaffected by his negligence.[22] 'Bad faith' usually means dishonesty.[23] However, in *Twinsectra Ltd v Yardley*, in the context of knowing assistance in a breach of trust, the House of Lords underlined the requirement that a dishonest person must not only engage in discreditable conduct but must either know that according to prevailing opinion it is discreditable or deliberately shut his eyes to facts which would reveal the prevailing condemnation to him.[24] If this subjective requirement narrowed the notion of dishonesty, the crucial question is whether it also narrows that disqualification from the defence of disenrichment. It seems that it does not.

In *Niru Battery Manufacturing Co v Milestone Trading Ltd*[25] a bank received a payment from Iran for the credit of one of its customers. It was sent under a letter of credit in respect of a cargo which the bank knew had not been shipped. The bank nonetheless allowed itself to be persuaded by its customer that in the light of the troubled history of the contract and the customer's assurance that he was making arrangements for a substitute shipment, the best thing would be to release the money to him. The money was released and lost. The bank at no stage consulted the Iranian side. The question was whether the bank's disenrichment gave it a defence. Moore-Bick J found that it had behaved discreditably but not

[21] [2002] 1 All ER Comm 193 (PC) [40]–[45], comparing the New Zealand experience where such balancing is attempted. In *National Bank of Egypt v Oman Housing Bank* [2002] EWHC 1760 (Comm), [2003] 1 All ER (Comm) 246, 251–2 David Steele J expressly endorsed the need for a bulwark against inquiries into relative fault.

[22] The irrelevance of the claimant's negligence, discussed above, 5–7, was reaffirmed in *Scottish Equitable plc v Derby* (n 7 above) [19]–[25], esp [24] (Robert Walker LJ with whom Keene and Simon Browne LJJ agreed).

[23] Sale of Goods Act 1979 s 61(3): 'A thing is deemed to be done in good faith within the meaning of this Act when it is in fact done honestly, whether it is done negligently or not.'

[24] [2002] UKHL 12, [2002] 2 AC 164, Lord Millett dissenting. The New Zealand Court of Appeal subsequently showed itself wary of accepting the narrow, subjective notion of dishonesty: *US International Marketing Ltd v National Bank of New Zealand* 28 October 2003, noted by TM Yeo (2004) 120 LQR 208.

[25] [2002] EWHC 1425 (Comm), [2002] 2 All ER (Comm) 705.

dishonestly in the subjective *Twinsectra* sense. But he was not prepared to narrow the disqualification. He preferred to open up a gap between dishonesty and bad faith. He emphasized that he was not disqualifying it on the ground of negligence. It was disqualified because it had not acted in good faith. The objective element of dishonesty sufficed for a finding of disqualifying bad faith. So the bank had no defence.

On appeal Moore-Bick J was upheld, but the Court of Appeal took a much less satisfactory line.[26] The bank remained disqualified and hence liable despite its 100 per cent disenrichment. However, the Court of Appeal softened the test for disqualification. Deliberately invoking recent cases on liability for knowing receipt, the Court held that an enrichee would be disqualified whenever it would be inequitable or unconscionable to plead the defence.[27] Such words offer no guidance at all. Worse still, they offer no protection against the descent into comparative fault which *Dextra Bank* was anxious to prevent.

The disqualification has to be narrow. *Twinsectra* subjective dishonesty is too narrow. At first instance Moore-Bick J's decision essentially distinguished between subjective and objective dishonesty and made the disqualification turn on the objective dishonesty which would have satisfied Lord Millett in the *Twinsectra* case, where he dissented on this very point. Conduct condemned by prevailing standards is objectively dishonest. Subjective dishonesty requires in addition knowledge of that condemnation, though not necessarily endorsement of it. Robin Hood was subjectively dishonest for, although he thought it good to steal from the rich to give to the poor, he knew that prevailing opinion condemned it. Moore-Bick J's bad faith was objective dishonesty. If that is watered down so as to enlarge the disqualification, it is inevitable that defendants will contest the claimant's right to discount his own carelessness. The Court of Appeal showed no sensitivity to that dynamic.

If, applying the correct test, you are not disqualified from the defence, you will either have believed yourself entitled to the enrichment in question or you will have understood yourself obliged to deal with it in some way. In the former case, where you believe yourself entitled, you will have the defence however capriciously you disenrich yourself. Suppose that, against all advice, you invest in a failing company, which duly fails. Your unreasonableness will not cost you the defence. The answer would have

[26] [2003] EWCA Civ 1446.

[27] [148]–[149] and [162] (Clarke LJ), [182]–[185] and [192] (Sedley LJ). Butler-Sloss P agreed with both judgments.

been the same if you had thrown the money in the fire or, like Cleopatra, had allowed a priceless pearl to dissolve in a glass of wine.

In the other case, you are not disqualified from the defence but honestly believe that you are under a duty to pass the money to a person other than yourself. It may be that you are persuaded that you must hand it over to a third party or that you know the money was not due and must be sent back to the payer as soon as you can find time to do it.[28] In the latter case you may come under a duty of care in the meantime, as one who knows he has the management of another's money. If the money is lost before you have done that which you know that you must do, you may be liable if you have failed in that duty. Although negligence does not disqualify you from the defence of disenrichment, you may in such a case have incurred an independent liability in negligence.

In *National Bank of New Zealand v Waitaki International Processing (NI) Ltd*[29] the bank persuaded itself that it owed Waitaki $500,000. In the teeth of warnings and protests, it insisted on paying it over. Waitaki nonetheless never believed other than that the bank had made a mistake. It knew that the money would have to go back. It deposited it with a finance house to earn interest, taking a sound security. Later it agreed to vary the security. The new security proved hopelessly inadequate. All the money was lost. The New Zealand courts found that Waitaki had failed in its duty when the security was varied. The security it took would at the time have been suitable for up to two-thirds of the sum, from which it was taken to follow that Waitaki was liable for a third of the loss. It was entitled to the defence of disenrichment but, by virtue of the breach of duty, it was independently liable for one-third of the loss.[30]

The New Zealand judges then went on to make the kind of apportionment from which the English courts have so far abstained. They said that the obstinately mistaken bank was more at fault than the defendants and should therefore bear all but 10 per cent of the loss. An English court would have started from the proposition that the bank, despite its obstinacy, would have been able to recover in full if the defendants had not been disenriched. However, the defendants had been 100 per cent disenriched and were not disqualified from the defence. Against the defence there

[28] *Thomas v Houston Corbett and Co* [1969] NZLR 151 (NZCA); *African Diamond Exporters Pty Ltd v Barclays Bank International* [1978] (3) SA 699 (A), discussed by D de Visser 'Responsibility to Return Lost Enrichment' [1992] Acta Juridica 175, 194–6.

[29] [1999] 2 NZLR 211 (NZCA).

[30] Compare the measure used in such circumstances against trustees: Trustee Act 1925 s 9.

had to be set their independent liability in negligence for 33 per cent of the loss.

Nearly all the cases in which the defence has been tested have been cases of mistake, but the defence is general. When value is transferred to you, not by mistake, but on a specified basis, you necessarily know that, depending on how things turn out, you may have to repay a like sum. This bears on what good faith will allow you to do in reliance on having the money in your hands. If you are paid £5,000 in advance for a garage to be built, it may causally be true that but for the advance you would not have taken an expensive Mediterranean holiday. The question will be whether good faith allows that kind of reliance. Almost certainly it does not. There are nevertheless some circumstances in which you can use up the enrichment without being disqualified from pleading the disenrichment. Money paid for a contractual reciprocation can safely be used to meet preparatory expenses. In *BP Exploration Co (Libya) Ltd v Hunt (No 2)*[31] Robert Goff J said that the statutory allowance for such expenses incurred 'in, or for the purpose of, the performance of the contract'[32] should be regarded as a statutory example of the defence.

In this connection, *Goss v Chilcott*[33] is problematic. Goss mortgaged his land to obtain a loan which his brother-in-law wanted. On his instructions, the lenders paid the money directly to the brother-in-law. The mortgage was later rendered void by alterations of the deed. The Privy Council held that the lenders nonetheless had a good claim for money paid on a basis which failed. Goss had no defence despite his disenrichment in favour of the brother in law. Since the nullified contract was a contract of loan, from the outset he knew that the money had to be repaid.

This outcome may have to be reviewed. Arguably it fails to separate the cause of action in unjust enrichment from the nullified contract. It also undermines the ground upon which it is now said that the ultra vires depositors in *Sinclair v Brougham*[34] could have been allowed their personal claim in unjust enrichment without stultifying the law's position in relation to the contract. It is the availability of the defence of disenrichment which chiefly differentiates the action in unjust enrichment from the action in contract.[35] The lenders in *Goss v Chilcott* could not sue in contract. They had to fall back on unjust enrichment. The money had

[31] [1982] 1 All ER 925, 925–78 (Robert Goff J).
[32] Section 1(2) of the Law Reform (Frustrated Contracts) Act 1943.
[33] [1996] AC 788 (PC).
[34] [1914] AC 398 (HL).
[35] *Westdeutsche Landesbank Girozentrale v Islington LBC* [1996] AC 669 (HL) 711–14 (Lord Browne-Wilkinson).

been paid on a basis which had failed. Falling back to unjust enrichment meant falling back to a claim which, against objectively honest enrichees, is fragile. The defendant was objectively honest. In that respect the court might be said to have dropped its guard.

(b) Policy-Motivated Deviations

Sometimes an honest defendant may find that the defence is excluded altogether on the ground that it would undermine a policy to which the law is committed. We will see below that claims in unjust enrichment are sometimes disallowed because they would stultify another commitment made by law. The same is true of this and other defences. It appears, for example, that, where people, usually wives, are induced to give domestic security for business borrowing,[36] the protective policies operating in favour of the security-giver deny the defence to the lender, usually a bank, which takes the security. The lending bank which is compelled to give up its security will inevitably have disenriched itself in response to the security given, in making the required advance or not calling in existing debts. If it could avail itself of the defence, the protection of the domestic security-giver would be utterly destroyed.

The other side of this penny is that in rare cases a defendant may be allowed the defence even in circumstances which would normally disqualify him. A minor's contracts are voidable at his option. The minor cannot, however, retain surviving enrichment.[37] That proposition restricting his liability to surviving enrichment, taken with the underlying protective policy, must entail allowing him, without inquiry into his honesty, all the disenrichments caused by his enrichment.

(c) Necessity of a Broad Defence

In conclusion it may be wise to gather together the issues which are implicated in the scope of the defence and which in the end require that the defence be broad and disqualification narrow. The line must be drawn at bad faith on the part of the recipient, in the sense of objective dishonesty. A wider disqualification would exclude even those whose honest beliefs are carelessly formed, for want of the inquiries which a reasonable person would make. That path would lead to two bad consequences. First, it would narrow the defence to the point at which it might be

[36] Exemplified by *Barclays Bank plc v O'Brien* [1994] 1 AC 180 (HL).

[37] Minors Contracts Act 1987 s 3(1), which, however, does not expressly say that it is talking about surviving property or proceeds: G Jones (ed), *Goff and Jones on Restitution* (6th edn Sweet & Maxwell London 2002) 25–6.

necessary to reintroduce restrictions in the cause of action itself. Secondly, it would generate inscrutable inquiries into comparative fault. So long as only those in bad faith are disqualified, the consequence is that, so far as the enrichment has been eliminated, as between parties in good faith the claimant bears the risk of the loss. That seems reasonable enough, and it is perfectly compatible with his initially having a claim which both yields a strict liability and is indifferent to his own negligence.

If even the careless defendant were disqualified from the defence the risk of loss would to that extent lie on him, which would seem monstrous if the rule were maintained, even after disenrichment, that the claimant's own negligence was irrelevant. In New Zealand, where the attempt has been made to apportion the loss in proportion to the fault of the parties, the outcomes appear entirely arbitrary, because the claimant's negligence in the enrichment and the defendant's negligence in the disenrichment are in truth incommensurable.

As we have seen, in *Dextra Bank and Trust Company v Bank of Jamaica* the Privy Council foresaw the need to take precautions against such developments.[38] For a short while the strength, breadth and clarity of the defence appeared to have been put beyond doubt. The more recent decisions of the Court of Appeal have undermined that confidence. They appear to favour a softer-edged version of the defence, and they show little or no sensitivity to either the trade-off between liberal grounds for restitution and vigorous defences or the trigger which sets in motion the descent towards arbitrary exercises in comparative fault.

B. DISIMPOVERISHMENT

In the common case enrichment of the defendant entails a loss to the claimant. The question has therefore arisen whether the defendant should be relieved of liability if the claimant manages to recoup that loss from third parties. This defence is usually discussed as 'passing on'. Does the fact that the claimant has passed on the loss deprive him of the right to recover the defendant's enrichment? In England, and also in Australia, there appears to be no such defence except under statutes concerned with claims to the return of taxes which turn out not to have been due. The broad wording used by those statutes makes it more appropriate to discuss them later, in connection with the defence which is designed to prevent an action in unjust enrichment from unjustly enriching the claimant.

[38] *Dextra Bank* (n 13 above) [43]–[44].

The defence of disimpoverishment was raised in the swaps litigation and was rejected. In those cases the question arose from the practice of hedging. Banks which enter into interest swaps often hedge by immediately making a back-to-back swap with another counter-party. In the second swap the bank takes the opposite position. The hedge then ensures that very penny lost under the first swap comes back under the second and, vice versa, that every penny won under the first swap is paid out under the hedge. The bank runs no risk. It makes money only through fees. When all the local authority swaps turned out to be void, such a bank, as winner under the swap and hence as defendant in the action in unjust enrichment, would invoke the hedge as a relevant disenrichment. This was unsuccessful because the hedge was not made in reliance on the relevant enrichment actually received but on the contract under which it might be received.[39]

By contrast a hedged bank which found itself the loser in the first swap and thus became the claimant in unjust enrichment would find its hedge used by the defendant public authority to defeat the claim. The authority's argument would be that the claimant bank, having hedged, had passed on the loss. It had disimpoverished itself.

This defence was firmly rejected by the English Court of Appeal,[40] as it had already been in Australia when an insurance company which had paid void taxes was said to have recouped by raising premiums.[41] The High Court of Australia has since strongly reasserted its rejection of the defence.[42] In jurisdictions such as England and Germany which do not insist that the claimant be identified as the person who suffered a loss corresponding to the defendant's gain, the premiss of the defence is false, for the claimant need not have suffered any loss. Loss is simply irrelevant. Canada takes the opposite position. It does require the claimant to have suffered the corresponding loss. In Canada the defence succeeds, though under heavy criticism because it encounters other difficulties.[43]

[39] Now that anticipatory disenrichment clearly suffices, this requires a more elaborate explanation: *Dextra Bank* (n 13 above) [39].

[40] *Kleinwort Benson Ltd v Birmingham City Council* [1997] QB 380 (CA).

[41] *Commissioner of State Revenue v Royal Insurance* (1994) 126 ALR 1 (HCA).

[42] *Roxborough v Rothmans of Pall Mall (Australia) Ltd* (2001) 185 ALR 335 (HCA), Kirby J dissenting, noted M McInnes (2002) 118 LQR 212–14

[43] *Air Canada v British Columbia* (1989) 59 DLR (4th) 161 (SCC) powerfully criticized by P Michell 'Restitution, Passing On, and the Recovery of Unlawfully Demanded Taxes: Why *Air Canada* Doesn't Fly' (1995) 1 U Toronto Faculty L Rev 130. For similarly adverse criticism of the recognition of the defence in European law: B Rudden and W Bishop, 'Gritz and Quellmehl: Pass it on' (1981) 6 ELR 243.

Everyone takes steps to adjust to a minus. The success of such steps is generally impossible to measure and often irrelevant, as where the loss is made good by extra work or efficiency savings. It is no business of a mistaken payee that the payer renounced his annual holiday to recoup the payment which he incorrectly thought to have been due. Even in a seemingly clear case, as where a tax is passed on in prices, it remains uncertain to what extent the addition to the price frightens away customers or constrains the profit margin. If the market is buoyant and the trader strong, it may be possible to conclude that the loss has been passed on. This shows the complexity of the inquiry. A weaker trader behaving in the same way in the same market may well have failed to disimpoverish itself.[44]

Moreover, even if it were certain that the loss had been successfully passed on, the quality of the defendant's enrichment as one which ought to be given up would remain absolutely unaffected. This becomes vividly apparent when the matter is tested against a defendant who still has surplus assets. The retort that the claimant has made good the loss inflicted by his mistaken payment does nothing whatever to strengthen the defendant's right to retain the enrichment. The passing on is *res inter alios acta* (something done between other parties) and as such irrelevant to the legal relations between the present litigants.

Statute apart, the objections to the defence of disimpoverishment, legal and factual, thus seem overwhelming. The rejection of the defence is therefore likely to endure. We will revert to the statutory version of the defence below. As we shall see, the fact that it comes under another name—unjust enrichment of the claimant—may be no more than a deception and, deception or not, cannot overcome the very real difficulties which have so far led to its rejection at common law.

C. OVERLAPPING NOMINATE DEFENCES

The statutory version of passing on is only one of several defences with names of their own which overlap with disenrichment or disimpoverishment. As in that example, it is often not clear whether the nominate

[44] In *Waikato Regional Airport v Attorney General* [2003] UKPC 50 the NZ government, having imposed ultra vires charges on the regional airports, tried to defend itself by arguing that the airports had passed on the charges to the airlines. The Privy Council observed that such evidence as there was suggested that the market was too fragile to allow the charges to be fully and effectively passed on [77]–[78]. Their Lordships, finding the factual basis of the attempted defence not to have been made out, abstained from pronouncing on the principal question of whether the defence had been finally rejected.

defence really is an unjust-related defence distinct from disenrichment or disimpoverisment. That in turn depends on whether or not it has an independent rationale. For example, it is one form of disenrichment to confer a valuable benefit on the claimant in exchange for the enrichment which he now seeks to recover. But it is clear that, in the case of such exchange benefits, something else is going on beyond mere disenrichment, not least because the demand for counter-restitution can be made by people who would be disqualified from the defence of disenrichment. A different rationale must therefore be operating. By contrast, when we come to 'ministerial receipt' we will see that it is more doubtful whether it ever offers anything more to the defendant than the defence of disenrichment.

The tidiest tactic is to let disenrichment and disimpoverishment do all the work that they can do and then to ask whether the overlapping nominate defence really offers something more or different. Estoppel, for instance, can seem to turn on disenrichment because of the requirement of detrimental reliance, but it actually depends on quite different premisses and gives a more absolute defence. Again bona fide purchase for value from a third party supposes disenrichment of the defendant in the form of expenditure towards that party. It too has a second string to its bow. However, it cannot be assumed from the fact that a defence has its own name that it necessarily has a distinct rationale. Puzzles of this kind, and the discipline of first exhausting disenrichment and disimpoverishment in order to test the question whether the nominate defence really does anything more in its own name, will be considered when overlaps with unjust-related defences are encountered in the next chapter.

D. CONCLUSION

This chapter has only considered those defences which go directly to one or other limb of 'enrichment at the expense of the claimant'. The next chapter deals with all those which admit the enrichment at the claimant's expense but seek directly to trump the claimant's case that that enrichment is unjust. Making that division between the two chapters has involved cutting in two the most important defence of all, namely change of position. That has become disenrichment here, while in the next chapter it will recur as a non-disenriching defence. Whether or not there are any relevant non-disenriching changes of position, and even though this division flies in the face of present judicial practice throughout the common law world, it is absolutely essential to maintain this separation of disenrichment.

The reasons are, first, that extant enrichment is the essential element in the peculiar normativity of unjust enrichment. With the disenrichment of the defendant the picture changes completely. The law is no longer relocating a gain but allocating a loss. Someone must now come out worse off than they were at the beginning of the story. And, secondly, non-disenriching changes of position need to be considered on the basis that disenrichment is no longer in question. If the defendant is not disqualified from the defence of change of position, and nonetheless has no defence of disenrichment, it follows that he is still sitting on the enrichment received. It is very difficult to make a case for keeping an extant enrichment to which one was not entitled. Only the isolation of non-disenriching changes of position makes it starkly apparent how rare such a defence must be.

The other consequence of the line drawn between this chapter and the next is the exposure of the overlaps between those that are, or by name purport to be, unjust-related and those that are enrichment-related or at-the-expense-related. To avoid confusion in that overlap, the essential discipline is only to apply the unjust-related defences to the situation which obtains after those which attack enrichment at the expense of the claimant have already done their work. That makes for clarity of analysis and compels the analyst to identify the rationale of the unjust-related defence which is supposed to offer more or different protection.

10

Unjust-Related Defences

The defences which trump the claimant's argument that the enrichment at his expense is unjust are numerous. There is a danger of incoherence. It is important, therefore, to recognize that they belong in just four groups, according to the interest which they serve. First, there are those which aim to ensure that the successful claimant will not himself end up unjustly enriched. Secondly, there is the finality group which aims to protect the social and individual interest in putting an end to litigation. Thirdly, there is the stultification group. To stultify the law elsewhere is to contradict it for no good reason. These defences aim to prevent the law of unjust enrichment from making nonsense of the law's considered positions in other areas. Finally, the fourth group is once again a miscellaneous residue, in this case a small one.

This makes a more orderly picture. The groups tell us that there are in effect just three big defences. A claimant in unjust enrichment will be defeated where and to the extent that he would himself be unjustly enriched if he succeeded. Again, he will be defeated if his claim breaks the rules of finality in litigation. Thirdly, he will be defeated if his claim would make unexplained nonsense of a position deliberately taken by the law in another area. These three leave a tiny handful of singletons, each with its own rationale.

A. UNJUST ENRICHMENT OF THE CLAIMANT

There appear to be three situations in which the law has so far taken steps against the unjust enrichment of the claimant. If he has received exchange benefits from the defendant, he must make counter-restitution. Secondly, if he has both gain-based and loss-based claims against the defendant, he must not so combine them as to count some items twice. Thirdly, under statute, if he is seeking overpaid tax he cannot recover if he has already recovered it by rolling it on to his customers or other similar third parties. The third case is different from the other two. In them it is true that according to the rules of the law of unjust enrichment itself the claimant would be unjustly enriched at the defendant's expense. In the third case that is not so. The statutes which speak of unjust enrichment of the claimant can do so only by illegitimately switching from the law's conception of unjust enrichment to the colloquial meaning of the phrase. We will return to that.

1. COUNTER-RESTITUTION

Where a benefit has been received by the claimant from the defendant in exchange for the enrichment which he is seeking to recover from the defendant, that exchange-benefit can be seen as a disenrichment of the defendant or as a disimpoverishment of the claimant. Since disimpoverishment is not a recognized defence, there is no need to dwell on that perspective.

(a) Justifying the Requirement of Counter-Restitution

There is nothing to prevent the defendant pleading the exchange as a disenrichment. However, that general defence cannot account for the way in which the requirement of counter-restitution behaves. For example, even a fraudster is not disqualified from insisting on counter-restitution. Moreover, the defence that counter-restitution is impossible has historically been absolute, whereas disenrichment diminishes the liability step-by-step as the enrichment disappears. It is therefore perfectly clear that this defence does do more than disenrichment. The explanation must be that exchange benefits conferred on the claimant trigger a genuinely different rationale, so that, while they could be treated as disenrichments, they also have a second string to their bow.

The search for that separate rationale begins with the observation that where there has been an exchange it must be true that, if one side recovers the value which he has transferred, the basis of his own receipt of the exchange-benefit must also have failed. In short, if the defendant is unjustly enriched at his expense, so also is the claimant enriched at the defendant's expense. I give you gold in exchange for money. The contract is invalid. The basis of my receipt of the money fails. You can claim restitution. But, necessarily, the basis of your receipt of the gold also fails.

That bilateral unjust enrichment shows that both sides have claims. It does not entirely explain why the requirement of counter-restitution should be insisted on in such a way as compulsorily to bind both claims together. Each party could be left to its own claim. But nowadays, as is illustrated in all the swaps cases,[1] that is not allowed, and the effect is to reduce them to a single claim for the difference in value between the two performances. The defendant's enrichment in the swaps cases was the rolling balance between the payments on both sides.

The reason for tying the two claims together is explained by German jurists. They have shown that the two-claim approach can produce bizarre results. One claimant may fortuitously encounter an obstacle or bar which the other escapes, with the consequence that for very slight reasons the parties to the one exchange may end up in very different situations. For example, if the law does not focus on the one enrichment which consists in the difference between the two performances, one party may be able to use the disenrichment defence and the other not. In the common law the old way of escaping from these problems was the very fierce rule that denied restitution altogether unless the parties could be put back into exactly their original position. Under that regime 'counter-restitution impossible' was a peremptory and absolute defence. That blunt instrument has been given up. The same problems are now evaded by applying, in money, what German law calls the '*Saldo*' theory (*Saldo* being an old Italian banking word for a balance or difference, here borrowed to denote the balance or difference between the exchanged performances).[2] In short restitution is allowed subject to pecuniary counter-restitution, thus achieving restitution of the difference.

(b) Condition or Defence?

Under the old regime the requirement of counter-restitution in *specie* frequently provided the defendant with a permanent defence. At common law substitutionary counter-restitution in money was not permitted. The defence was that counter-restitution had become impossible, and it became impossible when that which had been received could not be given back in the form in which it had been received. Equity always took a rather more flexible view. It would not regard counter-restitution as

[1] The swaps cases are described in Chapter 5 above, 108–12.

[2] BS Markesinis, W Lorenz, and G Dannemann, *The German Law of Obligations Vol I: The Law of Contracts and Restitution* (OUP Oxford 1997) 764–6; R Zimmermann and J du Plessis, 'Basic Features of the German Law of Unjustified Enrichment' [1994] Restitution L Rev 14, 41–2; D Reuter and M Martinek, *Ungerechtfertigte Bereicherung* (Mohr Tübingen 1978) 595–7; H-G Koppensteiner and ER Kramer, *Ungerechtfertigte Bereicherung* (2nd edn de Gruyter Berlin 1988) 136–7.

impossible if it could be satisfactorily done in money.[3] And against a fraudster it would be robust in concluding that pecuniary counter-restitution would be satisfactory.[4] To an innocent defendant counter-restitution impossible might yet be available as a rigid and an absolute defence.

However, in *O'Sullivan v Management Agency and Music Ltd* the Court of Appeal played down the notion that equity's flexibility was available only against fraudsters.[5] A pop star was there allowed to rescind his contract with his managers and to recover all that they had received under it, but he himself had to make pecuniary counter-restitution in respect of the management and promotion services which he had received over a long period. The defendants could be said to have been in breach of fiduciary duty, but no emphasis was placed on that wrong as the justification for compelling them to accept money in place of services which could not of course be given back in kind.

The same resourcefulness is apparent in *Mahoney v Purnell*,[6] where the exchange was vitiated by undue influence. An elderly man had released his shareholding in a hotel company to his son-in-law in exchange for an annuity. It was no longer possible to reverse the exchange *in specie*, but, reducing both restitution and counter-restitution to money, the court gave judgment for the father-in-law for the £200,000 difference in value between that which he gave and that which he received.

This is typical of the kind of difference between law and equity that cannot be allowed to persist in the modern law. Either the law—the law as a whole—can tolerate counter-restitution in money, or it cannot. Sensing the absurdity, the judges now appear to have eased the common law out of its former rigidity. It used to take the view that a failure of contractual reciprocation had to be literally total, but this intransigent position has now been relaxed to an extent which shows that the flexible Chancery attitude to counter-restitution has now prevailed. Squeamishness about making money allowances for benefits which the claimant received from the defendant therefore appears to be a thing of the past. If this is right,

[3] *Erlanger v New Sombrero Phosphate Co* (1878) 3 App Cas 1218 (HL), 1278–9 (Lord Blackburn). Compare the flexibility of *Atwood v Maude* (1868) 3 Ch App 369 with the unnecessary rigour of *Whincup v Hughes* (1871) LR 6 CP 78. E McKendrick, 'Total Failure of Consideration and Counter-Restitution: One Issue or Two' in P Birks (ed), *Laundering and Tracing* (OUP Oxford 1995) 217, 231–8.

[4] *Spence v Crawford* [1939] 3 All ER 271 (HL).

[5] [1985] QB 428 (CA).

[6] [1996] 3 All ER 61.

the consequence is that it becomes doubtful whether there is ever a permanent defence of counter-restitution impossible.

Professor Burrows rightly observes that, since the courts are used to all the difficulties of valuation in money, the case in which counter-restitution will be regarded as impossible is unlikely to be encountered. Indeed he regards the defence as working only to ensure that the necessary money allowances are made by the claimant.[7] The law is not really that there is defence but that it is a condition of restitution that the amount recovered be reduced to allow for benefits received by the claimant.

This relatively new flexibility is witnessed in the string of cases on void interest swaps, where both performances consisted in the payment of money. Hobhouse J, who heard the early cases at first instance and whose approach was then applied in every case, proceeded on the basis that, as interest rates fluctuated and payments went back and forth, there was all along just a single rolling enrichment consisting in the difference between the value of the two performances.[8] In *Goss v Chilcott* the Privy Council subsequently accepted that wherever the mutual performances present no insuperable problems of valuation, the common law would always follow the same approach as that adopted by Hobhouse J.[9]

Again, the Court of Appeal has shown that it no longer regards valuation of part performances as an insuperable problem. In *DO Ferguson & Associates v Sohl* contractors had failed to finish the fitting out of a shop.[10] Their repudiatory breach was accepted by the owner, who had already paid a large sum. The Court of Appeal held that the incomplete work which had been done by the defaulting builders could be valued and set against the amount which the owner had paid. He therefore recovered the difference.

(c) Occasional Departures from the Requirement of Counter-Restitution

There are some situations in which a claimant appears to be exempt from the routine requirement of counter-restitution. Having obtained restitution, he is then left to answer for the enrichment which he received in

[7] A Burrows, *The Law of Restitution* (2nd edn Butterworths London 2002) 541; cf A Burrows and E McKendrick, *Cases and Materials on the Law of Restitution* (OUP Oxford 1997) 822.

[8] *Westdeutsche Landesbank Girozentrale v Islington LBC* [1994] 4 All ER 890, 941.

[9] [1996] AC 788 (PC).

[10] (1992) 62 Building L Rep 95 (CA).

exchange in an independent action, or not at all.[11] *Guinness Plc v Saunders* was such a case.[12] In the background was serious malpractice during a competitive takeover bid. When the dust had settled the claimant company recovered a large payment made to a director for special services in connection with the bid. It was not denied that those services had been rendered. Yet the company obtained restitution without making counter-restitution. The agreement to pay had been irregularly made, with persons not authorized to speak for the company. The company believed that it was contractually bound to pay the huge fee, but in fact it was not. There was no contract at all between the company and the director.

The reason why the company did not have to make counter-restitution would appear to be that the work in question should have been done by the director *qua* director. There was a mechanism for fixing special remuneration for exceptional duties, which had not been used. Additionally, it was certainly a factor in the court's decision that it would be wrong to spread any kind of safety-net beneath a misbehaving fiduciary.

The principle may be that a defendant cannot claim counter-restitution in respect of a benefit which he ought never to have traded. One who sells a car which is not his normally fails to make the buyer owner. The seller must make restitution of the price as having been received on a basis which has failed. The buyer may have had months of use before the true owner came on the scene. The seller gets no allowance for having provided that benefit. Counter-restitution is not required. The reason is probably that, since the car was never his, the claim belongs, if to anyone, to the true owner who has now appeared.[13]

2. ELECTION

It sometimes happens that the same story discloses both loss-based and gain-based claims. This can happen in two ways. It may be that the claimant has a cause of action for a wrong which gives rise to both kinds

[11] The German courts also sometimes move from the 'balance-theory' to the 'two-claims-theory': Markesinis et al (n 2 above) 765–6.

[12] [1990] 2 AC 663 (HL), noted Birks [1990] LMCLQ 330. It is not easy to reconcile this with the liberal allowance for work and skill made against a fiduciary in breach of duty where the action was brought for that wrong as such: *Boardman v Phipps* [1967] 2 AC 46 (HL). There was no cause of action in *Boardman* other than the wrong, but in *Guinness* there was also an unjust enrichment.

[13] *Rowland v Divall* [1923] 2 KB 500 (CA); *Butterworth v Kingsway Motors Ltd* [1954] 1 WLR 1286. This and other cases like it are problematic in another respect in that they fail to explain why the buyer's right to terminate the contract is not reduced to a right to claim damages under what is now the Sale of Goods Act 1979 s 11(4).

of remedial right. In such a case it has been held the defendant is entitled to insist that the claimant elect to take judgment on one or the other. In other words, one bars the other, though it is for the claimant to decide which.[14] This appears to be an effective instrument to ensure that there is no double-counting. If you recover a gain made by a wrongdoer, you clearly diminish your loss arising from the same wrong. And if you recover your loss arising from the wrong you will thereby diminish the gain. If the claimant recovered both full loss and full gain he would be unjustly enriched at the expense of the defendant.

The other situation in which a claimant has both loss-based and gain-based claims is where a single story reveals two distinct causative events and the claimant relies on one for a compensatory claim and on the other for a restitutionary claim. For example, when a contract is terminated for the defendant's repudiatory breach the victim of the breach will be able to claim compensation for the breach and restitution for the unjust enrichment which consists in the receipt of money on a basis which has subsequently failed. This produces the same danger of double counting. It is necessary not to overlook the fact that had the contract been discharged by full performance this claimant would have paid the price. Hence his claim for expectation damages clearly cannot be cumulated with recovery of the price as paid on a basis which failed.[15]

One rule will probably serve for both these cases. However, it appears more clearly from the second group that election is no more than a blunt instrument to anticipate the danger of unjustly enriching the claimant. The better rule would seem to be that there must be no double counting. Professor Sir Guenter Treitel rightly comes down against election before judgment. He concludes that it is only necessary to say that the claimant must not obtain both full compensation and full restitution.[16]

3. A STATUTORY DEFENCE IN TAX CASES

There is no general defence of disimpoverishment or 'passing on'. However, the legislature has taken the view that there is a special problem in relation to taxes such as VAT which roll from one person to another. In such cases it is systematically the case that a claimant will very probably have passed on the burden of the tax by the time it is discovered that on ordinary principles it might be recovered as not having been due. A much

[14] *United Australia Ltd v Barclays Bank Ltd* [1941] AC 1 (HL); *Tang Man Sit v Capacious Investments Ltd* [1995] 1 WLR 430 (PC).

[15] *Baltic Shipping Co v Dillon (The 'Mikhail Lermontov')* (1993) 176 CLR 344 (HCA).

[16] GH Treitel, *Remedies for Breach of Contract* (OUP Oxford 1988) [97].

litigated example arose from an error induced by the Commissioners of Customs and Excise in relation to the supply of teacakes to Marks & Spencer. Owing to inaccurate advice given by the Commissioners to the manufacturers, Marks & Spencer for many years paid VAT on teacakes, which should all along have been zero-rated. When the truth came out the claim for overpaid VAT came to more than £3m. But, as to 90% of the claim, the Commissioners succeeded in invoking the statutory defence to the effect that the restitution would unjustly enrich the taxpayer on the ground that to that extent Marks & Spencer had in turn charged VAT to its retail customers.[17]

The Law Commission recommended a generalization in respect of all rolling indirect taxes, so that the taxing authority should be in every such case be allowed to show that repayment would unjustly enrich the claimant.[18] The relevant provisions were all amended by the Finance Act 1997.[19]

The statutory description of this defence, and hence its name, is unjust enrichment of the claimant. This accounts for its presence here in the first group of unjust-related defences. The fact that it is expressed in these very wide terms has encouraged some ingenious arguments as to why, on facts having nothing whatever to do with passing on, restitution to the taxpayer might be said unjustly to enrich him.[20] However, it seems likely that the defence will be confined to passing on. It is certain that, as between the parties, in this context the phrase unjust enrichment is not being used in its narrow technical sense. There is no unjust enrichment of the claimant at the expense of the Crown or the particular taxing authority. On the contrary, the Crown is *ex hypothesi* unjustly enriched at the expense of the claimant, having received a payment not due. And repayment would not make the claimant unjustly enriched at the Crown's expense, because the claimant's enrichment would be perfectly explained as having accrued in the discharge of the Crown's debt.

[17] *Marks & Spencer Plc v Commissioners of Customs and Excise (No 5)* [2003] EWCA Civ 1448, [2004] 1 CMLR 8 [17], [74]–[85]. The statutory defence arises under s 80(3) of the Value Added Tax Act 1994.

[18] Law Commission of England and Wales, *Restitution: Mistakes of Law and Ultra Vires Public Receipts and Payments* (Law Com No 227 1994), paras 10.44–10.47, recommendations 20 and 21.

[19] It now applies in VAT cases, under Value Added Tax Act 1994 s 80(3), as amended by the Finance Act 1997 s 46. Similar: Customs and Excise Management Act 1979 s 137A(3) (excise duties); Finance Act 1994 Schedule 7 para 8(3) (insurance premium tax); Finance Act 1996 Schedule 5 para 14(3) (landfill tax), all amended by Finance Act 1997 Schedule 5.

[20] *Customs and Excise Commissioners v McMaster Stores (Scotland) Ltd (in receivership)* 1996 SLT 935.

In this context the term 'unjust enrichment' is used to assert that the Crown should remain unjustly enriched at the claimant's expense on account of the fact that the claimant would be unjustly enriched either in a lay sense—he would get an unearned windfall—or, reverting to the technical sense, at the expense of third parties. The lay sense is unmanageable, in much the same way as non-disenriching changes of position are unmanageable: sympathy for the defendant, however generated, does not in the end justify his retention of extant enrichment to which he is not entitled. And the technical sense which draws in third parties simply puts its finger on a major weakness of the condemned defence of disimpoverishment, namely that by barring a claim between claimant and defendant it seeks to solve—and cannot—a problem which can only be solved in an action between third parties and the claimant (now as defendant).

The likely outcome is that this statutory defence will be exposed as no more than a covert version of the defence of disimpoverishment because it has no acceptable rationale distinct from that defence. Unfortunately its being statutory does no more than establish it by force. It does not cure its rational defects. So far most judges have rightly been extremely suspicious of any defence to the effect that the public purse must not be unnecessarily disrupted.[21] An alternative future judgment on this statutory defence may be that it was a covert attempt to introduce a defence on those dangerous lines.

B. FINALITY

There are five distinct finality defences. Each asserts, with different degrees of absoluteness, that the matter is closed and must not be reopened: *interest rei publicae ut sit finis litium* (it is in the public interest that there be an end to disputes).

[21] In *Deutsche Morgan Grenfell Group plc v IRC* [2003] 4 All ER 645 (Ch D) 655–6 Park J downplayed the notion that such a defence could find a foothold in *Kleinwort Benson Ltd v Lincoln CC* [1999] 2 AC 349, 381–2 (Lord Goff). In *Waikato Regional Airport v Attorney General* [2003] UKPC 50, [2003] All ER (D) 399 (Jun) [82] the Privy Council addressing a similar argument confined itself to saying that the sums in question, though very large indeed, were not of the order calculated to disrupt the finances of the government of New Zealand. Contrast *Air Canada v British Columbia* (1989) 59 DLR (4th) 161, Wilson J dissenting.

1. *RES JUDICATA*

Payment made under a valid judgment cannot be recovered unless the judgment is set aside, even if the judgment was obtained by fraud.[22] Once a judgment which has been paid is set aside, the right to restitution arises automatically and does not depend on the court's making an order for repayment.[23] This is a case of subsequent failure of basis. The payment was due when paid, its basis was the judgment. It has been repeatedly said[24] that Lord Mansfield violated the sanctity of *res judicata* in *Moses v Macferlan*.[25] In fact he was careful not to. His premiss was that Moses could have sued for compensatory damages for breach of contract without in the least impugning the judgment of the lower court. He upheld Moses' restitutionary action to recover the sum received by Macferlan as an alternative recourse for breach of contract.[26]

2. CAPITULATION AFTER INITIATION OF LEGAL PROCEEDINGS

This defence is no more than an extension of the last. Even where there is no judgment to be set aside, payments made after litigation has begun cannot be recovered. In the words of Lord Halsbury in *Moore v Fulham Vestry*, 'The principle of law is, not that money paid under a judgment, but that money paid under the pressure of legal process cannot be recovered.'[27] There a summons had been taken out to compel the claimant, as a frontager, to make a statutory contribution to a road improvement. He capitulated. After he had paid he discovered that his holding was not within the contributing class. His claim for restitution was refused. This strict rule is displaced in cases in which the party seeking to take advantage of it acted in bad faith, as for instance in snatching at a

[22] *De Medina v Grove* (1846) 10 QB 152, (1847) 10 QB 172; *Huffer v Allen* (1867) LR 2 Ex 15. For a recent example of an appeal out of time where, but for the judgment, a claim could have been made for failure of basis, see *Barder v Caluori* [1988] AC 20 (HL). Contrast *Dublin v The Ancient Guild of Brick and Stone Layers* [1996] 1 IR 468, where an arbitrator's award had not been set aside.

[23] *Commonwealth v McCormack* (1984) 155 CLR 273 (HCA); cf DM Gordon, 'The Effect of Reversal of Judgment on Acts Done between Pronouncement and Reversal' (1958) 74 LQR 517, 521–4; D Friedmann, 'Valid, Voidable, Qualified and Non-Existing Obligations: An Alternative Perspective on the Law of Restitution' in A Burrows (ed), *Essays in the Law of Restitution* (OUP Oxford 1991) 247, 265–6.

[24] *Phillips v Hunter* (1795) 2 H Bl 402, 414, 126 ER 618, 625 (Eyre C J); *Brisbane v Dacres* (1813) 5 Taunt 143, 160, 128 ER 641, 648 (Heath J).

[25] (1760) 2 Burr 1005, 97 ER 697.

[26] Above, 13–15.

[27] [1895] 1 QB 399, 401. Cf *Hamlet v Richardson* (1833) 9 Bing 644, 131 ER 756.

mistake made by the other.[28] Otherwise one who settles at the door of the court is made to bear all risks.

3. CONTRACT FOR FINALITY

A contract for finality made before the initiation of legal proceedings may be a compromise, a settlement, or a release.[29] There are shades of difference between these overlapping terms, but for present purposes they can all be considered together. Under whichever name, a party who has closed the matter in question for good consideration will not be able to reopen it so long as the contract remains in place. However, this bar is in two ways less absolute than that which is created by *res judicata* or capitulation. First, at least in respect of claims unknown to the parties at the time of the contract, a fierce *contra proferentem* construction may deprive the defendant of the protection which he thought he had secured.[30] Secondly, the contract is vulnerable, like all contracts, to vitiating factors such as misrepresentation, pressure, and undue influence. Spontaneous mistake will very rarely undermine any bargain, more rarely still since *Solle v Butcher* was condemned.[31] Once the exercise of construction concludes that there was a contract for finality, as opposed to a mere assent to pay or quantification of the amount to be paid, and that that contract covers the claim in question, it has to be accepted that a bargain of this kind, like any other, may turn out very badly for one or other party. It will certainly not suffice to avoid a compromise or release that one party bought off what with hindsight turned out to be a non-existent claim.[32]

It has sometimes been suggested that, even if there is no contract, but only a payment in submission to an honest claim, the honest claim itself provides a defence.[33] If that were right, the difficult exercise of construction would be much less important. But it cannot be right.[34] If it were, many mistaken payments would be irrecoverable. Even such a classic case

[28] *Ward v Wallis* (1900) 1 QB 675.

[29] NH Andrews, 'Mistaken Settlements of Disputable Claims' [1989] LMCLQ 431.

[30] *Bank of Credit and Commerce International v Ali* [2001] UKHL 8, [2002] 1 AC 251.

[31] *Great Peace Shipping Ltd v Tsavliris Salvage (International) Ltd* [2002] EWCA Civ 1407, [2002] 4 All ER 689.

[32] *Callisher v Bischoffsheim* (1870) 5 QB 449; *Bell v Lever Brothers Ltd* [1932] AC 161 (HL).

[33] Goff and Jones promoted this view in earlier editions, chiefly, it would seem, as an alternative explanation of the mistake of law cases. In the latest edition it makes only a shy appearance: G Jones (ed), *Goff and Jones on Restitution* (6th edn Sweet & Maxwell London 2002) [1–070].

[34] S Arrowsmith, 'Mistake and the Role of "Submission to an Honest Claim" ' *Essays in the Law of Restitution* in Burrows (n 23 above) (1991) 17–38.

as *Kelly v Solari*[35] would have to be decided differently, for nothing could be more certain than that the insurers there made their mistaken payment to the widow in response to an honest claim by her.

4. ESTOPPEL

Contracts for finality are just one application of the law of contract. Estoppel based on a representation that the defendant's entitlement has been checked and confirmed operates in a similar way. Once the estoppel is perfected, the representation becomes binding and the defence takes effect. In 1983, *Avon CC v Howlett*[36] showed that the detrimental reliance which perfects the estoppel and gives a complete defence may be less than amounts to a 100 per cent disenrichment. A local authority had overpaid a teacher's sick pay. It recovered nothing despite the teacher's putting in evidence reliance expenditure substantially less than the overpayments. The defence of disenrichment only reduces the recipient's liability step-by-step, as the enrichment is eliminated. Estoppel logically gives an absolute defence, just like a contract.

Although the two defences pursue entirely different goals, the courts are now reluctant to allow estoppel any role at all in this context. Three recent cases have come to the brink of excluding it as a matter of law.[37] In *Scottish Equitable plc v Derby* a lump sum in respect of a pension was massively overpaid. Representations were subsequently made that the amount paid was correct. Partial detrimental reliance followed. The Court of Appeal held, upholding Harrison J below, that estoppel could not be invoked where, in comparison with change of position, it would produce a disproportionate outcome. The Court was also attracted by an 'ingenious argument' to the effect that, since the defence of change of position entitled one to charge disenrichments to the claimant, they could not be regarded as detrimental reliance for the purpose of perfecting any estoppel.

It cannot be right formally to exclude the application of estoppel, rarely as it may now be made out. It is about holding people to their representations and is as such very close to contract. One could not exclude contracts for finality. The legitimate way to prevent overkill is, in the absence of extreme facts, to construe these representations as most reasonable people would understand them, namely as prospectively

[35] [1841] 9 M & W 54, 152 ER 24. [36] [1983] 1 WLR 605 (CA).
[37] *Phillip Collins Ltd v Davis* [2000] 3 All ER 808, 823–6; *Scottish Equitable plc v Derby* [2001] 3 All ER 818 (CA) 828–31; *National Westminster Bank v Somer* [2002] 1 All ER 198 (CA) 212–15, 217–18, 220.

revocable in the event of the representor's discovering a mistake. 'We have checked this out and you may rely on us that all is in order' should be construed as implying the additional words, 'unless and until we notify you to the contrary.' That construction would bind the payer in the meantime and, in the common case, produce the same outcome as the defence of change of position.

An absolute estoppel will be very rare. An estoppel construed to be prospectively revocable will not produce results disproportionate in comparison with the entirely different defence of change of position. If this is the way the law stands, it avoids the present predicament in which the courts find themselves where, even if they have found the necessary facts, they are driven to disapply what is, in theory, a perfectly good defence. It is important to remember that estoppel is about holding a person to his word.

In relation to contract we speak constantly of a person binding himself. The metaphor in 'estoppel' is not much different. It is also a metaphor for lost freedom.[38] One who is estopped is no longer free to go back on his representation. There is no reason why a defence which bears on enrichment and determines the extent to which a person has been disenriched should displace a defence based in compelling a claimant to keep his word. The contrary view has a now obsolete historical explanation. In the period before the defence of change of position was secure, estoppel was not infrequently invoked, and stretched, to do at least some of the work.[39] Nowadays there is no pressure to torture estoppels out of unwilling facts. Each defence has its own natural sphere.

5. LIMITATION AND LACHES

Here the fragmentation of the law of unjust enrichment, and its consequent concealment, is shown up at its worst. Although the Law Commission has recently engaged in a simplifying and modernizing project which may or may not result in a new Act, the primary source for time limits is still the Limitation Act 1980, which contains no provision at all for unjust enrichment. This speaks volumes for the state of the law of unjust enrichment a decade before *Lipkin Gorman v Karpnale Ltd*.[40] The legislator could not see it.

[38] The *OED* shows that an estoppel, in origin French, is a bung or cork or stopper, inhibiting the freedom of wine or other liquid.

[39] Goff and Jones (n 33 above) [40–010].

[40] [1991] 2 AC 548 (HL).

The consequence of this blindness has been that each of the wandering fragments has looked for its own foothold in the limitation regime. However, more recently the judges have slowly been putting this right. Subject to unequivocal statutory exceptions, as for instance the two-year time limit on claims under section 10 of the Civil Liability (Contribution) Act 1978 and the three-year limit for recovering VAT by virtue of section 47(1) and (2) of the Finance Act 1997,[41] the case law has now brought the law to the brink of achieving a uniform limitation period for unjust enrichment of six years.

In *Westdeutsche Landesbank Girozentrale v Islington LBC* Hobhouse J was once again confronted with an argument that the proper inference from the fact that the 1980 Act laid down no time limit for such claims was that they could be brought without limit of time. This provoked an elaborate exercise in statutory interpretation designed to prove that so far as such claims were made at common law they were covered by section 5, which on its face says nothing at all about them. Its words are: 'An action founded on simple contract shall not be brought after the expiration of six years from the date on which the cause of action accrued.' Hobhouse J adopted an earlier analysis to the effect that 'simple contract' had been intended to include quasi-contract and implied contract and continued to do so even after those fictions had been outgrown.[42]

Of equal or greater importance was Hobhouse J's application of the six-year period to the claimant's equitable claim. In the background the historical position is that equitable claims knew no fixed limitation period. That is still the default rule for those equitable claims which have neither been expressly brought within the statute nor subjected by the judges to a statutory period by analogy. Hobhouse J held that when the defendants received the payments under the void swap they became trustees of the money and, synonymously, the claimant payer acquired an equitable beneficial interest in it. This was the necessary foundation for his conclusion that the defendants had to pay compound interest, on the basis that they had used trust money for their own purposes. But he rejected the argument that the equitable claim should be handled for limitation purposes as a claim in the law of trusts.

[41] The retrospectivity of this three-year limitation—it applies to all claims whether or not they arose after the Act came into force—came under the microscope in *Marks & Spencer* (n 17 above).

[42] *Westdeutsche* (n 8 above) 943. Compare *Maskell v Horner* [1915] 3 KB 106, where a stallholder paid market dues under duress of goods for some twelve years and recovered for six; also *Re Diplock* [1948] Ch 465 (CA) 514.

Later the House of Lords reversed this part of Hobhouse J's judgment, holding that the claimant bank had acquired no more than a personal claim at common law. But this reversal did not touch the way in which, on the premiss that the claimants did have an equitable proprietary interest, Hobhouse J handled the limitation issue. In the *Westdeutsche* case it was, he said, 'common ground' that the same limitation period applied to both the equitable and the common law claim.[43] And a little later in *Kleinwort Benson v South Tyneside MBC*, which was another case in the same series, there was no trace of concession by the parties. He then said, 'The six-year limit provided for in section 5 of the Limitation Act 1980 applies to an action for money had and received and by analogy to an equivalent equitable action.'[44]

In similar spirit other cases have also refused to allow equitable claims to escape the 1980 Act and the six-year limitation period. Thus in *Paragon Finance Plc v D B Thakerar & Co*[45] and *Coulthard v Disco Mix Club Ltd*[46] the courts have said that a right to an account growing out of contract will not escape the six-year period simply because the accountant is in equity's eyes a fiduciary. In the latter case the manager and promoter of the plaintiff's music recording process, though a fiduciary, was held not to be accountable beyond the sixth year. These cases are not immediately in point because the causative event in question is not unjust enrichment, but they offer important indirect support to Hobhouse J's application of the six-year period for common law claims in unjust enrichment to analogous equitable claims. They show that there is no judicial sympathy for claimants who seek to exploit the deplorably persistent historical duality of our law. There are clear cases, but on the margin an equitable claim will succumb to the common law analogy.

Strong forces are thus operating to ensure that the six-year period laid down for contract applies to unjust enrichment. The same period applies to torts, by section 6, and thus to many cases of restitution for wrongs, also to statutory dues, by section 9. However, it is too soon to say that all equitable claims arising from unjust enrichment will be caught in one net. The equitable doctrine of laches remains a long-stop where no statutory period applies. It probably remains possible for particular equitable claims to fall through to the default regime of laches and acquiescence.

[43] *Westdeutsche* (n 8 above) 943.

[44] [1994] 4 All ER 972, 978.

[45] [1999] 1 All ER 400 (CA), disapproving Laddie J in *Nelson v Rye* [1996] 1 WLR 1378, so far as he held that no statutory period applied to an account due from a musician's manager.

[46] [1999] 2 All ER 457.

'Laches', pronounced 'laitches', denotes slackness or remissness. There is no fixed period. The judge has to ask himself whether the staleness of the claim seriously disadvantages the defendant to a degree which, weighed in the balance against the claimant's entitlement to justice, requires the action to be discontinued.[47]

The time limit, whatever it is, normally runs from the accrual of the cause of action, here the receipt of the enrichment, to the commencement of the action. In special cases the clock is stopped. Thus section 28 of the 1980 Act prevents time running against a person under a disability such as mental illness or minority, and section 32 provides that in cases of fraud, concealment, or mistake, the clock will not run until the plaintiff has discovered the true facts or could with reasonable diligence have done so.[48] The fraud or concealment may have been perpetrated not by the defendant but by his predecessor in title, but in that case the extension of the limitation period will not operate against a bona fide purchaser for value.[49]

It was to obtain the benefits of the extended limitation period under section 32(1)(c) that, in *Kleinwort Benson Ltd v Lincoln CC*,[50] Kleinwort Benson argued, successfully, that payments made under a void contract in the belief that it was valid could be recovered for mistake of law.[51] By way of an analysis alternative to failure of basis, it characterized its claim as one which sought relief for mistake. Their Lordships agreed and held that, until the House of Lords decided that local authority interest swaps were void, it was not reasonably possible for the claimants to discover their mistake. Time did not begin to run till then.

On deeper reflection it may become clear that mistake could not properly be said to have been an ingredient in the cause of action but, if so, it might yet be held that, where a claimant was indeed mistaken, the mistake's not being relevant to the cause of action was not fatal to its entitlement to the benefit of section 32(1)(c). *Kleinwort Benson* is doubly

[47] Laddie J's judgment in *Nelson v Rye* [1996] 1 WLR 1378, 1392–5 remains a superb statement of the operation of the doctrine, even though it was subsequently held that he should have applied the six-year period under the Act: n 45 above.

[48] On reasonable diligence, see *Peco Arts Inc v Hazlitt Gallery Ltd* [1983] 1 WLR 1315 (Webster J).

[49] Section 32(2) and (3); *Baker v Medway Building and Supplies* [1958] 2 All ER 532 (Danckwerts J), [1958] 1 WLR 1216 (CA). There the defendant was presented as a donee from a fraudster but was allowed to amend its defence to allow it to plead bona fide purchase.

[50] [1999] 2 AC 349 (HL).

[51] This has since been 'unenthusiastically' applied by Park J in *Deutsche Morgan Grenfell Group Plc v IRC* [2003] EWHC 1779 (Ch), [2003] 4 All ER 645 (Ch D) [37], [41]–[42].

vulnerable. It is difficult to agree either that the claimant was any more mistaken than a person who gets soaked because he mispredicted the weather, or, if it was mistaken, that that mistake was an essential ingredient of the cause of action.[52]

C. STULTIFICATION

To stultify the law is to make a fool of it. If without good reason an action in unjust enrichment were to contradict a considered position elsewhere, the unreasoned contradiction would stultify the law. This danger is averted by raising a defence to a claim in unjust enrichment which would otherwise be available. This is a single defence with diverse manifestations. The examples which follow should not be regarded as exhaustive.

1. BONA FIDE PURCHASE FROM A THIRD PARTY

Where the defendant enrichee receives the enrichment from a third party but has given value in exchange to that third party, he can be allowed that value under the head of disenrichment. In the *Lipkin Gorman* case there was no contract between the casino and the gambler because gambling contracts are always void even when the casino is licensed. Under the head of disenrichment the defendant casino was only allowed the sums laid out when the gambler won. There was no allowance under that head for the provision of the gambling service, presumably because nothing that was provided was provided specially for any one particular gambler.[53]

(a) Valid Contract Between Recipient and Third Party

If the contract between the casino and the gambler had not been void, the picture would have been very different. Suppose that the gambler had instead been addicted to extravagant evenings at the Ritz. If the claimant solicitors had sued the Ritz as having received their money from the addict, the Ritz would have had the defence of bona fide purchase from a third party. That defence is absolute. It does not matter that the food and wine supplied may have been available elsewhere for one-tenth of the price which customers of the Ritz have to pay. The cost to the Ritz is not in question. All that matters is that, through a valid contract, it bona fide gave value for what it received from a third party.

[52] Above, 109–12.
[53] [1991] 2 AC 548 (HL) discussed above, 155–6.

This is one of those cases where we have to determine whether this nominate defence has any rationale other than disenrichment. Does it really require to be classed as an independent unjust-related defence? The question is whether the result just described is entirely explicable in terms of disenrichment. It may be that it can. The reason is that, within the valid contract, it is impossible to say that the values exchanged were not exactly equal. Ambience and get-up attract high spenders. Champagne has a different value in different places. So it may be that, in the law of unjust enrichment, the defence of bona fide purchase, which applies only in respect of valid contractual exchanges with the third party, is no more than a special manifestation of disenrichment. At all events, so far as disenrichment will do the work the special manifestation needs no other name. The tactic recommended at the end of the last chapter, it will be recalled, is to exhaust the defence of disenrichment before asking whether a nominate defence adds anything to the picture. Using this approach we may find that it is always true that, where the defendant has acquired the enrichment under a valid contract with a third party, that which he has given is always equal in value to that which he has received. In other words he has always and instantly disenriched himself completely.

There is authority against this analysis of the defence of bona fide purchase in the law of unjust enrichment. Lord Goff himself said that the absoluteness of the defence set it apart from disenrichment:

> [W]e cannot simply say that bona fide purchase is a species of change of position. This is because change of position will only avail a defendant to the extent that his position has been changed, whereas, where bona fide purchase is invoked, no inquiry is made (in most cases) into the adequacy of the consideration.[54]

The only question not quite closed down by this is whether we ever inspect the adequacy of consideration within a valid contract between the defendant recipient and a third party—even when applying the defence of disenrichment. Lord Goff's view would seem to be that, in the hypothetical in which the addict drinks away his employer's money at the Ritz, the hotel, were it to rely on disenrichment rather than bona fide purchase, would have to accept a disembodied market valuation of its offerings. Its bill for £2,000 might then turn out to conceal a change of position—a disenrichment—of only £200. But it is not clear where one would find that disembodied valuation. Cosmetics sold for £50 are sometimes said to include a 90 per cent profit factor, and yet their value is not £5 but £50. If

[54] [1991] 2 AC 548, 580.

in fact the value of that which is supplied at the Ritz is what it charges, namely £2,000, the defence of disenrichment will arrive at the same conclusion as the defence of bona fide purchase, namely that the Ritz cannot be liable at all. This difficult issue remains to be finally decided.

However, if we accept Lord Goff's view that the two defences must be regarded as quite different, there is certainly an available explanation of bona fide purchase which has nothing to do with disenrichment but which deprives it of its generality. When bona fide purchase is explained in this second way it belongs in, and only in, the field of *nemo dat quod non habet*, and as a defence to personal claims in unjust enrichment it is a member of the stultification family of the unjust-related defences. In short, in this version the defence is part of the compromise between sanctity of property and security of transactions.

In pursuit of that compromise some proprietary claims are killed off as against a bona fide purchaser for value. For example, at common law the ownership of money is invariably sacrificed to the bona fide purchaser. That is to say, an adverse interest in money is extinguished every time it is received honestly from, and for value given to, a non-owner. The same outcome attaches to a number of other transactions with non-owners.

Under the money exception to *nemo dat*, the Ritz in honestly giving value to the addict would thus have cleared off any proprietary interest in the money on the part of the solicitors. If you pay for your lunch with my ten pound note, the restaurant becomes the unencumbered owner of the note.[55] That exception to *nemo dat* would be stultified if the recipient of the money were nonetheless liable to a *Lipkin Gorman* personal claim. It would be absurd and contradictory to say that, in the interest of the currency of money, the property in the money would pass to the Ritz, while at the same time preserving a personal claim to the value of that money. Such a regime would do nothing to ensure confidence in the currency of money. Clearly, the personal claim has to be killed off by the defence of bona fide purchase in order to avoid the stultification of the proprietary exception to *nemo dat*. It has to be killed off in order to support the commitment of the law of property to the bona fide purchaser of money.

On this view of the nominate defence, it is not general. It does not apply to every single case in which, honestly and for value, the defendant has received my money from a third party. Outside the few special

[55] *Miller v Race* (1758) 1 Burr 452, 97 ER 398; *Clarke v Shee and Johnson* (1774) 1 Cowp 197, 98 ER 1041; D Fox, 'Bona Fide Purchase and the Currency of Money' [1996] CLJ 547.

contexts in which it is expressly imposed by statute,[56] it has no place other than in situations in which an exception to *nemo dat* needs to be protected. English law takes a pepper and salt approach. There is no general doctrine, as there is in Italian law, giving good title to bona fide purchasers of moveables.[57] The bona fide purchaser of the legal title in a thing destroys adverse equitable interests. Again, there are specific situations in which the Sale of Goods Act 1979 and related legislation give a purchaser from a non-owner a good title.[58] To make such a purchaser answer to the owner in unjust enrichment would stultify these concessions to the security of transactions.

By contrast, if you bartered my ring for champagne, my ownership of the ring would survive. The defence of bona fide purchase, in this version, would have no role. If I brought an action in unjust enrichment against the recipient of the ring, that recipient could plead disenrichment and, if it is correct to say that values are always equal within a valid contract, it would have been 100 per cent disenriched, but it could not plead bona fide purchase in its anti-stultification version, because the context is not one in which English law insists on a compromise between sanctity of ownership and security of transactions. Sanctity of ownership simply prevails.

Professor Burrows holds that bona fide purchase is a general defence to claims in unjust enrichment, but at the same time he accepts that it is not just a special manifestation of disenrichment.[59] That is not an easy position to hold. According to what is said above, once the defence is cut away from disenrichment it can only operate in a pepper and salt way, where there must be no stultification of an exception to *nemo dat quod non habet*. But Professor Burrows finds a third, and general, rationale. He argues that unjust enrichment always shows respect for the sanctity of contract and that the defence is merely an aspect of that deference, manifested in relation to the contract between the defendant and the third party from whom he acquired. This would salvage the generality of the defence against claims in unjust enrichment, which is indeed widely assumed.

However, it is not completely clear that respect for contract can yield a sufficient rationale. If it did, bona fide purchasers would always get a good title, but we know that they do not. At the proprietary level the

[56] As for example in connection with stopping the limitation clock. See n 49 above and text thereto.

[57] Italian Civil Code, Article 1153.

[58] Sale of Goods Act 1979 ss 21, 23–5.

[59] A Burrows, *The Law of Restitution* (2nd edn Butterworths London 2002) 588–90.

contract with the third party is only respected in particular situations. It seems to follow that it is only in those same situations that the personal claim in unjust enrichment is cut off in order to protect the priority which the law there accords to the security of transactions.

(b) Disqualification

If and so far as the defendant who has received from a third party relies on disenrichment and succeeds by arguing that it is undeniable that he has suffered a 100 per cent disenrichment, disqualification should be determined on the same basis as was discussed above for the defence of disenrichment.[60] The enrichee, whatever words he uses, is then relying on the defence of disenrichment. All the disenrichment rules must apply.

When the defendant is relying on bona fide purchase as an absolute defence given to support the security of transactions and, so far as personal claims are concerned, to complete and protect the law's chosen exceptions to *nemo dat quod non habet*, disqualification turns on the rules of the exception in question. Here there appears to be an ineradicable difference between common law and equity. Common law exceptions to *nemo dat* require bona fides in the sense of honesty.[61] We have seen that the House of Lords has recently narrowed the notion of dishonesty by insisting that it be confined to 'subjective dishonesty' where the actor not only acts discreditably but knows that prevailing opinion would judge him to be so doing.[62] Although the context was different, and was indeed equitable, there is no suggestion that the redefinition of dishonesty was context-specific. If that redefinition proves correct, the defence of bona fide purchase from a third party has been enlarged. We have also seen that it has proved possible to break the equation of good faith and honesty.[63] It will, however, be difficult even to explore that line in any case in which the equation is statutory.

This difficulty does not touch the equitable defence of bona fide purchase into the very name of which, when spelled out in full, is built the additional requirement contained in the words 'without notice'. The full name is 'bona fide purchase for value without notice'. 'Purchase for value' is not pleonastic for 'purchase' is used in a sense now otherwise obsolete in which it denotes every acquisition other than by inheritance.

[60] Above, 213–9.

[61] Thus the Sale of Goods Act 1979 s 61(3) expressly says that wherever the Act requires bona fides what it requires is honesty, whence it follows that a defendant can be negligent without being dishonest.

[62] Above, 214.

[63] Above, 214–8.

'Without notice' has long been understood as 'without constructive notice' which in turn means without such notice as one would have had if one had asked the questions which a reasonable person would have asked.[64] In brief, the starting point above the technicalities is that a defendant who has to rely on the equitable defence in order to destroy an adverse equitable interest or to meet a personal claim which would stultify the destruction of that interest must show not merely that he was honest but also that he was not careless in failing to discover the claimant's interest. The law is the same for land and personal property, but, in asking what inquiries ought reasonably to have been made, one must expect very different answers. The standard of reasonableness recognizes that commerce would come to a halt if anything like house-buying inquiries were insisted upon.

2. MINISTERIAL RECEIPT

As with bona fide purchase, the question is whether there is a nominate defence called 'ministerial receipt' which offers the non-beneficial recipient more than the general defence of disenrichment. At common law, where a recipient knows that he has not received for his own benefit but merely to pass on to another, as where he is an agent acting for a principal, most cases hold that, although a restitutionary claim lies against the principal even before the agent has paid over, the agent himself will also be liable in two situations: where he has not paid over to, or to the order of, the principal, and where, although he has paid over, he did so when he already knew of the claimant's entitlement to restitution.[65] A common example is a bank which receives money for the credit of a customer. In such a case the bank falls within the general rule that a merely paper attribution to the principal's account does not in itself count as payment over. Until the credit has been withdrawn by the customer the bank is entitled to correct the account unilaterally.[66]

In the early editions of *Goff & Jones*, before the defence of change of position was secure, the agent's defence was presented as a bridgehead

[64] Embodied in s 199 of the Law of Property Act 1925, replacing s 3 of the Conveyancing Act 1882.

[65] *Gowers v Lloyds and National Provincial Bank* [1938] 1 All ER 766 (CA); *Australia and NZ Banking Group Ltd v Westpac Banking Corporation* (1988) 164 CLR 662 (HCA); cf *Portman Building Society v Hamlyn Taylor Neck* [1998] 4 All ER 202 (CA).

[66] In addition to the cases in the previous note, unequivocal on this point is *Admiralty Commissioners v National Provincial Bank* (1922) 127 LT 452, which is one of the foundation stones of M Bryan 'Recovering Misdirected Money from Banks: Ministerial Receipt at Law and Equity' in FD Rose (ed), *Restitution and Banking Law* (Mansfield Oxford 1998) 161–88.

from which the law could advance to the general defence.[67] Attention was drawn to cases such as *Bayliss v Bishop of London*.[68] Under a statutory scheme the Bishop had administered the insolvency of the rector of a parish within his diocese. In taking in the revenues of the parish he had received certain payments made by mistake. He had applied the entire fund in accordance with the requirements of the statutory scheme. He nevertheless had to make restitution. He could not be an agent because he had no principal. He could not take advantage of the agent's defence. Nowadays the Bishop's disenrichment would certainly be set against his enrichment. He would not be liable. But here all we seem to be saying is that agents and non-agents alike have that defence, and 'knowing of the claimant's entitlement to restitution' is no more than disqualification from the general defence on the ground of bad faith.

On the Chancery side the approach looks quite different. In *Agip (Africa) Ltd v Jackson* it was held that a ministerial recipient, one who receives under an obligation to account to another and not for his own benefit, can be liable for dishonestly assisting a breach of trust but cannot incur any personal liability for receiving.[69] If this ultimately translates to a proposition to the effect that a ministerial recipient cannot be liable in unjust enrichment at all, it will constitute a defence more absolute than disenrichment. And it will be more consonant than is the common law with the principle that the agent creates legal relations between others and himself drops out. German law at this point remains strictly faithful to that principle.[70]

It is certainly not tolerable for English law to take two positions on this matter. However, it might be wrong to jump too easily to the conclusion that the Chancery position provides an unequivocal foundation for a distinct and more absolute defence. The combination of the liability for knowing assistance and the vindication of traceably surviving enrichment narrows the gap between it and the common law. In the *Agip* case the defendant accountants, although they were regarded as exempt from personal liability for receipt, had to surrender the enrichment traceably surviving in their hands and, having been found to have been dishonest, were personally liable for the claimant's loss so far as they had assisted in the misdirection of money by a fiduciary. We will not be sure that

[67] R Goff and G Jones, *The Law of Restitution* (1st edn Sweet & Maxwell London 1966) 482–5.

[68] [1913] 1 Ch 127 (CA).

[69] [1990] Ch 265 (Millett J) aff'd [1991] Ch 547 (CA).

[70] H Dörner, 'Change of Position and *Wegfall der Bereicherung*' in W Swadling (ed), *The Limits of Restitutionary Claims: A Comparative Analysis* (BIICL London 1997) 64, 67.

'ministerial receipt' adds anything to disenrichment until it is held that no claim in unjust enrichment, personal or proprietary, can be brought against an agent recipient.

3. ILLEGALITY

In most cases in which illegality is a defence to unjust enrichment the reason is not to be found in the turpitude of the claimant. Even dishonest claimants are these days rescued from disaster.[71] It must nevertheless be that there are still exceptional degrees of turpitude such as would immediately compel the court to have nothing to do with the case. If *C* gave *D* money to place a bomb on a plane or to procure a child for sexual abuse, *C*'s claim would fail at square one: *ex turpi causa non oritur actio* (from a disgraceful cause arises no action). We might explain this as simple revulsion, but we might also see it as the recognition, and evasion, of an extreme form of stultification. The mission of the courts would be inexplicably contradicted if their help was extended to claimants of this kind. If anything would stultify the law it would be the sight of a court assisting a claimant of that kind.

(a) Lever and Safety-Net

These extreme cases aside, if the enrichee turns out to have a good defence, his victory is rather to be attributed to the danger of stultifying the law's refusal to enforce an illegal contract made between the parties. In this context the risk of such stultification is endemic in allowing an action in unjust enrichment. The same risk attaches to allowing any other non-contractual action, as, for example, conversion. All non-contractual actions, and especially actions in unjust enrichment, routinely provide a lever to compel performance and a safety-net in case that indirect compulsion fails. Suppose *C* makes a charitable donation to *D* and in return *D* undertakes to secure an honour for him, and then no honour is forthcoming.[72] Or, again, suppose that *C* deposits a share certificate with *D* as security for a foreign currency loan, in breach of exchange control legislation, and no loan is made.[73] In such cases the very availability to *C* of an action to recover that which he transferred will both reduce the risks of the illegal transaction and provide a threat which will indirectly compel performance.

[71] *Tinsley v Milligan* [1994] AC 340 (HL); *Tribe v Tribe* [1996] Ch 107 (CA).

[72] *Parkinson v College of Ambulance* [1925] 2 KB 1.

[73] *Bigos v Bousted* [1951] 1 All ER 92.

In *Boissevain v Weil*[74] the defendant had failed to repay a loan which had been made in violation of exchange control regulations. A claim to recover the sum as having been paid on a basis which had failed was disallowed by the House of Lords. Lord Radcliffe said that the non-contractual claim could not be allowed because it would stultify the law.[75] In that particular case it would have given the lender exactly what his illegality prevented him from getting by an action in contract. The danger arising from the lever and safety-net is not confined to extreme cases of that kind. It extends just as much to cases in which the two contractual performances are entirely different, so that recovery of the value of the one performance looks on its face nothing like compelling the other to make the illegal performance. The lever and the safety-net will nonetheless threaten to stultify the law.

The question in any one case must be whether the danger inherent in the lever and the safety-net should prevail, with the result that the action will be denied. Stultification is contradiction without a reason, here contradiction without reason of the law's refusal to enforce the contract. In the particular case there may on closer inspection be no contradiction, or there may be a reason for allowing the non-contractual action which weighs heavier than the fear of the lever and the safety-net. If the contradiction is real and there is no good reason to override it, the defendant will win. He himself may be very unattractive. All the same, in order to save the law being made a fool of, he has to be allowed his defence. That is the spirit in which we should understand the second maxim recurrent in this field: *in pari delicto potior est conditio defendentis* (when the parties are as bad as each other, the defendant has the stronger position). There is no doubt that the trend of the modern law has been to try to avoid arriving at the point at which that maxim has to be applied, but the ride has been very bumpy and the case law is in a mess.

(b) Two Ends of the Spectrum

At one end of the spectrum the correct conclusion may be that the policy behind the illegality in question would indeed be stultified if the claimant were allowed any non-contractual recourse, whether for unjust enrichment or under any other head. For example, in *Wilson v First County Trust Ltd*[76] Mrs Wilson had pledged her BMW car for a loan of £5,000.

[74] [1950] AC 327 (HL).

[75] Ibid 340.

[76] [2003] UKHL 40, [2003] 2 All ER (Comm) 491; compare *Dimond v Lovell* [2002] 1 AC 384 (HL).

The written contract did not comply with the requirements of the Consumer Credit Act 1974. She failed to repay the loan. Not for the first time the House of Lords affirmed that the disciplinary policy of the Act meant that the non-compliant lender could have no action at all. Its contract was void, and that nullity could not be circumvented by an action in unjust enrichment. She, for her part, was even entitled to recover possession of her car.[77]

At the other extreme the conclusion may be that to allow an action in unjust enrichment would compliment and fulfil the policy underlying the illegality. If the illegality is designed to protect people such as the claimant from making the payment or transfer which is in issue, clearly the law will be reinforced and not contradicted by the court's recognizing the right to restitution. Thus a statutory prohibition on taking premiums for accommodation leases is likely to arise from a policy of protecting tenants from market forces. Restitution of illegal premiums positively helps.[78] Once a court concludes that restitution would further the protective policy underlying the invalidity, there will be no question of stultification. A protective policy which is assisted by restitution is perhaps the strongest and simplest reason for denying any stultification and allowing the non-contractual action.

(c) Other Situations of Merely *prima facie* Stultification

Sometimes the lever and safety-net arguments are very weak and the parties cannot sensibly be said to be as bad as each other (*in pari delicto*). For example, the claimant may only have become involved in the illegality under pressure[79] or because of a mistake such as concealed the illegality from him.[80] Such innocents cannot as a class exploit the non-contractual claim as a lever, and they merit its availability as a safety-net. There is therefore no need to bar their claims.

Sometimes a *prima facie* stultification is explained and negatived by a greater evil which has to be avoided. To allow an illegal immigrant to sue for the value of his work seems to stultify the refusal to enforce his

[77] *Wilson* (n 76 above) [49], [121]–[123], [172].

[78] *Kiriri Cotton Co Ltd v Dewani* [1960] AC 192 (PC)—tenants protected from exploitative premiums for accommodation leases; compare *Kasumu v Baba-Egbe* [1956] AC 539 (PC)—protection of ethnic land against sale to outsiders.

[79] *Smith v Bromley* (1760) 2 Douglas KB 696, 99 ER 41; *Smith v Cuff* (1817) 6 M & S 160, 105 ER 1203.

[80] *Oom v Bruce* (1810) 12 East 225, 104 ER 87; *Hughes v Liverpool Victoria Friendly Society* [1916] 2 KB 482. Mistake of law will probably now suffice. *Mohamed v Alaga & Co* [1999] 3 All ER 699 (CA) seems to confirm this.

contract, but to refuse the non-contractual action would leave the immigrant with no remedy at all and open the way to slave-labour.[81] Again, the greater evil is sometimes a grossly disproportionate forfeiture. We have just seen that if the policy behind the illegality requires it, the courts will not flinch from such a forfeiture. But the demands of the policy have to be unequivocal. When the grant of a temporary interest or limited interest is tainted with illegality, as for instance because it infringes financial regulations or seeks to evade tax or deceive creditors, the courts, though they have so far stopped short of relying directly on the disproportion, usually find a way of ensuring that the taint does not in the end deprive the claimant of the entire interest. In this group properly belong all the cases on fraudulent concealment of assets. In substance these invariably entail temporary transfers, although in form they often involve out-and-out alienations.[82]

(d) Withdrawal

It is clearly in the public interest that parties should abandon illegal projects. It used to be said that there was therefore a *locus poenitentiae*—a space for repentance—and that voluntary withdrawal was rewarded with a right to restitution immune to the defence based on *in pari delicto*. Although voluntary withdrawal is very rare, nothing less deserves any such reward. Indeed it is for two reasons senseless to treat involuntary withdrawal, which usually means refusal of the other side to play out the illegal game, in the same way as voluntary withdrawal. First, if one who is foiled may have restitution, he thereby has both lever and safety-net. Secondly, if one really wanted to foil the illegal purpose, the preferred rule would be against recovery. Why bother to perform, if one may keep it anyway?

It is not difficult to find cases which show that there is no reward for involuntary withdrawal. In *Bigos v Bousted*[83] the defendant had received a share certificate by way of security for an illegal loan. She refused to make the loan. Prichard J refused the claim in respect of the certificate. A right to recover the share would have cut the risks of ignoring the exchange controls and worked as a powerful lever to induce performance. In *Berg v Sadler and Moore*[84] a tobacconist who had displeased his trade association and been put on a stop-list attempted to obtain supplies by false pretences.

[81] *Nizamuddowlah v Bengal Cabaret Inc* 399 NYS 2d 854 (1977).

[82] *Bowmakers Ltd v Barnet Instruments Ltd* [1945] KB 65 (CA); *Tinsley v Milligan* [1994] AC 340 (HL); *Tribe v Tribe* [1996] Ch 107 (CA).

[83] [1951] 1 All ER 92.

[84] [1937] 2 KB 158 (CA).

Between his payment and their supply, the wholesalers saw through his impersonation of another tobacconist. They kept his money, giving nothing for it. The court denied him restitution. On these particular facts a restitutionary action could never act as a lever, since one cannot lever a person who has seen through one's deceit. The modern practice of the courts makes it impossible to say that he lost the ground of turpitude. So here, if it was right to bar recovery, the explanation must lie in the safety-net. The safety-net alone suffices to stultify the law, or was thought at that time to do so. At all events in these cases we see that involuntary or frustrated withdrawal does not suffice to evade *in pari delicto*, and that seems right.

Nevertheless, voluntary withdrawal before performance has repeatedly been stretched to include involuntary withdrawal, with predictably bizarre consequences. In *Tribe v Tribe*[85] a father had transferred shares to his son to hide them from creditors. The black cloud of insolvency in fact blew over. The danger having passed, the father asked his son to retransfer the shares. The son refused. The Court of Appeal held that because no creditors had actually been defrauded the father still enjoyed the privilege of withdrawal and restitution. In so holding the Court helped the father complete the illegal transaction and, for the future, provided both lever and safety-net for those tempted to hide assets. That cannot be right.

More recently in *Collier v Collier*, a very similar case, another Court of Appeal distinguished *Tribe v Tribe* on the very orthodox ground that in *Collier* some creditors, though not those originally intended, had indeed been defrauded.[86] However, the Court, although critical of the confused state of the case law in this area, gave no indication that *Tribe v Tribe* had taken the doctrine of *locus poenitentiae* far beyond its natural limit. If *Tribe v Tribe* can be defended, it must be because forfeiture of shares in substance transferred only for a temporary purpose is disproportionate and, as such, an evil which outweighs the danger of stutification. There is no stultification when there is a good reason for embracing the prima facie contradiction.

(e) Proprietary Rights: The Game of Cards

The law is seriously disfigured by the proposition, strengthened by the House of Lords in *Tinsley v Milligan*,[87] that, even if the Court knows that

85 [1996] Ch 107 (CA).

86 [2002] EWCA Civ 1095 (CA). Compare *Kearley v Thomson* (1890) 24 QBD 742, which insists that no part of the illegal purpose must have been achieved.

87 [1994] AC 340 (HL).

the parties have been engaged in an illegal agreement so that an inquiry into stultification would be expected to ensue, the terms of the debate change dramatically if the claimant seeks to establish a proprietary rather than a personal right. Unless the claimant can get himself within the *locus poenitentiae*, in which case he will be entitled to restitution by virtue of his withdrawal, the debate as to the exigibility of the proprietary right will be concluded by the legal equivalent of a game of cards. That is to say, the party who has to play the illegality card first will lose.

In *Tinsley v Milligan* itself two women contributed to the purchase of a house, agreeing that *T* would take the paper title, so that *M* could pretend to be penniless and entitled to housing benefit. In due course the parties fell out, and *T*, with the paper title, denied that *M* had any interest in the house. However, *M* could prove her contribution to the price and, since the relationship between the two women was not one which generated a presumption of advancement, could thereby establish a resulting trust without playing the illegality card. It was *T* who had to rely on illegality to undermine that entitlement. So *M* won.

In *Tribe v Tribe* the relationship of father and son did generate a presumption of advancement, so that the father would have had to play the illegality card to destroy the gift to the son. Faced with the necessity of pleading the intent to defraud creditors, the father would have lost, had he not been squeezed within an over-extended privilege of withdrawal.

Collier v Collier also involved a transfer to defraud creditors. The parties were father and daughter. Again there was a presumption of advancement. Here the father did lose. He had to play the illegality card before his daughter in order to trump the presumption of advancement, and he could not turn to the *locus poenitentiae* even as extended by *Tribe v Tribe*. As we have just seen, he had lost the privilege of withdrawal because he had used the arrangement with his daughter to defraud a creditor, albeit not the one originally in view.

This is anti-rational law. The question whether to offer these dishonest, asset-hiding claimants both lever and safety-net is being taken on irrelevant and fickle criteria. Even in these cases which play with the supposed immunity of property rights to the maxim which tells us that when both are equally bad the position of the defendant is the stronger, the story begins with an illegal contract between the parties. Somehow the law must be taken back to the real question, whether there is a sufficient reason to justify contradicting the law's attitude to that contract, which is certainly illegal and void.

More use needs to be made of the proposition that there is no stultification where there is a good reason for granting restitution despite the lever and the safety net and, in particular, of the good reason which consists in the need to prevent the greater of two evils. The *prima facie* stultification of the law can be justified in these cases by the need to prevent a grossly disproportionate civil forfeiture. We saw earlier that the policy behind the illegality can mean that a weighty forfeiture has to be tolerated, but it is unlikely that, if the question were put, the House of Lords would agree that DHSS fraud rendered it necessary or tolerable to allow Ms Tinsley to deprive Ms Milligan of her most important asset. It is an important feature of all these cases that, in substance, the arrangement between the parties was temporary, as a bailment is temporary, while the forfeiture, where it bites, is of the loser's entire interest.

It is important to emphasize that the previous paragraphs speak of cases where there has been a contract between the parties which is void for illegality and the claimant wants back the enrichment which passed under that contract. In such cases there is a stultification issue to be confronted. Nothing which has been said touches those cases in which there is no contract and no stultification issue. Thus a thief's possession is a better possession than that of anyone who takes from him or without his consent. He can bring conversion.[88] Similarly if the possessor is a bailee with a temporary or, as the common law traditionally says, a special property, when that special property expires by effluxion of time there is no doubt that his continuing to hold the thing will expose him to an action for conversion by the bailor without regard to the contract which has expired.[89]

4. INCAPACITY

The cases on ultra vires interest swaps, which now dictate the whole structure of the English law of unjust enrichment,[90] exemplify a contractual nullity which is not stultified by consequent actions in unjust enrichment. Moreover, in overruling *Sinclair v Brougham*[91] in the

[88] *Costello v Chief Constable of Derbyshire* [2001] 3 All ER 150 (CA); compare *Armory v Delamirie* (1722) 1 Str 506, 93 ER 664. This may not hold good in cases of extreme turpitude, nor where the subject matter is unlawful to possess.

[89] This partly explains *Bowmakers Ltd v Barnet Instruments Ltd* [1945] KB 65. However, there is a neglected stultification issue where the bailments in question had been brought to an end by termination for breach rather than by passage of time or in some other automatic way.

[90] Cf the discussion of the interest swaps above, 108–12.

[91] [1914] AC 398 (HL).

Westdeutsche case,[92] the House of Lords indicated that, so far as ultra vires can be said to survive at all in relation to commercial companies, their Lordships did not contemplate this as being peculiar to public authorities.

Sinclair v Brougham concerned a bank which was being run by a building society which had no power to do banking business. In the liquidation of the building society the customers of the bank were ultra vires lenders. As the case was decided they had no personal claims at all. They could not sue in contract, because their contracts were ultra vires and hence void. And they could not sue in unjust enrichment because, in modern terms, claims in unjust enrichment, for failure of basis, would stultify the doctrine of ultra vires.

With the limited weapons then at their disposal their Lordships struggled to the conclusion that the lenders nonetheless had equitable proprietary claims in respect of traceably surviving enrichment. Further, to allow that kind of claim, with its quite different measure of recovery, would not stultify the law's commitment to the ultra vires doctrine. The protective incapacity did not require the building society to be allowed to sit on traceably surviving enrichment. In the *Westdeutsche* case, however, the House of Lords held that both limbs of *Sinclair v Brougham* were wrong.

In the view of the *Westdeutsche* majority, a transfer under a contract void for want of corporate capacity gave the transferor no equitable proprietary claim, and the depositors ought to have been allowed their personal claim in unjust enrichment. With the defence of change of position in place, it had become apparent that even the personal claim in unjust enrichment did not have the same content as the claim on the contract of loan. We might now say that, if *Sinclair v Brougham* decided that a claim limited to traceably surviving enrichment could not stultify the law's nullification of the contract for incapacity, *Westdeutsche* preferred the same proposition rephrased in terms of abstractly surviving enrichment. Change of position, in its disenrichment limb, thus confines the liability in unjust enrichment.[93]

In the case of the minority of natural persons there is no doubt that the policy of the law is to protect the minor. Contracts made by minors are unenforceable against the minor. The adult clearly cannot take advantage

[92] *Westdeutsche Landesbank Girozentrale v Islington LBC* [1996] AC 669 (HL) 710–14, 718, 738.

[93] This assumes the removal of the shadow cast by *Goss v Chilcott* [1996] AC 788 (PC), discussed above, 217–8.

of the invalidity. Before the Infants Relief Act 1874 was repealed in 1987, loans and sales to minors were absolutely void. Even the strongest language of nullity did not mean that an adult who sold goods to a minor too cheaply could reverse the transaction.

Here too the crucial proposition is that the protection of the minor is not subverted by making him give up still surviving enrichment. The Minors' Contracts Act 1987 section 3(1) now says the court 'may, if it is just and equitable to do so, require [the minor] to transfer to the [other] a property acquired by the minor under the contract, or any property representing it'. The adult's common law rights are not displaced by the statute. The common law remained somewhat obscure. It probably always meant to allow a similar measure of recovery, restricted to enrichment surviving in his hands.[94] It may now never be decided whether, in parallel with the paragraphs immediately above, the modern extrapolation from the confused common law would be that the minor remained liable to the extent of his abstractly surviving enrichment, or, in other words, that, with heavily modified rules of disqualification, he remained liable in unjust enrichment subject to a defence of disenrichment.

If the minor's protection were understood as protection only against contractual liability, then the discussion of claims in unjust enrichment would be correctly placed here, for the only question in regard to them would be whether a claim in unjust enrichment would stultify that protection from contractual liability. But it seems more probable that minors are protected from burdensome debt howsoever arising.[95] In that case minority is a defence to claims in unjust enrichment as such. On that assumption the discussion does not belong here. It does not depend on stultification but directly on minority. We will return to it below.[96]

5. INFORMALITY

Failure to comply with a requirement of writing generally renders a contract unenforceable. The word 'unenforceable' is used precisely to indicate that the contract is good but gives rise to no action to enforce it. In such a case, therefore, there is no invalidity sufficient to give rise to a

[94] The adult's right to restitution of the still surviving enrichment appears to have been tied to 'fraud' in only the loosest equitable sense of that term: *Clarke v Cobley* (1798) 2 Cox 173, 30 ER 80; *R Leslie Ltd v Sheill* [1914] 3 KB 607; cf *Marlow v Pitfield* (1719) 1 PWms 558, 24 ER 516; *Lewis v Alleyn* (1888) 4 TLR 650.

[95] The liability *ex delicto* in *Bristow v Eastman* (1794) 1 Esp 172, 170 ER 317 should nowadays be understood as restitutionary damages for the wrong, not as debt.

[96] Below, 261–3.

prima facie right to restitution of value transferred. Invalidity will only supervene, and the restitutionary right arise, if the good but unenforceable contract becomes terminable in the ordinary way, as for instance for repudiatory breach.[97]

The case in which, before more recent hesitations, the High Court of Australia appeared to have recognized unjust enrichment was of this kind. In *Pavey & Matthews Pty Ltd v Paul*[98] the claimants were builders who had completed work for the defendant, Mrs Paul. She refused to pay the sum which they maintained was due. The New South Wales Builders Licensing Act 1971 rendered all building contracts unenforceable unless written. In response to her refusal to pay, the builders were in principle entitled to a claim in unjust enrichment for the reasonable value of their work. The Court addressed the question whether allowing that action would subvert the policy of the Act. It decided that it would not. The desirable certainty promoted by the requirement of writing was sufficiently sanctioned by depriving the builder of his claim in contract. It did not require to be reinforced by barring even his claim in unjust enrichment, thus leaving him unpaid for work actually done and accepted.[99]

Some formal requirements stand on the borderline with illegality. Whatever it is called, if the formal requirement which is ignored is perceived to have a disciplinary and protective purpose in the presence of the danger of serious abuses, a court may take the view that actions in unjust enrichment would stultify the law and must be barred, even in a case in which the defendant has not been disenriched.[100]

Under the head of illegality above, we considered cases within the Consumer Credit Act 1974, such as *Dimond v Lovell*.[101] That case tested a question vital to the business of supplying short-term replacements for vehicles damaged by negligent driving and, obliquely, illustrated the consequences of this higher degree of disciplinary formality. Profitability depended on the supplier of the substitute car being able to charge the tortfeasor's insurer a high price for meeting the victim's need. The contract with the victim therefore included terms to the effect that the supplier of the substitute would manage the victim's claim against the

[97] *Thomas v Brown* [1876] 1 QBD 714. On invalidity, see above, 125–7.

[98] (1987) 162 CLR 221 (HCA).

[99] For the long history: D Ibbetson 'Implied Contracts and Restitution: History in the High Court of Australia' (1988) 8 OJLS 312–27. Compare AT Denning (later Lord Denning), '*Quantum Meruit* and the Statute of Frauds' (1925) 41 LQR 79.

[100] *Orakpo v Manson Investments Ltd* [1978] AC 95 (HL).

[101] [2002] 1 AC 384 (HL); cf *Wilson v First County Trust Ltd* [2003] UKHL 40, [2003] 2 All ER (Comm) 491, discussed above, 248–9.

tortfeasor and that the hire would not be payable until damages were paid. In this test case Mrs Dimond's insurer successfully set out to show that she was not liable to pay the suppliers for the car and therefore could not include the hire in the list of her losses.

The insurer's argument was that, structured as it was, the contract of hire was a regulated credit agreement within the Consumer Credit Act 1974 but failed to comply with the requisite formalities. The suppliers countered that if she was not liable to them in contract she must be liable in unjust enrichment since she had had the use of their vehicle knowing that it was not offered gratuitously. The House of Lords took the contrary view. In a field notorious for exploitation and extortion the Act had set out to protect the public from abuse and to discipline potential abusers. Reinforcement was called for, not dilution. The consequences of non-compliance with the statutory requirements must not be diluted by recourse to a non-contractual claim.

It can happen that a contract is expressly rendered void, and not merely unenforceable, for non-compliance with formal requirements. Unwritten contracts for the sale of land have been made void by section 2 of the Law of Property (Miscellaneous Provisions) Act 1989. It has already been thought necessary to say that that is not such a nullity as indicates that after execution the parties are liable to make mutual restitution.[102] This cannot be said to have been fully explored yet. However, it is predictable that this instance of nullity will serve as a vivid illustration that the fifth question can resist the notion that invalidity must automatically give rise to mutual restitution. If as the Act says there is no contract at all the parties must have *prima facie* rights to restitution. If at the same time the law is that they have no such rights it must be because the prima facie right to restitution meets a defence. Where the aims behind the invalidity would be confounded by restitution, the enrichee-defendant will have a stultification defence. It is here that the anxieties of Sir William Evans have to be met.[103]

6. WHERE A NATURAL OBLIGATION SURVIVES THE INVALIDITY

In *Moses v Macferlan* Lord Mansfield was careful to say that a claimant who had discharged an obligation in ignorance of the fact that it could not

[102] *Tootal Clothing Ltd v Guinea Properties Ltd* (1992) 64 P & CR 452.

[103] Sir William Evans, *Essays On the Action for Money Had and Received, on the Law of Insurances, and on the Law of Bills of Exchange and Promissory Notes* (Liverpool 1802) 37 ff [reprinted [1998] Restitution L Rev 1, 12 ff].

be enforced against him would not be able to recover simply because the money was technically not due. The invalidity on which he had to rely might have left him morally or 'naturally' bound. This is what Lord Mansfield said:[104]

> [This action] lies only for money which *ex aequo et bono* the defendant ought to refund. It does not lie for money paid by the plaintiff, which is claimed of him as payable in point of honour and honesty, although it could not have been recovered from him by any course of law: as in payment of a debt barred by the Statute of Limitations, or contracted during his infancy, or to the extent of principal and legal interest upon an usurious contract, or for money fairly lost at play; because in all these cases the defendant may retain it with a safe conscience, though by positive law he was barred from recovering.

So long as the bar against restitution for mistake of law was in place, little was heard of this, but, even though the notion of a natural obligation can become an unruly horse, it is now important. The law of unjust enrichment would itself be stultified if the criteria which normally identify an unjust enrichment were allowed in an exceptional case to compel restitution of an enrichment which was not unjust. The claimant cannot say that the money was not due if, behind the technicalities of the law, there was still a moral obligation to pay. In such a case the defendant must be allowed a defence.

D. RESIDUAL CASES

Putting on one side the defences related to enrichment at the expense of the claimant, most of the unjust-related defences aim to avoid unjust enrichment of the claimant himself, to achieve finality, or to avoid stultifying the law. A miscellany remains.

1. NON-DISENRICHING CHANGES OF POSITION

The defence of change of position is always expressed in very wide and imprecise terms, to the effect that the defendant will have a defence to the extent that in changed circumstances it would be inequitable to require full restitution. We have already dealt with changes of position which eliminate all or part of the enrichment.[105] Delay is covered by the

[104] *Moses v Macferlan* (1760) 2 Burr 1005, 1012, 97 ER 676, 681. The same idea worked to the benefit of the claimant in *Larner v London CC* [1949] 2 KB 683 (CA), where a putatively obligatory payment was held nonetheless obligatory for being natural, not legal.

[105] Above, 208–19.

Limitation Act 1980 and the law relating to laches and acquiescence. Supervening hardships which were not induced by the enrichment, such as unemployment, ill-health, and marital breakdown, have rightly been held not to be relevant.[106] There is clearly very little room, therefore, for any kind of non-disenriching change of position. All the same the discovery of an example is not to be ruled out.[107]

In *Kleinwort Benson Ltd v Lincoln CC*[108] the parties had been engaged in a void interest swap. The swap had gone the full distance. It was a closed swap. The claimant bank successfully sought to recover on the ground of its mistake as to the capacity of the Council. However, after that mistake was made, the contract, invalid as it was, was fully performed and the disappointment latent in the mistake never eventuated. Like a bomb safely defused, the mistake was spent. This looks like a plausible example of a non-disenriching change of circumstance rendering it inequitable to seek relief for the mistake, but the House of Lords said that the cause of action was complete at the moment of the payment, and that was that.[109] Unfortunately, the point was not explicitly argued in terms of change of position. It is just possible that, if it had been, the House of Lords would have directly confronted the question whether there can ever be a non-disenriching version of the defence.

In *Commerzbank AG v Gareth Price-Jones*[110] the defendant banker maintained that he had stayed with Commerzbank because he believed he would be paid a guaranteed annual bonus of £515,000. In due course he had indeed received that sum, in two instalments, one of £250,000, the other £265,000. In fact Commerzbank had only meant to raise a first offer of £250,000 to £265,000. It had never intended to pay both. The Court of Appeal recognized its right to recover £250,000.

Mummery LJ, with whom Sedley LJ agreed, used language which accepted the need to divide the inquiry in two. He said that there had been no disenrichment. The banker's assets were still swollen by the full amount of the mistaken payment. The question thus became whether, having proved no loss to set against the enrichment, he could nonetheless say that his staying with the bank was a sufficient change of position to render full restitution inequitable. The answer was, not that there could be no such thing as a non-disenriching change of position, but that the

[106] *Scottish Equitable plc v Derby* [2001] 3 All ER 818 (CA) 828.

[107] R Nolan, 'Change of Position' in P Birks (ed) *Laundering and Tracing* (OUP Oxford 1995) 135, 172–5.

[108] [1999] 2 AC 349 (HL). [109] Ibid 386, 409, approving *Baker v Courage* [1910] 1 KB 56.

[110] [2003] EWCA Civ 1663, introduced at 212 above, text to n 15.

defendant had not shown anything 'sufficiently significant, precise, or substantial in extent'.[111]

Munby J, by contrast, very emphatically asserted that the defence was not confined to disenrichment. He condemned attempts to restate or explicate the straightforward question whether in the circumstances it was inequitable for the claimant to recover in full. Judges should keep their distance from 'over-refined analysis'.[112] In the end, however, having sailed very close to the rocks of relative fault,[113] he too concluded that on these facts equity and justice were quite plainly on the side of the bank.

Commerzbank AG v Gareth Price-Jones clearly keeps open the possibility that a defendant who has not been disenriched may yet be able to advance a relevant change of position. Nevertheless, it is certainly necessary to separate disenrichment from other manifestations of the defence. The strict liability characteristic of unjust enrichment is tied to extant enrichment. So long as the defendant is still enriched there is no question of allocating a loss, only of relocating a gain. It is extraordinarily difficult to come up with convincing reasons for keeping an extant gain to which one has no claim. Neither fault on the part of the claimant nor innocence on the part of the defendant weakens the demand for restitution.[114] Disenrichment changes everything. What was a question of relocating a gain immediately becomes a question of allocating a loss.

Non-disenriching changes of position may yet be found. They have to be tested against the premiss of *Commerzbank*, namely that the defendant's assets are still swollen. He still has the unjustified units of value. Plausible hypotheticals usually turn out to have an unacknowledged foundation in disenrichment. 'This mistaken £100,000 persuaded us that we could at last start a family' might found a good defence if the wife was already pregnant, but not if she was merely trying to become pregnant. The difference is that in the former case there is already a financial commitment, in the latter no more than a plan which must be postponed if not achievable on a more limited budget. No rational system could allow the couple to pursue their ambition on the strength of money to which they were not entitled. The example shows that there is also a problem of quantification. If there were a judge whose notion of fairness told him

[111] Ibid [40].

[112] Ibid [48]. The rejection of analysis is powerfully criticized by A Burrows, 'Clouding the Issues on Change of Position' [2004] CLJ 276–9; cf P Birks, 'Change of Position: The Two Central Questions' (2004) 120 LQR 373–9.

[113] Ibid [79]–[80].

[114] Compare recently *Scottish Equitable plc v Derby* (n 106 above) [19]–[37].

that the couple should not suffer the disappointment of an unkind claim to restitution he would have to decide just how much of the claimant's money might equitably be allocated to fund their efforts.

If valid examples are found they will be very rare indeed. They leave the defendant to enjoy extant enrichment to which he is not entitled. No better example could be found of the unwisdom of rejecting rational analysis. Unanalysed intuition hidden behind words such as 'inequitable' or 'unconscionable' leads straight towards intolerable results.

2. TURPITUDE

We have seen that most cases of illegality are best understood in terms of the imperative not to allow an action in unjust enrichment to stultify the law's condemnation of the contract. Even dishonesty does not now elicit the revulsion expressed in the maxim *ex turpi causa non oritur actio* (no action arises from a disgraceful cause). Nevertheless, at a certain extreme degree of turpitude that maxim will be triggered. The consequence will be that the claimant's action will be rejected at square one. There is no question of allowing recovery of money paid to procure a child for sexual abuse. This could be kept within the stultification family, in that it would contradict every possible statement of the mission of courts of justice. But it stands more easily here as one of a number of residual unjust-related defences. It allows the defendant to invite the court to say that on the simple ground of revulsion no action can arise.

3. MINORITY

Minors are not bound by their contracts. The ground rule is, by statute, that the minor's contract is voidable at his option. This meets the need to protect the inexperienced from bad bargains. The question whether a minor also has a defence to claims in unjust enrichment could not be directly faced so long as unjust enrichment was buried in, and was, contract. If the minor were protected only from contractual liability, the answer to the unjust enrichment question would turn on whether the claim in unjust enrichment would stultify the protection from contract. An inquiry of that kind has to be made to determine the minor's liability in tort. He can be liable in tort when that liability does not subvert his protection from contract.

In fact the better view seems to be that the minor is protected, not just from contractual liability, but also from claims in unjust enrichment, save so far as the enrichment traceably survives. If that is right the minor has as good a defence to a claim in respect of a mistaken payment of a debt not due as to a claim for the return of money paid to him for a performance under a contract which he chooses to avoid.

In *Bristow v Eastman*[115] a minor had embezzled money from his employer. In modern terms the case could be analysed as either a restitutionary claim in respect of his wrong as such or as a claim in unjust enrichment in respect of money taken from the employer without the employer's knowledge. The court upheld it only in the former character, as a claim *ex delicto*. Again in *Cowern v Nield*[116] a minor who had been paid for a consignment of cattle feed which he failed to supply was allowed a defence to a claim in unjust enrichment for failure of basis. The defence was good even though the claim would not have yielded the same performance as was due under the contract. No doubt this result could be explained in terms of stultification of the protection from contractual liability, but Goff and Jones argue that the case was wrongly decided precisely because, in their view, the protection is from contractual liability and would not have been stultified if the adult had recovered in this case.[117] That takes a very narrow view of stultification.

However, stultification may not be in point at all. The outcome is absolutely right on the assumption that *Cowern v Nield* and *Bristow v Eastman* together stand for the proposition that the protection of the minor applies directly to all non-tortious indebtedness and to tortious indebtedness only so far as the action would subvert his protection from all and any non-contractual indebtedness.

The defence which the minor has to claims in unjust enrichment is not absolute. Restitution must stop where repayment begins.[118] He must give back surviving enrichment but must not be made to repay that which has already gone. It would be possible, therefore, to synthesize the old cases so as to present them as giving the minor what has now become the general defence of disenrichment, with a special privilege against disqualification. The present statutory judicial discretion to order the return of property received or representing that which was received can and should be operated consistently with that basic principle. The

[115] (1794) 1 Esp 172, 170 ER 317.

[116] [1912] 2 KB 419. Contrast a loan not repaid: *R Leslie Ltd v Sheill* [1914] 3 KB 607 (CA).

[117] G Goff (ed), *Goff & Jones on Restitution* (6th edn Sweet & Maxwell London 2002) [25–008].

[118] *R Leslie Ltd v Sheill* (n 116 above) 618.

long-established rule which makes the minor liable in respect of money traceably applied to the discharge of debts which were enforceable against him, as for instance in respect of the reasonable value of necessaries, is also part of that picture.[119] There is an unresolved tension between the two concepts of wealth which remains to be resolved. The minor certainly should not be liable to any extent greater than his abstractly surviving enrichment. On the other hand the question whether he can be liable at all if there is no traceable discrete enrichment is not now clear.

E. CONCLUSION

The 'absence of basis' method of deciding whether an enrichment at the expense of another is unjust can arouse anxieties. It worried Sir William Evans at the beginning of the 19th century. And it worried commentators who foresaw and tried to prevent its coming victory in the swaps cases. Those anxieties would be well founded if it seemed likely to degenerate into a dogma to the effect that invalidity entailed automatic restitution of value transferred. Sir Guenter Treitel, whose support for this approach antedates the swaps cases, says that that danger will not eventuate because the invalidity is only a starting point.[120] In other words the answer to the third of the five questions (unjust) establishes no more than a *prima facie* liability. The most important issue underlying this chapter has been whether the unjust-related defences are sufficiently dynamic to ensure that that is true.

The defences which have been reviewed, especially those in the stultification family, leave much to be desired. They need tidying up. Nonetheless they appear to be sufficiently vigorous and well-established to ensure that the law of unjust enrichment will retain its flexibility under the 'no basis' regime. The law will not be driven to produce outcomes which make nonsense either of its own mission or of considered positions taken in other areas such as the law of contract.

As was emphasized at the beginning of this part, the debate which watches over the fine tuning of the law of unjust enrichment has now largely moved from the third (unjust) to the fifth (defences) of the five questions. The two chapters of this part have shown that, even if it cannot

[119] *Marlow v Pitfield* (1719) 1 PWms 558, 24 ER 516; *Lewis v Alleyn* (1888) 4 TLR 650.

[120] Sir Guenter Treitel, *The Law of Contract* (11th edn Sweet & Maxwell London 2003) 1058, 1060.

be said that the law is entirely ready to bear that burden, there is no reason to think that the raw materials cannot be developed to be at once orderly, intelligible, and flexible. That optimistic prediction depends on the development being controlled for the first time by a principled understanding of the law of unjust enrichment as a whole and, in particular, of what we have been calling the peculiar normativity of extant enrichment. The fifth question is the last question but not by any means the least.

Part VI

Competing Terminology

11

Competing Generics

The obscure vocabulary which used to do the work of unjust enrichment is still constantly in use. Again and again we encounter the action for money had and received, the action for money paid, quasi-contract, constructive trust, and so on. Throughout the earlier chapters this ghostly inheritance from the past has so far as possible been suppressed. The law of unjust enrichment does not need it and is indeed impeded by it. The two chapters of this final part review the relationship between the old language and the new. The principal reason for mastering the old vocabulary is to transcend it. Sometimes that means getting rid of it altogether. Sometimes it is more a matter of making sure that it does no more than its legitimate work.

This chapter deals with terms which have directly competed with unjust enrichment in the naming and organization of this area of the law or, more accurately, an area of law approximating to or including this one. The next chapter turns from the generic vocabulary to the fragments which used to do most of the day-to-day work. The line between competing generics and persistent fragments cannot be cleanly drawn.

As competing generics from the past this chapter considers quasi-contract and implied or constructive contract. It then turns to modern competition, under which head it deals with restitution and with variations on unjust enrichment itself. Of these, restitution sticks out as making no pretence of being an event-oriented term, but it is undoubtedly a competitor. For some 70 years it has managed both to overstretch the language of unjust enrichment and to push it into second place.

A. OUTDATED GENERICS

1. QUASI-CONTRACT

Quasi-contract has a very shallow root in the common law. The term originated in the first life of Roman law, deserved no respect, and endured only because in its second life, from the 11th century, the Roman law library acquired the incontestable authority of scripture. In the common law the term 'quasi-contract' played almost no part at all until, in the last years of the 19th century, the first hesitant attempts to map the terrain beyond contract and tort produced books under this borrowed and barely translated Latin name.

The two earliest books on quasi-contract were written in America.[1] They were the precursors of the *Restatement of Restitution*. In England the first edition of Pollock's *Law of Tort* in 1882 revealed its author's awareness of the gap to be filled, for in the preface he acknowledged that a book on tort added to a book on contract did not amount to a complete law of obligations.[2] The term 'quasi-contract' was seen as an improvement on 'implied contract', to which we will come next. In his preface Keener acknowledged Pollock and Anson's lead in preferring 'quasi-contract' to 'implied contract'. Ironically the Roman term had itself been partly responsible for the all too robust heresy of implied contract.

(a) The Roman Origin

In the second century AD, coming in his *Institutes* to obligations, Gaius began with a proposition to the effect that every obligation arose either *ex contractu* (from a contract) or *ex delicto* (from a wrong). However, he almost immediately encountered the obligation arising from a mistaken payment. This forced him to admit that the classification in terms of two causative events was not exhaustive.[3]

In another book, excerpts from which are preserved in Justinian's *Digest*, he said instead that obligations arose from contracts, from wrongs, or from miscellaneous other events. The identification of that miscellany was the beginning of the story which ultimately produced the law of unjust enrichment. However, although they made progress in that direction within their action of debt and knew the argument that one person should not be unjustly enriched at another's expense,[4] the Romans never

[1] WA Keener, *A Treatise on the Law of Quasi-Contracts* (Baker Voorhis New York 1893); FC Woodward, *The Law of Quasi-Contracts* (Little Brown Boston 1913).

[2] F Pollock, *The Law of Tort* (Stevens & Co London 1882), following F Pollock, *The Law of Contract* (Stevens & Co London 1876).

[3] Gaius, *Institutes* 3.89–3.91.

[4] '*Iure naturae aequum est neminem cum alterius detrimento et iniuria fieri locupletiorem* (It is fair according to the law of nature that nobody should be enriched by loss and injustice to another)' (Pomponius D.50.17.206). Compare, slightly different, '*Nam hoc natura aequum est neminem cum alterius detrimento fieri lucupletiorem* (For this is by nature fair, that nobody should be enriched by another's loss)' (Pomponius D.12.6.4).

identified unjust enrichment as an independent category. Instead Gaius himself, or possibly someone later intervening in his text, tried to impose order on the residual miscellany by asserting that in some instances within it the obligation could be said to arise *quasi ex contractu*, as though from a contract, and in others *quasi ex delicto*, as though from a delict.[5]

Nearly four centuries after Gaius, when Justinian's commissioners compacted the law library in Constantinople and produced the *Corpus Juris Civilis*, the Emperor's new edition of the *Institutes* adopted this quasi-resolution of the residual miscellany: 'Every obligation arises from a contract or as though from a contract or from a wrong or as though from a wrong.'[6] The category of obligations arising as though from a contract (*quasi ex contractu*) included, with the obligation from receipt of a mistaken payment, the obligations from uninvited management of another's affairs, from guardianship, from involuntary co-ownership, and from wills in respect of the payment of legacies.[7]

It is as certain as anything could be that the phrase 'as though from contract' was coined to indicate similarities with particular contracts while at the same time emphasizing that there was no contract: as though upon a contract despite there being none. Mistaken payments, for instance, were not contracts but lived beside the contract of loan (*mutuum*) as a cause of indebtedness and gave rise to the same action, the *condictio*.[8] However, it was only one short step from 'as though upon a contract' to 'upon a sort-of-contract', from *quasi ex contractu* to quasi-contract. This step was first taken by Theophilus, a professorial member of Justinian's commission and one of the three who had been responsible for Justinian's *Institutes*, of which he also produced a Greek version. It was there that we find the first transition from 'as though from a contract' to 'from a quasi-contract'.[9]

In the second life of Roman law, when Justinian's compacted law library had become the foundation of the *ius commune* of Europe, some civilian jurists forged from this distortion a theory that the source of the obligation in these cases was a presumed or implied contract. The effect

[5] Gaius, *Aurea* bk 3, D.44.7.5 pr–3. The doubt whether this passage is genuine Gaius arises from the presence of interpolations in the *Digest*, but modern Romanists are slow to affirm the interpolation-hunting of their predecessors. Gaius probably did coin these *quasi* phrases, though without expecting them to do 2000 years of taxonomic service.

[6] Justinian, *Institutes* 3.13.2.

[7] Ibid 3.27. Compare, in 13th-century England, Bracton folio 100, SE Thorne (ed), *Bracton on the Laws and Customs of England* (Selden Society and Belknap Press of Harvard University Cambridge Mass 1968) vol 2, 287.

[8] Above, 130–1.

[9] Theophilus, *Paraphrase* 3.27.3 and 5.

was to push these figures back into the very category from which the Romans themselves had intended to exclude them.[10]

(b) Half-Hearted Borrowing

From the early 17th century English judges occasionally borrowed the Roman term.[11] In *Moses v Macferlan* itself Lord Mansfield invoked it to give respectability to the extension of the action of *assumpsit* to non-promissory debts. '*Assumpsit*' means 'he promised' and cannot naturally reach a debtor who never did. Macferlan had sued Moses in the teeth of an undertaking not to do so. Moses then alleged that Macferlan thereby became indebted to him in the sum which he had wrongfully obtained. The action which Moses brought was a sub-form of the action of *assumpsit*.[12] Macferlan objected that, having obtained the money 'by adverse suit', he could not possibly be said to have promised to repay. Lord Mansfield's answer defended the fictionalization of the allegation of a promise by saying that even the Romans had claims 'as it were upon a contract':

> If the defendant be under an obligation, from the ties of natural justice, to refund, the law implies a debt and gives this action, founded in the equity of the plaintiff's case, as it were upon a contract (*quasi ex contractu*, as the Roman law expresses it).[13]

It was not until the late 19th and early 20th century, in the period before the American Law Institute's *Restatement of the Law of Restitution*,[14] that the need made itself felt in earnest for the common law to make sense of its treatment of the miscellaneous causative events in the Gaian miscellany beyond contract and tort. An article in 1888 by the American legal historian James Barr Ames may have contributed to the resurgence of 'quasi-contract'.[15] Like the English scholars mentioned above, in relating

[10] P Birks and G McLeod, 'The Implied Contract Theory of Quasi-Contract: Civilian Opinion in the Century before Blackstone' (1986) 6 OJLS 46, esp 68–77.

[11] JH Baker, 'The History of Quasi-Contract in English Law' in WR Cornish and others (eds), *Restitution, Past, Present, and Future* (Hart Oxford 1998) 37.

[12] *Assumpsit* and its sub-form *indebitatus assumpsit* are discussed below, 286–90.

[13] (1760) 2 Burr 1005, 1009, 97 ER 676, 678.

[14] On the *Restatement* see below, 277–81.

[15] JB Ames, 'The History of Assumpsit: Implied Assumpsit' (1888) 2 Harvard L Rev 53, 64. On this see D Ibbetson, 'Unjust Enrichment in English Law' in E Schrage (ed), *Unjust Enrichment and the Law of Contract* (Kluwer The Hague 2001) 33, 45. In the Astor Lecture for 2004 given in Oxford on 6 May 2004 Professor Andrew Kull, reporter for the new *Restatement of Restitution*, made Ames the true father of the intellectual developments which ultimately produced the 1937 *Restatement*.

the history of implied *assumpsit* to the modern law he took the view that a return to the Roman term would be an improvement on 'implied contract'.[16]

Just as the textbook writers who set out to tame the law of tort left equitable wrongs on one side, so those who wrote on quasi-contract also assumed a restriction to the common law. Within that boundary, it was clear that the matter of unjust enrichment was prominently included, but quite how many of the other events in the residual miscellany were to count as belonging to quasi-contract remained unclear and impossible of proof. 'Quasi-contract' says only that the matter is not contract. So far as it suggests that there is a sort of contract, it deceives, unintelligibly. A quasi-sparrow is not a sparrow. In what respect it might resemble sparrows is left to speculation. Despite this conceptual uncertainty, six important books were ultimately written on quasi-contract.[17] The last was Stoljar's second edition, as late as 1989.

Professor Stoljar was deeply learned, kind, and far-seeing. Towards the end of his life, already unwell but undiminished, he walked me round Lake Burley Griffin in Canberra vigorously defending his decision not to modernize his title. Neither restitution nor unjust enrichment appealed to him. He has therefore become a hero to later sceptics.[18] However, on this point he was as wrong as he was adamant. There will be no more books on quasi-contract. A deceptive name is a constant impediment.

2. IMPLIED OR CONSTRUCTIVE CONTRACT

From Blackstone onwards the orthodoxy for common lawyers was that obligations arising from a mistaken payment and from all the events which the books just mentioned wrapped up in the Roman cloak of 'quasi-contract' were based on implied contract. We have already seen that some civilians did the same,[19] but no civilian jurisdiction was committed to the fiction of implied contract as comprehensively as the common law. As late as 1914, in *Sinclair v Brougham*, Lord Haldane LC,

[16] Discussed immediately below.

[17] WA Keener (1893); FC Woodward (1913); RM Jackson (1936—a history); JH Munkman (1950); PH Winfield (1952); SJ Stoljar (1964, 1989). There were also a number of American casebooks produced for courses on quasi-contract. One notable example is JS Scott (Voorhis New York 1905).

[18] This is witnessed by his prominence in the judgment of Gummow J in *Roxborough v Rothmans of Pall Mall Australia Ltd* (2002) 76 ALJR 203 (HCA).

[19] Note 10 above and text thereto.

struggling to maintain the position abandoned by Gaius in the second century, said:

> Broadly speaking, so far as proceedings *in personam* are concerned the common law of England really recognizes (unlike the Roman law) only actions of two classes, those founded on contract and those founded on tort. When it speaks of actions arising *quasi ex contractu* it refers merely to a class of action in theory based on a contract which is imputed by a fiction of law. The fiction can only be set up with effect if such a contract would be valid if it really existed.[20]

This attempt to manage with just two categories of causative event could not but cripple the law of unjust enrichment. It short-circuited the inquiry required by *Sinclair v Brougham* itself before the question was even put. In that case the court needed to ask whether, not within contract but outside it, a party could recover value transferred under a void contract. On the orthodox view there was nothing to turn to. The question presented itself as whether one could turn to contract to recover under a void contract, and the answer then seemed all too obvious. One could not imply a contract where an express contract would be inexorably void. The same mind-set left us unable to say to what extent a minor could be liable in unjust enrichment. Here too we find the explanation for the astonishing fact that even in 1980 a new Limitation Act made no provision for unjust enrichment. There was no such category.

This implied contract heresy had at least three roots. One was certainly the use of *assumpsit* to recover non-promissory debts. The courts connived in that adulteration of the 'he promised' action because they were unwilling to put obstacles in the way of claimants who wanted to escape disadvantages inherent in the old action of debt, including trial by oath-taking rather than jury.[21] The radical modernization of pleading in the 19th century did little to alter long-standing habits of mind. The fiction of implied *assumpsit* lived on.

The second was Blackstone, whose *Commentaries* embraced the implied contract theory of this kind of non-contractual liability with enthusiasm. It fitted neatly with his fondness for social contract explanations of all burdens imposed by law. Even punishment for crimes could be explained as having been agreed to in the social contract.[22]

[20] [1914] AC 398 (HL) 415.

[21] JH Baker, *An Introduction to English Legal History* (4th edn Butterworths London 2002) 342, 368–9.

[22] Blackstone 3 *Commentaries* 158, 161–2 (citing to the first edition).

The third, subtly implicated in both the other two, was the influence of the Roman term 'quasi-contract' and the fact that some civilian jurists had themselves used that term as a springboard to their own implied contract heresy. The civilians who taught that quasi-contract was presumed or implied contract provided the intellectual cover for the adulteration of *assumpsit* and for Blackstone's enthusiasm for implied contract.

These three forces drove implied contract deep into the English legal mind. The line between implication in fact and implication in law was blurred or ignored. Practitioners became habituated to finding this non-contractual material in the books on contract. This continued far into the 20th century. Ten years after the publication of the *Restatement of Restitution* the first post-war edition of *Chitty on Contract* still juxtaposed the obligation to return mistaken payments with *The Moorcock*[23] and the discussion of terms to be implied in contracts for the purpose of giving them business efficacy.[24]

Attempts to blow away the web of falsehood and to introduce the law to the notion of unjust enrichment met with extraordinarily vehement opposition. Sir William Holdsworth boldly declared that 'the English principle based upon a contract implied by the law makes it more possible to work out some definite rules than the continental system or the system advocated by Lord Wright.'[25] In the sixties *Goff & Jones* finally launched an all-out attack on contracts 'implied in law':

> [T]he assertion that the requirement of implied contract leads to certainty is unintelligible. When is a contract to be implied? No logical answer can be given to the question when recourse should be had to a fiction. Moreover, study of the cases reveals that emphasis on implied contract, and the spurious connection with contract which it implies, has inhibited discussion of substantive issues.[26]

There was no answer to that. The implied contract heresy has been once and for all seen off and with it the more pretentious but slightly less dishonest 'constructive contract', which was also found.[27] It is still

[23] (1889) 14 PD 64 (CA).

[24] *Chitty on Contract* (20th edn Sweet & Maxwell London 1947) 68–119. This was maintained in the 21st edition (1955). In the 22nd edition, under the editorship of the great Dr John Morris, 'Quasi-Contract and Restitution' was finally set apart as Part 8 of Volume 1 (General Principles).

[25] Sir William Holdsworth, 'Unjustifiable Enrichment' (1939) 55 LQR 37, 51, replying to Lord Wright of Durley, '*Sinclair v Brougham*' (1938) 6 CLJ 305.

[26] R Goff and G Jones, *The Law of Restitution* (1st edn Sweet & Maxwell London 1966) 9.

[27] Especially in America: *Words and Phrases* vol 8A (West Publishing Co St Paul Minn 1951) 508–11 with its cumulative supplement (Thomson-West 2002) 341.

capable of little local come-backs, but it will not recover. A mistaken payee does not contract to repay. The only reason for subscribing to the contrary falsehood was the difficulty of knowing where else to put the mistaken payer's case and how exactly to explain it.

B. MODERN COMPETITORS

1. UNJUSTIFIED OR UNCONSCIONABLE ENRICHMENT

In the phrase 'unjust enrichment' the word 'unjust' is only weakly normative. For the most part it merely gathers up the law's reasons, not being contracts or wrongs, why an enrichment should be given up to a person at whose expense it was received. There is nonetheless a perceptible difference between being weakly normative and having no active role at all. The weakly normative 'unjust' is a constant reminder of the conclusion which the rules aim to reach. In the occasional case the rules require incremental development, to allow restitution on new facts or prevent it when old rules misfire.[28] The law has to retain the marginal energy to ensure that in such a case dogma does not take over. Inert language such as 'restitution-yielding enrichment' or 'restorable enrichment'[29] would discourage this kind of creative self-criticism and encourage stasis.

(a) Unjust or Unjustified?

Given that the chosen adjective has only this weakly normative role, there is nothing to choose between 'unjust' and 'unjustified'. German scholars writing in English certainly prefer the latter, which is a closer translation of the word chosen by the relevant title in their code (*ungerechtfertigte Bereicherung*). In his path-breaking comparative articles, Professor Nicholas clearly thought 'unjustified' safer than 'unjust' because it was less likely to excite the scorn of a judiciary easily provoked by the least hint of an invitation to do palm-tree justice.[30] That misplaced irritability having abated, 'unjust' appears to have won the day among

[28] For example, strict liability was intolerable and crudely inhibited until the defence of change of position was revived (above, 208–19) and fear that invalidity might automatically require restitution has to be met by sensitive handling of the defence of stultification (above, 240–58). Flexibility is nowadays often a matter for the defences.

[29] Preferred, and said to be normative, by R Grantham and C Rickett, *Enrichment and Restitution in New Zealand* (Hart Oxford 2000) 58–60.

[30] B Nicholas, 'Unjustified Enrichment in Civil Law and Louisiana Law' (1962) 36 Tulane L Rev 605, 605–6 (continued 37 Tulane L Rev 49).

authors writing in English.[31] It has the advantage of being shorter and more flexible.

The truth is, however, that it makes no difference whatever whether one speaks of unjust enrichment or of unjustified enrichment. But for the need to retain a trace of normativity, one might just as well speak of pink enrichment. The chosen adjective must serve as a peg on which to hang the reasons, not being contracts or wrongs, why an enrichment should be given up, and it must be weakly normative in order to encourage fine-tuning.

(b) Unjust or Unconscionable?

Likewise there would be no objection whatever to 'unconscionable enrichment' if those who preferred it could be relied on to remember that it must mean 'enrichment retained contrary to good conscience' and not 'enrichment obtained contrary to good conscience'. Lord Mansfield spoke in those terms, of money which could not in conscience be retained.[32] We have repeatedly emphasized that liability in unjust enrichment has to be strict unless for some specific and clearly articulated reason a requirement of fault is injected. In general it is not fault-based. It is unconscientious not to give up that which ought to be given up. Unconscientiousness is no more than a conclusion derived from premisses in which it initially has no active role.[33]

Under that discipline, the use of 'unconscientious' or 'unconscionable' would not alter the nature of the inquiry into the reasons why an enrichment must be given up even in the absence of contract or wrong. If these words are dangerous, it is only because they are stronger than 'unjust' and less able to accept a passive role. It must be regarded as very likely that the use of either of these words would in practice usher in an inappropriate requirement of fault in the manner of the acquisition.[34]

(c) A Step Too Far

If Dr Kremer is to be believed, the High Court of Australia nevertheless not only prefers the language of conscience but, in addition, has decided

[31] Ibbetson treats the selection of 'unjust' as more or less accidental, possibly initiated by Ames's choice in his discussion of the ingredients of quasi-contract: Ibbetson (n 15 above) 52, referring back to 45–7.

[32] *Moses v Macferlan* (1760) 2 Burr 1005, 1012, 97 ER 676, 681.

[33] Above, 5–9.

[34] A warning: *Citadel General Assurance Company v Lloyds Bank Canada* (1997) 152 DLR (4th) 411, 435 (La Forest J); cf NJ McBride and P McGrath, 'The Nature of Restitution' (1995) 15 Oxford Jo Leg Stud 33, answered by L Ho, 'The Nature of Restitution—A Reply' (1996) 16 Oxford Jo Leg Stud 517.

to take a long step beyond the unsafe preference for a stronger adjective. It has decided not to base its approach on enrichment at all.[35] It attaches no special importance to enrichment. The intention must therefore be to submerge unjust enrichment in the law of equitable compensation for unconscionable behaviour, which itself would have to be located in the law of wrongs.

Although everyone should by now be constantly trying to reduce to an absolute minimum the dreadful legacy of duality between law and equity, a new outbreak has allowed it to become almost orthodox that outside the traditional boundaries of the law of tort bad conduct gives rise to a right to compensation in equity. 'Equitable compensation' is nothing other than damages awarded for a wrong where the wrong for reasons incomprehensible outside legal history is a meta-tort and not a tort. In order to empty unjust enrichment into this Chancery extension of the law of wrongs, Lord Mansfield's echo of the Roman '*aequitas*' in *Moses v Macferlan* is being made to suggest either that he was referring to equity in the sense of Chancery law or, if he was not, that his *aequitas* was and is one and the same as Chancery's equity.[36]

This is a distortion of history and a denial of the Roman sub-structure of Lord Mansfield's contribution in this field.[37] Much more importantly, it seeks to ignore or override the *raison d'être* of the law of unjust enrichment as a distinct category, which is that, subject to the defence of disenrichment, an irresistible claim to restitution of enrichment can be made out on very weak facts, not connoting fault and incapable of engendering any right to recover consequential loss. The peculiar normativity of extant enrichment is not to be denied.

Enrichment is the key to this unique liability. If it is true that the present High Court of Australia intends to deny that truth, the experience of every other jurisdiction suggests that it will later have to change its mind. The price of extending the law of wrongs instead of recognizing a law of unjust enrichment will be that in some cases claimants will obtain compensation when they should not, and in others they will be denied restitution when it should have been granted.

[35] B Kremer, 'Restitution and Unconscientiousness: Another View' (2003) 119 LQR 188, 189: 'Notions of "enrichment" or "unjustness" do not and should not enter into consideration'. Cf (2002) 76 ALJR 203 [71] (Gummow J).

[36] (2002) 76 ALJR 203 (HCA) [83]–[89] (Gummow J).

[37] The notion that Lord Mansfield was borrowing equity in any sense other than fairness, called *aequitas* in Latin, has been repeatedly rejected: below, 289–90.

In summary, it does not matter much which adjective is used to qualify 'enrichment' so long as it does not import a requirement of fault. 'Enrichment' itself might possibly find a synonym or near-synonym, such as 'benefit'. Under the semantic surface, however, this indispensably independent area of law turns on the indisputable proposition that it takes very slight facts to require the relocation of an extant gain. That is why it had to be extracted from the law of contract and sort-of-contract and why it cannot now be poured into the law of wrongs and meta-wrongs.

2. RESTITUTION

The common law's first serious attempt to modernize and unify this area of the law without invoking fictions was made under this name. In 1933, a fateful year in the history of Western civilization, the American Law Institute commissioned Professors Austin Scott and Warren Seavey to produce a restatement which was completed in 1936 and published in the following year as the *Restatement of the Law of Restitution*, with the subtitle *Quasi Contracts and Constructive Trusts*.[38] The gestation of the Scott and Seavey project merits close attention and will one day be the subject of an important work of modern legal history. The *Restatement* was warmly welcomed in England by influential reviewers, especially Lord Wright of Durley.[39] It seemed clear that the Anglo side of the Anglo-American common law must follow the American lead.[40] *Goff & Jones on Restitution* was ultimately the English response, much delayed by the War. Its first edition was published in 1966.[41]

(a) Missing the Mark

Both the *Restatement* and *Goff & Jones* were magnificent achievements. They hugely improved the understanding of a large area of law which was previously embedded in fictions and antique nomenclature. Equally important was the benefit to other subjects. Contract and trusts are the better for not having to pretend to explain alien matter.

A century earlier the great reformers of the 19th century had abolished the forms of action, thus sweeping away the ancient framework of the

[38] American Law Institute, *Restatement of Restitution* [:] *Quasi Contracts and Constructive Trusts* (American Law Institute Publishers St Paul Minn 1937).

[39] Lord Wright of Durley (1937) 51 Harv LR 369, reprinted in *Legal Essays and Addresses* (CUP Cambridge 1939) 34–65; cf PH Winfield (1938) 54 LQR 529.

[40] This exhortation is present not only in Lord Wright's review (n 39 above) but also in his speech in *Fibrosa Spolka Akcyjna v Fairbairn Lawson Combe Barbour* [1943] AC 32, 61.

[41] Robert Goff and Gareth Jones, *The Law of Restitution* (Sweet & Maxwell London 1966), now 6th edn (Sweet & Maxwell London 2002).

common law.[42] Stability had to be maintained by a strengthened doctrine of precedent. This bought time for the law to develop its substantive rationality. The golden age of the textbook ensued. Textbooks and competition between textbooks were the means by which, one by one, the familiar categories of the law were put in intellectual order. The law of unjust enrichment missed that modernizing boat. Contract and trusts were both left with an assertive cuckoo in their nest. The upshot was that in the 20th century the *Restatement* and *Goff & Jones* still had essentially 19th-century work to do. It was through them that late in time the courts and law schools throughout the common law world began to recognize the need to think systematically about this neglected area of the law.

In America the flame for some reason flickered and almost went out. The response-oriented name drew the study of restitution into books and courses on remedies. But on the Anglo side, *Goff & Jones* bred courses and textbooks in every major common law jurisdiction. It brought the Restitution Law Review into existence and fathered literally hundreds of important articles in leading law journals around the world. It made for a time of excitement and discovery. It is an astonishing fact of legal history that a whole continent should have remained hidden and unmapped until well into the 20th century.

Despite this enormous success, the law of restitution was seriously flawed from its beginning by a seemingly trivial error. The great work of rationalization was conducted within a category which was oriented towards the response, restitution, rather than the event, unjust enrichment. What was needed all along was the illumination of a neglected causative event; what emerged was an overlapping exposition of gain-based recovery.

The assumption seems to have been that restitution and unjust enrichment were two sides of the same square: unjust enrichment triggered restitution and only restitution, and restitution was triggered by unjust enrichment and only by unjust enrichment. In naming the response one therefore named the event. It became gradually more apparent that this was false. The illusion of mono-causality—that is, the illusion that every case of restitution was also a case of unjust enrichment—was only made possible by overblowing the notion of unjust enrichment. The non-contractual and non-tortious causative event described in this present book would never be clearly seen unless and

[42] Uniformity of Process Act 1832, Common Law Procedure Act 1852. JH Baker, *An Introduction to English Legal History* (4th edn Butterworths London 2002) 67–9.

until it was sharply differentiated from the response. Unjust enrichment in the *Restatement* is any event at all which gives rise to gain-based recovery.

Restitution is gain-based recovery, and gain-based recovery is multi-causal, not mono-causal. A book on gain-based recovery is therefore very different from a book on unjust enrichment properly so called, because unjust enrichment is only one of its causative events, albeit the most important. Professor Douglas Laycock was the first to put his finger on this point. In 1989 he wrote of the necessity of distinguishing between substantive and remedial restitution, meaning between cases in which the business of the law of restitution was to identify its own peculiar cause of action (unjust enrichment) and cases in which it was merely the response to other causes of action perfectly familiar long before the *Restatement*.[43] No explicitly multi-causal book on restitution appeared till a decade later. The first by a short head was by Ian Jackman,[44] followed a year later by a much larger work by Graham Virgo.[45]

Although not everyone is persuaded,[46] the multi-causalists are undoubtedly right. This truth is not affected by the fact that their own house is in disorder for want of agreement as to the identity of the plural causative events. That dissension will be ironed out. The present book assumes an event-based series in which the restitutionary right arises either from a manifestation of the consent of some grantor or independently of consent and, when independently of consent, from a wrong, from an unjust enrichment, or from some other event.[47] This is no more than a cut down version of a proposition which is true of all rights known to the law and realizable in court.

One of many questions which we have to be able to answer about all rights is, From what events do they arise? And the answer is, if we use a shorter form, that they arise from consent, as for instance in the making

[43] D Laycock, 'The Scope and Significance of Restitution' 67 Tex L Rev 1277 (1989).

[44] ID Jackman, *The Varieties of Restitution* (Federation Press Sydney 1998).

[45] G Virgo, *The Principles of the Law of Restitution* (OUP Oxford 1999).

[46] A Burrows, *The Law of Restitution* (2nd edn Butterworths London 2002) 5–7; cf A Burrows, 'Quadrating Restitution and Unjust Enrichment: A Matter of Principle' [2000] Restitution LR 257, 269; A Tettenborn, 'Misnomer—a Response to Professor Birks' in WR Cornish, R Nolan, J O'Sullivan, and G Virgo (eds), *Restitution, Past, Present and Future: Essays in Honour of Gareth Jones* (Hart Oxford 1998) 31–6, replying to P Birks, 'Misnomer' in the same volume 1–30. On 22 January 2003 Keith Mason, President of the NSW Court of Appeal gave notice in a lecture that there would be no change of standpoint in the second edition of K Mason and J Carter, *Restitution Law in Australia* (Butterworths Sydney 1995).

[47] P Birks, 'The Law of Restitution at the End of an Epoch' (1999) 28 U Western Australia L Rev 13, esp 17; cf P Birks (ed), *English Private Law* (OUP Oxford 2000) xxxv–li.

of a contract or conveyance, from wrongs, from unjust enrichments, or from various other events. The true mission of the law of restitution was all along to complete this event-based series by supplying its third column. It overstepped its mark. Among the many advantages of treating unjust enrichment in isolation is that it allows common lawyers to see that event-based series of causative events clearly and for the first time.

For the moment the category called restitution still has wider recognition than the category called unjust enrichment. So long as that continues, it will be necessary to be wary of the tendency to line it up with contract and wrongs as though it were, like them, a category of causative event. Professor Burrows, for example, has a very good book the title of which does line up these three.[48] It is difficult to handle a single series which mixes categories of causative event and categories of response. Restitution properly aligns with compensation and punishment, not with contract and wrongs.

There is nothing whatever wrong with writing on, or studying, restitution rather than unjust enrichment, so long as one never assumes that the two are the same. A study of gain-based recovery is no less valuable than a study of loss-based recovery, but both will necessarily be multi-causal. In the superb new edition of his textbook, Professor Burrows appears to suggest that multi-causalists must be opposed to work on restitution as such.[49] That is not so. The point is only that a study of gain-based recovery cannot complete the classification of rights by their causative event. Only a separate book on unjust enrichment can demonstrate the independence of the causative event typified by mistaken payment of a non-existent debt. Only within that smaller book will it be clearly seen that very slight facts not amounting to a wrong or contract will generate a right to restitution, the resulting liability being strict until disenrichment supervenes. At least until that proposition is secure, it has to be seen in isolation, without the ever-present distraction of other restitution-yielding events. Gain-based recovery for wrongs is an incompatible bedfellow. Analytically an unjust enrichment is never a wrong.

The mistake made in the 1930s crystallized in the choice of name, 'restitution' rather than 'unjust enrichment'. The German civil code was the first to affirm with absolute clarity that unjust enrichment was an indispensable category of the law. That was in 1900. More than a century

[48] A Burrows, *Understanding the Law of Obligations* [:] *Essays on Contract, Tort and Restitution* (Hart Oxford 1998).

[49] A Burrows (n 46 above) 6.

later we are still disputing a theorem which the German code regarded as having been tested and proved on the anvil of scholarly examination. That commitment was built on the past, on the pandectists and the historical school of Savigny. Behind them its root stretched back to Grotius, and behind him to the Spanish scholastics. It had nothing whatever to do with the grisly lunacy to come. But in 1933 of all years one could not be seen to be copying anything German. That may explain the choice of the response-oriented name, which put clear water between the *Restatement* and *Ungerechtfertigte Bereicherung* (unjustified enrichment) in the German code.

Whether there was a Scottish American behind that choice is not presently known, although Scots law provides the only precedent. In 1681 Viscount Stair, who was fond of response-based categories, committed Scots law to the same name for a very similar category.[50] There was no parallel Anglo-American tradition before the *Restatement* itself.

There is now to be a new *Restatement*. The American Law Institute has commissioned as the new reporter Professor Andrew Kull, of the University of Boston. They could not have chosen a better scholar to take on this exciting and intensely difficult job. The present plan is slightly to change the title. It will become *Restitution and Unjust Enrichment*. In the light of the discussion in this section, the conjunction is deeply puzzling. Restitution includes unjust enrichment. It is one of the causative events which bring restitutionary rights into being. The new title is a concession to past error, not a cure.

(b) 'Restitution' and 'Disgorgement'

Quite apart from the tension between event-based and response-based categories, 'restitution' is not the happiest of words for gain-based recovery. First, there is a disconcerting overlap with 'compensation'. When restitution is expressed to be of a person to a previous condition it usually denotes compensation for loss. The Latin phrase '*restitutio in integrum*' signifies such a restoration of a person to the position in which he was before a given event. He is to be made whole again.

Restitution of something to someone is the sense used in the modern law of restitution. Yet even this has one unwanted overtone. It tends to imply a giving back. Every giving back is a giving up, but not every giving

[50] Stair, *Institutions* 1.7, D Walker (ed), James Dalrymple Viscount Stair, *The Institutions of the Law of Scotland* (tercentenary edition of the 1693 text University Presses of Edinburgh and Glasgow) 154–63.

up of something to someone is a giving back. Nevertheless it is in this last sense that the books on restitution have to be understood. They mean the law of restitution to be the law of enrichments to be given up, in short the law of gain-based recovery. The functional equivalent in German law is '*Herausgabe*', from the verb '*herausgeben*'. These German words cover all givings up, whether or not they are givings back. English has 'surrender', which has distracting military overtones. The unattractive noun 'disgorgement' has not yet become a serious challenger.

James Edelman in his recent book on gain-based awards for wrongs draws a most important distinction within the law of wrongs according as the gain to be recovered by the victim is contemplated as, and confined to, a transfer wrongfully obtained from the claimant or simply as the profit derived from the wrong, irrespective of its source. He uses 'restitutionary damages' for the former, 'disgorgement damages' for the latter.[51] He demonstrates, beyond contradiction, that, from the standpoint of both measure and rationale, we have to make this distinction. But we do not have to make it in these particular terms. Edelman is not the only scholar to have sought to specialize the meanings of 'restitution' and 'disgorgement'.[52] However, even supposing it were possible to persuade people to divide the field between those words, the wisdom of the attempt is not evident. It is, moreover, no less unnatural to compel 'disgorgement' to exclude 'restitution (of something to someone)' than to make 'restitution' synonymous with 'disgorgement'.

The attempt to give each word its own sphere ignores the danger of new confusion as different courts and scholars interpret the distinction differently. Moreover, confining 'restitution' to givings back would complicate and prejudice the discussion of the second question in the five-question analysis of the law of unjust enrichment. That question explores the phrase 'at the expense of' as the vehicle for identifying a competent claimant.

The safest way forward will be to adhere to the slightly artificial equation of restitution and gain-based recovery, and to treat disgorgement as superfluously synonymous. This is emphatically not a rejection of Dr Edelman's distinction, merely an assertion that it must find other vocabulary. The available names for gain-based recovery must not divide the field. However uncomfortably, 'restitution' has been made to serve for

[51] J Edelman, *Gain-Based Damages* (Hart Oxford 2002) esp 65–80.

[52] Notably LD Smith, 'The Province of Restitution' (1992) 17 Canadian Bar Rev 672; cf Edelman (n 51 above) 78–80.

'gain-based recovery'; and 'disgorgement', which is more comfortable in that role, is its demotic synonym.

C. CONCLUSION

This review of the generic vocabulary serves to underline the necessity of the event-based category of unjust enrichment or, if one prefers, unjustified enrichment. It commits 'quasi-contract' and 'quasi-contractual' to the dustbin of history. These terms need to be known only to be avoided. Quasi-contract was understood to include, but was wider than, unjust enrichment. It has no useful work to do even in relation to those other events, which are best moved to the residual miscellany. The same is true of 'implied contract' so far as that phrase means 'contract implied in law' or 'constructive contract'. Even more powerfully than 'quasi-contract', 'implied contract' conceals and distracts. It makes it impossible to see and understand the independent normativity of unjust enrichment.

Finally, there will continue to be books on restitution, although they must be more explicitly multi-causal. We need studies of gain-based recovery, and gain-based recovery needs a single name. 'Disgorgement' is unlikely to take over. However, the great achievements of the law of restitution over the last 70 years have themselves delayed the recognition of the law of unjust enrichment. Unjust enrichment, or unjustified enrichment, is just one of the events which triggers a right to gain-based recovery. Books on restitution have proved unable to demonstrate its independence or necessity. It must have books to itself. The event-based classification of rights is incomplete without it: rights arise from consent, from wrongs, from unjust enrichment, or from other events.

12

Persistent Fragments

The everyday work of the law of unjust enrichment was never left entirely undone. It was picked up under a variety of heads, principally, on the common law side, under money had and received, money paid, *quantum meruit*, and *quantum valebat*, and, on the Chancery side, under constructive trust, resulting trust, and equitable lien. At least three more figures had a foot in both law and equity, namely account, rescission, and subrogation. These are the ten terms which are explained in this chapter. They have proved remarkably resilient. Their persistence would in some cases be inexplicable were it not that, until the language of unjust enrichment became available, there was nothing which could satisfactorily replace them. Even in *Lipkin Gorman v Karpnale Ltd*, in which the House of Lords first recognized the existence of the law of restitution of unjust enrichment, the claimant firm was contemplated as having brought an action for money had and received.[1]

The metaphor of fragments is convenient but slightly misleading. The modern law of unjust enrichment has not been put together as a broken vase is re-assembled from its shattered pieces but rather by extracting that which belongs to it from a number of different sources. It has not taken over all the work of any one of the fragments. This is obvious in relation to most of them. *Quantum meruit* and *quantum valebat*, for example, are usually responses to contract, but they also respond to unjust enrichment. Even the action for money had and received, which is far and away the largest and most prominent contributor, was not exclusively dedicated to restitution of unjust enrichment.

Sceptics have sometimes pointed this out as though it constituted proof that unjust enrichment could not be useful,[2] but one might as well argue that 'dog' is unsound because it fails to include 'cat'. Unjust enrichment is one category in the classification of events from which

[1] [1991] 2 AC 548 (HL). The phrase occurs 34 times in the report, eg 560, 564, 577–8.
[2] B Kremer, 'Restitution and Unconscientiousness: Another View' (2003) 119 LQR 188, 189, echoing Gummow J (2002) 76 ALJR 203 (HCA) [71].

rights arise. There is no exact correspondence between it and other kinds of category used in the historical development of the common law. Exactly the same is true of contract, except that, if one allows that a contract need not be synallagmatic, the first-generation of action of covenant belonged entirely to it. *Assumpsit* did not, although it would have done if it had not been adulterated after *Slade's case*. That story is told immediately below.

A. COMMON LAW

On the common law side money had and received, money paid, *quantum meruit* and *quantum valebat* are all ghosts from the forms of action. Better proof could not be found of Maitland's famous dictum, 'The forms of action we have buried, but they still rule us from their graves.'[3] The action for money had and received which Lipkin Gorman were thought of as bringing had been abolished a century and a half before the firm's gambling partner rifled their client account to feed his habit.

1. BACKGROUND: THE FORMS OF ACTION

The 'forms of action' were abolished in the 19th century.[4] Nowadays we plead our essential facts and conclude that they give rise to a cause of action. There is no longer a fixed list of claims in standard form. A form of action was essentially a winning proposition. You selected your standard proposition and undertook to substantiate it before a jury. The law's task was to say what facts, when led before a jury, would substantiate each proposition. As the judges developed the law within each actional envelope, some elements in the standard allegations were overstretched and became fictions. A layman would often see little relation between the formal claim and its substantiation.

Those actions which were already in place by the death of Edward I in 1307 can be thought of as first-generation actions. From the middle of that century, the list began to be supplemented by actions on the case, also called trespass on the case. For the early years of that development it is better to think of 'case' as an innominate supplementary technique rather than as a second list of actions, for it was only as a particular supplementation succeeded that it became identifiable as an action to

[3] AH Chaytor and WJ Whittaker (eds), FW Maitland, *The Forms of Action at Common Law* (CUP Cambridge 1965 [1909]) 2.

[4] Uniformity of Process Act 1832, Common Law Procedure Act 1852. JH Baker, *An Introduction to English Legal History* (4th edn Butterworths London 2002) 67–9, 90–6.

which a name could be given. Much of our modern law is derived from those successful actions on the case, and much of our legal history is the story of their shaking off their originally supplemental role and taking over the work of first-generation actions.

One of these successful actions on the case which settled down and acquired a name was the action of '*assumpsit* (he promised)'. In the 16th century the King's Bench began to allow this action even where the first-generation action of debt could have been brought. The judges of the Common Pleas resisted, thinking, not entirely without justification, that the fabric of the law would crumble if subsidiary actions were allowed to escape their supplementary role. After *Slade v Morley*, which ground to an inconclusive end in 1602, they seem to have abandoned their opposition.[5] That was a claim for the price of goods sold. A buyer incurs a debt but does indeed also promise to pay. The only objection to *assumpsit* in such a case had been the old rule protecting the primacy of the first-generation actions.

Wherever the 'he promised' action was brought to recover a debt it was known as *indebitatus assumpsit* (being indebted he promised). In the period after *Slade's case* it came to be accepted that the availability of *indebitatus assumpsit* was not to be confined to debts born of promises but extended even to debts arising by operation of law. That wide interpretation adulterated the 'he promised' action. It was done by allowing the allegation of a promise to become a fiction. We have seen that Lord Mansfield later dignified that development by invoking Roman law. The action lay, he said 'as it were upon a contract, *quasi ex contractu* as the Roman law expresses it'.[6]

2. MONEY HAD AND RECEIVED AND THREE OTHER ACTIONS

It is essential to see that the actions were indeed sets of words. Heavily abbreviated, the versions which follow convey the structure of each of those which contributed to the modern law of unjust enrichment. It is not necessary to give separate examples for both *quantum meruit* and *quantum valebant*. The reason is given below.

[5] (1602) 4 Co Rep 91. The best available report is now printed from manuscript sources in JH Baker and SFC Milsom, *Sources of English Legal History* (Butterworths London 1976) 420. Cf JH Baker (n 4 above) 344.

[6] Above, 270.

(a) Abbreviated Versions of the Relevant Actions

(i) Money Had and Received to the Use of the Plaintiff

[W]hereas the defendant was indebted to the plaintiff in the sum of £10 as so much money before that time had and received to the use of the plaintiff, and, being so indebted, he, in consideration thereof, afterwards undertook and faithfully promised to pay, yet he, contriving craftily and subtilly to deceive and defraud the plaintiff, hath not paid.

(ii) Money Paid to the Use of the Defendant

[W]hereas the defendant was indebted to the plaintiff in the sum of £20 as so much money before that time paid, laid out and expended to and for the use of the defendant at his special instance and request, and being so indebted he, in consideration thereof, afterwards undertook and faithfully promised to pay, yet he, contriving craftily and subtilly to deceive and defraud the plaintiff, hath not paid.

(iii) Quantum Meruit *and* Quantum Valebat

[W]hereas, in consideration that the plaintiff at the special instance and request of the defendant would entertain and board the family of the defendant in his house, the defendant did undertake and faithfully promise to pay to the plaintiff so much money for the same as he should reasonably deserve (*quantum meruit*), yet he, contriving craftily and subtilly to deceive and defraud the plaintiff, hath not paid.

The third of these models, for *quantum meruit*, which means 'as much as he deserved' or, in other words, 'reasonable remuneration', would turn into *quantum valebant* ('as much as they were worth' or 'reasonable value') where goods, rather than services, were in issue. *Quantum valebat* ('as much as it was worth') is the singular. This model, unlike the other two, is not an *indebitatus assumpsit*. It does not turn on the proof of a debt. It is an ordinary action of *assumpsit* alleging a promise to pay a reasonable sum for a requested service or requested goods.

(b) The Request-Based Models

In the first two models the allegation of a promise to pay was superfluous at least in the sense that the liability in debt was formally independent of the promise. There was nonetheless a marked difference between the two. In the first, the words which identified the cause of the debt contained no trace of contract. They required only that the defendant had received money for the benefit of the plaintiff (to the use of the plaintiff). In the second, for money paid, they said that the debt arose because the plaintiff had laid out money for the benefit of the defendant (to the use of the defendant) at the defendant's request.

It follows from the allegation of a request that a fully non-contractual indebtedness was more difficult to reach in that second case. A non-contractual liability was nevertheless achieved by blurring the line between implication in fact and implication in law. In *Exall v Partridge*[7] the question debated was whether an unequivocal benefit to a defendant would justify 'implying' a request. The answer was that the benefit was not sufficient in itself. In modern terms, enrichment alone did not suffice, the enrichment must also be unjust. The extra element was supplied by the fact that the claimant had not merely paid the defendants' rent but had done so under legal compulsion, in that their landlord had lawfully taken possession of the claimant's carriage as security for the rent when it was on the premises.[8]

The model for *quantum meruit* and *quantum valebat* made it doubly difficult to develop any non-contractual liability in respect of services and goods. Not only was there an allegation of request but also the allegation of a promise was not superfluously tacked on to another undoubted liability but was the one and only basis of liability which was alleged. Nevertheless, once again by blurring the line between promises implied in fact and promises implied in law it proved possible to arrive at a covert non-contractual liability. Here the fact that such a liability had been achieved was not overtly admitted until long after the abolition of the forms of action.[9]

(c) Money Had and Received

The first of the three models, the action for money had and received, is the principal source of the modern law of unjust enrichment, though confined to money. Its operative allegation was that the defendant was indebted to the plaintiff because he had received a sum of money for the benefit of the plaintiff—to the use of the plaintiff. If he was so indebted and had not paid, the rest of the allegations were deemed to have been substantiated. The root of that principal allegation runs back to the first-generation action of account, which lay against bailiffs of land and receivers such as rent collectors. The action of debt lay against such defendants instead of account whenever it was unnecessary to go through the quantification procedure provided by the action of account. Money

[7] (1799) 8 TR 308, 101 ER 1405. Cf *Brooks Wharf and Bulls Wharf v Goodman Bros* [1937] 1 KB 534 (CA).

[8] Above, 54–5.

[9] *William Lacey (Hounslow) Ltd v Davis* [1957] 1 WLR 932 may be the earliest English recognition of that truth.

had and received can thus be viewed as *assumpsit* brought instead of debt brought instead of account.

If things had worked out more narrowly, the core notion of receipt to another's use might have been confined to persons such as rent collectors who had been actually appointed by the claimant as receivers. If that had happened the action could not have done the work of unjust enrichment. In fact it was not so confined. It was not even confined to those who knew they were receiving to another's use, as where a third party gave me money to give to you. Crucially from the point of view of the later law of unjust enrichment, the law developed so that the words could be substantiated before the jury even by proof of facts on which the defendant receiver had thought he was receiving for himself and had intended to receive for his own benefit. In short there were facts on which the law took the view that a receiver should be treated willy nilly as having received for the benefit of the claimant.

On what facts would one be treated as receiving for another? In 1760, in *Moses v Macferlan*, Lord Mansfield gave the first coherent answer to that vital question. As was pointed out by Sir William Evans some 40 years later, his answer was largely borrowed from civilian learning about the non-contractual end of the spectrum of causative events which gave rise to the *condictio*, which was the Roman action of debt.[10] We noticed earlier that Blackstone copied part of his exposition almost verbatim into the third book of the *Commentaries*.[11] Lord Mansfield's answer to the question went like this:

> This kind of equitable action, to recover money which ought not in justice to be kept, is very beneficial and therefore much encouraged. It lies only for money which *ex aequo et bono* the defendant ought to refund. It does not lie for money paid by the plaintiff, which is claimed of him as payable in point of honour and honesty, although it could not have been recovered from him by any course of law; as in payment of a debt barred by the statute of limitations, or contracted during his infancy, or to the extent of principal and legal interest upon an usurious contract, or for money fairly lost at play: because in all these cases the defendant may retain it with a safe conscience, though by positive law he was barred from recovering. But it lies for money paid by mistake; or upon a consideration which happens to fail; or for money got by imposition (express or implied) or extortion

[10] WD Evans, *Essays On the Action for Money Had and Received, on the Law of Insurances, and on the Law of Bills of Exchange and Promissory Notes* (Liverpool 1802) 7–8, 25, reprinted in [1998] Restitution L Rev 1–33. He set out Lord Mansfield's sources fully in parallel in WD Evans (tr), *Pothier on Obligations* (Joseph Butterworth London 1806) vol 2, 378–81.

[11] Blackstone 3 *Commentaries* 162 (citing to first edition).

or oppression; or an undue advantage taken of the plaintiff's situation, contrary to laws made for the protection of persons under these circumstances. In one word the gist of this kind of action is, that the defendant, on the circumstance of the case, is obliged by the ties of natural justice and equity, to refund the money.[12]

This is a classic example of the common law's combination of high level principles and, beneath them, the more finely textured rules in which those principles are instantiated. Lord Mansfield begins and ends with an affirmation that the generic conception of the relevant event is unjust enrichment. In between he makes more concrete statements, the one negative, the other positive. These show that the generic conception cannot be directly applied but has to be mediated through the cases which illustrate the actual rules of liability. His references to equity have nothing to do with the Chancery. They reflect the fact the Roman texts refer the liability to make restitution to '*aequitas*' which signifies 'equity' in the non-technical sense of 'fairness'.[13]

3. NEEDLESS DELAY

With better luck it might have been a very short step from Lord Mansfield's civilian exposition of the action for money had and received to the modern law of unjust enrichment. There are four main reasons why it has taken nearly 250 years to reconnect.

(a) Tunnel Vision

As had happened in Rome too, the forms of action caused a species of tunnel vision. What could be seen for money received could not be seen at all for other enrichments received, which were pushed into other actions where the terms of the debate were, as we have seen, different and, on their face, more emphatically contractual. One might have expected that the law would have enlarged the scope of money had and received by allowing the claimant to plead a receipt of money to his use but to substantiate that allegation by proof of the receipt of money's worth. That trick was tried and very firmly rejected,[14] which meant that claims in respect of value received by the direct supply of services and goods could not but be driven to *quantum meruit* and *quantum valebat*.

[12] (1760) 2 Burr 1005, 1012, 97 ER 676, 679.

[13] *Miller v Attlee* (1849) 13 Jurist 431 (Pollock CB); cf *Sinclair v Brougham* [1914] AC 398 (HL) 417 (Viscount Haldane LC), 455–6 (Lord Sumner). This is discussed in detail by Winfield: PH Winfield, *The Province of the Law of Tort* (CUP Cambridge 1931) 129–31.

[14] *Nightingal v Devisme* (1770) 5 Burr 2589, 2 Wm Bl 684, 98 ER 361, 96 ER 401.

(b) Deeper Fragmentation

The impossibility of seeing the unity of the law of unjust enrichment went deeper than the division of labour between different forms of action at common law. Some of its work was done in different language in equity and some, even when done at common law, was not done in or by any one action. Thus at common law there was no single action for rescission, which was a 19th century conceptualization of certain aspects of the behaviour of several actions, chiefly conversion, general *assumpsit*, and money had and received. This technique for responding to unjust enrichment was therefore done almost invisibly in the interstices of the forms of action. Rescission was moreover not confined to the common law. It had its equitable equivalent, which, as we shall see immediately below, initially rested on a very different analysis.

(c) Social Contract and Implied Contract

It suited Blackstone's political theory, based as it was on the social contract, to build on the accidental history of *indebitatus assumpsit* and its false resonance with 'quasi-contract'. Although never quite without dissentients,[15] for nearly 200 years from publication of his *Commentaries* until the middle of the 20th century, English law swallowed hook, line, and sinker the maddening heresy of implied contract. Those who were bold enough to take pride in that approach also affected to regard Lord Mansfield's principle as a risible invitation to do intuitive justice.[16]

(d) Response-Based Progress in the 20th Century

The great success of the law of restitution in the 20th century, although it can be said to have been the springboard for the emergence of unjust enrichment, must also now be seen as having missed an opportunity. The emancipation of the law of unjust enrichment from the law of restitution is even now still incomplete. The reconnection with Lord Mansfield will not have been fully achieved until the difference between unjust enrichment and restitution is affirmed by the House of Lords.

[15] As for instance Cotton LJ in *Re Rhodes* (1890) 44 ChD 94, 105. Maine was very clear on this: HS Maine, *Ancient Law* (John Murray London 1861) 343–5. More detail in D Ibbetson, 'Unjust Enrichment in English Law' in E Schrage (ed), *Unjust Enrichment and the Law of Contract* (Kluwer The Hague 2001) 33, 44–6.

[16] 'Well-meaning sloppiness of thought' *Holt v Markham* [1923] 1 KB 504, 513 (Scrutton LJ). Cf *Baylis v Bishop of London* [1913] 1 Ch 127, 140 (Hamilton LJ, soon to become Lord Sumner).

B. CHANCERY

Although the institutional separation of law and equity finally came to an end in 1871, the inheritance of intellectual duality has proved difficult to overcome. Differences of language and technique still resist the unitary approach towards which we have to struggle. On the Chancery side unjust enrichment was redressed in various ways, as, for example, by imposing an undeclared trust or an automatic lien. Trusts and liens apart, there were other responses, notably account, subrogation, and rescission, which had one foot in the courts of common law and one in the Chancery. These will be considered here with their Chancery counterparts.

A distinction must again be taken between event and response. The Court of Chancery enlarged the grounds of invalidity of contracts and gifts. In that way it extended the range of the event which is, generically, unjust enrichment. Transactions induced by innocent misrepresentation, for example, were remediable only in equity. Likewise, duress at common law was extended by relief in equity for undue influence, which was in addition broad enough to reach the paralysis of autonomy which can overcome one party to a relationship dominated by the other. Most of the other species of impaired autonomy arising from personal or transactional disadvantage were also first relieved in that court. More recently, the dual response to spontaneous mistakes has been called in question. It is clear enough that mistaken gifts are voidable in equity,[17] but it now seems that spontaneously mistaken bargains, if they are valid at law, are not. This is because, rarely as it intervenes, the common law nullifies the contract in all cases in which the mistake is foundational, that is, where the truth of the mistaken belief was the necessary foundation of the bargain. Having attempted to offer supplementary relief, equity has been compelled to withdraw, because, short of relieving parties from bad bargains, there was no logical room for it to take its usual second bite.[18]

The present discussion of terminology need say no more about these contributions to the generic event which is unjust enrichment. In Part IV we reduced the analysis of responses to unjust enrichment to a simple division between rights *in personam* and rights *in rem*, with some subdivision of the latter. Chancery vocabulary in that sector does require

[17] *Lady Hood of Avalon v Mackinnon* [1909] 1 Ch 476; *Re Butlin's Settlement Trusts* [1976] Ch 251; *Gibbon v Mitchell* [1990] 1 WLR 1304.

[18] *Great Peace Shipping Ltd v Tsavliris Salvage (International) Ltd* [2002] EWCA Civ 1407, [2002] 3 WLR 1617 (CA). Above, 137–8.

some explanation. Its effect is that, within the law of unjust enrichment, we have far too many ways of saying that the claimant has a personal claim to restitution or, as the case may be, a property right.

1. RIGHTS *IN PERSONAM*

Nowadays, in the law of unjust enrichment, the language of accountability hardly ever adds anything at all. It only means that the defendant is under an obligation to pay, correlative with the claimant's personal right to demand payment. By contrast, the language of subrogation, in its core usage, does still do more than duplicate the simplest terminology.

(a) Account

The liability to account was and indeed is the characteristic liability of one who has the management of another's affairs. It is not properly speaking a liability to pay. It is a liability to account—to set out the story of one's management. The giving of that account will establish what sum, if any, is due. When that is done, the liability to account has done its work. The amount found due becomes a debt.

For the medieval landowner the bailiff was a key figure. The bailiff approximated to what we might now call a farm-manager. He was in day-to-day charge of the workforce, the planting and harvesting, and the marketing. At common law the bailiff was answerable to the first-generation action of account. The landowner who appointed him had a right *in personam*, that he account, and he was under a correlative obligation to account. The action of account would compel him to do so, a rare example of specific performance at common law. A receiver was likewise liable to the action, as where he had been given money to trade with or had been appointed to collect rents.

The *New Natura Brevium* marks an important growth point when it says 'A man shall have a writ of account against one as bailiff or receiver, where he was not his bailiff or receiver; for if a man receive money for my use, I shall have an account against him as receiver.'[19] The availability of the action against constructive receivers was the springboard for the development of the law of unjust enrichment. But that development actually proceeded, not in the action of account, but in *indebitatus assumpsit* and, more particularly, in the sub-sub-species called 'money had and received'.

[19] Sir Anthony Fitzherbert, *La Novelle Natura Brevium* (1534) as translated in 7th edn (London 1730).

The common law's action of account was obsolete by the end of the 17th century though it made an occasional appearance in the 18th.[20] Two things had happened. First, some of its work had been drawn directly into the action of debt when it was held that a claimant could proceed immediately to a claim in debt if he could quantify the amount owed due without going through the accounting procedure. When debt was later poured into *indebitatus assumpsit*,[21] the action for money had and received in turn took over that legacy of account. Although it developed a life of its own, the action for money had and received was essentially *assumpsit* brought instead of debt brought instead of account. Secondly, the procedures used by the Chancery for the taking of accounts had proved greatly superior to those of the old common law action. Where there was real accounting to be done the work was lost to the Chancery.

The Chancery made great use of accountability. The law and practice of accounting defined the accountant's liability for gains and losses. It is often said that damages could never be awarded in that court, but that should not be understood as meaning that it could never impose a liability to compensate for loss. Once a person was accountable, he might seek to write off a loss, as where an investment had failed, or claim to be allowed a disbursement, as for instance where he had paid a supposed beneficiary. Disallowing such an item was tantamount to imposing liability to pay damages. Where a court ordered that the person accounting must account on the basis of wilful default he would be charged in the account with sums which he ought to have received had he behaved properly. The sum ultimately found owing on the account was not 'damages'; it was an equitable debt which in effect included the court's quantification of his liability to compensate for bad management. In the same way the account could be made to yield a restitutionary award. If a trustee made a secret profit, intending it entirely for himself, he would be made to bring it into the account and would be charged with it, so that, again, the bottom line would include the giving up of that gain. The law of accounting and accountability thus went far beyond mere quantification of profit or loss. It embraced at the same time the very bases of the accountant's liability.

Some features of the modern law, even the all important defence of disenrichment and liability for profits, could be re-examined and explained in terms of accountability,[22] but accountablility is dying and

[20] The last was *Godfrey v Saunders* (1770) 3 Wilson 73, 95 ER 940.

[21] Above, 286–90.

[22] A glimpse is revealed in *Brown v Litton* (1711) 1 P Wms 140, 24 ER 329.

there is no point in trying to turn the clock back. In the modern law, the language of accounting merely introduces an unnecessary distraction, for two reasons.

On the one hand the language of liability to account usually signifies nothing more than an obligation to pay. For instance, when speaking of the liability of the mistakenly paid charities to repay the next of kin in *Re Diplock*,[23] Hanbury and Martin say that this shows that 'personal liability to account in equity can arise in the absence of constructive trusteeship'.[24] There was no accounting to be done by the charities. They simply had to repay the money they had received. If we say that they incurred an obligation from unjust enrichment, we have said all that the invocation of account is intended to convey.

On the other hand the courts themselves no longer show much interest in the law of accountability in the old sense, as defining the extent of the accountant's liability. The modern judge prefers to move straight to, say, the language of wrongs. Thus, in *Target Holdings Ltd v Redferns*[25] where an accountable fiduciary had paid a person who was not entitled to receive the money in his keeping, the House of Lords made no attempt to locate his liability in the context of accountability for the sum received. It treated the fiduciary as having committed a wrong for which it must make good the loss. And accounts of profits are mere exercises in quantification. Even the account that would have been ordered against the traitor Blake had he received any royalties would only have been directed to finding out what sum he had made from his breach of contract.[26] That is a mere shadow of the old account, parallel to countless inquiries into loss to quantify compensation.

The upshot is that accountability in equity boils down in almost every case, perhaps in every case, to nothing more than an obligation to pay compensation or make restitution for a wrong first recognized by the Court of Chancery or an obligation to make restitution for an unjust enrichment imposed by the Court of Chancery. Within the law of unjust enrichment, once the claimant has answered the first three questions of the five-question analysis, there is no longer any case in which there is a practical difference between the enrichee's being personally liable to make restitution and his being accountable.

[23] [1948] Ch 465 (CA).

[24] J Martin (ed), *Hanbury and Martin's Modern Equity* (16th edn Sweet & Maxwell London 2001) 315.

[25] [1996] 1 AC 421 (HL).

[26] [2001] 1 AC 268 (HL).

(b) Subrogation

The right to be subrogated is, when properly so-called, a right to maintain another's claim in that other's name. The claims in question are often not assignable. Otherwise one might be tempted to speak of a species of involuntary assignment. The right to control the other person's claim is a personal right which was always protected by the Court of Chancery's readiness to issue an injunction to prevent the right-holder from objecting to or interfering with the claimant's takeover of his litigation. It was, and is, perfectly adapted to the situations of 'imperfect discharge', as where an indemnity insurer pays a loss, leaving the insured with his right to sue the tortfeasor who caused the loss still intact, but with no incentive whatever to realize it.

In *Re Cleadon Trust Ltd*[27] a director had taken a risk that the company might or might not decide to reimburse his payment in respect of certain guarantees which the company had given. On account of the risk-taking the director had no right to reimbursement. However, in interpreting earlier cases, in particular *B Liggett (Liverpool) Ltd v Barclays Bank Ltd*,[28] the majority of the Court of Appeal gave the impression,[29] which persists, that failure perfectly to discharge the defendant's debt would be fatal. Under this head, it is not fatal. Subrogation proper is designed to cope with the very case in which there is no perfect discharge. The action is brought in the name of the original right-holder.[30]

It is not yet entirely clear how far subrogation proper will reach. For example, in *Barclays Bank Ltd v WJ Simms & Son Ltd*[31] the claimant bank paid a stopped cheque. The defendant builder, who received the money, was a creditor of one of the bank's customers. The bank was allowed to recover its payment directly from the builder. The debt had not been discharged. On the face of things, the bank could in the alternative have been subrogated to the creditor's unextinguished claim against the customer. It is not obvious that the one excludes the other.

The conceptual difficulties with subrogation arise in relation to the extension of the word beyond imperfect discharge to perfect discharge. Where the intervention of the now claimant, or, traceably, the application of his money, has discharged the defendant's debt, the satisfied creditor drops out, his right extinguished. At common law the intervener may

[27] [1939] Ch 286 (CA).

[28] [1928] 1 KB 48 (KB).

[29] Reinforced in *Crantrave Ltd v Lloyds Bank plc* [2000] QB 917 (CA).

[30] *Esso Petroleum v Hall Russell, The Esso Bernicia* [1989] AC 643 (HL).

[31] [1980] QB 677 (QB); cf *Khan v Permayer* [2001] Bankruptcy and Personal Insolvency Rep 95.

now have no claim at all, as where he intended a gift or took a risk whether he would or would not be repaid or was himself the principal debtor. If he was constrained to pay and was not himself the principal debtor, he has a direct right to sue in his own name for reimbursement. This right to reimbursement was asserted under the old action for money paid to the use of the defendant.[32]

The Court of Chancery allowed the language of subrogation to spill over into this completely different situation. This gave rise to false subrogation, which Mitchell calls 'reviving subrogation', so named to emphasize that a right that has been discharged is metaphorically revived for the purpose of being taken over by another. Equity, though it extended the language of subrogation, did not deny that the intervener now brought his own action in his own name. It would have been sufficient to say that the nature and content of his right was to be exactly the same as that which he had discharged. But the metaphor of placing one person in the shoes of another proved irresistible. It was even said that, if he preferred, the intervener could use the mechanism of subrogation proper, suing in the name of the discharged creditor. When statute reinforced the rights of sureties it assumed that, although their payment discharged the debtor and co-sureties, they should have this right to sue in the name of the paid off creditor.[33] In fact the right is not much used, since, when they can, people naturally prefer to sue in their own name.[34]

Reviving or false subrogation is sometimes used by way of metaphorical explanation of a personal claim which could be justified more simply and more openly in other ways. A loan to a minor can be recovered to the extent that it can traceably be shown to have been spent discharging a binding obligation to pay for necessaries. There is no real need to say that the lender is subrogated to the supplier's claim. It would be enough to say that the minor's burden is not increased and the policy of protection therefore has nothing against which to protect him. However, the principal attraction of reviving subrogation is its potential to make available, not the discharged creditor's personal claim, but his real and personal security rights.

While subrogation proper is a right *in personam* to be allowed to manage another's litigation, false subrogation cannot be so described, because the payee's claim has been extinguished. It is a fiction or metaphor

[32] Above, 287.

[33] Mercantile Law Amendment Act 1856 s 5.

[34] C Mitchell, *The Law of Contribution and Reimbursement* (OUP Oxford 2003) [14.27]–[14.31].

which can be used, albeit superfluously, to explain a direct personal claim against the discharged debtor.[35] It also provides a picturesque description of the intervener's entitlement to any securities held by the creditor, which are sometimes said to be kept alive for the intervener but are more correctly described as extinguished and then revived. However, that is matter for the next heading.

2. RIGHTS *IN REM*

(a) Reviving Real Security

In the case of subrogation proper the claimant would have no claim at all but for the right to be subrogated to his payee's right. In false or metaphorical subrogation that is not the case, because he always has his own direct personal claim against the defendant. The principal attraction is the revival of the security rights and priorities of the discharged creditor. It is certainly not the case that they revive automatically in every case where the paid-off creditor's rights are extinguished. It becomes a crucial question, therefore, to know when they will and when they will not. However, an exact answer cannot at the moment be given. In cases in which the claimant affirmatively intended to lend without security, and where the invalidity of the loan would therefore yield a fortuitous advantage simply because the money could be traced to the payment of a priority creditor, there is no revival of the creditor's priority.[36] The most recent cases suggest that in all other cases, so long as the claimant was not a gift-giver or a risk-taker, the claimant will be entitled to the priorities.[37]

If the cases on the proprietary response to unjust enrichment were in better shape, the correct proposition would be that where the claimant's money is traced into a corporeal asset and the facts are such that he is entitled to a proprietary interest in that asset, then, the facts remaining otherwise unchanged, where it is traced into the discharge of a debt, he

[35] It should therefore be impossible to deny reimbursement and, on the same facts, allow the claimant to succeed by reviving subrogation, as did Moore-Bick J in *Niru Battery Manufacturing Co v Milestone Trading Ltd (No 2)* [2003] EWHC 1032 (Comm), [2003] 2 All ER (Comm) 365.

[36] *Marlow v Pitfield* (1719) P Wms 558, 24 ER 516; *Lewis v Alleyne* (1888) 4 TLR 650. Cf for ultra vires loans to companies: *Re Wrexham Mold and Connah's Quay Rly* [1899] 1 Ch 440 (CA); *Baroness Wenlock v River Dee Co (No2)* (1887) LR 19 QBD 155 (CA).

[37] *Halifax v Omar* [2002] EWCA Civ 121; [2002] 2 P & CR 26, [53]–[55]; *Banque Financière de la Cité SA v Parc (Battersea) Ltd* [1999] 1 AC 221 (HL) is both liberal and, perhaps disconcertingly, flexible. The move in this direction is marked in Dr Mitchell's account by the Mercantile Law Amendment Act 1856 s 5: C Mitchell, *The Law of Contribution and Reimbursement* (OUP Oxford 2003) [14.14]–[14.16].

should be allowed the securities held by the creditor. However, if that proposition were rigorously applied a distinction would have to be taken between discharge as the original enrichment and as the substitute for an original enrichment. If the claimant's money is traced through substitutions to the discharge of the debt, the claimant should then have no more than a power to revive the real securities, which might mean that his priority would date only from the exercise of that power.[38] At the moment this picture can only be seen through a glass darkly.

(b) Rescission

The Latin verb '*scindere*' was a strong word, with overtones of force, for 'to cut' or 'to cleave', and '*rescindere*' meant 'to hack back' or 'to hack down' and, by transference, 'to cancel' or 'to annul'. It is not yet clear exactly how the word entered our law. The correct answer may be that it was a rationalizing 19th-century imposition upon practices differently described at law and in equity. It is frequently extended to include the termination of a transaction with only future effect, as where a contract is brought to an end for breach or by frustration. But termination and rescission should be distinguished, rescission being confined to annulment—cutting back from the beginning. The verbal noun 'rescission' denotes the process of rescinding, just as 'termination' denotes the act or process of terminating. As with most verbal nouns, process tends to merge with outcome.

The analysis of the right to rescind is nowadays much the same at law and in equity. It is a power or a bundle of powers, most obviously to nullify a contract, but also to alter the status of assets transferred under the voidable transaction, divesting the title of the recipient and vesting it in the transferor. The recipient meanwhile has a voidable title but can give a good title to a bona fide purchaser. It was somewhat surprisingly held in *Car & Universal Finance Co Ltd v Caldwell*[39] that, to exercise this power, it was not necessary to communicate with the recipient. It sufficed to make a suitably public manifestation of the intention to rescind. There the seller of a car to a fraudster had a common law power to rescind and had sufficiently exercised it by telling the police and the Automobile Association.

On the Chancery side this analysis is relatively new. The American

[38] Cf the discussion of substitutes, above, 198–201. *Halifax v Omar* (n 37 above) did not take this point.

[39] [1965] 1 QB 525 (CA).

Restatement of Restitution assumes an earlier model, namely that voidability in equity entails an immediate constructive trust. The recipient having being immediately turned into a trustee for the transferor upon the receipt of the asset, the transferor, on ordinary trust principles, is then in a position to insist on reconveyance of the legal title.[40] Now, however, there is said to be no immediate trust but only a power, and the only difference from rescission at law is that in equity the transferor's power, evasively called 'a mere equity', does not allow him to alter the legal status of the thing but only to create for himself an equitable interest in it and thus to turn the recipient into a trustee. Being fully entitled in equity, he can then call for the return of his legal title.[41] In relation to an asset transferred the modern analysis of equitable rescission thus has three steps—power, equitable interest, legal interest—while the earlier analysis had two, omitting the first.

'Rescission' is thus the exercise of a power to destroy the contract and revest the thing transferred or the outcome of that exercise. We discussed at some length the question whether concurrently and in some respects more durably the defendant also comes under a pecuniary obligation to pay over the value of his unjust enrichment.[42] We have also just noticed that it is now desirable to resist the temptation to describe that as a personal liability to account.

(c) Equitable Lien

A common law lien is a right to retain possession and thus resembles a pledge arising by operation of law, albeit with no right to sell. A garage has such a possessory lien over the car which it repairs. An equitable lien is, by contrast, an abstract charge over property which allows a creditor to apply for an order of sale, so that he can be repaid from the proceeds. It is essentially an equitable mortgage, distinguished from a mortgage in being by definition a creature of the law, not of the parties. There is no such thing as a lien arising by consent of parties.[43] It is difficult to propound

[40] *Restatement of the Law of Restitution* [:] *Quasi Contracts and Constructive Trusts* (American Law Institute St Paul Minn 1937) sections 163, 166. Cf R Chambers, *Resulting Trusts* (OUP Oxford 1997) 170–84 and R Chambers, 'Constructive Trusts in Canada' (part II) (2002) 16 Trust Law Intl 2, 15. See also above, 184 n 8.

[41] *Lonrho Plc v Fayed* [1992] 1 WLR 1, 11–12 (Millett J); *Bristol and West BS v Motthew* [1998] Ch 1, 22–23 followed in *Twinsectra Ltd v Yardley* [1999] Lloyd's Rep Banking 348, 461–2 (CA), in which this point did not arise in the subsequent appeal: [2002] UKHL 12, [2002] 2 WLR 802 (HL).

[42] Above, 173–9.

[43] *Re Birmingham* [1959] Ch 523.

any general theory to explain when either a common law or an equitable lien arises. They arise where they arise.

It is certainly true that, perhaps only because it was by definition an interest which arose by operation of law, the equitable lien did seem to be a weapon ideally suited for use in cases of unjust and wrongful enrichment. An unpaid vendor of land thus has an equitable lien on the land for payment of the price. And in cases of non-consensual substitution the earlier cases seem to have assumed that the interest in the substitute identified by tracing would be a lien.[44] *Foskett v McKeown*[45] has dispelled all doubts on this score, confirming that the claimant has a choice whether to take a lien or a beneficial interest. The proximity of resulting trusts in favour of a party who gratuitously supplies the resources for an acquisition necessitated that outcome, for a non-consensual substitution is nothing other than an acquisition with the resources of another. It cannot, however, be assumed that in every case the availability of a lien will give the lienor an option to claim in the alternative a beneficial proprietary interest.[46]

(d) Constructive and Resulting Trusts

The American *Restatement* promoted constructive trusts to its sub-title, indicating that that category of trusts was a major contributor to the law of restitution.[47] Indeed the sub-title can be read as an affirmation that the law of restitution has two principal contributors, quasi-contract from the common law and constructive trusts from equity. That is misleading in more ways than one. Constructive trusts are not always restitutionary, and restitutionary trusts are not always constructive trusts. Resulting trusts have an equal or greater claim. Their very name declares as much. The multi-causal understanding of restitution then has to add that not all restitutionary trusts, constructive or otherwise, arise from unjust enrichment.[48]

[44] *Re Hallett's Estate* (1879) 13 Ch D 696 (CA); *Re Oatway* [1903] 2 Ch 356.

[45] [2001] 1 AC 102 (HL).

[46] No more than a lien on payments reducing an insured loss: *Lord Napier and Ettrick v Hunter* [1993] AC 713 (HL).

[47] *Restatement* (n 40 above).

[48] Two two-part articles by Professor Chambers in large measure form the foundation of what follows: R Chambers, 'Constructive Trusts in Canada' (parts I and II) (2001) 15 Trust Law International 214 and (2002) 16 Trust Law Intl 2; and R Chambers, 'Resulting Trusts in Canada' (part I and II) (2002) 16 Trust Law Intl 104 and 138. These in turn develop Chambers, *Resulting Trusts* (OUP Oxford 1997).

(i) Constructive Trusts

'Constructive' here has nothing to do with 'helpful' or 'useful' as in 'constructive suggestion' or 'constructive contribution'.[49] As often in the law, the word can only be understood in terms of a contrast. The contrast is between something deemed and something genuine. The underlying verb is 'construe', not 'construct'. Constructive knowledge is knowledge which you are understood to have because you would have had it if you had asked the questions which a reasonable person would have asked. Constructive dismissal is dismissal without an order to go. A constructive contract serves to explain a non-contractual obligation the true reason for which is obstinately elusive. A constructive cat is very probably a dog permitted to go where only felines may.

In 'constructive trust' what is it precisely that is imaginary? 'Trust' has two senses. We slip from one to the other without noticing. In one it identifies the law's response to the event which in the other it denotes. We should distinguish between trust-as-response and trust-as-event. Suppose that *S* transfers money to *T* to be held for *B*. The trust-as-response is the recognition that all the benefits normally associated with that entitlement belong to *B*, the beneficiary, and the simultaneous reduction of *T*'s entitlement to a bare right, or, in other words, the proprietary split which reflects the fact that, in the days of the institutional separation of law and equity, the courts of common law would say that the money belonged to *T* but had to accept that the Chancery would see that *T* held for the benefit of *B*. Trust-as-response is this proprietary split. Trust-as-event is the act of trusting, the declaration by which *S* reposes trust in *T*.

Of the two meanings, trust-as-response, defined as the proprietary split between bare and beneficial interest, is dominant amongst lawyers.[50] That is what the word 'trust' first brings to mind. However, in the phrase 'constructive trust' it cannot be that the word 'trust' is being used in that sense. The trust-as-response is genuine, not imaginary: *T*'s entitlement really is reduced to a bare right and *B* really does acquire the beneficial interest. A constructive contract does not exist at all, a constructive trust

[49] *In Plus Group Ltd v Pyke* [2002] EWCA Civ 370 includes this notable semantic coincidence, that an accountable fiduciary narrowly escaped liability as a constructive trustee for profits made from a firm called 'Constructive Interiors'.

[50] Lord Browne-Wilkinson in *Westdeutsche Landesbank Girozentrale v Islington LBC* [1996] AC 669 (HL) 705–6 urged that 'trust' be withheld until in addition to the proprietary split the holder of the bare right also had management obligations. However, it is not possible to do without the word 'trust' to describe the proprietary split.

appears to be as good a trust as any other. This riddle is solved when we see that, in the phrase 'constructive trust', 'trust' is used of the event. In a constructive trust, what is constructive is not the proprietary split but the declaration of trust.

'Constructive trust' thus vouchsafes only the unhelpful negative information that the real causative event is not a declaration of trust, together with a tacit assurance that the real facts justify capturing the consequences of the pretended premiss. What are the actual events hiding behind the non-existent declaration of trust? The beginning of a positive answer can be found in *Attorney-General for Hong Kong v Reid*.[51] When a fiduciary takes a bribe a true trust-as-response arises from his wrong. Among the trusts-as-response which arise other than from declarations of trust, some evidently arise from a wrong. *Reid* is a wrong-based trust, restitutionary in effect and wrong-based in origin.

Every positive answer reduces the need for the negative of 'constructive trust'. A causative event which is 'not a declaration of trust' is no better known than a bird which is 'not an ostrich'. To say that in the *Reid* case there was a wrong-based trust is, moreover, just another way of affirming that in response to his wrong an equitable proprietary interest arose in the Hong Kong government, simultaneously reducing Reid's own title to a bare, non-beneficial right. From a different perspective a wrong-based trust is a wrong-based equitable proprietary right.

In the same way, we want to know whether there are any non-consensual trusts (trusts-as-response) which originate in unjust enrichment. That is a large part of the question debated in Chapter 8. There it was put in the form of an inquiry whether any unjust enrichments gave rise to proprietary interests. If a claimant in unjust enrichment acquires such an interest and it is an equitable beneficial interest, the defendant recipient must thereby be turned into a trustee. Thus *Chase Manhattan Bank NA v Israel-British Bank (London) Ltd*,[52] if it still stands, is authority for the proposition that a mistaken payer acquires an equitable beneficial interest in the money transferred, the legal property passing to the recipient. In other words, the recipient becomes the owner at law but is turned into a trustee. The beneficial interest jumps back, effecting restitution to the transferor. This is an unjust enrichment trust.

Although it is resulting in pattern, many trusts lawyers will still want to call this a constructive trust. Old terms die hard. While this one survives we have to remember that constructive trusts are genuine trusts

[51] [1994] 1 AC 324 (PC). [52] [1981] Ch 105 (Ch). Above, 186.

(trusts-as-response) arising from a variety of events other than a declaration of trust and, in particular, sometimes from wrongs, sometimes from unjust enrichment, and sometimes from miscellaneous other events. But the truth is that the term 'constructive trust' is already a fifth wheel on the coach. 'Unjust enrichment trust' says what needs saying. Unjust enrichment is the non-consensual causative event, and trust is the response in which an equitable beneficial interest arises and simultaneously reduces the recipient's legal title to a *nudum ius*, a bare right.

(ii) Resulting Trusts

If the traditional classification of trusts simply contradistinguished express and constructive trusts, there would be no further complications. We could conclude that constructive trusts are trusts arising by operation of law and that they sometimes respond to a wrong, sometimes to an unjust enrichment and sometimes to some other event. Unfortunately, the line between trusts arising from manifestations of consent and trusts arising independently of consent has to find its way through the additional categories of implied trusts and resulting trusts.

Implied trusts are easily laid aside. So far as they are trusts based on genuine intention to create a trust, they are juridically identical to express trusts. For the rest there is nothing which might be called an implied trust which is not either a resulting or constructive trust. Implied trusts therefore disappear.

Resulting trusts are more difficult. The name is a concealed synonym of 'restitutionary' in the unextended sense in which it was confined to giving *back*.[53] A resulting benefit is one returning whence it came. As 'constructive' has nothing to do with helpfulness or usefulness, so 'resulting' does not indicate outcome or consequence. The two Latin verbs for 'jump back' are '*resilio*' and '*resulto*'. In Latinate English 'resulting' meant, and here still means, 'jumping back'.

All trusts under which the beneficial interest jumps back to the settlor are resulting in pattern. If I transfer £1,000 to you on trust for myself, I make an express trust which is resulting in pattern. The beneficial proprietary interest jumps back to me. This is consent-based restitution within the law of trusts, just as is loan with the law of contract. However, as a matter of history one sub-set of jumping back trusts has especially attracted the name 'resulting'. It comprises those which have been regarded as arising with the help of a rebuttable presumption. The facts

[53] Cf above, 281–2.

generating the presumption are the failure of an express or genuinely implied trust and the receipt, outside that traditional list of gift-giving relationships, of a gratuitous benefit.

Thus the word 'resulting' refers naturally to the trust-as-response. Trusts which jump back are trusts-as-response in which the beneficiary is the person from whom the assets proceeded. But the classification of trusts as being express, implied, resulting, or constructive is a classification of trusts-as-response by trusts-as-event. How do trusts-as-response arise? They arise from express trusts-as-event (express declarations of trust), from genuinely implied trusts-as-event, from presumed trusts-as-event, and from fictitious trusts-as-event. This then requires a note to the effect that presumed trusts-as-event are called resulting trusts because the trust-as-response to which the presumption gives rise always carries the beneficial interest back to the person from whom it came.

To call this a presumption of resulting trust is to evade a crucial question. What fact is rebuttably presumed? Traditionally, it has been regarded as as a genuine intent to create a jumping back trust, and, on that traditional view, these trusts are consent-based trusts established with the help of a presumption. It makes no juridical difference whether we call them express or genuinely implied. But the traditional view has run into trouble. What are the other possibilities? If the fact presumed were a wrong or an ingredient which completed the picture of a wrong, they would be wrong-based trusts. If the fact is or indicates the absence of explanatory basis for the transfer, these are unjust enrichment trusts. The only other possibility is that they arise independently of consent, wrongs, and unjust enrichment, and must be placed in the fourth category, miscellaneous other events.

There is no question of analysing resulting trusts as arising from a wrong. The most recent discussion of this question in the House of Lords came down in favour of the traditional view that the fact presumed is an intent that the transferee hold on trust, which makes resulting trusts genuinely implied trusts in relation to which the claimant has the assistance of an evidential presumption of intent to create a jumping back trust.[54] By contrast, the position taken in this book is that these resulting trusts arise from unjust enrichment and that implied intent to create a trust is a Chancery fiction exactly parallel to the old implied contract theory of unjust enrichment at common law.[55] Its function has

[54] *Westdeutsche Landesbank Girozentrale v Islington LBC* [1996] AC 669 (HL) 708–9.

[55] Above, 146–8.

been to provide a familiar explanation of these restitutionary trusts, and its justification was, as usual, the inner conviction that there was a valid but elusive reason why the consequences of the false premiss should flow from the real facts. The proof of its fictitious nature is that it is not rebutted by affirmative evidence that the settlor never entertained an intention to create a trust for himself.[56] Where the presumption operates the true fact rebuttably presumed is always that a transferor did not intend a gift to the transferee. In general the context is such that, if gift is thus knocked out, the transfer is left without any explanation. The transferee is enriched *sine causa*.

The presumption arises on two sets of facts. One is the failure of an express trust to dispose of the entirety of the beneficial interest. The other is where the externalities suggest a gift. In both situations the outcome must be either a beneficial gift to the transferee or restitution to the transferor. Affirmative evidence of an intended trust for the transferor will normally be decisive: there will be an express trust, resulting only in pattern. The presumption does not then come into play.

In the absence of such evidence, the presumption is a presumption against gift. It presumes that the transferor has no *animus donandi*—no gift-giving intent or, as Professor Chambers would put it, no intent to benefit the transferee. In the case of a trust which fails, this presumption against gift to the trustee-transferee is probably redundant, because it coincides with the balance of probabilities. The basis of the transfer was that the transferee should hold on trust, and that basis has failed. If the transferee maintains that the transferor intended a default gift to him, the onus falls naturally on him to prove it. The presumption against *animus donandi* merely underlines that or, at most, eliminates the last vestige of doubt as to where the natural onus lies.

In the case of the apparent gift outside the list of gift-giving relationships, the balance of probability lies the other way. Although the transferee received the asset gratuitously or received gratuitously the wherewithal to acquire the asset, the presumption tells the court to start from the counter-probable position that there was no *animus donandi*. It follows that, unless the presumption is rebutted by the transferee, the basis of the transfer cannot have been gift. Since there is then no other explanatory basis in sight, it follows that the transfer is *sine causa*; it has no explanation. Restitution must follow and is effected by resulting trust.

[56] Above, 187–8.

Once unjust enrichment is accepted as an essential category of causative event in its own right, the need for a fictitious intention to create a trust disappears, in the same way as the need for an implied contract disappears once we accept that it is as an unjust enrichment that a mistaken payment must be given back. There is also no point within the law of unjust enrichment in distinguishing between constructive and resulting trusts. All that matters is that, amongst trusts (trusts-as-response) arising non-consensually, some arise from unjust enrichment. For example, the trust arising from the mistaken payment made in *Chase Manhattan Bank NA v Israel-British Bank (London) Ltd*[57] has not as a matter of history been called a resulting trust, but in terms of its causative event it is of the same kind as those which have. It is an unjust enrichment trust. The trusts which have been resulting trusts with a capital 'R'—those which have been fictitiously supposed to arise from presumed intent—are always unjust enrichment trusts. It is the unity of causative event which matters, not the labels used during the time when that causative event could not be named.

C. CONCLUSION

The final part of this book has catalogued the terminology of the age before the recognition of unjust enrichment. Much of it has hidden unjust enrichment on the edge of contract. In an institutionally dualist system, it was inevitable that the Chancery would do some of the work with its favourite instrument, the trust. Unconverted sceptics may now be preparing to empty it into a hidden corner of the law of wrongs. The independent normativity of unjust enrichment has been recurrently overlooked. Even those early 20th-century scholars who intended to ensure that it was brought to the surface managed to let it slip away into an undifferentiated law of restitution.

It is not easy to explain the long reluctance of the common law jurisdictions. The comparative law lesson has been there to learn. Even though Roman law contributed the misleading term 'quasi-contract' and on that unsound foundation some civilians developed their own version of the implied contract heresy, in every modern civilian system the law of unjust enrichment stands on its own feet, emancipated from its dependence on contract or any other event-based category. Moreover, once confronted with a few simple instances, such as a shop's overpayment of

[57] [1981] Ch 105 (Ch). Above, 186.

change, almost everyone sees both that extant gain at another's expense easily generates a strict liability and that that liability arises independently of any contract or wrong. And that, one would have thought, would have convinced common lawyers that the lesson of comparative law was worth learning.

Three great advantages flow from the secure recognition of the independence of the law of unjust enrichment. First and most obviously, a large body of cases becomes intelligible because, in place of distorting fictions, it acquires its own honest explanation. Secondly, a clearer picture of the law as a whole emerges because it becomes possible to see the complete series of causative events from which rights arise—consent, wrongs, unjust enrichments, and miscellaneous others, and that series of causative events can then be confidently related to other series which answer other questions, above all to the division between obligations and property which distinguishes between rights according to their exigibility. In short, a system with an independent law of unjust enrichment improves its rationality overall because it acquires a better grip on the map of the law. Thirdly, the internal rationality of the overworked consent-based categories is itself immediately improved by the removal of alien non-consensual matter to the law of unjust enrichment or to the fourth category of miscellaneous other events.

Imaginary contracts and imaginary declarations of trust have been a menace, unwanted cuckoos in otherwise well-organized nests. Imaginary wrongs will be no less disruptive. If the law of unjust enrichment were to slide into the law of wrongs there would be no way to capture the peculiar normativity of extant enrichment. A system which went down that route would find itself in a cul-de-sac. No system can manage without a minimum of four categories of causative event. Every right realizable in court arises from a manifestation of consent or, independently of consent, from a wrong, from an unjust enrichment, or from some other event. The residual fourth head can yield up more nominate categories, but the prior three are indispensable. The aim of this book has been to prove that that is as true of the third as of the first two. No system can manage without a law of unjust enrichment.

Index